Constitutional Law in the United States

Constitutional Law in the United States

Third Edition

Robert A. Sedler

This book was originally published as a monograph in the International Encyclopaedia of Laws/Constitutional Law.

Founding Editor: Roger Blanpain
General Editor: Frank Hendrickx
Volume Editors: André Alen & David Haljan

Wolters Kluwer

Published by:
Kluwer Law International B.V.
PO Box 316
2400 AH Alphen aan den Rijn
The Netherlands
Website: www.wolterskluwerlr.com

Sold and distributed in North, Central and South America by:
Wolters Kluwer Legal & Regulatory U.S.
7201 McKinney Circle
Frederick, MD 21704
United States of America
Email: customer.service@wolterskluwer.com

Sold and distributed in all other countries by:
Quadrant
Rockwood House
Haywards Heath
West Sussex
RH16 3DH
United Kingdom
Email: international-customerservice@wolterskluwer.com

Printed on acid-free paper

ISBN 978-90-411-9052-9

e-Book: ISBN 978-90-411-9058-1
web-PDF: ISBN 978-90-411-9064-2

This title is available on www.kluwerlawonline.com

Printed and Bound by CPI Group (UK) Ltd, Croydon, CR0 4YY.

FSC
MIX
FSC® C103993

The Author

Robert A. Sedler (born September 11, 1935) is Distinguished Professor of Law at Wayne State University, Detroit, Michigan, where he teaches the courses in Constitutional Law and Conflict of Laws (Private International Law). Prior to coming to Wayne State University in 1977, he was Professor of Law at the University of Kentucky. He has also held permanent or visiting appointments at the law schools of Cornell, Washington University of St. Louis, the University of Iowa, the National University of Ethiopia, and Saint Louis University. He received his Bachelor of Arts degree from the University of Pittsburgh in 1956 and his Juris Doctor degree from the same institution in 1959. Professor Sedler has published extensively in Constitutional Law and in Conflict of Laws. He is the author of four books, numerous articles in legal periodicals, chapters in books, and other writings.

In addition to being a law professor and academic commentator, Professor Sedler has been an active constitutional lawyer. He has litigated a large number of constitutional cases, including two cases in which he appeared before the Supreme Court of the United States. He has also testified on constitutional issues before committees of the United States Congress. Professor Sedler is a member of Phi Beta Kappa and the Order of the Coif. He was named a Gershenson Distinguished Faculty Fellow at Wayne State for 1985–1987 and received the Donald H. Gordon Award for Excellence in Teaching in 1988. From 2000–2005, he held the Gibbs Chair in Civil Rights and Civil Liberties. In 2005, he was elected to the Wayne State University Academy of Scholars, an organization comprised of the University's leading scholars. Election to the Academy is the highest honor that can be bestowed on a faculty member at Wayne State University. Professor Sedler served as the President of the Academy during the 2007–2008 academic year.

The Author

Table of Contents

Table of Contents

List of Abbreviations

CIA	Central Intelligence Agency
ERISA	Employee Retirement Income Security Act
FMIA	Federal Meat Inspection Act
FMLA	Family and Medical Leave Act
GATT	General Agreement on Tariffs and Trade
LIA	Locomotive Inspection Act
NAFTA	North American Free Trade Act
NATO	North Atlantic Treaty Organization
NVRA	National Voter Registration Act
PPACA	Patient Protection and Affordable Care Act
RLUIPA	Religious Land Use and Institutionalized Persons Act

Preface

In this survey of American Constitutional Law, the author has attempted to explain the nature and operation of the American constitutional system to an international audience. The author has found this to be a rather formidable undertaking. The United States Constitution dates back to 1787, with the first ten amendments comprising the Bill of Rights added in 1791. There have been only seventeen additional amendments since then. Moreover, a number of the very important features of the American constitutional system do not find their source in the text of the Constitution. The American constitutional system as we know it today was not planned, but came about as a result of historical circumstance and gradual evolution. It is a constitutional system that consists of sovereign states, each with its own system of laws and its own courts, and each possessing the general regulatory and taxation power, and of a sovereign federal government, again with its own laws and its own courts, and whose enumerated powers under the Constitution have been construed very broadly by the United States Supreme Court. While the Constitution provides for federal supremacy in the event of a conflict between the exercise of federal power and the exercise of state power, such conflicts are comparatively few in number, and the overriding feature of the American constitutional system with respect to domestic matters is concurrent power between the federal government and the states. Such a degree of dual sovereignty between different levels of government will not be found in most other constitutional systems.

The organization of the federal government (which is replicated in the organization of the state governments) is also highly unusual. This organization reflects an eighteenth century concept of separation of powers and checks and balances that was considered necessary by the Framers of the Constitution to prevent and limit the abuses that they feared would result from the concentration of governmental power in a single individual or institution. Thus, the Constitution provides for three separate and independent branches of the federal government, each of which exercises specified powers and each of which is designed to be a "check" on the other branch. In this sense, the organization of the federal government in the United States is commonly referred to as a "Presidential system," as opposed to the more familiar "Parliamentary system" that has long existed in most other democratic countries. (It may be noted, however, that today some other democratic countries, such as France and the Russian Federation have moved to a form of a "Presidential system" while still retaining to varying degrees, the essential features of a "Parliamentary system."). And even within the legislative branch, the Congress, checks and balances continue to operate. There are two Houses of Congress, both of which must concur in legislation, and in order for the legislation to become law, it must be approved by the President, or enacted by a two-thirds vote of both Houses over his opposition.

The most significant feature of the American constitutional system, of course, which for a long time differentiated it from most other constitutional systems and which still differentiates it from a number of constitutional systems today, is judicial review and the constitutional protection of individual rights against governmental action. Because of judicial review, there is the judicial enforcement against the government of the individual rights guarantees of the Constitution. The power of judicial review—the power of the courts to declare laws and governmental action unconstitutional—has been recognized in the United States ever since 1803 and is an indispensable feature of the American constitutional system. By far the great majority of constitutional cases in the United States involve claims of governmental violation of the individual rights guarantees of the Constitution. It should not be surprising, therefore, that over half of this rather lengthy work is devoted to a consideration of the constitutional protection of individual rights in the American constitutional system.

A study of American constitutional law is necessarily a study of the United States Supreme Court and of its constitutional function of defining the meaning of the Constitution and of interpreting and applying its provisions. It is precisely because the American Constitution is so old and because so many of its provisions, particularly those protecting individual rights, are very general and broadly phrased, that operationally the primary source of American constitutional law has come to be the Supreme Court's interpretation of the Constitution. It is for this reason that we will explain American constitutional law in terms of the decisions of the United States Supreme Court interpreting and applying the Constitution. It is these decisions that authoritatively promulgate the constitutional doctrine that must be applied by the lower federal courts and the state courts in constitutional cases. It is also these decisions that authoritatively determine all questions relating to the existence of federal and state governmental power and to the constitutional protection of individual rights against governmental action. Our focus then will be on the constitutional doctrine that has been promulgated by the Supreme Court and on the decisions that the Court has reached in the application of that doctrine. The doctrine and decisions serve as precedents for the resolution of constitutional cases arising in the future.

The doctrine and precedent that has emerged from the decisions of the Supreme Court in the different areas of constitutional law over a long period of time comprise what may be referred to as the "law of the Constitution." Most of the constitutional cases coming before the Supreme Court today, important as some of them may be in terms of public policy and societal impact, involve the application of the "law of the Constitution to particular constitutional questions," some quite narrow, arising from new laws and new kinds of governmental action. In deciding these cases, the Court will sometimes expand or contract existing doctrine and precedent, and will occasionally overrule a particular precedent. However, the essential nature of the "law of the Constitution" that has evolved from nearly two centuries of constitutional interpretation remains intact, and such change as there is occurs mostly around the edges. To put it another way, the structure of the "law of the Constitution" has now been established, and constitutional cases are litigated, analyzed and decided within the framework provided by that structure. The structure does not change, and the doctrine and precedents that comprise that structure are the starting point for the analysis and determination of all the constitutional questions that come before the American courts. For this reason,

Preface

American constitutional law may be considered to be relatively settled, and it is possible to state that law somewhat authoritatively in the present work.

Although the American Constitution is over 200 years old and reflects eighteenth century notions of democratic government, it is the Constitution under which the American people have chosen to live. Not only is the Constitution very difficult to amend, but the "political will" is more disposed to live under the Constitution as it exists rather than to try to change it. Under that Constitution, for example, the President is elected by an Electoral College, consisting of Electors from each of the states, rather than by popular vote. Thus, in the 2000 Presidential election, the world was treated to the spectacle of the result of the election for the American President—arguably the most powerful position in the world—depending on how "punchcard" ballots would be counted in the State of Florida. The President was again elected by the Electoral College in 2004, 2008, 2012, and 2016 with voting in most places by electronic voting machines, and the 2000 spectacle was forgotten. However, the 2016 Presidential election was extremely close, and although Donald Trump won the electoral vote and so was elected President, the losing candidate, Hilary Clinton, received about one and one-half million more popular votes than President Trump. So too, given the fact that when the Constitution was promulgated, international law was in its infancy, it should not be surprising that international law is not a part of American constitutional law. Indeed, a treaty stands only on the same footing as a federal law, so that if a treaty is in irreconcilable conflict with a later enacted federal law, the federal law controls, even though this effective repeal of a treaty may put the United States in violation of its obligations under international law. In the modern Constitutions of democratic nations today, norms of international law are often made an integral part of the constitutional system, and treaties prevail over inconsistent domestic laws. On the other hand, because the American Constitution itself provides for protection of individual rights against governmental action, Americans can rely on the Nation's courts to provide effective protection for those rights while the citizens of many other democratic nations are limited to the somewhat lower level of protection provided by international human rights norms and institutions.

This survey of American constitutional law has been updated to the Supreme Court's decisions of its 2015 term, ending in June 2016. The Court does not reconvene until October of each year, and at the time the work went to the publisher in January 2017 there have been no new significant constitutional decisions of the Supreme Court. Thus, the work contains the latest constitutional decisions of the United States Supreme Court.

Acknowledgments

This work could not have been completed without the assistance of many other people. Wayne State University Law Librarian, Jan Bisset, provided invaluable research assistance for this edition. Previous Wayne State University Law Librarians, Heather Braithwaite Simmons and Carol Parker provided invaluable research assistance for earlier editions.

Charles S. Owen, a lawyer who specializes in Immigration Law, reviewed the sections on Acquisition and Loss of Citizenship and Control of Entry on Aliens and Deportation of Aliens, and suggested changes that were incorporated into those sections. Michelle Gullett acted as my research assistant for the technical part of the 1994 original volume. She used her extensive computer skills to number the paragraphs, to correct case citations, to prepare a Table of Cases, a Table of Constitutional Provisions, and a Table of Statutes keyed to paragraph numbers, and to assist in the preparation of the Selected Bibliography and the Index. Her excellent work on the technical part of the 1994 original edition made for easy updating in the later editions. Considerable additional work on the technical part of the 2012 edition was performed by my research assistant at the time, Jason Kanter. Jonathan Akari, my current research assistant, provided important research assistance by reviewing and summarizing United States Supreme Court decisions for the 2013, 2014, and 2015 Terms of the Court. June Frierson, my secretary at the time of the 1994 original volume, and Olive Hyman, my secretary at the time of the 2000, 2004, and 2011 supplements, and the 2012 and 2014 editions, and the current edition provided very helpful assistance.

Prof. Dr. Andre Alen, the Constitutional Law Editor of the International Encyclopaedia of Laws, has worked very closely with me throughout the project. Professor Alen helped me to organize the structure of the work, which has been continued in the updates, and reviewed an initial draft. He made suggestions as to some additional areas of coverage, with which I agreed. The final version of the work owes much to his editorial contribution. Mr. David Haljan, of the Institute for Constitutional Law, Catholic University of Leuven, provided important assistance for the 2005 edition. Mr. Joeri Lauwers, Assistant to the General Editor of the International Encyclopaedia of Laws, provided important assistance for the 2012, 2014 editions and for the current edition.

As always, Rozanne Sedler, now my wife of 57 years, provided encouragement for this undertaking, and endured its preparation as no one else possibly could.

General Introduction

§1. Constitutional History of the United States

1. The constitutional history of the United States begins with the Declaration of Independence from Great Britain in 1776. Upon the Declaration of Independence, each of the thirteen colonies (Massachusetts, New Hampshire, Vermont, Connecticut, Rhode Island, Delaware, New York, Pennsylvania, Virginia, South Carolina, North Carolina, Maryland, and Georgia) became "free and independent states." This meant in American constitutional theory that each of the newly independent states succeeded to the sovereignty formerly exercised by the British Crown over domestic matters. As a part of this sovereignty, each state had its own system of laws and its own courts, each state could levy its own taxes, each state had its own militia and was responsible for its own defense. Thus, each state obtained its sovereignty by way of succession upon declaring Independence from Great Britain, and it was not necessary to have a national Constitution in order to give the states sovereignty. This historical source of state sovereignty remains fully in effect today. In the American constitutional system, state sovereignty is "given," and the states retain all the powers that they possessed at the time of the adoption of the national Constitution,[1] except to the extent that the Constitution may prohibit or restrict a particular exercise of state power.

2. Following Independence, the states entered into a loose form of union under the Articles of Confederation. There were many problems with this arrangement, precisely because it permitted each state to act like a "sovereign nation." The states would impose custom duties on goods coming in from other states, and generally would try to promote their own economic well-being at the expense of the residents of the neighboring states. Dissatisfaction with the Articles of Confederation led to the calling of a Constitutional Convention in 1787 to consider amendments to the Articles.[2] However, the delegates to the Constitutional Convention decided to abandon the Articles of Confederation completely and to adopt an entirely new Constitution for the "United States of America." Upon the ratification of the Constitution by nine states in 1788, it became the "Supreme Law of the Land."[3]

In American constitutional theory, the source of the Constitution is the "People of the United States." The Preamble to the Constitution reads: "We the People of the United States, in Order to form a more perfect Union, establish Justice, insure domestic tranquility, provide for the common defence, promote the general Welfare, and secure

1. We will hereafter refer to the National Constitution simply as "the Constitution," which is the generally understood meaning of the term in the United States.
2. Each of the states except Rhode Island sent delegates to the Convention.
3. New Hampshire became the ninth state to ratify the Constitution on Jun. 21, 1788.

the Blessings of Liberty to ourselves and our posterity, do ordain and establish this Constitution for the United States of America." As the Supreme Court stated in the famous case of McCulloch *v.* Maryland:[4] "The government of the Union then is emphatically and truly a government of the people. In form and in substance it emanated from them. Its powers are granted by them, and they are to be exercised directly on them, and for their benefit."

3. The primary function of the new Constitution was to establish a *federal government* with three branches—the legislative branch, the executive branch, and the judicial branch—and to allocate power among these branches. The Constitution also provided for representative democracy: the members of the legislative and executive branches of the federal government were to be chosen by the people, directly or indirectly, and thus were made electorally accountable to them. Finally, the Constitution imposed a few limitations upon the exercise of state governmental power, designed to promote "national unity," and provided for federal supremacy in the event of a conflict between the exercise of federal power and the exercise of state power.

4. During the debates in the state ratifying conventions, much concern was expressed about the need to limit the power of the newly formed federal government, so that it would not be able to interfere with individual rights, such as freedom of speech and freedom of religion. The proponents of the Constitution promised that a Bill of Rights would be promulgated after ratification of the Constitution, and in September, 1789, Congress approved twelve amendments to the Constitution and sent them to the states for ratification. Ten of the proposed amendments were ratified on December 15, 1791, and these amendments became known collectively as the Bill of Rights. The Bill of Rights is considered a part of the structure of constitutional governance established by the original Constitution because, as the Supreme Court has stated, the Bill of Rights was promulgated "practically contemporaneous with the adoption of the original."[5]

5. Apart from the Bill of Rights, there have only been seventeen other amendments to the Constitution during its 200-year history.[6] The most important of these has been the Fourteenth Amendment, adopted in 1868 during the "Reconstruction Period" following the Civil War. The primary historical purpose of the Fourteenth Amendment was to prevent discrimination against the newly emancipated black citizens, but its provisions go far beyond prohibiting racial discrimination. Most significantly, the Fourteenth Amendment's due process clause has been held to "incorporate" the principal

4. 17 U.S. 316, 404–05 (1819).
5. The Slaughterhouse Cases, In re 83 U.S. 36, 67 (1873).
6. Two of these amendments canceled each other out. The Eighteenth Amendment, adopted in 1919, prohibited the use of alcoholic beverages in the United States. After the disastrous experience with "Prohibition," the Eighteenth Amendment was repealed by the Twenty-First Amendment in 1933.

guarantees of the Bill of Rights so as to make them binding on the states as well as on the federal government.[7]

In 1992, Michigan became the 38th state to approve a constitutional amendment that was first promulgated and sent to the states for ratification in 1789. This amendment, now the Twenty-Seventh Amendment to the Constitution, prevents Congress from voting itself an immediate pay raise. Under the Twenty-Seventh Amendment, any pay raise for Congress cannot take effect until after the next election for the House of Representatives. No time limit for ratification was imposed when the amendment was first sent to the states for ratification (later amendments typically contained a seven-year period for ratification), and when Michigan ratified the amendment, Congress, concerned about voter reaction that it was unwilling to accept a limit on its "privileges," immediately voted to "accept" the ratification.

Other amendments will be discussed in the text as relevant.

§2. An Overview of the Form of Government

6. As indicated by the above discussion of the constitutional history of the United States, the United States is a *strong federal system* in which both the states and the federal government exercise sovereignty over domestic matters. (As we will see, the federal government has the exclusive power over foreign affairs.) The structure of the federal government, with three separate and independent branches, is replicated on the state level. The citizens of each state elect their own executive, called a Governor, and their own legislatures, and each state has its own system of courts.[8]

7. In Part II, Form of Government, we will discuss the workings and operation of the federal government. This will include a detailed discussion of the powers of the Legislative, Executive and Judicial Branches, as well as the principle of separation of powers. In Part III, The State and Its Subdivisions, we will discuss the operation of the American federal system and the interaction between federal and state power.

§3. The Territory and Population of the United States

8. For constitutional purposes, the United States consists of fifty states, the District of Columbia, and four territories. The continental United States (forty-eight states) stretches from the Atlantic Ocean on the east to the Pacific Ocean on the west and covers approximately 3,000 miles (4,800 kilometers). It occupies all of the central

7. The other two "Reconstruction Amendments" were the Thirteenth, adopted in 1865, which prohibits slavery or involuntary servitude in the United States, and the Fifteenth, adopted in 1870, which prohibits racial discrimination in voting. Discrimination in voting on the basis of sex is prohibited by the Nineteenth Amendment, adopted in 1920. The last major amendment to be ratified was the Twenty-Sixth Amendment in 1971, which prohibits discrimination in voting against citizens who are 18 years of age or older.

8. Municipal governments are established in each state pursuant to state law and derive their powers solely from the state. Thus, for constitutional purposes they are "creatures of the state" and do not have a separate status in the American constitutional system.

portion of North America, and is bounded by Canada on the north and by Mexico on the south. The state of Alaska occupies the large northwestern section of North America, and the state of Hawaii, a chain of islands, is located in the Pacific Ocean. The nation's capital, Washington, is located in a separate federal district, the District of Columbia, which is on the east coast, between the states of Maryland and Virginia, and is commonly referred to as "Washington, D.C." The territories of the United States are Puerto Rico and the Virgin Islands, located in the Caribbean Sea, and Guam and the Northern Mariana Islands, located in the Pacific Ocean.[9] The residents of the territories, like the residents of the states and the District of Columbia, are United States citizens. (However, because Members of Congress are elected from the states, the residents of the territories and the residents of the District of Columbia do not have any representation in Congress. So too, because the President is elected by electors from each of the States, the residents of the territories are not able to vote for the President, and a constitutional amendment was necessary to give the residents of the District of Columbia the right to vote for President). The United States also exercises protectorate jurisdiction over an assortment of islands in the Pacific Ocean, the residents of which are not United States citizens.

9. The population of the fifty states and the District of Columbia, as of January 1, 2017, according to the latest projection of the United States Census Bureau, stood at 324,310,011, up from 308,745,538, in the 2010 census. The population is projected to increase during subsequent years, with a projection of approximately 335,000,000 in 2020 and 363,000,000 in 2030. The racial composition of the United States is predominantly white (Caucasian), with a substantial "non-white" component. According to the United States Census Bureau, as of July 1, 2015, counting race alone or race in combination, whites comprised 255,081,137, or 77.1% of the total population. The next largest racial group consists of blacks (African-American), who comprised 46,282,080, or 13.3% of the total population. Asians totaled 20,984,374, or 5.6% of the total population. American Indians and Alaska Natives, who were included in a substantial number of persons reporting "in combination" in addition to "alone," totaled 6,623.94 or 1.2% of the total population. Native Hawaiian and Other Pacific Islander also included a substantial number of persons reporting "in combination" and totaled 1,505,910 or 0.2% of the total population. Some 19,107,368 Americans, or 6.2% of the total population, listed their race in the census as "other," and 13,218,733 or 4.2% of the total, listed their race as "combination-white, combination black, or combination other." In addition, 57,078,650 persons, or 17.6% of the total population identified themselves in the census as being of "Hispanic or Latino origin."[10] This is up from 50,477,594 or 16.3% of the total population, that identified as "Hispanic or Latino" in the 2010 census, making Hispanics-Latinos the largest and fastest growing minority group in the United States. The United States then, while predominantly white, is a

9. Puerto Rico and the Northern Mariana Islands are self-governing commonwealths, exercising many of the powers exercised by American states, but not subject to the constitutional obligations of the states. The Virgin Islands and Guam are governed as territories, with fewer powers than the self-governing commonwealths.

10. Persons of "Hispanic or Latino origin" may be of any race, but the largest number of them are white. The largest group of "Hispanic or Latino origin" persons are from Mexico. The remainder of "Hispanic or Latino origin" persons are primarily from Puerto Rico and Cuba, with smaller numbers from Central America and South America.

very heterogeneous nation, populated by large numbers of "non-white" persons, and the "non-white" population is growing at a proportionately larger rate than the white population.[11]

10. The states of the United States vary tremendously in size and population. Alaska, which is not connected to the continental United States, is the largest state in terms of land, Texas, in the southwest, is the second largest, and Rhode Island, in the northeast, is the smallest. According to the 2016 projections of the United States Census Bureau, the state populations range from a high of 39,250,017 in California to a low of 563,626 in Wyoming. The ten largest states in population after California, according to the 2016 projection, are as follows: Texas—27,862,596; Florida—20,612,439; New York—19,745,289; Illinois—12,801,539; Pennsylvania—12,784,227; Ohio—11,614; Georgia—10,310,371, North Carolina—10,146,788, and Michigan—9,928,300. Alaska is located in the far northwest part of the North American continent and borders Canada. California is located in the far west; Texas in the southwest; Florida, Georgia, and North Carolina in the southeast; New York and Pennsylvania in the northeast; and Illinois, Ohio, and Michigan in the north-central. The Mississippi River, which runs the length of the United States, north-south, is traditionally considered the east-west dividing line.

11. There are many different religious organizations in the United States. The largest number of persons, about half of those reporting a religion, belong to a variety of Protestant denominations, the next largest number, about a fourth of those reporting a religion, belong to the Roman Catholic church. Slightly less than 2% of the population is Jewish. The number of persons adhering to other religions, such as Islam, Buddhism, and Hindu is on the increase, and it is estimated that members of these religions comprise approximately 2.3% of the population. All told, about 80% of the population identifies itself as belonging to a religion.

Part I. Sources of Constitutional Law

Chapter 1. The Constitution as the Only Source of Constitutional Law

11. The Constitution of the United States—the original Constitution together with its amendments—analytically is the only source of American constitutional law.[12] The original Constitution consists of seven articles. Article I deals with the Legislature,[13] Article II with the Executive, and Article III with the Judiciary. Article IV deals primarily with matters concerning relations between the states and relations between the states and the federal government. Article V sets forth the process for amending the Constitution. Article VI, the "Supremacy Clause," provides for the supremacy of the Constitution over any other law and for the supremacy of federal power over state power in the event of a conflict between the exercise of federal power and the exercise of state power. Article VII covers ratification of the original Constitution.

12. As stated previously, the first ten amendments, popularly called the Bill of Rights, are considered a part of the structure of governance established by the original Constitution. The "Reconstruction Amendments," adopted between 1865 and 1870, following the American Civil War, provide extensive protection for individual rights against state governmental action. Some other amendments prohibit discrimination in voting. The remaining amendments deal with the internal structure of the federal government.

13. Under Article V, the Constitution is deliberately made very difficult to amend. In order for an amendment to be adopted, it must be approved by a two-thirds vote of both Houses of Congress, and then ratified by three-fourths of the states. Article V also provides for amendment of the Constitution by a constitutional convention called

---

12. It should be noted, however, that some important features of the American constitutional system do not find their source in the Constitution. As is discussed in Part III, Ch. 1, upon Independence, each of the new American states succeeded to the sovereignty formerly exercised by the British Crown over domestic matters. State sovereignty, therefore, is a "given" in the American constitutional system, and the states do not depend on the United States Constitution for their power over domestic matters.

Within each state, the state constitution correspondingly is analytically the only source of the constitutional law of that state.

13. The articles are not always internally consistent, in that sometimes an article covers additional matters as well. For example, while Art. I deals with the federal Legislature, Art. I, s. 10, imposes some limitations on the exercise of state power.

for this purpose upon the application of two-thirds of the states, but this method of amendment has never been used.

Chapter 2. Constitutional Interpretation: The Role of the Supreme Court

14. Not only is the Constitution over 200 years old and deliberately made very difficult to amend, but many of its provisions are very general and broadly phrased. This is particularly true of the major provisions protecting individual rights against governmental action, such as the First Amendment's guarantee of freedom of speech and the Fourteenth Amendment's guarantees of due process of law and equal protection of the laws. It has become the function of the Supreme Court in the American constitutional system to *define the meaning of the Constitution* and to interpret and apply its provisions. Judicial review of the constitutionality of laws and other governmental action has existed in the United States ever since the Supreme Court's seminal 1803 decision of *Marbury v. Madison.*[14] That case "declared the basic principle that the federal judiciary is supreme in the exposition of the law of the Constitution, and that principle has ever since been respected by this Court and the Country as a permanent and indispensable feature of our constitutional system."[15]

15. What this means operationally is that the primary source of American constitutional law is the interpretation of the Constitution by the Supreme Court. While the text of the Constitution is the starting point for such interpretation, it is precisely because so many provisions of the Constitution are general and broadly phrased that the actual meaning of those provisions depends on how they have been interpreted and applied by the Supreme Court.[16] As a practical matter then, "American constitutional law" will be found in the decisions of the Supreme Court interpreting and applying the Constitution.[17]

---

14. 5 U.S. 137 (1803).
15. *Cooper v. Aaron*, 358 U.S. 1, 18 (1957).
16. It is a matter of considerable academic debate in the United States and to a degree among the Members of Court itself as to how the Court should proceed in interpreting the Constitution. Much of this debate has revolved around how much weight the Court should give to the purported "intention of the Framers" as to the meaning of a particular constitutional provision and around whether it is "legitimate" for the Court to engage in what has been called "constitutional policymaking." In practice, however, the Court's constitutional interpretation goes far beyond merely ascertaining the purported "intention of the Framers," and there can be no doubt that the Court does in fact engage in "constitutional policy-making." On the subject generally, *see* Sedler, *The Legitimacy Debate in Constitutional Adjudication: An Assessment and a Different Perspective*, 44 Ohio State L.J. 93 (1983).
17. These decisions are reported in the United States Reports, an official publication of the Supreme Court itself, and in two major unofficial publications, The Supreme Court Reporter, published by West Publishing Company, St. Paul, Minnesota, and United States Supreme Court Reports, Lawyers' Edition, published by Lawyers Cooperative Publishing, Rochester, New York. There are also many online services that report Supreme Court decisions. As a result, there is complete and often contemporaneous access to Supreme Court decisions by the general public.

Chapter 3. Constitutional Supremacy

16. The Constitution is the "highest law in the hierarchy of laws." Under the Supremacy Clause, Article VI, section 2, "The Constitution … shall be the supreme Law of the Land." The Constitution supersedes any other law, federal or state, and any treaty or international obligation of the United States. Thus, an American court, if faced for example, with a conflict between the Constitution, as interpreted by the Supreme Court, and a provision of a treaty into which the United States has entered, would have no choice but to declare the treaty provision inoperative. While this might place the United States in violation of its obligations under international law, this cannot constitutionally be a concern of the court, which is required by the Supremacy Clause to apply the Constitution over any other legal norm. In other words, in the United States, the only source of constitutional law is the Constitution itself, as it has been interpreted by the Supreme Court.[18]

18. Likewise, within each state, the state constitution, as interpreted by the highest state court, is the only source of state constitutional law, and the state constitution is the "highest law in the hierarchy of [state] law."

Chapter 4. Nonconstitutional Sources of Law

17. While the Constitution, as it has been interpreted by the Supreme Court, is the only source of constitutional law in the United States, the function of the Constitution in what may be referred to generically as the American legal system is a very specific one. The specific function of the Constitution is to define the nature and limits of governmental power and to protect individual rights against governmental action. The Constitution does not apply to the actions of private entities and is not the source of most of the legal rules that are applicable in the American legal system. Most of the sources of law in the American legal system then are nonconstitutional. We will now briefly discuss the nonconstitutional sources of law in the American legal system and their hierarchical relationship.

18. The nonconstitutional sources of law in the American legal system and their hierarchical relationship result from the fact that the United States is a strong federal system, with each state having its own system of laws and its own court system. We will first consider the sources of law and their hierarchical relationship within each state.

Within each state, of course, the state constitution is the highest law in the hierarchy of state law, and legislation enacted by the state legislature must be consistent with the state constitution.

Legislation is next in the hierarchy of state law. Legislation not only regulates individual conduct in relation to the state, such as state criminal laws, but may also apply to regulate the legal relationships between private persons. However, except for Louisiana, which follows the civil law tradition, American state legislatures generally have not enacted comprehensive codes in most areas of private law. Most of the applicable law in private law areas, such as contracts, torts, and property, is the common law that has been developed in each state by the judicial decisions of the highest state court. Under the principle of *stare decisis*, the highest state court follows its prior decisions in subsequent cases, so that these decisions have binding precedential effect and control the decision in subsequent cases presenting the same issue. The result is that within each state the courts have developed common law rules that apply in most areas of private law. These common law rules may be superseded by legislation, which stands higher in the hierarchy of state law than common law rules. So, when a court is looking for a legal rule in order to resolve a dispute between private persons or a civil dispute between the state and a private person, it will first look to see if there is legislation that is applicable to the resolution of the dispute. If there is no legislation applicable to the resolution of the dispute, the court will resolve the dispute in accordance with applicable common law rules.

A final source of state law is administrative law, which refers to rule-making, adjudication and informal action by administrative agencies, acting pursuant to legislative authority.

19. On the federal level, most federal law consists of legislation enacted by Congress. Another source of federal law is treaties entered into by the President with the concurrence of two-thirds of the Senate. Under the Supremacy Clause, Article VI, section 2, legislation and a treaty are of equal constitutional status, so that subsequent legislation prevails over an inconsistent provision in a treaty. In some areas, federal courts may develop "federal common law" with respect to matters coming within the power of the federal government, but "common law" is much less important on the federal level than on the state level. As on the state level, a final source of federal law is administrative law, and as we will see, federal administrative law is very extensive and plays a very important role in the exercise of the federal government's regulatory power.

Part II. Form of Government

Chapter 1. General

§1. Introduction

20. As has been emphasized, the United States has a *strong federal system*, in which both the states and the federal government exercise sovereignty over domestic matters. The powers of the states and the relationship between the federal government and the states will be discussed in detail in Part III. The remainder of the discussion in Part II will be limited to the federal government.

21. The Constitution provides for three separate and independent branches of the federal government: (1) the Legislative Branch (Congress); (2) the Executive Branch (the President);[19] and (3) the Judicial Branch (the Supreme Court and the lower federal courts). Under the principle of separation of powers, neither branch can exercise the power that properly belongs to another branch. The Constitution, in this respect reflecting the Framers' fear of a concentration of power, also provides for a system of checks and balances, in which each branch acts as a "check" on the other.

§2. Political Parties and the Operation of the American Political System

22. The Constitution makes no formal provision for political parties, and the Framers, who were fearful of the harm that could be caused by "factions," did not contemplate a constitutional system in which political parties would exist. Political parties, however, began to be formed soon after the Constitution was adopted, and have always been a prominent feature of the American political scene.

---

19. Administrative agencies are considered part of the Executive Branch for constitutional purposes. However, Congress has provided for two kinds of federal administrative agencies. There are independent regulatory administrative agencies and commissions that are established by Congress. They operate pursuant to Congressional authorization and are not subject to control by the President. Then there are federal departments and agencies that established by Congress but headed by a federal officer appointed by the President, such as cabinet members and so are subject to Presidential control. *See* Part II, Ch. 3, para. 69, *infra* .

23. During most of the Nation's history, there have been two major political parties, and minor political parties have not played an important role. Ever since the 1860s, the two major political parties have been the Democratic Party and the Republican Party, and it is common to refer to the "two-party system." Since these parties are national parties, and run candidates in national, state and local elections, they must necessarily be broadly based and, at least until recent times, were only somewhat ideological. The Democratic Party generally is more "liberal," and the Republican Party generally is more "conservative" in the popular sense. The Democratic Party is more disposed to favor social welfare programs, governmental economic regulation, progressive taxation, and a degree of wealth redistribution. It relies more on the support of intellectuals, religious liberals, labor unions, lower middle-income and low-income persons, and minority groups. The Republican Party, in turn, is more hesitant to adopt social welfare programs, generally favors lower taxes and less governmental economic regulation, and is more concerned with protecting existing property and wealth interests. It relies more on the support of business groups, upper and middle-income and persons, religious conservatives, and whites. The Democratic Party is more "liberal" on social issues, such as abortion and marriage for same-sex couples, while the Republican Party is more "conservative" on social issues.

24. The above comparison of the positions of the two parties is somewhat generalized. In past years, both parties contained "liberals," moderates, and "conservatives," and until more recent years, it was common to speak of the "liberal wing" and the "conservative wing" of both parties. However, in more recent years, the electorate has become much more polarized, and the parties have reflected this increased polarization. The Democratic Party has become more "liberal," and the Republican Party has become more "conservative." As a result, it is more accurate today to refer to the "liberal" and "moderate" wings of the Democratic Party and to the "conservative" and "moderate" wings of the Republican Party. The "liberal" wing of the Democratic party is more dominant within the party, although the "moderate" wing is still very strong. The "conservative" wing of the Republican Party is much more dominant within the party, and the influence of the "moderate" wing has been considerably reduced. Nonetheless, the positions of the parties vary to a degree from state to state. In a state where the voters are more "liberal," such as California and New York, Republicans likewise usually are more "moderate" than Republicans in "conservative" states, such as Mississippi or Utah, and in "conservative" states, such as Indiana or Missouri, Democrats conversely are likely to be more "moderate" than Democrats in "liberal" states. Even more significantly, despite the increased polarization of the electorate, party affiliation is generally less important in the United States than in most other democratic nations, because voters frequently vote "more for the candidate than for the party." This tendency of voters to "vote for the candidate" is enhanced by the fact that, as will be pointed out in the next section, party candidates are usually selected by the voters themselves in a party primary. So, every candidate must have broad appeal to the constituency whose votes the candidate is seeking, and must take positions that would be supported by that constituency.

25. In the national Congress, there has been very little political party discipline. Again, each candidate must be elected independently in the candidate's home district or state, and must be responsive to the wishes of the candidate's constituency. While the respective parties try to take a uniform position on various issues, whether a particular Member of Congress joins that position will depend on local or regional considerations, the Member's own views, and the Member's responsiveness to pressures from lobbies and interest groups. Often the President has some degree of influence over Members of Congress from the President's own party, but even here there are limits to the President's influence, particularly when the Member is asked to support a position that will not be popular in the Member's home district or state. In a number of cases, the vote on key issues will break down on regional lines or interparty lines, with "moderates" of both parties voting together in opposition to the position of "liberal" Democrats or "conservative" Republicans. In more recent years, however, there has been a greater tendency among members of both parties toward voting on party lines on a number of issues.

For much of the last half-century, prior to the 1994 elections, the Democratic Party had a majority, in both Houses of the Congress. The Republican Party did not have a majority in the House of Representatives from 1956 to 1994, and from 1956 to 1994, the Republican Party only controlled the Senate during six years of the Reagan Administration, from 1980 to 1986. The election of 1994 changed this pattern. The Republicans made sweeping gains in that election and came away with control of both Houses of Congress in that election. They retained control of both Houses through the 2004 election except for a brief period in 2002 when the Democrats obtained control due to the defection of a Republican Senator. However, in the 2006 election, the Democrats turned things around and obtained a majority in the House, and with the help of two Independents, obtained a 51-49 majority in the Senate. The Democrats scored a sweeping victory in the 2008 elections, electing Barack Obama as President and substantially increasing their majorities in the House and the Senate. After that election, the Democrats held a 257-178 majority in the House, and with the support of two Independents and a party switch by one Senator, held an effective 60-40 majority in the Senate.

However, in the 2010 elections, referred to as the midyear elections, it was the Republicans who scored the sweeping victory. Sixty-three seats in the House of Representatives changed hands from the Democrats to the Republicans, giving the Republicans a 242-193 majority in the House of Representatives. The Republicans also picked up six Democratic seats in the Senate, reducing the Democratic majority of 53-47. In addition, the Republicans made significant gains in the races for state governors and the state legislature, and in a number of states controlled both houses of the state legislature and the Governor's Office. After that election, the Republicans led the Democrats 30-20 in Governors.

There were a number of factors that may have contributed to the sweeping Republican victory in the 2010 elections. The American economy still had not recovered from the severe recession, with unemployment hovering around 10%. The President and the Democratic-controlled Congress were subject to strong criticism for failing to being about significant improvement in the economy. In addition, the Democratic-controlled Congress, over virtually complete Republican opposition, enacted a major health care reform measure, which when fully implemented in 2014, will have changed significantly the operation of the current health care system and will require most people to carry health insurance. The health care reform measure, then and now referred to as Obamacare, is very controversial, and it was strongly attacked by the Republican candidates for Congress. Finally, a new conservative movement, the Tea Party, has emerged in the United States, and the Tea Party provided strong support for Republican candidates. These factors coalesced for the benefit of the Republican Party in the 2010 elections.

26. The facts that the Republican Party ousted the Democratic Party from its long time control of the House of Representatives in 1994, that the Democrats regained control of the House in the 2006 elections, and that the Republicans took back control of the House in the 2010 elections, clearly demonstrate that in the United States, there is truly a two-party political system.

In the 2012 Presidential elections, the tide shifted back to the Democrats. President Barack Obama was reelected by close to 5 million popular votes—a substantial margin in a politically divided Nation—and won the Electoral College (which is what counts, *see* paragraphs 57–60, *infra*) by a vote of 332-206, with 270 being needed to win. The Democrats gained two seats in the Senate and eight seats in the House, maintaining control of the Senate, but leaving control of the House with the Republicans.

In the 2014 election, the tide shifted back to the Republicans, and they made sweeping gains. Republicans generally do better that the Democrats in off-year elections (the years where there is no Presidential race), because the voter turnout is significantly lower in those elections, and the voters tend to be "older, whiter, and more affluent." In the 2014 election, the Republicans wrested nine Senate seats from the Democrats, giving them a 54-46 majority. They made a gain of thirteen seats in the House of Representatives, increasing their majority to 247–188. They also made gains in the state legislative and gubernatorial races.

The Democrats expected to win the 2016 Presidential election. Although President Obama, who enjoyed high favorability ratings, was barred from running for a third term (American Presidents can only serve a total of two terms, *see* paragraph 56, *infra*), the nation had made a fairly good recovery from the 2007–2009 recession, with unemployment now under 5% and a substantial number of new jobs being created every month. The favored candidate for the Democratic nomination was Hillary Clinton, who had been the Secretary of State during President Obama's first term. She was challenged for the nomination by Senator Bernie Sanders of Vermont, an Independent who voted with the Democrats. Sanders made a strong appeal to white working class Americans and others who had not fully shared in the economic recovery. He claimed that American trade deals, such as the North American Free Trade Act (NAFTA) between the United States, Canada and Mexico, were causing a loss of manufacturing jobs and other jobs traditionally held by non-collegiate workers. He also made a strong appeal to younger voters for a "political revolution." Clinton won the nomination after a hard-fought nomination process.

On the Republican side, a surprise candidate was Donald J. Trump, a prominent billionaire land developer and television celebrity. Trump also appealed to the white working class Americans and contended that the "Washington elite" was "out-of-touch" with the "American Heartland." He also contended that the United States had lost its status in the world because of the failed foreign policy of the Obama Administration, and that he would "make America great again." He attacked "radical Islam" and threatened to ban Muslim immigration into the United States. He also attacked the illegal aliens living in the United States, especially those from Mexico, threatened widespread deportation of illegal immigrants, and proposed to build a "wall" between the United States and Mexico, and to compel Mexico to pay for it. Although Trump had never held public office and had no experience in government, he was widely popular with the Republican primary voters, and won one victory after another. One by one, the more traditional Republican candidates dropped out of the race, and Trump secured the Republican nomination.

The Presidential campaign can only be described as "vicious and personal." The candidates attacked each other constantly. Trump claimed that Clinton endangered national security when she was Secretary of State by using her private e-mail server for official business instead of the official State Department server. Clinton attacked Trump for his treatment of women and for his unprecedented refusal to release his federal income returns.

In the United States, there is no direct popular election of the President. The President is elected by the Electoral College on a state-by-state basis (*see* paragraphs 57–60, *infra*), and the so-called popular vote is irrelevant. Clinton won the popular vote by close to three million votes, 65,853,625 or 48%, to Trump's 62,985,106, or 46%. But Trump won the Electoral Vote, and thus the Presidency, by 304 to 227. All told, Trump carried thirty states to Clinton's twenty states. This included six states won by Obama in 2012, Iowa, Ohio, Florida, Pennsylvania, Michigan, and Wisconsin. In three of those states, Florida, Pennsylvania, and Michigan, which Clinton had been expected to win, Trump won by a very small margin – 77,000 votes out of millions cast – but this gave him forty-six electoral votes, which provided his margin of victory. Close to 8 million voters voted for third-party candidates. The Democrats gained two Senate seats and six House seats, but the Republicans remained in control of both chambers. Thus, the Republicans now control both House of Congress and the Presidency, as the Democrats did following the 2008 election.

In the last half-century, the Republicans and the Democrats divided the Presidential elections 10–6 in favor of the Republicans, with the Republicans winning the Presidential election (commonly referred to as "winning the White House") in 1952, 1956, 1968, 1972, 1980, 1984, 1988, 2000, 2004, and 2016, while the Democrats won the Presidential election in 1960, 1964, 1976, 1992, 1996, 2008, and 2012. This division of Presidential elections has occurred throughout the entire twentieth century and continued into the twenty-first. Of the thirty Presidential elections held between 1900 and 2016, the Republicans won sixteen and the Democrats won fourteen. The aggregate popular vote in those elections was also fairly evenly divided between the two parties.

The 2000 Presidential election between Republican candidate George W. Bush and Democratic candidate Albert Gore was extremely close. The result turned out to depend on which candidate received the largest number of votes in the State of Florida. Bush had a lead of only a few hundred votes, and there was much controversy over a recount of the ballots, which ultimately was resolved by the Supreme Court in Bush's favor, so he became the President. *See* paragraph 60, n. 56 *infra*. In the 2004 election, President Bush won reelection over the Democratic candidate John Kerry by about 3 million votes out of approximately 122 million votes cast. In the 2008 election, however, the Democratic candidate, Barack Obama, defeated the Republican candidate, John McCain, by nearly 10 million votes out of approximately 131 million votes cast. In the 2012 election, the number of voters declined slightly to approximately 129 million, and Barack Obama defeated the Republican candidate, Mitt Romney, by approximately 5 million votes. In the 2016 election, the number of voters had increased significantly to 137,098,601 and as stated above, Hillary Clinton won the popular vote to close to 3 million votes, but lost the electoral vote and thus the Presidency to Donald Trump.

On the state level, prior to the 1990s, the Democrats typically elected a majority of the Governors, and controlled both houses of the legislature in many more states than did the Republicans. This changed in the 1990s, with increasing Republican strength in a number of states, particularly in the South. At one time a majority of the Governors have been Republican, and another time a majority have been Democrats. At the present time, in large part because of the victories of the Republicans in the 2010 and 2014 elections, things have changed, and the Republicans clearly have the advantage on the state level. At the present time, there are thirty-three Republican Governors and seventeen Democratic Governors. In the past, control of the state legislatures was likewise typically divided, with the Republicans controlling both houses in some states, the Democrats controlling both houses in some other states, and control being divided in a number of states, with one party controlling one house of the state legislature and the other party controlling the other house. Control of one or both houses in a number of states often shifted after each election. At the present time, however, the Republicans control both houses of the state legislature in thirty-one states, compared to Democratic control of both houses in twelve states. Control is divided in only six states, and one state, Nebraska, has a non-partisan one-house legislature. In terms of controlling the state legislature and the Governor's office, there are now twenty-four Republican-controlled state governments, compared to five Democratic-controlled state governments, twenty divided control state government, and one non-partisan state government.

The state legislatures draw Congressional districts after each census. (*See* paragraph 35, *infra*) While Congressional districts must be drawn with "strict mathematical equality," computerization enables the legislature to identify very precisely the likely political composition of the different districts. Since the Republicans control significantly more state legislatures than the Democrats, they have used their power to redistrict to create more "Republican leaning" districts than Democratic ones. The result is that large numbers of Republican Members of the House of Representatives run in "safe" districts, which will make it much for difficult for the Democrats to gain control of the House in the 2018 election and other future elections until the districts are redrawn after the 2020 decennial census. And we see the anomaly of states that were won by President Obama in the 2008 and 2012 Presidential elections and that typically vote Democratic in Presidential elections having Republican-dominated Congressional delegations.

It is clear that in the United States, there is a strong two-party system. Clearly the Republican Party is in the ascendency at the present time, but this may change in the future. The strong two-party system will continue, and neither party is likely to become the dominant party in the long run.

27. Most of the minor parties that run candidates for public office get very few votes. Occasionally, a "third party," featuring a well-known candidate, has made a run at the Presidency, but the "third party candidate" has had only limited influence on the outcome of the election. The "high-water mark" of third party candidacy for the Presidency would appear to be the 1992 Presidential election, where Ross Perot, a billionaire industrialist, captured 19% of the popular vote, compared to Bill Clinton's 43% and George Bush's 38%. However, it appears that Perot drew votes away from Clinton and Bush in roughly equal numbers, so that the outcome of the election would have been the same even if Perot had not been a candidate. In the 1996 election, Perot ran again, but this time drew only 9% of the vote, compared to 49% for Bill Clinton, the Democratic President running for reelection, and 41% for Bob Dole, the Republican candidate. In the 2000 election, Ralph Nader ran as a third party candidate and received 2,882,995 votes or 2.74% of the total vote. Since Nader is very liberal, it has been assumed that if he had not been running, most of his votes would have gone to Gore, the Democratic candidate. The election was extremely close and the result depended on which candidate carried Florida, where Bush had a lead of only 574 votes in the final official count. *See* paragraph 60, n. 56, *infra*. Nader received 97,488 votes in Florida. Doubtless if Nader had not been running, the largest number of these votes would have gone to Gore, Gore would have carried the State of Florida, and Gore would have been elected President. In the 2000 election then, Nader, the third party candidate made the difference and tipped the election in favor of Bush, the Republican candidate, over Gore, the Democratic candidate. Nader ran again in 2004, and this time received only 240,896 votes out of some 122 million cast. In the 2008 election, he received only 590,101 votes out of some 131 million votes cast. All told, in the 2004 Presidential election, third party candidates received 1,157,859 votes or less than 1% of the total vote cast, in the 2008 Presidential election, they received 1,619,264 votes, about 1.2% of the total vote cast, and in the 2012 Presidential election they received 2,325,952 votes, about 1.8% of the total vote cast. In the 2016 Presidential election, where there was some dissatisfaction with both the Democratic and Republican candidates, third-party candidates received 7,804,212 votes, about 5.7% of the total vote cast.

On rare occasions, an independent candidate—usually a "disaffected" Democrat or Republican—has managed to win an election to a particular office, such as United States Representative or Senator, or Governor of a State. But for the most part, the United States has a "two-party" system, and candidates for public office are almost always elected under that system.

28. There are a large number and variety of lobbies and interest groups in American politics. The influence of lobbies and interest groups is magnified by their extensive political contributions to candidates. Since there is only limited governmental funding for campaigns, mostly at the Presidential level, candidates must raise very large sums of money on their own, and so rely heavily on political contributions. While federal and state laws regulate political contributions to some degree, especially by requiring that they be reported and published, the need of political candidates to raise large sums of money increases the influence of lobbies and interest groups in American political life. While candidates and incumbents often attack the "special interests," what they are really attacking are the "special interests" that support their opponent. Once elected, they will not be unresponsive to the lobbying of the "special interests" that provided them with financial support. In 2003, Congress enacted a comprehensive law imposing new limitations on contributions and expenditures. The Supreme Court has upheld the constitutionality of the limitations on contributions but has held violative of the First Amendment most of the limitations on expenditures. *See* paragraph 245, *infra.*

§3. The President as "Head of State and Head of Government"

29. In the United States, there is no head of state as distinct from head of government. Indeed, the concept of a head of state or a head of government would be inconsistent with the form of government established by the Constitution, which provides for three separate and equal branches of the federal government. In comparison with parliamentary systems, the American form of government is sometimes referred to as a "Presidential system." What this means is that in the United States, the President, all executive power is vested in the President, who performs both the functions that are performed by the head of state and by the head of government in parliamentary systems. But, in both the constitutional and popular sense, the President is a "political officer," and while the President performs the ceremonial duties that a head of state performs in other nations, he does so only because these ceremonial duties are related to the powers conferred upon the Executive Branch under Article II of the Constitution, such as receiving ambassadors of foreign nations.

30. However, as the only officer of the federal government who is elected on a nationwide basis, and the only officer who as an individual is also the head of one of the three branches of the federal government, the President is in a unique position to exercise enormous political and personal influence. And since the United States is a "global superpower," the worldwide influence of the President of the United States is also enormous. By virtue of that office, the President is necessarily a "global leader," and undoubtedly the single most important governmental official in the world. This is why American Presidential elections are watched closely in many foreign nations.

§4. The Principle of Representative Democracy

31. The underlying political principle of the form of government in the United States is the principle of representative democracy. The Constitution makes no provision for direct participation of the electorate in the formation of governmental policy, such as by way of initiative or referendum. The theory of representative democracy is that the people elect Members of Congress and, through the Electoral College, the President, and that the Members of Congress and the President are electorally accountable to the people who elected them. The Members of Congress and the President serve constitutionally fixed terms, and must run for reelection at the conclusion of their terms. There is no constitutional limit on the number of terms to which Members of Congress may be elected; the President is constitutionally limited to two terms of office by the Twenty-Second Amendment. In theory, if the people are dissatisfied with the performance of their representative officials, or simply want to make a change, they can do so at the next election. There is no provision for the voters to recall or remove an official prior to the expiration of the official's fixed term.

32. A number of state constitutions provide for initiative or referendum, and some provide for recall of officials prior to the expiration of their term. Thus, a form of direct participation exists at the state level, but the Constitution does not contemplate such direct participation at the federal level.

Chapter 2. The Legislative Power

§1. The Congress and the "Great Compromise"

33. Article I, section 1 provides that the legislative powers granted to the federal government shall be exercised by a Congress consisting of two branches, a House of Representatives and a Senate. This bicameral legislature is the result of the "Great Compromise" of the Constitutional Convention of 1787. The more populous states wanted greater influence in the proposed national legislature due to their larger population, while the less populous states feared that they would be overwhelmed by the more populous ones in the national legislature, and that their interests would be sacrificed for the benefit of the interests of the larger states. The "Great Compromise" resolved this conflict by establishing two branches, the House of Representatives, which would represent "people according to their respective numbers," and the Senate, which would represent the states as states in the national legislature.

34. Representation in the House of Representatives is based entirely on population, except that the Constitution guarantees that each state will have at least one Representative. Each state is entitled to two Senators, regardless of size. Thus, a state with a very small population, like Wyoming or Montana, will have only one Representative in the House, but two Senators in the Senate, while the largest state, California, now has fifty-three Representatives in the House, but the same two Senators in the Senate. For some time, the number of Representatives in the House has been fixed at 435, but the number of Senators increases whenever a new state is admitted to the Union. With the admission of Alaska and Hawaii in 1959, the number of Senators now stands at 100.

35. In order to ensure that the people will be represented in the House of Representatives "according to their respective numbers," the Constitution provides that a census must be taken every ten years.[20] Following the taking of the decennial census, the seats in the House of Representatives are assigned to each state on the basis of that state's population, and each state entitled to more than one seat, as all but a few are, is divided up into what are called Congressional districts. Congressional districts cannot cross state lines. After the decennial census, there is thus a reallocation of Congressional seats between the states based on each state's population increase or decrease in relation to the population increase or decrease of other states during the last decade. So, given the population shifts that have been taking place from the northeastern and midwestern parts of the United States to the southern and western parts of the nation, states that have had large population increases, such as California, Texas, and Florida, have gained proportionately in the allocation of Congressional

20. While the decennial census, which is conducted in the first year of each decade, i.e., 2000, 2010, is used to collect a great deal of information about the demographic, economic and social characteristics of the American people, and census data is used for a large variety of governmental and nongovernmental purposes, the sole constitutional reason for the decennial census is to "enumerate the whole Number of persons in each State" for the purpose of apportionment of representation in the House of Representatives.

seats, while states that have had relatively smaller population increases or whose population has remained constant, such as New York, Pennsylvania, Ohio, Illinois, and Michigan, have lost some seats. This process continued with the 2010 decennial census. Following the census, New York and Ohio each lost two seats, and Illinois, Iowa, Louisiana, Massachusetts, Michigan, Missouri, New Jersey and Pennsylvania each lost one seat. Texas gained four seats, Florida gained two seats, and Arizona, Georgia, Nevada, South Carolina, Utah, and Washington gained one seat each.

Within each state, the Congressional districts must be drawn in accordance with "strict mathematical equality," and there can only be very small population variances between districts. Again, the Constitution requires that representation in the House of Representatives be entirely on the basis of population, and there must be "equal representation for equal numbers of persons."[21] The states have the constitutional responsibility to redraw Congressional districts after each census in accordance with state law. While most states provide that Congressional districts shall be redrawn by the state legislature, the states have the constitutional authority to redraw the districts by means of an independent redistricting commission.[22] While Congressional districts must be drawn with "strict mathematical equality," computerization enables the legislature to identify very precisely the likely political composition of the different districts. This encourages a political party that controls both Houses of the state legislature and the Governor's office, to draw the Congressional districts in such a way as to strongly favor this party. *See* paragraph 26, *supra*. Since the Republicans control significantly more state legislatures than the Democrats, they have used their power to redistrict to create more "Republican leaning" districts than Democratic ones. The result is that large numbers of Republican Members of the House of Representatives run in "safe" districts, which will make it very difficult for the Democrats to gain until the districts are redrawn after the 2020 decennial census. And we see the anomaly of states that were won by President Obama in the 2008 and 2012 Presidential elections and that typically vote Democratic in Presidential elections having Republican-dominated Congressional delegations.

§2. Elections, Qualifications and Legal Status

36. Representatives serve a term of two years, Senators a term of six years.[23] Thus, there is an election for all members of the House and for one-third of the members

21. For cases implementing the principle of "precise mathematical equality," *see Kirkpatrick v. Preisler*, 394 U.S. 526 (1969); *Karcher v. Daggett*, 462 U.S. 725 (1983).
22. *Arizona State Legislature v. Arizona Independent Redistricting Commission*, 135 Sup.Ct. 2652 (2015).
23. Under the original Constitution, Senators were chosen by the legislature of the state they represented. This was changed by the Seventeenth Amendment in 1913, and today Senators are popularly elected.

of the Senate every two years.[24] The Constitution prescribes the qualifications for membership in terms of age, residence, and citizenship. A Representative must be 25 years old, a citizen of the United States for seven years, and a resident of the state from which the Representative is elected. The Constitution does not require that the Representative reside in the Congressional district from which the Representative is elected, but it would be "politically unthinkable" for a Representative not to do so. A Senator must be 30 years old, a citizen of the United States for nine years, and a resident of the State from which the Senator is elected. Because the Constitution prescribes the qualifications for membership in Congress in terms of age, residence and citizenship, neither Congress nor the states can impose additional qualifications, such as limiting the number of terms that a Representative or Senator may serve.[25] If there are to be term limits for Members of Congress, this must be done by a constitutional amendment.

37. As indicated by the different age and length of citizenship requirements, the Framers contemplated that the individual Senators would have more experience and stature than the individual Representatives. Today, given their fewer numbers and longer terms of office individual Senators are indeed likely to have more influence and power than individual Representatives, except for those Representatives who have achieved important leadership positions, such as the Speaker of the House and the leaders of the Democratic and Republican parties in the House. Not infrequently a Representative gives up a House seat in order to run for the Senate.

38. Representatives and Senators are elected in each state in accordance with state election laws.[26] Under the election laws of all the states, each political party nominates its candidates for Representatives and Senators through a party primary, held during the spring or summer of the election year.[27] The general election is always held during the first week of November. Where more than two candidates are running in a primary or general election (in the general election a third party may be running a candidate or a person may run as an independent), typically the candidate receiving

24. The election is held in the even-numbered year, and every fourth year coincides with the Presidential election. It is widely believed that a "strong" Presidential candidate "at the head of the ticket" will gain votes for the party's candidates for Senators and Representatives. However, in the 2012 election, the Democrats gained only eight seats, and in the very close 2016 election, the Democrats, which won the popular vote, gained only six seats.

25. *U.S. Term Limits, Inc. v. Thornton*, 514 U.S. 779 (1995) (states cannot constitutionally impose term limits on Members of Congress). *Cook v. Grailke*, 531 U.S. 510 (2001) (states cannot constitutionally require that the failure of United States Senators, Representatives or candidates for those offices, to support congressional term limits be noted on the ballot). *See also Powell v. McCormack, infra* , para. 38, n. 29 (The House of Representatives cannot refuse to seat a person who has been properly elected and who meets the age, residency and citizenship requirements of the Constitution).

26. Article I, s. 2 and Amen. XVII, s. 1 provide that "The electors in each State shall have the qualifications requisite for the most numerous branch of the State legislatures." Art. I, s. 4 provides that, "The Times, Places and Manner of holding elections for Senators and Representatives shall be prescribed in each State by the Legislature; but the Congress may at any time by Law make or alter such Regulations … ."

27. In some states, there is an "open primary," under which voters can choose the party primary in which they wish to vote. In other states, voters wishing to vote in a party primary must register as a member of one political party and can only vote in that party's primary.

the highest number of votes wins the election, although the candidate may only have received a plurality of the votes cast.[28] When a House or Senate seat becomes vacant before the expiration of the Member's term, such as by death or resignation, a special election is held to fill out the unexpired term. The Governor of the state may make a temporary appointment to fill a Senate vacancy until the special election is held, usually in the next even-numbered year. The Governor does not have this power with respect to a House vacancy, and the district will be unrepresented until the special election is held.

Article I, section 5, clause 1 provides that, "Each House shall be the Judge of the Elections, Returns and Qualifications of its own Members." So, if there is a dispute over which candidate was properly elected, the dispute is to be resolved by the House of Congress that is involved. But more frequently, there is a challenge to a disputed election in the state courts, and the House of Congress will wait until the challenge has been resolved by the state courts. In the 2008 election, there was a very close Senate race in the state of Minnesota, and with recounts and state court challenges, the seat remained vacant until the state Supreme Court issued its final ruling. The Senate then seated the candidate who had been declared the winner by the state Supreme Court. However, each House must seat any person who has been properly elected and who meets the age, residency and citizenship requirements of the Constitution. A House could not, for example, refuse to seat such a person, because it finds that that person has engaged in improper behavior.[29]

39. Members of Congress have no immunity from criminal prosecution or civil litigation during their terms of office, except for statements made during legislative debates or in the performance of their legislative duties.[30] Thus, instances have occurred where Members of Congress have been prosecuted for crimes while they were still serving in office, and civil suits may be brought against Members of Congress in the same manner as against any other person.

40. Each House of Congress may discipline its own Members, and by a two-thirds vote may expel a Member. Although the latter procedure has not been employed in recent times, there have been a number of recent instances in which individual Members have been censured or reprimanded for improper behavior by the House in which they serve. And the threat of such proceedings has caused some Members to resign or agree not to seek reelection.

---

28. Some states, however, require a run-off election between the two candidates receiving the highest number of votes. Usually, this will be for the primary election, but occasionally it is for the general election as well.

29. *See Powell v. McCormack*, 395 U.S. 486 (1969).

30. Article I, s. 6, provides that: "And for any Speech or Debate in either House, they shall not be questioned in any other Place." This immunity has been narrowly construed to be limited to statements made in connection with performance of official duties. Thus, a Member of Congress may not be sued for an alleged invasion of privacy resulting from public dissemination of a Congressional Committee Report, *Doe v. McMillan*, 412 U.S. 306 (1973), but may be sued for public statements or press releases outside of the Congress. *Hutchinson v. Proxmire*, 443 U.S. 111 (1979).

§3. The Organization and Workings of the Congress

41. The Constitution specifically regulates the organization and workings of the Congress. It directs that the House of Representatives choose a Speaker, who is to preside over the sessions of the House. It provides that the Vice-President presides over the Senate, without vote except to break a tie, and directs the Senate to choose a President Pro Tempore, who presides over the Senate in the absence of the Vice-President. (In practice, the Vice-President rarely presides over the Senate, except where it is anticipated that his vote may be necessary to break a tie.) Each House is also directed to choose its "other officers." Congress organizes itself every two years, in the first regular meeting after the Congressional election.

42. The Speaker of the House of Representatives is the most important figure in the House. The second most important figure in the House and the most important figure in the Senate is the Majority Leader, who is selected by the political party having a majority of the Members. There is also a Minority Leader in each House, who is also an important figure, given the absence of political party "discipline." Frequently, the Majority Leader and the Minority Leader in each House will succeed in negotiating a compromise with respect to proposed legislation, so that the compromise legislation will pass in that House.

43. Both the House of Representatives and the Senate operate under a committee system, and most of the work of each House is done through its committees. The committees hold hearings on proposed legislation and generally must give their approval to the legislation before it can be considered by the full body. It will be a very rare circumstance where proposed legislation will be considered by the full body if it has not been approved by the committee to which it has been referred. The chairs of the committees and subcommittees and the "ranking member" of the minority party on each committee and subcommittee are generally chosen by seniority, and exercise a great deal of influence. If the committee chair, for example, is strongly opposed to proposed legislation, it is unlikely that the legislation will be approved by the full committee. And it is common to refer to proposed legislation as being "killed in committee."

44. The Constitution, Article I, section 4, requires that the Congress "shall assemble at least once in every Year, and such meeting shall be on the 3rd day of January, unless they shall by law appoint a different day." Thus, a new session of Congress begins each January. Congress typically adjourns late in the year during the year when no Congressional election is scheduled, and in the early fall during the year when a Congressional election is scheduled. The leaders of Congress sometimes call it back for a special session after adjournment. The President has the power to call Congress back into session on "extraordinary occasions," and as might be expected from the constitutional language, this power is rarely exercised.

§4. The Legislative Process

45. In accordance with the constitutional principle of checks and balances, the legislative process prescribed by the Constitution in Article I, section 7 is a collaborative effort between Congress and the President. In order for proposed legislation to become enacted into law, it must be approved by both Houses of Congress and by the President, or approved again, this time by a two-thirds vote of both Houses, if it is disapproved or "vetoed" by the President.[31] The President may also propose legislation to Congress, although typically the "President's bill" is introduced by a Member of Congress from the President's political party.

46. Except for revenue bills, which must be introduced first in the House of Representatives, proposed legislation may be introduced in either House. When legislation is proposed and passed in one House, it is then sent to the other House for its consideration. If it passes the second House in identical form, it is then sent to the President for approval. More typically, similar bills are introduced in each House, and if both bills pass the respective Houses in a different form, they are referred to a conference committee, consisting of members from both Houses, which attempts to reconcile the differences. If the conference committee is successful, a single bill emerges, which then must be approved by both Houses and sent to the President.

47. As the above discussion demonstrates, the Constitution deliberately makes it very difficult for a bill to be enacted into law. In order for a bill to be enacted into law, there must be the concurrence between both Houses of Congress and the President, or there must be such strong support for the bill in the Congress that it can obtain the approval of two-thirds of each House and so be "veto-proof." The constitutionally imposed difficulty of enacting legislation promotes compromise within each House of Congress, between both of the Houses of Congress, and between Congress and the President. The necessity for compromise is heightened by the lack of political party discipline and is most apparent when one party controls one House of Congress and the other party the other House, or when one party controls the Congress, while the President is a member of the other party. In early 2013, the Republican-controlled House and the Democratic-controlled Senate (with backing from President Obama) could not agree on legislation appropriating funds for the fiscal year 2014, and could not even agree on a continuing resolution for the interim authorization of appropriations for the fiscal year 2014. And for the first time, the Republican-controlled House refused to agree to raise the debt limit for government borrowing, which was to expire shortly. The failure to appropriate funds resulted in a "shutdown" of the federal government except for certain vital services for a period of sixteen days. In the evening of the day before the debt limit was to expire, October 16, 2013, both Houses were able to agree on a continuing resolution funding the government until January 15, 2014, and raising the debt limit until February 7, 2014. The President signed the bill shortly after midnight on October 17 and the crisis was averted for the time being. In February 2014, Congress raised the debt limit through March 2015. Congress and the President subsequently agreed on appropriation bills, and the debt limit continued to be raised.

31. The President must approve or disapprove a bill in its entirety. The Constitution does not provide that the President has a so-called line item veto, by which the President may veto only a particular part of a bill with which he disagrees. Congress's attempt to effectively provide the President with a "line item veto" by delegating to him the authority to "cancel" certain spending and tax benefit measures that he had signed into law was held unconstitutional by the Supreme Court. *Clinton v. New York*, 524 U.S. 417 (1998).

Following the 2016 elections, the Republican Party controls both Houses of Congress and the President is a Republican.

§5. The Federal Legislative Power: The Powers of Congress

48. Article I, section 8, sets forth the powers of Congress. Other provisions of the Constitution, such as the "implementing clauses" of the Thirteenth, Fourteenth, Fifteenth, Nineteenth, Twenty-Fourth, and Twenty-Sixth Amendments, give the Congress additional powers. In the American constitutional system, the grant of legislative power to Congress has a twofold function, one relating to the federal system and the other relating to the principle of separation of powers.

49. As regards the federal system, the grant of legislative power to Congress means that the matter in issue is within the powers of the federal government. In American constitutional theory, the federal government can only exercise those powers over domestic matters that are enumerated to it in the Constitution. So, the enumeration of powers to Congress in Article I, section 8, and elsewhere, is an enumeration of the power in question to the federal government. As we will see subsequently, very few of the enumerated powers in Article I, section 8, are exclusive federal powers. This means that the states can exercise power over the same matter so long as there is no conflict between the exercise of federal power and the exercise of state power. For present purposes, the point to be emphasized is that the enumeration of these powers in Article I, section 8, brings the enumerated power within the authority of the federal government.

50. As regards the principle of separation of powers, the enumeration of these powers to the Congress in Article I, section 8, and elsewhere, also means that the matter in issue comes within the power of Congress, as opposed to the power of the President. Some of the powers enumerated in Article I, section 8, clearly relate to the operation of the federal government and establish these powers in the Congress. Such powers include the taxing and spending power, the power to establish federal courts below the Supreme Court, the power to declare war, the power to raise and support the armed forces and to regulate their operation, the power to call up the state militias into federal service, and the power to establish and legislate for the District of Columbia. The interaction between the exercise of Congressional power under Article I, section 8, and the exercise of Presidential power under Article II, will be discussed subsequently. Note, however, as pointed out above, that bills enacted by Congress must be approved by the President, or by two-thirds vote of each House of Congress over the President's objections, in order to become law. Thus, when we speak of the power of Congress, we necessarily include the power of the President to approve or disapprove proposed legislation.

51. The other powers enumerated in Article I, section 8, are powers over domestic matters, and, as pointed out above, the effect of the enumeration of these powers in Article I, section 8, is to make them powers of the federal government. These powers include the power to regulate interstate and foreign commerce, the power over immigration and naturalization, the power over bankruptcy, the power over patents, trademarks and copyright, the power to coin money, the power to fix the standard of weights and measures, and the power over the mails. Congress is also specifically given the power in Article I, section 8, clause 17, to make all laws "necessary and proper" for carrying into execution the enumerated powers of Article I, section 8, and the "necessary and proper" clause has been construed broadly by the Supreme Court to permit Congress to rely on a combination of enumerated powers to do something that is qualitatively different from that authorized by any particular enumerated power.[32]

In a recent case, the Supreme Court held that a federal law providing for the civil commitment of mentally ill, sexually dangerous federal prisoners following the completion of their sentences was a necessary and proper exercise of Congress' power to punish crimes against the United States.[33] In another recent case, the Court held that Congress had the power under the "necessary and proper" clause to require convicted sex offenders to register in the states in which they live, study and work, and to apply the requirement to convicted sex offenders who had completed their sentences.[34]

52. Like the "necessary and proper" clause, the enumerated powers of Article I, section 8, have been construed very broadly by the Supreme Court. This is particularly true with respect to the power over interstate and foreign commerce. The Supreme Court has interpreted the commerce power so broadly that today there is virtually no activity, no matter how "local," that cannot be reached by Congress under the commerce power. First, Congress can regulate the interstate movement of persons or things and the channels and instrumentalities of interstate commerce. So, whenever something has moved across state lines, such as a stolen automobile or a kidnapping victim, Congressional power may constitutionally be invoked,[35] and a number of ordinary crimes are made "federal crimes" when they involve activity that "crosses state lines." In addition, Congress can "follow the person or thing" across state lines after interstate commerce has come to an end. Thus, it can require that a retailer display federally mandated labels on goods that have moved in interstate commerce, although the retailer purchased the goods from an in-state wholesaler,[36] and can make it unlawful for a person who has been convicted of a felony offense to purchase a firearm that has moved in interstate commerce.[37] For the same reason, Congress can regulate all forms

---

32. *See McCulloch v. Maryland*, 17 U.S. (4 Wheat.) 316 (1819). The Court held in that case that under the "necessary and proper" clause, Congress could charter a federal bank that performed all the functions of any bank and so competed with state-chartered banks. The authority to charter a federal bank could be found in the taxing and spending power, the power to raise and support armies, and the power to regulate interstate commerce, among others.
33. *United States v. Comstock*, 560 U.S. 126 (2010).
34. *United States v. Kebodeaux*, 133 Sup.Ct. 2496 (2013).
35. *See* e.g., *Brooks v. United States*, 267 U.S. 432 (1925) (interstate transportation of stolen automobile); *Gooch v. United States*, 297 U.S. 124 (1936) (interstate transportation of kidnapping victim); *Hoke v. United States*, 227 U.S. 308 (1913) (interstate prostitution). Under the interstate movement aspect of the commerce power, Congress can exclude whatever it considers to be harmful from interstate commerce, such as lotteries, The Lottery Case, 188 U.S. 321 (1903), goods produced by prison inmates, *Kentucky Whip & Collar Co. v. Illinois Central R.R.*, 299 U.S. 334 (1937), or goods produced under sub-standard labor conditions, *United States v. Darby*, 315 U.S. 100 (1941).
36. *United States v. Sullivan*, 332 U.S. 689 (1948)
37. *Barrett v. United States*, 423 U.S. 212 (1976).

of transportation and communication that can be used in interstate commerce.[38] Second, Congress can regulate any economic activity, no matter how local, that when viewed cumulatively, has a substantial economic effect on interstate commerce. For example, in one case, the Supreme Court held that in regulating wheat production in order to control wheat prices, Congress could prohibit a farmer from feeding wheat that he grew on his own farm to his livestock. Since wheat grown on a large number of farms for livestock feed could have a nationwide effect on wheat prices, Congress in the exercise of the commerce power can require that a farmer not grow wheat on his land and buy his wheat at market instead.[39] What this means is that Congress has plenary power over the national economy.

In more recent years, a sharply divided Court has held that whenever Congress relies on the commerce power to regulate purely local non-economic activity, there must be some demonstration, to the Court's satisfaction, of precisely how that activity "substantially affects interstate commerce." In two cases, that demonstration could not be made, and the Court held that the regulation cannot be sustained under the commerce power. In *United States v. Lopez*,[40] the Court, in a 5-4 decision, held that Congress could not prohibit the mere possession of firearms within the vicinity of a school. In *United States v. Morrison*,[41] the Court, in another 5-4 decision, held that Congress could not use the commerce power to provide a federal civil remedy for victims of gender-motivated violence despite Congressional findings that such violence "affects interstate commerce" in a number of ways. The Court majority emphasized that state law provided a remedy for victims of gender-motivated violence and that to

---

38. The extent of the power of Congress to regulate the channels and instrumentalities of interstate commerce is illustrated by *Pierce County, Washington v. Guillen*, 537 U.S. 129 (2003), where the Court upheld a federal law protecting from discovery or introduction into evidence any reports or data compiled and collected by state agencies to identify potential accident sites or hazardous roadway conditions.
39. *Wickard v. Filburn*, 317 U.S. 111 (1942). *See also Hodel v. Virginia Surface Mining and Reclamation Association*, 452 U.S. 264 (1981), upholding Congress' exercise of the commerce power to regulate surface coal mining within each state. The applicable principle is that Congress can regulate any activity, no matter how local, if that activity, when viewed cumulatively, exerts a substantial economic effect on interstate commerce. Other examples of Congressional regulation sustained on this basis include the following: the regulation of rates charged by intrastate railroad carriers, which could affect the rates charged by interstate railroad carriers, *Houston, East & West Texas Ry. v. United States*, 234 U.S. 342 (1913); labor-management relations at a local manufacturing plant, since strikes at local manufacturing plants could affect interstate commerce, *National Labor Relations Board v. Jones & Laughlin Steel Corp.*, 301 U.S. 1 (1936); wages and hours of employees of businesses and employees of non-profit institutions, since labor costs can affect prices at which goods are sold in interstate commerce, and since work stoppages could interrupt the flow of goods across state lines, *United States v. Darby, supra* , *Maryland v. Wirtz*, 312 U.S. 183 (1968); prohibition of "extortionate extension of credit" in purely local activities because of dependence of nationally organized crime on revenues derived from this activity, *Perez v. United States*, 402 U.S. 146 (1971).
40. 514 U.S. 549 (1995).
41. 529 U.S. 598 (2000).

allow Congress to use the commerce power in this way would "completely obliterate the Constitution's distinction between national and local authority."[42]

However, the impact of these decisions appeared to have been limited by the Court's more recent decision in *Gonzales v. Raich*,[43] where the Court held 6-3 that Congress had the power to apply the federal law regulating controlled substances to prohibit the local cultivation and use of marijuana for medical purposes, even though such use was authorized by state law. The Court took a broad view of "economic effect" for commerce clause purposes, saying that Congress had a rational basis for concluding that home-consumed marijuana outside of federal control would affect price and market conditions and that a high demand for marijuana in the interstate market would draw home-grown marijuana into that market. The Court also made the point that where Congress is regulating a class of activities, such as marijuana use, and the class of activities is within the reach of federal power, the Court would not "excise individual components of that larger scheme."[44]

But in its most recent decision involving the power of Congress to regulate interstate commerce, *National Federation of Independent Business v. Sebelius*,[45] a sharply divided Court held in a 5-4 decision that Congress could not use the commerce power to require an individual to engage in commerce, here to purchase health insurance. The case involved a constitutional challenge under the commerce clause to the "individual mandate" provision of the Patient Protection and Affordable Care Act (PPACA), popularly known as "Obamacare," which, beginning in 2014, requires most Americans to maintain "minimum essential" health insurance coverage. While many persons will receive the required coverage through their employer or from a government program for older persons or for lower-income persons, those persons who do not receive health insurance through a third party are required to purchase insurance from a private company. The law heavily regulates the private insurance companies, including a prohibition on their denying coverage to people because of a preexisting illness and on imposing yearly or lifetime limits on coverage. Subsidies to reduce the cost of the insurance and available for persons at certain income levels. Those individuals who do not maintain the required coverage are required to pay a penalty, calculated as a percentage of household income, subject to a floor and a cap. The Court held that the imposition of the "individual mandate" requirement could not be sustained under the

---

42. Some federal laws have been interpreted as not applying to purely local non- economic activity in order to avoid a question as to the constitutionality of such application. *See Jones v. United States*, 529 U.S. 848 (2000) (federal arson law did not apply to the burning of an owner-occupied private residence that was not being used for commercial purposes); *Solid Waste Agency of Northern Cook County v. United States Army Corps of Engineers*, 531 U.S. 159 (2001) (federal clean water law did not apply to non-navigable, isolated intrastate waters that provided a habitat for migratory birds).
43. 545 U.S. 1 (2005).
44. 545 U.S. at 22. Since federal law prohibited the growing of marijuana for personal use, including medical use, federal law controlled as a matter of federal supremacy, and it did not matter that the use of marijuana for medical purposes was authorized by state law. *See also Taylor v. United States*, 136 S.Ct. 2074 (2016), where the Court held that Congress could make it a crime to rob or attempt to rob a drug dealer without showing that the drugs traveled across state lines, since Congress could regulate the market for drugs.
45. 132 Sup.Ct. 2566 (2012).

commerce power, because it did not regulate existing commercial activity, but compels people to become active in commerce by purchasing a product that they did not want to purchase. The Court distinguished all of the cases in which it had upheld the exercise of the commerce power on the ground that in those cases Congress was regulating existing commercial activity.[46] However, the holding in Sebelius is limited to the situation present in that case, where the law compels a person to become active in commerce, and so has little capacity for extension. Most exercises of the commerce power by Congress will be sustained under the rationale of the *Gonzales decision,* so that the *Sibelius* decision imposes only a very small limitation on the power of Congress to regulate interstate commerce.[47]

In *Sibelius*, Chief Justice Roberts, joined by Justices Ginsburg, Breyer, Sotomayor and Kagan, held that because the law imposed a "penalty" for noncompliance with the "individual mandate," requirement the law could be upheld as a proper exercise of Congress' constitutional power to tax under Article I, section 8, clause 1. It is well settled that Congress can use the power to tax, sometimes in conjunction with the power to spend, to achieve regulatory objectives. The Court has stated that, "Congress has substantive power to tax and appropriate for the general welfare, limited only by the requirement that it shall be exercised for the common benefit as distinguished from some mere local purpose."[48] Important benefit federal programs, including Social Security and Unemployment Compensation, have been upheld under the "taxing and spending" power.[49]

53. In other words, although in theory the federal government can exercise only those powers that are enumerated in the Constitution, the powers of Congress under Article I, section 8, have been construed so broadly by the Supreme Court that today there is very little activity that may not constitutionally be subject to federal regulation. In this sense, the constitutional power of the federal government may be considered to be plenary. However, as we will see subsequently, the states are generally free to

---

46. The main opinion on this issue was authored by Chief Justice Roberts. However, as will be pointed out subsequently, Chief Justice Roberts upheld the constitutionality of the "individual mandate" as a proper exercise of the "taxing and spending" power of Art. I, s. 8, cl. 1. Justices Scalia, Kennedy, Thomas and Alito, wrote a dissenting opinion, contending that the "individual mandate" could not be sustained under the commerce power, and could not be sustained under the "taxing and spending" power either, because Congress did not enact the "individual mandate" under the "taxing and spending" power.
47. The overwhelming number of laws enacted under the commerce power regulate economic activity, the channels or instrumentalities of interstate commerce or activity that has crossed state lines. The very small limitation on the commerce power applies only to the regulation of purely local noneconomic activity, and as in National Federation, to "non-commerce," so to speak.
48. *United States v. Gerlach Live Stock Co.*, 339 U.S. 725, 738 (1950).
49. *See Helvering v. Davis,* 301 U.S. 619 (1937); *Steward Machine Co. v. Davis,* 301 U.S. 548 (1937). Moreover, under the "taxing and spending" power, Congress has the broad authority to regulate any activity that has received federal funding. Thus, Congress may constitutionally prohibit the bribery of state and local governmental officials where the state or local government has received federal funds, as all states and local governments have. It is not a constitutionally necessary element of the offense that the bribery was in connection with a particular program receiving federal funds. *Sabri v. United States*, 541 U.S. 600 (2004).

regulate the same matters regulated by the federal government so long as there is no conflict between the exercise of state power and the exercise of federal power.

Chapter 3. The Executive Power

§1. The Presidency

54. Article II, section 1, provides that the executive power "shall be vested in a President of the United States of America." The American Presidency is a unique constitutional concept, unparalleled in the constitutional system of any other democratic nation, in which the entire executive power is lodged in the person of a single individual. Looking to the historical context in which the American Presidency was established, it may be said that the Framers of the Constitution conceived of the President as an electorally accountable officer who would combine in his person all the executive functions that were performed in Great Britain separately by the monarch and by the prime minister.[50]

55. There is no provision in the Constitution for anything like a "council of ministers" or a "cabinet." Under Article II, section 2, Congress has the power to establish "federal offices," and this provision contemplates that executive departments will be among the "federal offices" established by Congress. At the present time, Congress has established fifteen executive departments: the Departments of Agriculture, Commerce, Defense, Education, Energy, Health and Human Services, Housing and Urban Development, Interior, Justice, Labor, State, Transportation, Treasury, Veterans Affairs, and Homeland Security.[51] The heads of these departments and other executive branch officials to whom the president has accorded "cabinet rank," in practice constitute the Presidential Cabinet. However, the Presidential Cabinet has no constitutional status and no constitutional power. The President consults regularly with and seeks the advice of the Cabinet, but the final decision on any matter coming within the executive power resides entirely with the President. Again, it must be emphasized that under the American "Presidential system," the President is not in any way "responsible" to the Congress, and that the President alone exercises the executive power of the United States.

50. In constitutional theory, the President is simply a citizen who has been chosen to exercise the executive power of the United States, and by tradition is addressed only as "Mr President." (It is assumed that if a woman were elected to that office Xas none has yet been—she would be addressed as "Madam President.") In contradistinction to the British practice (and doubtless in reaction to it), Art. 1, s. 9 of the Constitution specifically provides that, "No Title of Nobility shall be granted by the United States."

51. The head of each department is designated the "Secretary" of the department, except for the head of the Department of Justice, who is designated the "Attorney-General of the United States."

§2. Election, Qualifications and Legal Status of the President

56. The President is elected for a term of four years, and under the Twenty-Second Amendment, no person can be elected to that office more than twice.[52] The President must be a native-born (as opposed to naturalized) citizen, at least 35 years of age, and a resident of the United States for 14 years.

Prior to President Franklin D. Roosevelt's running for a third term in 1940 and a fourth term in 1944, it had been an "unwritten tradition" that no President would serve more than two terms. The Twenty-Second Amendment was adopted after Roosevelt's death in office in April 1945, in reaction to his having broken this "unwritten tradition." If it had not been for the Twenty-Second Amendment, it is quite possible that President Ronald Reagan, who was very popular with the electorate, would have been elected to a third term in 1988.

57. While in the political sense, the President is "popularly elected" by the people of the United States, as a constitutional matter, there is an indirect election of the President. Constitutionally, the President is selected on a state-by-state basis by an Electoral College, the members of which are elected by the voters in each state. The Framers considered the office of the President too important to be entrusted to direct election by the people, fearing that a "demagogue" might be elected in this manner. So, they established a system by which electors voting in each state, would choose the "most qualified" person to be President, having in mind at the time George Washington, the Commander of the Continental Army during the Revolutionary War, who in fact was chosen to be the first President.

58. Under Article II, section 2, each state is entitled to a number of electors in the Electoral College "equal to the whole Number of Senators and Representatives to which the State may be entitled." The Twenty-Third Amendment makes the seat of government, the District of Columbia (Washington, D.C.), the equivalent of a state for purposes of representation in the Electoral College. At the present time, there are 538 electoral votes, with the smallest states and the District of Columbia having three electoral votes, and the largest state, California, having fifty-five electoral votes. Article II, section 2, also provides that the legislature of each state is to decide how its electors shall be chosen, and in every state, of course, the legislature has provided that the electors are to be chosen by popular vote. Congress is directed to provide a "uniform day" on which the electors are to be chosen and on which they are to cast their votes. The "election for electors," or more popularly, the Presidential election, is now held on the first Tuesday after the first Monday in November. After the electors have been chosen, they meet in their respective states on the first Monday after the second Wednesday in December, and cast ballots for the President. The vote totals in each state are then sent to the "President of the Senate" (actually the Vice-President) in Washington, D.C., who "in the presence of the Senate and the House of Representatives,"

52. If the Vice-President has succeeded to an unexpired term of the President and served more than two years of that term, the Vice-President can only be elected to one additional term. For example, when President Ford succeeded to the unexpired term of President Nixon, who resigned in August 1974, that term had more than two years to run before it expired in January 1977. If President Ford had been reelected President in the 1976 election (which he was not), he would not have been eligible to run for another term in 1980.

counts the vote totals from each state. The person having a majority of electoral votes is declared the President. If no person receives a majority of the votes, the matter is referred to the House of Representatives, which is directed to choose the President from the three persons having the highest number of electoral votes. The vote in the House of Representatives is taken by states, with each state having one vote, and the person receiving a majority of the votes by state is declared to be the President.[53]

59. In practice, of course, the Presidential election operates quite differently. The Democratic Party, the Republican Party, and various "third parties" run candidates for President, and the voters in each state vote for the candidate, although in theory they are voting for "electors who are pledged to vote for the candidate."[54] With the exception of two small states, all the states have provided that when a candidate "carries a state," that is, when a candidate receives more "popular votes" than any other candidate in the state, that candidate has won all the electoral votes of that state, regardless of the size of the candidate's margin in the popular voting.[55] The candidate who "carries" with a total of electoral votes adding up to 270 thus has been elected to be the President.

60. Since the President is elected by the Electoral College rather than by the voters directly, the candidates for President campaign with a view toward winning the necessary 270 electoral votes. For this reason, they do not campaign very much in smaller states or in larger states that are likely to vote for their opponent. In the 2000 election, for example, it was assumed that Gore, the Democratic candidate would win in California and New York while Bush, the Republican candidate, would win in his home state of Texas. It was also assumed that most of the states in the south would vote for Bush while most of the states in the northeast would vote for Gore. Both candidates campaigned very hard in "battleground" states, where each candidate had

---

53. The last time the election was "thrown into the House" was in 1824, when the House chose John Quincy Adams over Andrew Jackson. Jackson had received a majority of the popular vote, but did not receive a majority of votes in the Electoral College. The three highest vote getters in the Electoral College were Jackson, Adams, and William Crawford. The fourth candidate receiving votes in the Electoral College was Henry Clay, who had considerable support in the House. A number of his supporters voted for Adams, purportedly pursuant to a deal by which if Adams were elected, he would appoint Clay as Secretary of State. Adams was elected and subsequently appointed Clay to this position.

54. In most states, only the candidate's name appears on the ballot, although in some, the candidate's name is preceded in small print by "electors for" or the like.

55. In Maine the statewide winner receives two electoral votes, and the winner of each Congressional district receives one vote. In the 2016 election, Hillary Clinton, the Democratic nominee, carried the state and one Congressional district while Donald Trump, the Republican nominee, carried the other Congressional district. So Clinton ended up with three electoral votes and Trump with one. In Nebraska, prior to the 2008 election, the same candidate carried all five Congressional districts. In the 2008 election, the Democratic candidate, Barack Obama, carried one Congressional district, and thus received one electoral vote, while the Republican candidate, John McCain, carried the other four Congressional districts and thus received four electoral votes. These two states have only nine electoral votes between them.

a good chance of winning. The most important "battleground" state was Florida, and it turned out that the result in Florida determined the result of the election.[56]

It is thus irrelevant for constitutional purposes which candidate wins the "popular vote." The 2000 election was extremely close, both as to the popular vote and the Electoral College vote, and since Bush managed to win 271 electoral votes, it did not matter that Gore received about 500,000 more popular votes than Bush. This phenomenon had occurred three times before in American history. In the 1824 Presidential Election, Andrew Jackson received a majority of the popular vote, but not a majority in the Electoral College. The election was "thrown into the House," which voted for John Quincy Adams. In the 1888 Presidential election, the Democratic candidate, Grover Cleveland, won the popular vote, but the Republican candidate, Benjamin Harrison, won the vote in the Electoral College. In the 1876 Presidential election, the Democratic candidate, Samuel Tilden, won the popular vote, but the Republican candidate, Rutherford B. Hayes, won the vote in the Electoral College. The possibility that this phenomenon could occur, as well as the possibility that a strong "third party" candidate could "carry" enough states to "throw the election into the House," has prompted numerous academic proposals to abolish the Electoral College and provide for direct election of the President. At the present time, however, even after the controversial 2000 election, these proposals are not being seriously pursued, and as a constitutional matter, the President is still elected directly by the Electoral College and only indirectly by the People of the United States. In the 2004 election President George Bush maintained a 3 million lead in the popular vote and received 286 electoral votes to Democratic candidate John Kerry's 251 electoral votes (One Democratic Minnesota elector cast his vote for the Democratic Vice-Presidential candidate). In the 2008 election, the Democratic candidate, Barack Obama, defeated the Republican candidate, John McCain by 9 million, 7 hundred thousand popular votes, and by 365 to 173 electoral votes. In the 2012 election, President Obama defeated the Republican candidate, Mitt Romney by close to 5 million popular votes and by 332 to 206 electoral votes.

However, in the 2016 election, the Republican candidate, Donald Trump won the electoral vote 306 to 234 and thus the Presidency despite losing the "popular vote" to the Democratic candidate, Hillary Clinton, by 2.8 million votes. He accomplished this task by winning a number of smaller states, a few larger states, and three larger states that had traditionally voted Democratic, Pennsylvania, Michigan, and Wisconsin, by very small margins. By winning these three states, he secured their forty-six electoral votes, which were sufficient to give him the electoral vote majority. If Clinton had

---

56. The 2000 Presidential election brought to the forefront the matter of election of the President by the Electoral College instead of by popular vote. It treated the world to the spectacle of the result of the election for the American President—arguably the most powerful position in the world—depending on how "punchcard" ballots would be counted in the State of Florida. The controversy was finally resolved by the Supreme Court, which held that Florida's method of recounting votes violated the Fourteenth Amendment's equal protection clause and also held that under Florida law, there was no time for the recount to continue. Thus, Bush, who had been declared the winner in the original count, was awarded Florida's twenty-five electoral votes, and so obtained 271 electoral votes to Gore's 266 electoral votes, and was elected President. *Bush v. Gore*, 531 U.S. 98 (2000). One of Gore's electors abstained in protest of the Supreme Court's decision, which is why the number of electoral votes totaled 537 instead of 538.

carried those states with their forty-six electoral votes, she would have received the electoral vote majority and would have been elected President. All told, Trump carried thirty states to Clinton's twenty states and the District of Columbia. As the result of the 2016 election demonstrates, a candidate can win the election despite losing the "popular vote" with small margin wins in states with a large number of electoral votes.

61. The President, as the Supreme Court has stated, "occupies a unique position in the constitutional scheme," and thus is entitled to absolute immunity from civil liability for damages arising out of acts performed as President.[57] Other executive officials, however, generally are entitled only to qualified immunity, and may be held liable if the official's actions were "in violation of clearly established law."[58] While the President is immune from civil liability for damages arising out of the performance of his official duties, the President is not immune from legal process and can be compelled to comply with a judicial subpoena. The President can assert "executive privilege" with respect to the particular information requested by the subpoena, but—the validity of the claim of "executive privilege" must be determined by the courts.[59] When the testimony of sitting or former Presidents is subpoenaed or otherwise requested,

57. *Nixon v. Fitzgerald*, 457 U.S. 731 (1982). It has been assumed that the President, like any other legislative, executive or judicial official, does not enjoy immunity from criminal liability for crimes committed in the performance of official duties. President Ford, upon succeeding former President Nixon following Nixon's resignation in the "Watergate scandal," issued a blanket pardon for any crimes Nixon may have committed while serving as President. The President enjoys no immunity from civil suits during his term of office for private conduct unrelated to his official duties. *Clinton v. Jones*, 520 U.S. 681 (1997). In that case, the plaintiff, a former Arkansas state employee, filed a civil suit against President Clinton, seeking damages for acts allegedly committed against her while the President was Governor of Arkansas. Clinton's claim that the suit should be delayed until he left office, because defending the suit would interfere with the performance of his Presidential duties, was unanimously rejected by the Supreme Court. The suit was subsequently settled and did not come to trial. President Clinton's conduct in connection with his defense of the civil suit led to his impeachment. *See* para. 82, *infra* .

58. *Harlow v. Fitzgerald*, 457 U.S. 800 (1982).

59. *United States v. Nixon*, 418 U.S. 683 (1974). This case involved the famous "Watergate tapes," and arose out of a prosecution of seven of President Nixon's presidential aides and campaign staff for a conspiracy to obstruct justice in connection with the investigation of the break-in at the opposing party's headquarters in the Watergate Hotel in Washington, DC, during the 1972 Presidential election campaign. Nixon himself was named an "unindicted co-conspirator" in the case. The prosecutor moved the federal court hearing the case to issue a *subpoena duces tecum* to the President, requiring him to produce certain memoranda, papers and tapes relating to specific meetings between the President and others. The President's lawyers moved to quash the subpoena on grounds of "executive privilege." The Supreme Court held that the President could be required to respond to the subpoena and that it was for the court to decide whether the claim of "executive privilege" would be recognized in the particular case. The material would be viewed by the court in camera, and the court would exclude all material that it found to be privileged. Since the "Watergate tapes" clearly implicated the President in the obstruction of justice, the President, fearing impeachment and conviction, resigned from office, the only President ever to have done so in the Nation's history.

it is customary to permit the President to testify by way of a videotaped deposition rather than by appearing in court.[60]

§3. The Vice-President

62. The Vice-President is elected in the same manner as the President and must have the same qualifications. As a practical matter, each political party nominates a "ticket," consisting of a candidate for President and a candidate for Vice-President, and in theory the voters vote for electors who are committed to cast their electoral votes for the party's candidates for both offices.

63. The primary constitutional function of the Vice-President is to serve as "President-in-waiting." The Vice-President automatically succeeds to the Presidency in the event of the President's death, resignation, or removal from office.[61] The only other constitutional function of the Vice-President is to preside over the Senate, which the Vice-President rarely does in practice.

64. While the President typically promises to make the Vice-President "an important part of my administration," in times past, this promise usually "is honored more in the breach than in the observance." However, during the eight years of the George Bush Administration, the President relied heavily on his Vice-President Dick Cheney for advice and for a number of specific tasks. President Barack Obama has also relied on Vice-President Joe Biden in this way. The Vice-President attends cabinet meetings, frequently represents the United States at inaugurations and other ceremonial events in foreign nations, and performs specific tasks assigned to him by the President, but in past times had only limited power within the administration. As stated above, the influence of the Vice-President has increased with the last two Presidents. Above all, regardless of the Vice-President's influence within the administration, the Vice-President must always appear loyal to the President and must fully support the President's policies.

65. The Vice-Presidency has often operated as a "steppingstone" to the Presidency. In the twentieth century, four Vice-Presidents have succeeded to the Presidency upon

60. In *Nixon v. Administrator of General Services Administration*, 433 U.S. 425 (1977), the Court upheld against the claim of "executive privilege," a federal law directing a federal official to take custody of former President Nixon's presidential papers and tape recordings, to provide for their processing and screening, to return personal items to the President, and to establish the conditions upon which the remainder of the materials would eventually be made available to scholars and the general public.

61. The Twenty-Fifth Amendment, promulgated in 1967, establishes a procedure by which the President may voluntarily relinquish or involuntarily be made to relinquish the duties of office due to a temporary disability. During this time, the Vice-President performs the duties of the Presidency. This situation has never occurred.

the President's death,[62] and one upon the President's resignation,[63] and two former Vice-Presidents have been elected President in their own right.[64]

§4. The Appointment and Removal of Federal Officers

66. The appointment process established by the Constitution reflects both the constitutional principle of separation of powers and the constitutional principle of checks and balances. Congress establishes the federal offices, the President appoints the officers, and the President's appointments must be confirmed by a majority vote of the Senate.

67. An "officer of the United States" is one who "exercises significant authority pursuant to the laws of the United States."[65] Thousands of federal "officers," from Cabinet members on down, fall into this category. Within the class of "officers of the United States," there are in effect "principal" and "inferior" officers. This distinction is made by Article II, section 2 itself, which requires that "officers of the United States" be appointed by the President and confirmed by the Senate, but allows Congress to provide for the appointment of "inferior" officers either by the President or by the head of a department or by the courts.[66] However, Congress may not, consistent with

---

62. Theodore Roosevelt upon the death of William McKinley in 1901, Calvin Coolidge upon the death of Warren Harding in 1923, Harry Truman upon the death of Franklin Roosevelt in 1945, and Lyndon Johnson upon the death of John Kennedy in 1963.

63. Gerald Ford succeeded Richard Nixon, who resigned in 1974 in the wake of the "Watergate scandal."

64. Richard Nixon, who was Vice-President under Dwight Eisenhower, was defeated in his efforts to succeed President Eisenhower in the 1960 election, but was later elected in 1968. George Bush, who was Vice-President under Ronald Reagan from 1980 to 1988, was elected President in the 1988 election. George W. Bush's Vice-President, Dick Cheney, became Vice-President only after serving in other important offices, including as a Member of Congress and Secretary of Defense. Barack Obama's Vice-President, Joe Biden, was serving as United States Senator and Chairman of the Foreign Relations Committee when he was selected to run. In both cases, it was suggested that the relatively young Presidential candidates wanted a Vice-President who was significantly older and much more experienced than they were. It had been assumed at the outset that neither Vice-President would himself seek the Presidency in the future. This factor may have made it possible for the President to give them a more prominent role and greater influence in his administration.

65. *Buckley v. Valeo*, 424 U.S. 1, 126 (1976).

66. Under this provision, Congress may authorize the courts to appoint election supervisors, *Ex parte Siebold*, 100 U.S. 371 (1879), and to appoint commissioners to handle extradition matters. *Rice v. Ames*, 180 U.S. 371 (1901). In *Morrison v. Olson*, 487 U.S. 654 (1988), the Supreme Court relied on this provision to uphold the constitutionality of a law authorizing the Attorney-General to ask a designated panel of federal judges to appoint an "Independent Counsel" to investigate and, if appropriate, to prosecute certain high-ranking officials for alleged violations of the federal criminal law. The Supreme Court has also held that civilian judges of the Coast Guard Court of Criminal Appeals, an intermediate court in the military justice system, are "inferior" officers for purposes of the Appointments Clause, so that Congress could authorize their appointment by the Secretary of the Treasury, who is the department head in charge of the *Coast Guard. Edmond v. United States*, 502 U.S. 651 (1997).

the appointments clause, itself appoint "inferior" officers. Thus, the Court held unconstitutional a law that established a federal election commission and provided that a majority of the voting members of the commission were to be appointed by the Speaker of the House of Representatives and the President pro tempore of the Senate.[67]

68. The great majority of the employees of the federal government, of course, are not "officers of the United States," but civil service employees, who are subject to a "merit system" of employment and retention, and so are unaffected by a change of Presidential administrations. In addition, there are a large number of non-civil service or "political" employees, who are nonetheless not "officers of the United States" for constitutional purposes, so that their appointment does not require Senate confirmation.

69. Except as regards impeachment for misconduct, which will be discussed subsequently, the Constitution makes no provision for the removal of federal officers once they have been appointed by the President and confirmed by the Senate. In times past, the President has asserted the power to remove such officers, while Congress has contended that it alone has the power to provide a fixed term for federal officers and to establish the conditions for their removal. The Supreme Court has held that Congress has the power to provide a fixed term and establish the conditions for removal of federal officers, except to the extent that this would interfere with the President's ability to carry out his constitutional duties. In other words, there are some "purely executive" officers who must be removable at will by the President if he is to accomplish his constitutional role, but the removal of all other federal officers may be regulated by Congress. Thus, for example, Congress cannot restrict the President's power to remove the head of a cabinet-level executive department,[68] but can restrict the President's power to remove a member of an independent regulatory agency[69] or of a commission whose function it is to determine claims against the government.[70]

§5. The Powers of the President

70. Since the President exercises the entire executive power of the United States under Article II, the powers of the President are enormous, and our discussion of these powers will divide them into a number of categories.

I. Powers with Respect to Congress and the Legislative Process

71. Under Article II, section 3, the President is directed to "from time to time give the Congress Information of the State of the Union, and shall recommend to their

---

67. *Buckley v. Valeo*, 424 U.S. 1 (1976). Where the Appointments Clause was violated in the appointment of civilian judges to an intermediate court in the military justice system, any action taken by the court, here the conviction of an accused service member, was void and could not be given de facto effect. *Ryder v. United States*, 515 U.S. 177 (1995).
68. *Myers v. United States*, 272 U.S. 52 (1926).
69. *Humphrey's Executor v. United States*, 295 U.S. 602 (1935).
70. *Wiener v. United States*, 357 U.S. 349 (1958).

consideration such Measures as he shall judge necessary and expedient." It has become a fixed custom for the President to deliver a "State of the Union" address to a joint session of Congress after their session has begun in January. Typically, the President will set forth his legislative proposals in the "State of the Union" address, and proposed legislation embodying these proposals will be introduced in Congress by a member of the President's political party. As we have discussed previously, the legislative process is a collaborative effort between Congress and the President. The President may veto legislation with which he disagrees, and legislation may be enacted over the President's veto only by a two-thirds vote of both Houses of Congress.[71]

II. The Appointment Power

72. The appointment process for federal officers has been discussed previously in §4. The President must appoint all "officers of the United States," and the President also has the power to appoint ambassadors and all federal judges, including Justices of the Supreme Court. All Presidential appointments must be confirmed by majority vote of the Senate. When the Senate is not in session, the President has the power to make a "recess appointment," which continues until the end of the next session of Congress. In recent years, the Presidents have used this power to appoint judges and other federal officials in circumstances where the Senate had long delayed voting on their nomination.[72]

III. The Pardoning Power

73. The President has the power to "grant reprieves and pardons for offenses against the United States," except for impeachment.[73] The pardoning power has been construed very broadly to include the power to commute a sentence imposed as punishment for crime as well as to pardon the offense itself,[74] the power to pardon the

---

71. *See* para. 44 *supra* . If the two Houses of Congress cannot agree on when to adjourn, the President has the constitutional power to "adjourn them to such Time as he shall think proper." This situation has not occurred in recent memory. In addition, as we have discussed previously, after Congress has adjourned for the year, the President has the power to call Congress back into sessions on "extraordinary occasions," although as might be expected from the constitutional language, this power is rarely exercised.
72. In a case challenging the President's use of the power to make "recess appointments," the Court held that the term "the recess" applied to both intra-session and inter-session recesses, but that a recess lasting less than ten days was presumptively too short to trigger the exercise of this power. In the case before it, the Court held that pro forma sessions counted as sessions and that the recess at issue was only three days and so was invalid. *National Labor Relations Board v. Canning*, 134 S.Ct. 2550 (2014).
73. As will be discussed more fully subsequently, impeachment involves the removal from office of a "civil officer of the United States," and does not involve any punishment in the penal sense. The officer convicted by the Senate following the impeachment is only removed from office and disqualified from holding any further federal office.
74. *Perovich v. Biddle*, 274 U.S. 480 (1927).

in the House, voting in favor of filing the impeachment charges, and with virtually all the Democrats voting against it. The trial in the Senate took place at various times in January and February 1999. The evidence in the trial consisted solely of the voluminous report filed by an Independent Counsel appointed to investigate the President's conduct (the Independent Counsel law, authorizing the appointment of an Independent Counsel to investigate the conduct of the President and certain other federal officials in specified circumstances, expired in July, 1999, and was not renewed), and the depositions of three witnesses, which were taken outside of the Senate and were available for review by the Senators. In February 1999, the Senate voted to acquit the President on both charges. The vote on the charge of committing perjury before the grand jury was fifty-five in favor of acquittal and forty-five in favor of conviction, and the vote on the charge of obstruction of justice was fifty in favor of acquittal and fifty in favor of conviction, both far short of the constitutionally required two-thirds vote for conviction. While the proceedings in the Senate were not as openly partisan as the proceedings in the House, most of the votes on procedural matters were along party lines, and with the exception of one vote on one count, all of the votes for conviction came from Republican Senators. Public opinion surveys taken throughout the proceedings in both Houses showed that a substantial majority of the public opposed removing the President from office.

The public opposition to the Clinton impeachment makes a future Presidential impeachment highly unlikely except in circumstances where there is strong evidence of a serious abuse of official power or a serious breach of official duty. This type of evidence was present in 1974, when the House was considering impeachment proceedings against former President Nixon, *see* paragraph 81, *supra*, and public opinion surveys showed that when the House Judiciary Committee recommended the filing of impeachment charges against Nixon, a substantial majority of the public favored removing Nixon from office. He resigned before the bill of impeachment was voted on by the House.

83. In practice, impeachments are very rare, since federal officers (other than judges, who enjoy life tenure) who are charged with serious misconduct are likely to resign or be removed by the President.[89]

89. Apart from the two Presidential impeachments, there have only been seventeen other impeachments in American history. One of these cases involved a Supreme Justice, who was acquitted, one involved a Senator (it is recognized today that Members of Congress cannot constitutionally be impeached), and one involved a Secretary of War, who was acquitted. The remaining fourteen cases involved federal judges. Eight of the judges were removed, three were acquitted, three resigned before the trial.

Chapter 4. Separation of Powers and Conflicts Between Congress and the President

§1. The Principle of Separation of Powers

84. Under the principle of separation of powers, each branch of the federal government can only exercise the powers given to it under the Constitution and cannot exercise the powers given under the Constitution to another branch. Whenever one branch purports to exercise the powers that under the Constitution belong to another branch, there has been a violation of the principle of separation of powers, and such action is unconstitutional. We have seen an example of this situation in the discussion of the appointment of federal officers in Chapter 3, §4. Since the Constitution provides that "primary" federal officers must be appointed by the President and that "inferior" officers must be appointed by the President, a head of a department or the courts, Congress has no power whatsoever to appoint any federal officers. This being so, a provision of a law that authorized the Speaker of the House of Representatives and the President pro tempore of the Senate to appoint a majority of the members of the Federal Election Commission was held to be unconstitutional.[90]

§2. Direct Conflicts

85. Likewise, the question of "which branch has the power" comes into play whenever there is a direct conflict between Congress and the President with respect to a particular exercise of governmental power. In this circumstance, Congress asserts its authority to deal with the matter in issue under the powers provided to it under Article I, section 8, and the President asserts his authority to deal with the same matter under the powers provided to the executive branch under Article II, sections 2 and 3. Again, we saw an example of this situation in the discussion of the removal of federal officers in Chapter 3, §4. The President asserted that he had the power to remove the officer in question while Congress asserted that it alone had the power to provide a fixed term of office and to establish the conditions for the removal of the officer. The Court, it will be recalled, resolved this conflict by upholding the President's power to remove officers whose duties are predominantly "political or executive," and upholding Congress' power to control the removal of officers whose duties are predominantly, "quasi-judicial" and "quasi-legislative."[91]

86. When challenges are made to the exercise of Presidential power as being beyond his authority under Article II, sections 2 and 3, as we discussed in Chapter 3, §6.V., the Court has often been able to reject the challenge by looking to the President's power to "execute the laws" under Article II, section 3, and finding that the Presidential

90. *Buckley v. Valeo*, 424 U.S. 1 (1976).
91. *See* para. 69, *supra* .

action in question was authorized by Congress. This means of avoiding the question of the President's authority is not possible only when the President, asserting his power under Article II, sections 2 and 3, has taken action that directly conflicts with action that has been prescribed in a federal law. This situation is exceedingly rare in practice, but occurred in *Youngstown Sheet & Tube Co. v. Sawyer* (The Steel Seizure Case).[92] The Court's decision in that case indicates that where there is a direct conflict between the exercise of Congressional power and the exercise of Presidential power, at least in matters not directly involving military action or foreign affairs, the exercise of Congressional power must prevail.

87. That case involved the validity of a Presidential order directing the Secretary of Commerce to take possession of most of the nation's steel mills to avert a nationwide steel strike during the Korean War. The President justified the order on the basis of his power as Commander-in-Chief of the Armed Forces, contending that continued steel production was necessary to the war effort. Not only was the use of the seizure technique not authorized by any federal law, but to the contrary, federal law specifically provided a method of dealing with this situation, and when that law was under consideration by the Congress, Congress had expressly refused to authorize governmental seizure as a means of avoiding a nationwide strike. The Court held that the matter in issue related to the exercise of legislative power, and that the President's power as Commander-in-Chief of the Armed Forces could not be relied on to supplant what was otherwise within the legislative power. As the Court stated: "The power of Congress to adopt such public policies as those pro-claimed by the order is beyond question. … The Constitution does not subject this lawmaking power of Congress to presidential or military supervision or control."[93]

In an oft-cited concurring opinion, Justice Robert Jackson set forth a three-part analysis of the nature of Presidential power in relation to Congressional power: (1) When the President acts pursuant to Congressional authorization, Presidential authority is at the maximum, since it includes all the authority that the President possesses in his own right plus all the authority that Congress can delegate. (2) When the President acts in absence of either a Congressional grant or a Congressional denial of authority, the President can rely on his own independent powers, but there is a "zone of twilight" in which both the President and the Congress may have concurrent authority, so the President's action more likely may be sustained. (3) When the President takes measures incompatible with the expressed or implied will of Congress, Presidential power is at its lowest ebb, since then the President can only rely on his own power minus any constitutional powers of Congress over the matter, and the Court can uphold Presidential

92. 343 U.S. 579 (1952).
93. 343 U.S. at 588.

power only by disabling Congress from acting upon the subject.[94] Since the third situation was presented here, Jackson found that the President's action was unconstitutional.[95]

The third situation was also presented in the very recent case of *Zivotofsky v. Kerry*, but here the Court upheld Presidential power by finding that Congress was disabled from acting upon the subject.[96] Under the Constitution, Article II, section 3, the President is given the power to "receive Ambassadors and other public Ministers," and this provision has been interpreted as giving the President the sole power to recognize foreign governments and the territorial boundaries of a foreign state. *See* paragraph 441, *infra.* It has long been the practice of American Presidents to refuse to recognize Israel's annexation of Jerusalem, and to maintain that the status of Jerusalem can be determined only as a part of the final peace settlement of the Israeli-Arab conflict. As a result, the American Embassy is located in Tel Aviv rather than Jerusalem. In addition when a child is born to American citizen parents in Jerusalem, the place of birth on the child's passport is listed simply as "Jerusalem" rather than as "Jerusalem, Israel." Ordinarily, the passport lists the foreign county as the childs' place of birth, such as "Paris, France." Congress enacted legislation requiring that when a child was born to American citizen parents in Jerusalem, the child's passport must list the place of birth as "Jerusalem, Israel." In *Zivotofsky,* the Court held that the legislation was unconstitutional as an improper interference with the President's power to recognize foreign governments.

§3. The Power over War and Military Intervention

88. War powers constitute one field where the separation and delimitation of powers is most controversial. It is dealt with extensively in Part V, Chapter 1, §2.

§4. Judicial Organization: The Dual Court System

89. In the United States, there is a dual court system of state courts and federal courts. This dual court system is an essential part of American federalism, and is the result of the historical circumstances in which American federalism developed. Since upon Independence in 1776, the states succeeded to the sovereignty formerly exercised

94. *Ibid.* at 637–638.
95. The third situation was presented in the more recent case of *Medellin v. Texas*, 552 U.S. 491 (2008). The International Court of Justice had rendered a decision that the United States had violated the Vienna Convention on Consular Relations, which requires law enforcement officials to inform arrested foreign nationals of their right to notify their consulate of their detention. The State of Texas had not done this with respect to a Mexican national who had been arrested and convicted in Texas. President George W. Bush sent a memorandum to the Texas state courts advising them that they must adhere to this decision. Since the Vienna Convention is not a self-executing treaty, it requires implementing Congressional legislation, *see* para *infra* , and none had been enacted. Because this was so, the Court held that the decision of the International Court of Justice was not binding domestic law, and the President did not have the power under Art. II to order the state courts to reopen a state court criminal judgment.
96. 135 S.Ct. 2076 (2015).

by Great Britain over domestic matters, it followed that each state would have its own system of laws and its own court system. This fundamental attribute of state sovereignty was in no way affected by the adoption of the Constitution in 1787, and today each state continues to have its own system of laws and its own court system. However, when the federal Constitution was adopted, provision was made for a system of federal courts to "exercise the judicial power of the United States." In the United States today then, there is a dual system of state and federal courts, sometimes with overlapping jurisdiction, so that in some circumstances a party may be able to choose whether to bring the case in a state court or in a federal court.

I. The State Courts

90. The state courts may best be described as courts of unlimited jurisdiction. They adjudicate civil and criminal cases, develop the "common law" of that state through judicial decisions, and interpret and apply the laws enacted by state legislatures and local governments. The state courts are also required by the Supremacy Clause of the federal Constitution, Article VI, section 2, to apply the Constitution and federal laws when relevant in cases coming before them for decision and to hear suits based on the federal Constitution and federal laws, except as Congress may provide otherwise. The state courts then are courts of unlimited jurisdiction, with the power and responsibility to hear cases arising under state law, and to a large extent, to hear cases arising under federal law.[97]

91. Typically, a state court system consists of a court of general jurisdiction or "trial court,"[98] an intermediate appellate court, and a state Supreme Court. Cases from the trial court can be appealed as of right to the intermediate appellate court, and in most circumstances a further appeal to the state Supreme Court must be granted by leave of that court. In some of the less populated states, there is no intermediate appellate court, and all cases may be appealed directly from the court of general jurisdiction to the state Supreme Court. The state Supreme Court is the final authority on all the questions of state law. While, as we will see, the United States Supreme Court can review state court decisions involving question of federal law, it has no power to review their decisions on questions of state law.

92. The selection and appointment of state court judges varies considerably from state to state. In most states, lower court judges are popularly elected for a term of years, and in a number of states, appellate judges are popularly elected as well. Frequently, but not always, these judges are elected on a nonpartisan ballot, that is, they do not run as candidates of political parties, but in some states judges must run in partisan elections. Some states provide for the appointment of judges, usually by the Governor. In some states, judges are initially appointed for a term of years, and

97. Usually, there is also a court of limited jurisdiction below the court of general jurisdiction. Congress has provided that any suit against a federal official may be removed by that official to federal court, as it always will be, so as a practical matter of such suits are always brought in federal court.

98. Usually, there is also a court of limited jurisdiction below the court of general jurisdiction.

then run unopposed "on their record," so to speak, with the voters deciding whether or not they wish to retain the judge for another term.

II. The Federal Courts

93. Article III, section 1, of the Constitution, the "judicial article," provides that "the judicial Power of the United States shall be vested in one Supreme Court, and in such inferior courts as the Congress may from time to time establish." Thus, only the Supreme Court is provided for in the Constitution, and Congress has control over the establishment and organization of the lower federal courts. For many years now, the federal court system has consisted of courts of general jurisdiction, called District Courts, and appellate courts, called Courts of Appeals. These courts are organized geographically and cover all of the United States and its territories. At the present time, there are ninety-three District Courts, and thirteen United States Courts of Appeal, one for each of eleven "circuits," one for the District of Columbia, and the Federal Circuit, which hears patent, copyright and other specialized kinds of federal matters. Each Court of Appeal hears appeals from District Courts within its "circuit," and the Court of Appeals for the District of Columbia hears appeals from the District Court for the District of Columbia, where a large number of cases involving suits against federal officers and administrative agencies originate.

94. Article III, section 2, defines the "judicial power of the United States," and the federal courts only have jurisdiction to hear cases coming within the "judicial power of the United States." These cases include, of course, cases arising under the Constitution, laws, and treaties of the United States. They also include admiralty and maritime cases, and other "federal specialty" cases, i.e., cases involving areas of law that come within the specified powers of Congress, such as patent, copyright and trademark cases, and bankruptcy cases. Finally, federal jurisdiction extends to "diversity of citizenship" cases, which are cases where the parties are from different states, or where one of the parties is a foreign national. The "diversity of citizenship" jurisdiction of the federal courts is an historical anomaly, going back to the time of the Constitution when the Framers feared that state court judges might be hostile to the claims of nonresidents and foreigners, and so provided that such cases could be brought or transferred[99] to the assumedly "neutral" federal court. While Congress has restricted the exercise of diversity jurisdiction to some degree,[100] it has not abolished it, and many cases are brought in federal court today solely on the basis of diversity of citizenship.[101]

---

99. Federal law generally authorizes either party to "remove" a case that has been filed in a state court where that case could have been filed in the federal court in the first instance. However, a defendant sued in a state court in its home state on the basis of diversity of citizenship cannot "remove" the case to federal court.

100. The cases must involve at least USD 75,000, and there must be complete diversity, i.e., all the plaintiffs and all the defendants must be residents of different states or of an American state and a foreign nation.

101. In such cases, federal law requires that the federal courts apply the substantive law of the states in which they sit, including that state's conflict of laws rules.

95. The Supreme Court of the United States is the highest court in the federal court system. While Article III, section 1, makes provision for a Supreme Court, it does not say anything about its composition, so it is up to Congress to determine the Court's composition. Ever since the nineteenth century, the Court has been composed of nine Justices, although for a brief period of time after the Civil War it had ten. It is extremely unlikely that Congress would change the number of Justices. The Framers were very much concerned about an independent judiciary, so they provided that all federal judges would be appointed with life tenure,[102] and that their compensation could not be diminished during their terms of office.[103]

96. Article III, section 2, authorizes the Supreme Court to exercise original jurisdiction in cases affecting foreign ambassadors and consuls and cases in which a state is a party.[104] Otherwise, the Supreme Court only exercises appellate jurisdiction. While Congress is given the power to regulate the Court's appellate jurisdiction, and in theory could remove some cases or all cases from the Court's appellate jurisdiction, it has not done so, and the Court is authorized to review any case decided by the lower federal courts and any case decided by the state courts that involves a federal question or any other question coming within the "judicial power" of the United States. As noted previously, the Supreme Court cannot review a decision of a state court on a question of state law, because questions of state law are not within the "judicial power of the United States."

§5. Judicial Review

I. The Principle of Judicial Review and the Role of the United States Supreme Court

97. Although Article III does not expressly provide for judicial review, the principle of judicial review has been firmly established in the American constitutional system ever since the foundation case of *Marbury v. Madison*, decided in 1803.[105] There the Supreme Court held that the federal courts have the power under Article III

102. Article III, s. 1, provides that federal judges shall hold their offices "during good Behaviour," which means that they have life tenure, but are subject to impeachment and removal for "bribery, treason, or other high Crimes and Misdemeanors," in the same manner as any other "civil Officer of the United States."

103. In recent years, the Court has been called upon to define the meaning of "diminished compensation." Applying the long-standing principle that is generally applicable, nondiscriminatory taxes can be applied to the salaries of federal judges whether they were appointed before or after the enactment of the tax, the Court held that the federal Medicare tax, which is imposed on all wage-earners, could be applied to judges appointed before the tax was enacted, but that a law applying the social security tax to federal judges alone was unconstitutional, notwithstanding that Congress subsequently increased their pay. *United States v. Hatter*, 532 U.S. 557 (2001).

104. In practice today, original jurisdiction is exercised primarily in boundary disputes between states. In such cases, the Court appoints a master to hear the evidence and make recommendations to the Court.

105. 5 U.S. 137 (1803).

to review and declare unconstitutional Congressional legislation and federal executive action. The Court subsequently held that Congress could also authorize the Supreme Court to review the judgments of the highest court of a state on questions of federal law, and that under the Supremacy Clause, Article VI, section 2, the Supreme Court's decisions on questions of federal law are binding on the state courts.[106] Thus, the Supreme Court is the ultimate interpreter of the meaning of the Constitution and federal law, and its decisions on these questions are binding on the other branches of the federal government and on the states. As the Court has stated: "In 1803, [Marbury] declared the basic principle that the federal judiciary is supreme in the exposition of the law of the Constitution, and that principle has ever since been respected by this Court and the Country as a permanent and indispensable feature of our constitutional system."[107]

98. The significance of judicial review in the American constitutional system and the role of the Supreme Court in American public life cannot be overemphasized. In the United States, judicial review and constitutional supremacy are synonymous. Judicial review has meant that the provisions of the Constitution, as interpreted by the Supreme Court, are legally enforceable norms, constraining the actions of the legislative and executive branches of the federal government and of the states. It has long been "politically accepted" that it is the role of the Supreme Court in our constitutional system to define the meaning of the Constitution, and this being so, it would be "politically unthinkable" for Congress or the President to act in defiance of the Supreme Court's constitutional rulings.[108] And precisely because the provisions of the Constitution protecting individual rights have been construed very broadly by the Supreme Court, many important social and moral issues, such as a woman's right to an abortion and the right of same-sex couples to marry, end up being resolved by the Supreme Court as a matter of constitutional interpretation. Again, this result is "politically accepted" by the American people, even though there may be strong disagreement with the Court's decision in a particular case. In addition, because the judiciary has the power to review and declare unconstitutional any governmental action, a person injured or threatened with injury by such action can challenge that action in the courts. It is thus an essential feature of the American constitutional system that the individual can "take the government to court" and can invoke the Constitution against the actions of the government. In the final analysis, in the United States, judicial review and constitutional supremacy are intertwined, and operationally as well as theoretically, the Constitution is the "Supreme law of the land."

---

106. *Martin v. Hunter's Lessee*, 14 U.S. 304 (1816).

107. *Cooper v. Aaron*, 358 U.S. 1, 18 (1958).

108. For example, in 1974, the Supreme Court, rejecting the President's claim of "executive privilege," held that the then President Nixon was required to comply with a federal court subpoena that he turn over tapes that revealed his complicity in a "cover-up" of a burglary of the offices of the opposition political party. *United States v. Nixon*, 418 U.S. 683 (1974). The decision was rendered at a time when impeachment proceedings were being threatened against him. Despite the impact of these revelations, which led to his resignation from office a few weeks later, he apparently concluded that it would be "politically more dangerous" to appear to be defying a Supreme Court ruling than to have his complicity revealed by the tapes.

II. Limitations on Judicial Review

99. Crucial to an understanding of the operation of judicial review in the United States is the matter of limitations on judicial review. The United States Supreme Court is not a "constitutional court," but an "ordinary court" in the federal judicial system. This means that it functions as any other court and can only hear "cases and controversies." Thus, its decisions on constitutional questions, like the decisions of the lower federal courts, are made only in the context of actual litigation between parties with adverse legal interests. This being so, the Supreme Court and the lower federal courts have no constitutional power to issue advisory opinions, and Congress cannot, for example, ask the Court for an advisory opinion on whether a proposed law would be constitutional. If Members of Congress have doubts as to a proposed law's constitutionality, they may decide to vote against it for that reason, or the President may decide to veto a proposed law because of doubts as to its constitutionality. But it is only after a law has been enacted and then has been challenged in court by a person who is adversely affected by the law, that the federal courts have the power to authoritatively determine its constitutionality.

100. The fact that the federal courts can only hear "cases and controversies" has given rise to certain kinds of limitations on judicial review, which may be referred to as "constitutional limitations." In addition, precisely because the power of judicial review can have such a significant impact on governmental action and policy, the Supreme Court has imposed certain other limitations on judicial review by the federal courts even when a "case or controversy" is otherwise presented. These may be referred to as "self-imposed" or "prudential" limitations on judicial review. Third, there are certain limitations on judicial review that arise when the federal courts are asked to review the constitutionality of state laws or governmental action. Some of these limitations find their source in the Eleventh Amendment, which prohibits the federal courts from entertaining suits by individuals against a state, while others relate to federalism-type considerations and recognition of the role of the states in our constitutional scheme. Finally, the Court has developed certain principles of constitutional interpretation that are designed to avoid unnecessary or inappropriate judicial review.

101. The above limitations on judicial review are extensive and are very important in actual constitutional litigation. The first line of defense by the government or other defending party in a constitutional challenge very often will be that the case is not justiciable. Justiciability is an umbrella term referring to all limitations on judicial review. Because of the importance of limitations on judicial review in American constitutional litigation, we will discuss them in some detail.

A. Constitutional Limitations

102. The constitutional limitations on judicial review stem from the fact that the jurisdiction of the federal courts is constitutionally limited to "cases and controversies." The essential element of a "case or controversy" is the existence of two opposing parties with presently adverse legal interests. In addition, the Court has held that the "case or controversy" provision requires that a party seeking to challenge the constitutionality or the legal validity of a law or governmental action have standing to do so, which generally means that the party must show that the party has or will suffer individualized injury due to the challenged law or governmental action.

1. Adverse Parties and Mootness

103. In order for there to be a "case or controversy," the parties before the court must have presently adverse legal interests, that is, both parties must stand to gain or lose something from the court's decision as to the validity of the challenged law or governmental action. If only one party stands to gain or lose something, while the other party does not, the requirement of adverse parties is not satisfied, and a case or controversy is not presented.[109]

104. A case is not moot if the court's decision in favor of the plaintiff will result in some relief for the plaintiff, even though the decision will not restore the parties to the situation as it existed before the challenged governmental action occurred. In *Church of Scientology of California v. United States,*[110] the Court held that an appeal from an order requiring a state court clerk to comply with an Internal Revenue Service summons for the production of tapes in the clerk's custody did not become moot because of the clerk's compliance with the order. The tapes recorded conversations between parties and their attorneys, and the claim was that the summons was invalid. The Court noted that while return of the tapes would not provide a fully satisfactory remedy for the invasion of privacy that had occurred, the court could effectuate a partial remedy by ordering the Internal Revenue Service to destroy or return any and all copies of the tapes it had in its possession. The availability of this partial remedy was sufficient to prevent the case from becoming moot.[111]

105. A case is not "moot" if there is still a continuing controversy between the parties before the court, even though the immediate problem that gave rise to the controversy has ceased to exist. In such a circumstance, the issue presented is said to be "capable of repetition, yet evading review." So, if a pregnant woman brings a challenge to a state law prohibiting abortion, the case does not become "moot" if she

109. This proposition is illustrated by *Muskrat v. United States*, 219 U.S. 346 (1911). In 1902, Congress made a "final" allotment of federal lands to certain Cherokee Indians. In 1906, Congress enacted another law, increasing the number of allottees entitled to shares of the land. The law also authorized four named allottees under the 1902 law to bring a suit against the United States on behalf of the 1902 allottees to determine the validity of the 1906 law increasing the number of allottees. The case lacked adverse parties and so could not be heard by the federal courts, because the United States as an entity had no interest adverse to the 1902 allottees. As a result of the 1902 law, the land in question no longer belonged to the United States, so if the 1906 law were invalidated, the United States would not gain anything. The adverse parties were the allottees under the 1902 Act and the allottees under the 1906 Act, and any litigation involving the validity of the 1906 Act would have to be undertaken between these parties.

110. 506 U.S. 9 (1992).

111. *See also Arizonans for Official English v. Arizona*, 520 U.S. 43 (1997) (employee's constitutional challenge to state law making English the only language that could be used by state employees in carrying out their official duties became moot when the employee left her state employment); *Camreta v. Greene* 563 U.S. 692 (2011) (when school officials appealed from a decision that they were required to get a warrant before interviewing a student and the student moved away from the school district, never to return, the case became moot).

procures an abortion or carries the pregnancy to term before the case has been resolved. In the normal course of things, she could again become pregnant and could again seek an abortion, which continued to be prohibited by the challenged law. There is thus a continuing controversy between her and the official charged with enforcement of the law prohibiting abortion, and the court will determine the constitutionality of that law, even though she is not seeking an abortion at the present time.[112]

2. Standing

106. In order to have standing to challenge the validity of a law or governmental action, the plaintiff must show that the plaintiff suffers injury in fact having a fairly traceable causal connection to the challenged law that is likely to be redressed by a favorable decision invalidating the law. In the absence of a showing of standing, a "case or controversy" is not presented.

107. The injury in fact must be direct, identified, and differentiated as to the particular plaintiff, although the same injury may be shared by a large number of persons.[113]

The injury required for standing is not limited to economic interests, and includes injury to intangible interests, such as the "aesthetic, conservational and recreational interests" of users of a national park, who would have standing to challenge the proposed construction of an entertainment facility in that park.[114] The injury may be one that is presently being suffered or may be one that is clearly threatened. A very clear example of present injury in fact is where a party refrains from engaging in allegedly constitutionally protected conduct because that conduct is prohibited by a law and the party fears prosecution or other sanction if the party engages in that conduct, such as a physician

---

112. *Roe v. Wade*, 410 U.S. 113 (1973). *See also Friends of the Earth, Inc. v. Laidlaw Environmental Services*, Inc., 528 U.S. 167 (2000) (claim against waste water treatment plant for violation of federal environmental laws due to noncompliance with its permit did not become moot once plant came into compliance, since it was possible that plant would fail to comply with its permit in the future); *City of Eire v. Pap's A.M.*, 529 U.S. 1382 (2000) (controversy over the validity of a city ordinance regulating nude dancing did not become moot when the business ceased to provide nude dancing, since the business could decide to resume nude dancing in the future); *Chafin v. Chafin*, 133 S.Ct. 1017 (2013) (appeal from court order in custody dispute directing the return of the child to Scotland did not become moot by the fact that the mother had returned with the child to Scotland, since there was the possibility that the court could enter an enforceable re-return order).

113. In *Warth v. Seldin*, 422 U.S. 490 (1975), low-income residents living in an urban area brought a challenge to the alleged refusal of an adjacent suburban area to permit the construction of any low-income housing there.

114. *See Sierra Club v. Morton*, 405 U.S. 777 (1972). *See also Friends of the Earth, Inc. v. Laidlaw Environmental Services*, 528 U.S. 167 (2000), where people who had ceased to use a river because of a fear of harmful effects from discharged pollutants by a waste water treatment plan had standing to challenge the plant's alleged violation of federal environmental laws.

who is challenging a law restricting or prohibiting abortion.[115] Clearly threatened injury in fact will be found where a party has actually engaged in the conduct prohibited by the challenged law and alleges a credible threat of prosecution as a result, such as the physician who has committed an abortion in violation of a law prohibiting abortion and who alleges that the prosecutor plans to bring a prosecution against her for such violation.[116]

The matter of "direct, identified and differentiated" injury in fact to the particular plaintiff was involved in two efforts to challenge the constitutionality of a law giving the President a "line item veto." In *Raines v. Byrd*,[117] the Court held that members of Congress did not have standing to challenge the law prior to the time the President exercised a "line item veto" despite their claim that the existence of the provision for a "line item veto" would dilute the significance of their vote on bills that were subject to the exercise of the "line item veto." In *Clinton v. City of New York*,[118] the Court found standing to challenge the law for a city and for health care providers when the President exercised the "line item veto" to cancel a waiver for certain state taxes levied against the health care providers, and for a farmer's cooperative when the President exercised the "line item veto" to cancel tax deferral relief for sales of stock in food refiners and processors to cooperatives.

Legislators have standing to challenge actions that impair the effectiveness of their vote. Thus, legislators who voted against a measure in a 20-20 tie had standing to challenge the authority of the Lieutenant-Governor to cast a vote to break the tie, resulting in passage of the measure.[119] And very recently, the Court held that state legislators could assert a challenge to a voter initiative that removed the authority to

---

115. *See Doe v. Bolton*, 410 U.S. 179 (1973). The injury in fact may be the deprivation of the opportunity to compete for a governmental benefit. It is not necessary that the party show that if the challenged law or governmental action is declared unconstitutional, the party would actually receive the benefit. Thus, a contractor that regularly bid on government contracts had standing to challenge the constitutionality of a law that would prevent it from bidding on a certain percentage of the contracts that were "set aside" for contracting firms owned by racial minorities and women. Northwestern Florida Chapter of the *Association of General Contractors of America v. City of Jacksonville*, Florida (1993). Likewise white students who were not admitted to a public university, but who showed that minority students with their qualifications would have been admitted, had standing to challenge the university's admissions preference for minority students. *Gratz v. Bollinger*, 539 U.S. 244 (2003).
116. *See also Susan B. Anthony List v. Driehaus*, 134 S.Ct. 2334 (2014), where the Court held that advocacy organizations had standing to challenge a state law prohibiting certain false statements in the course of a political campaign where their intended future dissemination of information criticizing votes on legislation was arguably prohibited by the law, the law had been enforced in the past, and any person with knowledge of the purported violation could file a complaint that could lead to a possible criminal prosecution. In *Clapper v. Amnesty International*, USA, 133 Sup.Ct. 1138 (2013), the Court held that the assertion of lawyers and human rights, labor, legal, and media organizations that there was an objectively reasonable likelihood that their communications with foreign contacts would be intercepted in the future under provision of federal law allowing surveillance of noncitizens believed to be located outside of the United States did not satisfy the requirement that the threatened injury be "certainly impending."
117. 521 U.S. 811 (1997).
118. 524 U.S. 417 (1998).
119. *Coleman v. Miller*, 307 U.S. 433 (1939).

redistrict legislative districts from the legislature to an independent redistricting commission.[120]

Recently the Supreme Court dealt with two cases involving appeals from federal court decisions holding unconstitutional state and federal laws that refused to recognize same-sex marriage. In one case, after a federal court held unconstitutional a California constitutional amendment refusing to recognize same-sex marriage, the Governor and state Attorney-General refused to take an appeal from the decision. The state supreme court permitted the proponents of the state constitutional amendment to take the appeal in order to defend the law's constitutionality. The Supreme Court held that simply because they were proponents of the law, they did not suffer a personal and particularized injury by the court's declaring the law unconstitutional, and so were asserting only a general interest in upholding the constitutional validity of the law, which was insufficient to confer standing.[121] The second case[122] involved a constitutional challenge to a federal law that denied any federal benefits to a couple in a same-sex marriage. The plaintiff and her deceased same-sex spouse were legally married in the State of New York, where the couple resided. She was denied the spousal exemption from the federal estate tax and asserted her constitutional challenge in a suit for a tax refund against the United States. The federal District Court held the challenged portion of the federal law unconstitutional, and the United States Attorney-General declined to take an appeal from that decision. However, the United States also stated that it would continue to enforce the challenged law until it had been held unconstitutional by the Supreme Court. The Supreme Court held that a continuing controversy remained between the plaintiff and the United States, so that there remained a case or controversy within the constitutional jurisdiction of the Supreme Court. The Court then directed that a special committee of the United States House of Representatives, which had been permitted to appear in the case as *amicus curiae*, defend the case and decided the case on the merits. *See* paragraph 330, *infra*.

108. Even though the plaintiff can identify a particular injury, the plaintiff must also show both that the injury bears a fairly traceable causal connection to the challenged law or governmental action, and that this injury is likely to be redressed by a favorable decision invalidating the law or governmental action. Both of these required elements

---

120. *Arizona State Legislature v. Arizona Independent Redistricting Commission*, 135 S.Ct. 2652 (2015).

A party who has been assigned a claim has standing to sue in federal court, even when the assignee is a "collection firm" that has promised to remit the proceeds of the claim to the assignor. *Sprint Communications Co. v. APCC Services, Inc.*, 554 U.S. 269 (2008). Likewise, federal law authorizes individuals to bring "qui tam" actions for civil penalties and damages against any person who has procured payment on a false claim against the United States. The person bringing the action receives a portion of the recovery. Standing under the law was upheld on the ground that the person bringing the claim is the assignee of the government's claim.

An organization has standing to sue in its own right when it can establish that it or its members are suffering present or clearly threatened injury in fact. *See Alabama Legislative Black Caucus v. Alabama*, 135 Sup.Ct. 1257 (2015), where a civil rights organization with a statewide membership had standing to allege that legislative redistricting was "racially gerrymandered" and so unconstitutional. *See* para. 365, *infra* .

121. *Hollingsworth v. Perry*, 133 Sup.Ct. 2652 (2013).

122. *United States v. Windsor*, 133 Sup.Ct. 2675 (2013).

of standing are illustrated by a case where the Internal Revenue Service reduced the level of services to poor persons that a hospital was required to provide in order to receive a federal tax exemption. The plaintiffs were poor persons who had been receiving medical services at a particular hospital and who alleged that after the Internal Revenue Service issued the ruling, the hospital cut back on its services to poor persons. The Court held that this allegation was insufficient to satisfy the "causation" and "redressibility" elements of standing. In order to satisfy the "causation" element, the plaintiffs would have to allege and prove if challenged that the hospital had reduced the level of services to poor persons because of the Internal Revenue.

109. Service ruling and that "but for" that ruling, it would not have reduced the level of services. In order to satisfy the "redressibility" element, the plaintiffs would have to allege and prove that if the ruling were invalidated, the hospital would restore the level of services it had previously been providing to poor persons rather than give up the tax exemption. Since the plaintiffs failed to make either of these allegations, they lacked standing to challenge the validity of the Internal Revenue Service ruling.[123]

110. As a general proposition, a federal taxpayer lacks standing as a taxpayer to challenge the constitutionality of the expenditure of federal funds, and the same is true of a state taxpayer seeking to the challenge the constitutionality of the expenditure of state funds. The individual taxpayer's interest in the expenditure of such funds is said to be "comparatively minute and indeterminate."[124] However, older cases that have never been overruled by the Supreme Court have held that a taxpayer of a local governmental unit, such as a city, does have a "direct and immediate" interest in the expenditure of local funds, so under current doctrine such a taxpayer has "taxpayer standing" to challenge the expenditure of local funds as unconstitutional.[125] The Supreme Court has also allowed "taxpayer" standing to challenge the expenditure of governmental

123. *Simon v. Eastern Kentucky Welfare Rights Organization*, 426 U.S. 26 (1976). Compare *Duke Power Co. v. Carolina Environmental Study Group*, 438 U.S. 59 (1978). There a federal law limited the liability of nuclear power plants for "mass disasters" to USD 550,000,000. The plaintiffs were opposed to nuclear power development and sought to have this liability-limiting law declared unconstitutional. They alleged that a particular nuclear power plant was polluting the waters that they used for recreational purposes. This allegation was sufficient to satisfy the injury in fact requirement. They further alleged, and the trial court found as a fact, that "but for" the limitation of liability under federal law, this particular nuclear power plant would not have been built. The trial court further found that if the law were declared unconstitutional, the operator would close the plant. Therefore, the plaintiffs satisfied the "causation" and "redressibility" requirements, and so had standing to challenge the constitutionality of the federal law limiting the liability of nuclear power plants. (The Supreme Court, while upholding the plaintiffs' standing, also held that the law was constitutional.) *See also Utah v. Evans*, 536 U.S. 452 (2002), where the Court held that a state had standing to challenge Census calculations of the population of the states for the 2001 census, on the basis of its claim that if those calculations had not been used, the state would have obtained an additional seat in the House of Representatives. Although the census officials could not themselves award the state an additional seat, the Court found that if the calculations were declared invalid (which they were not), the President and relevant Congressional officials would award the state an additional seat.

124. *Frothingham v. Mellon*, 262 U.S. 447 (1923) (federal); *ASARCO, Inc. v. Kadish*, 490 U.S. 605 (1989) (state); *Daimler-Chrysler Corp. v. Cuno*, 547 U.S. 332 (2006).

125. *See Crampton v. Zabriskie*, 101 U.S. 601 (1879).

funds in aid of religion as constituting an impermissible "establishment of religion," in violation of the First Amendment.[126] While this exception is difficult to reconcile with the general prohibition against "taxpayer" standing, it nonetheless remains viable at the present time.[127]

111. The Court has also held that a citizen's interest in constitutional governance is an abstract rather than a concrete and differentiated interest, so that any injury to that interest, such as by the enactment of an allegedly unconstitutional law, does not amount to "injury in fact" for standing purposes. Thus, the Court does not permit "citizens' suits" to challenge the constitutionality of a law or governmental action.[128] In some circumstances, this means that there will be no one with standing to challenge a particular law or governmental action, and in those circumstances, according to the Supreme Court, "[t]he absence of any particular individual or class to litigate these claims gives support to the argument that the subject matter is committed to the surveillance of Congress and ultimately to the political process."[129]

At the same time, the Court has recognized that Congress can create federal statutory rights, the injury to which constitutes "injury in fact" for standing purposes. For example, federal civil rights laws have been interpreted as creating an individual

---

126. *Flast v. Cohen*, 392 U.S. 83 (1968).

127. This exception has been construed very narrowly. It only applies where there has been an actual expenditure of government funds authorized by Congress or a state legislature. Thus, it does not apply where a federal agency gave away surplus federal property to a religious institution, *Valley Force Christian College v. Americans United for Separation*, 454 U.S. 464 (1982), or where the President issued an executive order to ensure that faith-based community organizations would be able to apply for federal financial support for activities that were not inherently religious. *Hein v. Freedom From Religion Foundation, Inc.*, 549 U.S. 1109 (2007). The Court has also held that taxpayers lack standing to challenge dollar-for-dollar tax credits for contributions to organizations that provide scholarships to children attending religious schools. The Court said that a tax credit is not equivalent to a religious tax and so does not cause the injury to the taxpayer that was the basis of *Flast. Arizona Christian School Tuition Organization v. Winn*, 131 Sup.Ct. 1436 (2011).

128. However, a person has been charged with a federal criminal offense under a federal statute can challenge the constitutionality of that statute as being beyond the power of Congress under Art. 1 and as violative of state sovereignty under the Tenth Amendment. Since the statute is being invoked against that person in a criminal case, that person suffers injury in fact from the existence of that statute and so can challenge the constitutional authority of the Congress to enact it. *Bond v. United States*, 131 Sup.Ct. 2355 (2011).

129. *United States v. Richardson*, 418 U.S. 166, 179 (1974). In that case, the Court held that Richardson, as a citizen and taxpayer, did not have standing to challenge the provision of the Central Intelligence Agency Act (CIA), which permits CIA expenditures to be hidden in the federal budget. In the companion case of *Schlesinger v. Reservists Committee to Stop the War*, 418 U.S. 208 (1974), the Court held that an organization opposed to American involvement in the Vietnam War did not have standing to challenge the constitutionality of Members of Congress serving in the Armed Forces Reserve. The Court also held that the "case or controversy" provision precludes Congress from statutorily authorizing "citizen's suits" against governmental agencies to compel their compliance with the federal Constitution or laws. *Lujan v. Defenders of Wildlife*, 504 U.S. 555 (1992). Such "citizen standing" has been authorized in a number of environmental laws, such as the Endangered Species Act, and in *Lujan*, the Supreme Court held that such a suit could only be brought by a citizen who otherwise satisfies the "injury in fact" requirement.

right to interracial associations in the housing context. This being so, a white resident of an apartment complex from which blacks had been excluded, suffers injury in fact to this interest as a result of such exclusion and has standing to bring a civil rights action against the apartment complex to enjoin it from committing racial discrimination.[130]

In *McConnell v. Federal Elections Commission*,[131] a large number of plaintiffs, including the national committees and Congressional and Senatorial committees of the Democratic and Republican parties, supporters of political candidates and various advocacy groups, brought suit to challenge the constitutionality of a number of the provisions of the Bipartisan Campaign Reform Act of 2002. While a sufficient number of plaintiffs had standing to challenge all of the provisions of the law, the Court found that some of the plaintiffs lacked standing to challenge particular provisions of the law. Specifically, the Court held that: (1) a Senator whose current term did not expire until 2009 could not show clearly threatened injury in fact from and so lacked standing to challenge a provision denying a candidate the benefit of a lower charge for broadcast advertising on the condition that forty-five days before a primary election or sixty days before a general election, the candidate could not run broadcast ads making reference to another candidate for the same office; (2) voters and candidates could not challenge provisions that increased the permissible limits for contributions on the ground that they did not want to solicit large contributions, because their alleged inability to compete with candidates obtaining large contributions was not due to the provisions of the law, but to their own wish not to solicit large contributions, so that the injury of which they complained was not fairly traceable to the challenged law; (3) voters and candidates could not challenge provisions allowing a candidate to obtain larger contributions if the candidate's opponent chooses to spend a certain amount of personal funds, because none of the plaintiffs was a candidate in an election affected by this provision.

---

130. *Trafficante v. Metropolitan Life Insurance Co.*, 409 U.S. 205 (1972). *See also Federal Election Commission v. Akins*, 524 U.S. 11 (1998), holding that Congress could confer standing on any 'aggrieved' person who suffered the harm of the "inability to receive information" as a result of a decision of the Federal Election Commission that the disclosure and reporting provisions of a federal election were not applicable to a private organization. In that case, a group of voters who opposed the policies of a particular organization were found to have a standing to challenge the Commission's refusal to require the organization to make disclosures concerning its membership, contributions and expenditures.

In *Department of Commerce v. United States House of Representatives*, 525 U.S. 316 (1999), Congress conferred standing to challenge a proposed statistical adjustment to the census on "any person aggrieved by the use of any statistical method in violation of the Constitution or any provision of law, in connection with the 2000 census or later decennial census, to determine the population for purposes of the apportionment or redistricting of Members of Congress." The Court held that a resident of Indiana had standing to challenge the use of a statistical adjustment upon a showing that it was "virtually certain" that Indiana would lose a seat in the House of Representatives under the proposed statistical adjustment.

In *Massachusetts v. Environmental Protection Agency*, 549 U.S. 497 (2007), the Court, relying on a federal law authorizing certain challenges to actions by this agency, held that a state could assert a challenge to the refusal of the agency to issue regulations governing greenhouse gas emissions by motor vehicles.

131. 540 U.S. 93 (2003).

B. Self-Imposed Limitations

112. A question of self-imposed limitations on judicial review arises only after the court is satisfied that a "case or controversy" is presented, i.e., that there are two presently adverse parties and that the plaintiff has standing. The two most important self-imposed limitations on judicial review are ripeness and the political question doctrine.

1. Ripeness

113. One aspect of ripeness relates to the abstract posture in which a constitutional question is presented in the particular case. Where this is so, the court may conclude that it is better to defer consideration of the constitutional question until a later time when the constitutional question will be presented more concretely. Presumably this means in another case, after something else has occurred, or, in the same case where the plaintiffs will have presented specific evidence as to how the challenged law or governmental action has operated in practice. In one case that the Supreme Court held should have been dismissed on "ripeness" grounds, an independent political party challenged a state requirement that it execute a "loyalty oath" in order to get on the ballot. The party alleged that such a requirement "chilled" its free speech rights and so violated the First Amendment. But the party was challenging the law only "on its face," and there was no specific showing of how the party had been injured by the "loyalty oath" requirement, since it had always been able to appear on the ballot. In these circumstances, the Court held that the claim of a constitutional violation was not "ripe," because it was presented in too abstract a context.[132]

114. The result in this case may be compared to the result in another case, where the Court held that it was not proper to dismiss the case on "ripeness" grounds. That case involved a constitutional challenge to a federal law that imposed a USD 555,000,000 on the recovery of damages caused by a nuclear disaster. The government argued that the case was not "ripe" unless and until a nuclear disaster occurred, and the statutory limit was found to be inadequate to pay all the claims. The Court noted that the question presented was purely one of law, so that it would not be in a better position to resolve the question "later than it is now." In other words, the question would not be presented more concretely after a nuclear disaster occurred, and it was in the public interest that the question of the liability of private nuclear power companies for nuclear disasters be resolved in advance of the time when such a disaster might occur.[133]

132. *Socialist Labor Party v. Gilligan*, 406 U.S. 583 (1972).

133. *Duke Power Co. v. Carolina Environmental Study Group*, 438 U.S. 59 (1978). To the same effect, *see Susan B. Anthony List v. Driehaus*, para. 107, n. 116, *supra* , where the Court held that a challenge to a ban on certain false statements during a political campaign was ripe prior to the time that the ban had been invoked against the plaintiffs, because the issue involved a pure question of law and denying prompt judicial review would have forced the organizations to choose between refraining from core political speech and risking costly proceedings and possible criminal prosecution.

2. The Political Question Doctrine

115. The political question doctrine is based on separation of powers concerns. The Supreme Court has concluded that in the American constitutional system, there are certain kinds of constitutional questions, including some involving the validity of state governmental action, that cannot be, or at least should not be, resolved by the judicial branch of the federal government. These kinds of questions are referred to as "non-justiciable political questions," and a case presenting such a question will not be heard by the federal courts.

116. The Court has stated that there are six factors that must be considered in determining whether a particular question is a non-justiciable political question. These are as follows:

(1) whether there is a textually demonstrable constitutional commitment of the issue to Congress or the President;
(2) whether there is a lack of judicially discoverable and manageable standards for resolving it;
(3) whether the question cannot be decided without an initial policy determination of a kind clearly for nonjudicial discretion;
(4) whether it is impossible for a court to undertake independent resolution of the question without expressing a lack of respect due the coordinate branches of the federal government;
(5) whether there is an unusual need for unquestioning adherence to a political decision already made;
(6) the potentiality of embarrassment from multifarious pronouncements by the different branches of the federal government on the same question.[134]

117. The first factor, a textually demonstrable constitutional commitment of the issue to Congress or the President, is the most important one, and analytically involves substantive constitutional interpretation. This means that, as a matter of substantive constitutional law, the determination of the question at issue comes within the exclusive authority of Congress or of the President, and so is not within the constitutional power of the courts to resolve. For example, the grant of power to the President under Article II, section 3 to "receive Ambassadors and other public Ministers" has been interpreted to vest the power to recognize a foreign government exclusively within the President. There is thus a textually demonstrable constitutional commitment of the issue of recognition of foreign governments to the President, and the courts lack the constitutional authority to review the President's decision to recognize or to refuse to recognize a particular foreign government. Another example of a question that has been constitutionally committed to the "political branches" of the federal government is the question of whether an American state has a "republican form of government," as is required by Article IV, section 4 of the Constitution. This being so, the federal courts are precluded from determining whether a state's use of the initiative procedure to permit the direct enactment of laws by the electorate is consistent with a "republican form of government."[135]

---

134. *Baker v. Carr*, 369 U.S. 186, 217 (1962).
135. *Pacific States Tel. & Tel. Co. v. Oregon*, 223 U.S. 118 (1912).

Among the other questions that have been held to be constitutionally committed to the "political branches" of the federal government are questions relating to the process of amending the Constitution,[136] questions relating to the procedures employed by the Senate in conducting an impeachment trial,[137] and questions relating to the operation of a state government's "militia."[138] On the other hand, although Article I, section 5, provides that each House of Congress is to be the "judge of the elections, returns and qualifications of its own members," the Court held that this provision is not a textually demonstrable commitment to the Congress of the question of whether Congress can refuse to seat a Member elected by the voters who otherwise possesses the constitutional qualifications for membership.[139]

118. The other five "political question" criteria clearly illustrate the operation of the political question doctrine as a self-imposed or prudential limitation on judicial review. They relate to the determination of when it is inappropriate for the courts to resolve a particular constitutional question because of the nature of the question itself, and the results of the cases indicate that the political question doctrine is to be invoked sparingly. The leading case in this regard is *Baker v. Carr*,[140] where the Court formulated the political question criteria. There voters in the State of Tennessee challenged the apportionment of the Tennessee legislature into legislative districts that varied widely in population, so that the votes of voters residing in "overpopulated districts" were worth less than the votes of voters residing in "underpopulated districts," claiming that such an apportionment violated the Fourteenth Amendment's equal protection clause. The state's invocation of the political question doctrine was rejected, since none of the "political question" criteria were shown to be applicable. It did not matter that the case involved a "political" question in the popular sense or that the resolution of the constitutional question could—and did—have far-reaching "political"

136. *See Coleman v. Miller*, 307 U.S. 433 (1939).
137. *Nixon v. United States*, 506 U.S. 224 (1993). As a result of the *Nixon* decision, it was assumed during the impeachment proceedings involving President Clinton that under the political question doctrine the question of what constitutes a "high crime and misdemeanor" was not subject to judicial review.
138. *Gilligan v. Morgan*, 413 U.S. 1 (1973). Each state has its own military force or "militia," which is called the National Guard. Under Art. I, s. 8, cl. 16, Congress has ultimate authority over the National Guard, and the President can call the National Guard into federal service. In 1970, the Ohio National Guard was sent by the Governor to maintain order on a state university campus following a student protest against the invasion of Cambodia during the Vietnam War. During a confrontation with the students, the Guard opened fire, and four students were killed. Their survivors brought a suit against Ohio state officials, seeking an order that would require a change in the method of the training the Guard to prevent a repetition of this kind of fatal incident. The Supreme Court held that the training of the National Guard was within the exclusive authority of Congress, so that the suit had to be dismissed under the political question doctrine.
139. *Powell v. McCormack*, 395 U.S. 486 (1969). In that case, the House of Representatives, by majority vote, refused to seat a Member who met the age, citizenship and residency qualifications for membership in the House prescribed by Art. I, s. 2, cl. 2. After rejecting the contention that the determination of the issue was textually committed to the House, the Court held that the House's refusal to seat the Member was violative of Art. I, s. 2, cl. 2, and ordered the Member to be seated.
140. *Supra*, para. 116, n. 134.

consequences.[141] Since none of the "political question" criteria were shown to be applicable, and since a case or controversy was presented, the federal courts were required to hear the case and to determine the constitutional question at issue.

119. Where the political question doctrine as a self-imposed limitation on judicial review has the most efficacy is in the areas of foreign affairs and military matters, and most of the other five "political question" criteria promulgated in *Baker v. Carr* seem to be oriented toward these areas. Because of the consequences of a judicial decision in these areas, it may be more appropriate that such questions be resolved by the "political" branches of the federal government. Moreover, the kinds of constitutional questions arising in these areas sometimes involve a potential conflict between Congress and the President, and the argument can be made that this conflict should not be resolved by the courts, but by the "political" branches themselves as coequals. Finally, where the conflict between the branches is only potential, "ripeness" considerations may also operate to prevent judicial review.

120. This kind of situation is illustrated by *Goldwater v. Carter*.[142] When President Carter established diplomatic relations with China in 1978, he also terminated a defense treaty with Taiwan. A few Senators brought a suit against the President, contending that the President lacked the power to terminate the treaty without Congressional approval. The Supreme Court held that the suit should be dismissed, but there was disagreement among the Justices on the reasons for the dismissal. Four Justices, in a plurality opinion by former Chief Justice Rehnquist, took the position that the case presented a non-justiciable political question. Rehnquist emphasized that the case involved an important question of foreign relations and said that because there was no constitutional provision expressly governing treaty termination, there were no judicially manageable standards by which the courts could resolve the question. He also noted that the courts were being asked to settle a dispute between "coequal branches of our government, each of which has resources available to protect and assert its interests." Justices Powell and Brennan, in concurring opinions, strongly disagreed with the plurality's invocation of the political question doctrine. They contended that the question was one of decision-making authority between the branches and so was purely a question of constitutional interpretation, capable of being resolved by the courts. However, while Brennan would have resolved the question on the merits in favor of Presidential authority, Powell would have dismissed the case on "ripeness" grounds. He contended that differences between the President and Congress should ordinarily be resolved by the political process, and that the courts should not intervene until each branch has "taken action asserting its constitutional authority." Since neither House of Congress had expressly taken action rejecting the President's claim of authority to terminate the treaty, Powell would hold that the constitutional issue was not "ripe."

---

141. As will be discussed subsequently, the Court has held that legislative apportionment must take place in accordance with the principle of "one person, one vote," so that legislative districts must be reasonably equal in population. The effect of this holding was to require reapportionment of virtually all state legislatures and to make any legislative reapportionment subject to constitutional challenge under the principle of "one person, one vote." *See* paras. 362–368, *infra*.

142. 444 U.S. 996 (1979).

121. A similar situation was presented in a lower court case arising in connection with the Gulf War, when a group of Members of Congress brought a suit against the President, seeking an injunction to prevent him from initiating military action against Iraq without first securing a declaration of war or other explicit Congressional authorization for such action. The court rejected the President's contention that the issue presented a non-justiciable political question, but, relying on Justice Powell's opinion in *Goldwater v. Carter*, found that the claim was not "ripe," because Congress as a whole was not seeking relief against an alleged interference by the President with its power to declare war.[143] The court's decision to dismiss the case on "ripeness" grounds turned out to be well-advised, since the President obtained Congressional authorization before taking any military action against Iraq.[144]

122. In summary, there are really two parts to the political question doctrine. The first part, a textually demonstrable constitutional commitment of the question to the "political branches" of the federal government, is analytically a matter of substantive constitutional interpretation. If the Supreme Court interprets the Constitution as entrusting the matter in issue to the exclusive authority of Congress or the President, the matter cannot constitutionally be determined by the courts. Under this part of the political question doctrine, a question going to the recognition of a foreign government, for example, is non-justiciable, because the Constitution entrusts this question to the exclusive authority of the President.[145]

123. The second part of the political question doctrine relates to that doctrine as a self-imposed or prudential limitation on judicial review. It means that certain kinds of questions, because of their nature, are more appropriately resolved by the "political branches," and it involves the application of the other five political question criteria promulgated in *Baker v. Carr*. This part of the political question doctrine operates primarily in the areas of foreign affairs and military matters, and sometimes operates in connection with "ripeness." On the whole, this part of the political question doctrine has been applied sparingly, except for recognition of the fact that where there is a potential conflict between the President and the Congress, these branches may have to resolve the conflict as coequals. A point to be emphasized is that the political question doctrine cannot be invoked simply to enable the federal courts to avoid resolving

143. *Dellums v. Bush*, 752 F.Supp. 1141 (D.C. 1990).

144. The matter of the President taking military action without Congressional authorization will be discussed in paras. 439–447. It will be pointed out there that when a question involves a conflict between Congress and the President over a matter of foreign affairs, the courts are likely to treat it as a "non-justiciable political question," saying that the President and Congress should resolve it as coequals, or at least, that the courts will not resolve it until a direct conflict is actually presented.

145. In *Zivotofsky ex rel. Zivotofsky v. Clinton*, 132 Sup.Ct. 1421 (2012), parents of a child born in Jerusalem sought an injunction ordering the Secretary of State to identify the child's place of birth for purposes of a passport and other official documents, as "Jerusalem, Israel," pursuant to a federal law requiring such action on the part of the Secretary of State. The Court rejected the government's argument that suit was barred by the political question doctrine, as involving recognition of a foreign government. The law was limited to the description of the place of the child's birth on official documents and would not affect the President's power to make decisions with respect to the status of Jerusalem.

difficult and controversial questions that may have a profound impact on American society.

C. Limitations on Judicial Review of State Action

124. There are additional limitations on judicial review when the federal courts are asked to review the constitutionality of state laws or governmental action or to interfere with state court proceedings in order to protect federal rights.

1. The Eleventh Amendment

125. One set of limitations arises from the Eleventh Amendment, which prohibits the federal courts from exercising jurisdiction in suits brought by individuals to enforce claims under federal law against the government of an American state. The Eleventh Amendment was adopted in 1798 in reaction to a Supreme Court decision holding that the states were subject to suit in the federal courts on the theory that grant of federal court jurisdiction over certain matters superseded the sovereign immunity from suit that the states had possessed prior to the adoption of the Constitution. The Supreme Court has held that the Eleventh Amendment confirms the proposition that the states' sovereign immunity from suit derives from the structure of the Constitution itself. As the Court has stated: "[i]t follows that the scope of the States" immunity from suit is demarcated not by the text of the Amendment alone, but by fundamental postulates implicit in the constitutional design.[146] Thus, although the Eleventh Amendment by its terms refers to suits brought against a state by citizens of another state or a foreign nation, it has long been interpreted to extend to suits brought against a state by its own citizens. The effect of the Eleventh Amendment then is to bar all suits by private entities against a state.[147] Moreover, Congress is constitutionally precluded from abolishing a state's sovereign immunity, so as to make the state subject to suit by a private entity on a federal claim either in a federal court or in a state court.[148]

As a result of the Court's holding to this effect, numerous provisions of federal law have been invalidated in their application to the states. These have included: a federal statute interpreted as authorizing suit by private entity against state for trademark violation and invalidating federal statute abrogating state sovereign immunity in suits by private entity for patent infringement claims;[149] a federal statute subjecting states

146. *Alden v. Maine*, 527 U.S. 706 (1999).

147. *Hans v. Louisiana*, 134 U.S. 1 (1890). The Eleventh Amendment applies only to suits against the state government itself, and not to suits against subordinate units of state government, such as municipalities or other units of local government. The Supreme Court has also held that the Eleventh Amendment did not apply to a suit against a railroad owned by the Port Authority of New York, an independent entity created by a bi-state compact between the states of New York and New Jersey. *Hess v. Port Authority Trans-Hudson*, 513 U.S. 30 (1994).

148. The Court's current interpretation of the Eleventh Amendment began with *Seminole Tribe of Florida v. Florida*, 517 U.S. 44 (1996) (invalidating federal statute authorizing federal court suit by a private entity to compel a state to comply with a duty imposed by federal law).

149. *Florida Prepaid Postsecondary Education Expense Board v. College Savings Bank*, 527 U.S. 666 (1999).

to suit in state court for claims under federal Wage and Hours law;[150] the application of a federal law prohibiting age discrimination in employment to suits by state employees against state agencies;[151] the application of federal law prohibiting employment discrimination against persons with disabilities to suits by state employees against state agencies.[152]

There is an exception where Congress has acted under its Fourteenth Amendment enforcement powers to protect an individual's federal constitutional rights from state governmental action. In this situation, the Court reasoned that since the Fourteenth Amendment was enacted after the Eleventh Amendment, the grant of enforcement powers to Congress would have the effect of enabling Congress to abrogate state immunity to the extent that this was necessary to protect Fourteenth Amendment rights. So, Congress, in the exercise of its Fourteenth Amendment enforcement powers, may authorize an award of damages against the state for the violation of rights protected by the Fourteenth Amendment.[153]

In *Nevada Department of Human Resources v. Hibbs*,[154] the Court held that Congress could constitutionally authorize an award of damages against a state for a violation of the federal Family and Medical Leave Act (FMLA), 29 U.S.C. sec. 2601. The Court found that the law was an appropriate response to remedy and deter sex discrimination in the administration of employment leave benefits by state agencies. Similarly, in *Tennessee v. Lane*,[155] the Court held that Congress could constitutionally abolish state sovereign immunity in a suit under Title II of the Americans with Disabilities Act,[156] prohibiting discrimination against persons with disabilities with respect to the provision of public services and access to disabilities, in a suit by paraplegics who contended that they were denied access to state courts that were not wheelchair accessible. Here too the Court held that Congress could find that in many states across

---

150. *Alden v. Maine*, *supra* n. 146.
151. *Kimmel v. Florida Board of Regents*, 528 U.S. 62 (2000).
152. *Board of Trustees of University of Alabama v. Garrett*, 531 U.S. 356 (2001). *See also Federal Maritime Commissioner v. South Carolina State Ports Authority*, 535 U.S. 473 (2002), where the Court held that the Eleventh Amendment also prevents a federal administrative agency, here the Federal Maritime Commission, from adjudicating a cruise ship's complaint that the state port authority violated federal law by denying the cruise ship permission to berth at the agency's port facilities and so should be required to compensate the cruise ship. A state, however, waives its Eleventh Amendment immunity when it chooses to remove a case from state court to federal court. *Lapides v. Board of Regents of University System of Georgia*, 535 U.S. 613 (2002).
153. *Fitzpatrick v. Bitzer*, 427 U.S. 445 (1976).
154. 538 U.S. 721 (2003).
155. 541 U.S. 509 (2004).
156. 42 U.S.C. sec. 12132.

the country, many persons were being excluded from courthouses and court proceedings because of their disabilities.[157]

More importantly, the Supreme Court has held that a suit seeking only prospective injunctive relief to protect federal constitutional rights brought against a state officer, such as the Governor or Attorney-General, is not a suit against the "state" for Eleventh Amendment purposes, although the action of the state officer is otherwise "state action" for constitutional purposes.[158] As a practical matter, then, the Eleventh Amendment does not prevent judicial review of the constitutionality of state laws or governmental action in the federal courts. Rather, the essential effect of the Eleventh Amendment is to prohibit the abrogation of the state's sovereign immunity in suits by private entities for damages or monetary relief against the state or state officers acting in their official capacity, or in suits for the enforcement of non-constitutional federal law claims.[159]

2. Abstention

126. The other limitations relate to the existence of the dual court system of state courts and federal courts. One of these limitations is the abstention doctrine, which is a postponement rather than a relinquishment of federal court jurisdiction. Recall that only the state courts can authoritatively interpret state law. Sometimes, when a constitutional challenge is brought to a state law or governmental action, a question of state law may also be present. The abstention doctrine holds that where a decision on the state law question could avoid or modify the federal constitutional question, the federal court should abstain from deciding the federal constitutional question until the state courts have had the opportunity to decide the state law question. The plaintiff in the federal action is directed by the federal court to bring an action in

157. But in *Coleman v. Court of Appeals of Maryland*, 132 S.Ct. 1327 (2012), the Court held that a provision of FMLA relating to the employee's self care could not be sustained under the Fourteenth Amendment, so that the Eleventh Amendment provided the states with immunity from such suits. Moreover, a state does not waive its Eleventh Amendment immunity by accepting federal funds, even though acceptance of federal funds imposes certain conditions on the state. *See Sossamon v. Texas*, 563 U.S. 277 (2011) (State cannot be held liable in damages for a violation of the Religious Land Use and Institutionalized Persons Act (RLUIPA), 42 U.S.C. sec. 2000cc, which requires recipients of federal funds to make "reasonable accommodation" for religious practices of prison inmates).

158. *Ex parte Young*, 209 U.S. 123 (1908). In *Verizon Maryland, Inc. v. Public Service Commission of Maryland*, 535 U.S. 635 (2002), the Court, applying *Ex parte Young*, allowed a suit by a local exchange carrier against members of the Maryland Public Service Commission in their official capacities to enjoin enforcement of a decision of the Commission that was claimed to be in violation of federal law. The Court has also held that under *Ex parte Young*, a federal court can hear a suit for prospective relief against state officials brought by an agency of the same state. *Virginia Office for Protection and Advocacy v. Stewart*, 563 U.S. 247 (2011).The holding of *Ex parte Young* also applies to federal court enforcement of a consent decree entered into by state officials. *Frew v. Hawkins*, 540 U.S. 431 (2004).

159. Thus, the federal courts cannot order state officials to pay illegally withheld welfare payments, *Edelman v. Jordan*, 415 U.S. 651 (1974), or require the state to issue notices to persons that welfare payments were illegally withheld. *Green v. Mansour*, 474 U.S. 64 (1985). Nor can the federal courts entertain any suits against state officials involving non-constitutional federal law claims. *See* n. 3, *supra* .

the state court for a determination of the state law question. If the decision on the state law question by the state court does not succeed in avoiding the federal constitutional question, the parties return to the federal court for a resolution of that question.

127. The rationale behind this kind of abstention is the policy of avoiding unnecessary constitutional adjudication, which will be discussed in more detail shortly. If the decision of the state court on the state law question will dispose of the case, the federal court will not be required to decide the constitutional question. And even if the decision of the state court on the state law question does not dispose of the case entirely, it may modify or narrow the constitutional question, thereby serving another policy which will also be discussed in more detail shortly, that of deciding a case on the narrowest possible constitutional ground.

128. The rationale behind this kind of abstention is illustrated by the case of *Railroad Commission of Tex. v. Pullman Co.*,[160] where the doctrine, sometimes referred to as "Pullman abstention," was first promulgated. There, railroads sought an injunction in a federal court against a regulation of a state administrative agency requiring that all sleeping cars be in charge of a conductor. The railroads claimed that the order was not authorized by state law and alternatively, that if it was authorized by state law, it was unconstitutional. If the administrative agency lacked the authority to issue the order under state law, then the state court's decision to that effect would end the controversy between the parties, and there would be no need for the federal court to pass on the hypothetical question of whether such an order, if authorized by state law, would be unconstitutional. Another situation where abstention is clearly proper is where a challenge is made to a state law on the ground that it reaches activity allegedly protected by the federal Constitution, and it is not clear whether the state law actually applies to the activity claimed to be constitutionally protected. Here abstention is proper in order to enable the state court to render an authoritative interpretation of that law. Again, if the state court holds that the state law does not apply to the allegedly constitutionally protected activity, the controversy between the parties is ended.

129. Abstention is also proper where the challenged state law or governmental action could be violative of a specific provision of the state constitution relating to the internal governance of the state, and thus having no analogue in the federal Constitution.[161] However, abstention is not proper merely because there is a state constitutional provision that tracks federal constitutional provisions protecting individual rights, such as a guarantee of free speech or equal protection of the laws. As the Supreme Court has said, to permit abstention on this basis would "convert abstention from an exception into a general rule."[162] Note finally in this regard that a party seeking to challenge a

---

160. 312 U.S. 496 (1941).

161. *See Harris County Commissioners Court v. Moore*, 420 U.S. 77 (1975). There, the plaintiffs alleged that the state's apportionment of electoral districts for minor courts violated the "one person, one vote" principle of the Fourteenth Amendment's equal protection clause. Specific state constitutional provisions dealt with the tenure and removal of the judges of these minor courts, and the apportionment of the electoral districts was arguably violative of these provisions. This being so, abstention was proper to enable the state courts to resolve the state law question, and if they held that the redistricting did violate those provisions, there would be no need for the federal court to determine the federal constitutional question.

162. *Examining Board of Engineers v. Flores de Otero*, 426 U.S. 572, 598 (1976).

state law or governmental action as violative of the federal Constitution has a choice of forum. The party can bring the suit in the state court, which is required to hear it under the Supremacy Clause, or the party can bring the suit in the federal courts. The state courts do not have the "first opportunity," so to speak, to pass on a federal constitutional challenge to a state law or governmental action. Indeed, they do not have this opportunity at all if the party chooses to bring the suit in a federal court.

3. Concurrently Pending Proceedings: The Younger Doctrine

130. Another limitation on federal court judicial review of state laws or governmental action relates to the concurrent jurisdiction of federal and state courts to determine federal constitutional claims. Under the doctrine of *Younger v. Harris*,[163] a federal court may not, in the absence of exceptional circumstances, grant injunctive or declaratory relief against the enforcement of a state law that is being enforced against the federal plaintiff in a pending state court criminal proceeding or certain civil proceedings that are akin to criminal proceedings or that are in furtherance of the state courts' ability to perform their judicial functions. In *Younger*, a party who was being prosecuted in a state court for a violation of a state criminal law, brought suit in a federal court for a declaration that the law under which he was being prosecuted violated his freedom of speech rights under the First Amendment, and an injunction against the continuation of the prosecution. The Supreme Court held that the federal courts were precluded from interfering with the pending state court prosecution because: (1) the federal plaintiff had an adequate remedy to assert his federal constitutional rights by way of defense to the pending state court proceeding; (2) considerations of "comity and federalism" dictated that the federal courts respect the authority of the state courts to protect federal constitutional rights in the cases pending before them. If, however, the state court proceeding has been brought by state officials in bad faith for the purpose of harassing the federal plaintiff and inhibiting the plaintiff's exercise of federal constitutional rights, then it is the prosecution itself that causes the injury, and the federal courts can enjoin the prosecution.[164]

As a general proposition, the *Younger* doctrine does not apply to concurrently pending civil proceedings. The federal courts are required to exercise the jurisdiction conferred on them by Congress, and they are not authorized to refuse to exercise that jurisdiction simply because a case involving the same matter is pending in the state courts. The only exception to this proposition is where the state court proceeding is akin to a criminal prosecution or the matter in issue involves the state's interest in

163. 401 U.S. 37 (1971).

164. So long as the criminal prosecution was brought in good faith, it does not matter whether the federal proceeding was brought before or after the state initiated the criminal proceeding. *Hicks v. Miranda*, 422 U.S. 332 (1975).

enforcing the judgments of its courts.[165] The rule against federal court intervention in a pending state court proceeding also applies to civil proceedings, including those between private parties.[166] It also does not matter whether the federal proceeding was brought before the state court proceeding. So long as the subsequent state court proceeding was brought in good faith, the federal plaintiff now has an adequate state court remedy by way of defense to that proceeding, and federal intervention is barred.[167]

131. The rule against federal court intervention in state criminal proceedings only applies to pending state court proceedings. As stated earlier, a party has a choice of a federal forum in which to vindicate that party's federal constitutional rights. So, if state officials have threatened to prosecute a party under a state law if that party engages in certain conduct, that party has shown threatened injury in fact for standing purposes, and can seek relief against the threatened prosecution in federal court.[168] By the same token, when a party has been prosecuted under a state criminal law in state court, and that prosecution has been completed, the party can then bring a suit in federal court for a declaration that the law under which the party was prosecuted is unconstitutional and an injunction against future prosecutions under it.[169]

D. Avoiding Unnecessary or Inappropriate Judicial Review

132. Over the years, the Supreme Court has developed certain principles of constitutional interpretation designed to avoid unnecessary or inappropriate judicial review.[170] The most important of these principles is that a court should not decide constitutional questions "in advance of the necessity of deciding them." We saw the operation of this principle earlier as the basis for refusing to decide a case on "ripeness" grounds and as the basis for "*Pullman* abstention," where the decision of a state court on a state law question could avoid the federal constitutional question. This principle

---

165. *Sprint Communications, Inc. v. Jacobs*, 134 S.Ct. 584 (2013). Under these exceptions, a federal court could not enjoin a state court civil prosecution to enforce its obscenity laws, *Huffman v. Pursue, Ltd.*, 420 U.S. 592 (1975), or the issuance of a state court judgment pending the appeal of that judgment in the state court system. *Pennzoil Co. v. Texaco, Inc.*, 481 U.S. 1 (1987). In *Sprint*, the Court held that *Younger* abstention did not apply to preclude a federal court from deciding whether federal law preempted a ruling of a state administrative agency concerning fees for internet long distance service.

166. *Pennzoil Co. v. Texaco, Inc.*, 481 U.S. 1 (1987).

167. *Hicks v. Miranda*, 422 U.S. 332 (1975).

168. *Steffel v. Thompson*, 415 U.S. 452 (1974).

169. *Wooley v. Maynard*, 430 U.S. 705 (1977). The subsequent federal court suit was not barred by res judicata, because the parties were different: the state court suit had been brought by the state against the subsequent federal plaintiff as defendant, and the subsequent federal suit was brought by the plaintiff against the state official charged with enforcement of the law. (Recall that the "state" and a "state officer" are distinct entities for purposes of the Eleventh Amendment, although the action of the "state officer" is "state action" for constitutional purposes.) Since res judicata does not apply, it does not matter that the federal constitutional question could have been, but was not litigated in the state court proceeding; if it had been litigated, collateral estoppel would apply to bar its relitigation in the subsequent federal court action.

170. *See* generally the discussion in *Rescue Army v. Municipal Court of City of Los Angeles*, 331 U.S. 549, 569 (1947).

also means that the courts should avoid deciding a constitutional question "if the record presents some other ground upon which the case may be disposed of." An application of this principle is reflected in a rule of statutory interpretation: where a law is challenged as unconstitutional, the courts must first determine whether an interpretation of the law is fairly possible by which the constitutional question can be avoided. For example, suppose that a law prohibits membership in "illegal organizations." A person charged with a violation of the law argues that the First Amendment protects "innocent" membership in otherwise "illegal organizations," and the argument is a plausible one. In order to avoid having to decide whether the First Amendment does protect "innocent" membership in "illegal" organizations, the court should try to interpret the law, if fairly possible, to exclude "innocent" membership from its prohibitions.

133. A related principle is that a court should decide constitutional questions on narrow rather than on broad grounds, and that its constitutional decision should not be "in broader terms than are required by the precise facts to which the ruling is to be applied." Typically, this principle means that rather than decide whether or not a law is unconstitutional in all its applications, the courts will only determine that it is unconstitutional as applied to the facts of the particular case. It also means that where only a part of a law is invalid, the law should be held unconstitutional only to the extent of that invalidity.[171]

134. For a discussion of judicial review of administrative action, reference is made to Part IV, Chapter 4 *infra*.

---

171. *See* e.g., *Brockett v. Spokane Arcades, Inc.*, 472 U.S. 491 (1985) (Law prohibiting dissemination of "obscene" materials should not have been invalidated "on its face," although definition of "obscenity" was partially invalid); *Ayotte v. Planned Parenthood of New England*, 546 U.S. 320 (2006) (where only one provision of a law requiring notification to a minor's parent or guardian of her intention to have an abortion was unconstitutional, the injunction against enforcement should be limited to the unconstitutional provision, and the court could not enjoin enforcement of the entire law).

Chapter 5. Independent Nonpolitical Agencies

135. There are a large number of administrative agencies in the federal government, and they play an extremely important role in implementing federal regulatory policy.[172] From a constitutional standpoint, administrative agencies are federal offices that have been established by Congress, whose function it is to administer and enforce Congressional laws in a specific regulatory area. A number of the executive departments, headed by a Secretary or other cabinet-level official (*see* Chapter 3), are like administrative agencies in this sense. Most of the administrative agencies, however, are "independent agencies," variously designated as "Commission," "agency," "Board," or "Service," and the officials heading them are variously designated as "Commissioner," "Member," or "Director." The officials heading these agencies are "principal officers of the United States," within the meaning of Article II, section 2, appointed by the President and confirmed by Congress. Unlike the "departmental agencies," which are part of the "Presidential Administration," and so subject to direct Presidential control, the "independent agencies" are not subject to direct Presidential control. Congress prescribes their power and authority, fixes a term for their members, appropriates the funds for their operations, and can regulate their structure and procedures. As discussed previously, the President cannot remove members of "independent agencies" prior to the expiration of the term fixed by Congress, and cannot interfere in their day-to-day operations or determine their policies.

136. Most of the administrative agencies, both "departmental" and "independent," have been given rule-making authority by Congress, that is, they promulgate regulations within the area of their statutory authority, and these regulations take effect in accordance with procedures established by Congress.[173] All the administrative agencies have also been given adjudication authority, that is, they can adjudicate certain claims involving the application of the laws that they administer.[174] In practice, much of the activity of administrative agencies, both rule-making and adjudication, takes the form of "informal agency action." This is a generic term, referring to anything other than formal rule-making and formal adjudication. "Informal agency action" includes, for example,

172. Most state governments also make use of administrative agencies, although the degree of authority they exercise varies considerably from state to state.

173. These procedures are set forth in the Administrative Procedure Act, 5 U.S.C. sec. 553. The basic approach to rule-making under the Act is "notice and comment." The agency gives public notice of its intention to promulgate a proposed rule and invites public comment. After considering the public comments, the agency compiles a rule-making record, and prepares a statement of the basis and purpose of the rule, which is generally published along with the final rule. In some circumstances, Congress has required that the agencies promulgate rules in accordance with the procedures specified in 5 U.S.C. secs. 556 and 557, a process known as "formal rule-making."

174. Some agencies have the authority only to engage in "informal" adjudication. The procedures governing "formal" adjudication are set forth in the Administrative Procedure Act, 5 U.S.C. secs. 554–557. These hearings are more informal than a court trial, but are somewhat similar in that there is the presentation of evidence, representation by counsel, and a written decision. The hearings are presided over by an Administrative Law Judge (who is an employee of the agency and not a judicial officer), who makes findings and renders the initial decision. The final administrative decision is rendered by the agency.

processing claims for benefits under a program administered by the agency, taking actions that by law require agency approval, and agency decisions whether or not to undertake particular activity within the agency's authority. Congress has provided for judicial review of both rule-making and adjudication actions of administrative agencies, and judicial review of administrative action will be discussed in Part IV, Chapter 4.

137. Some of the major federal administrative agencies are the Federal Trade Commission, the Federal Energy Regulatory Commission, the National Labor Relations Board, the Federal Aviation Agency, the Occupational Safety and Health Administration, the Nuclear Regulatory Commission, the Equal Employment Opportunity Commission, the Federal Maritime Administration, and the Securities and Exchange Commission.

Part III. The State and Its Subdivisions

Chapter 1. The American Federal System

138. We have previously discussed the historical development of the American federal system and have described the form of government of the United States as being a strong federal system. We will now explain in more detail the constitutional basis and operation of the American federal system.

139. It is very important to remember that the American federal system, as it now exists, began with the states. Upon Independence, all of the thirteen colonies became "free and independent states," which meant that they succeeded to the sovereignty formerly exercised by the British Crown over domestic matters. To put it another way, each state obtained its sovereignty by way of succession upon declaring Independence from Great Britain, and it was not necessary to have a national Constitution to give the states power. State sovereignty is thus a "given" in the American constitutional system. As a part of this sovereignty, each state has its own system of laws and its own courts and possesses the general regulatory and taxation power. In the constitutional sense then, American states are "independent sovereigns" and cannot be considered "subdivisions" of the national state.[175]

140. In constitutional terms, as stated in the Preamble, the national state we call the United States of America is conceived of as a "Union of the People of the United States." One component of this Union is the states, and the other component is the federal government that was established by the Constitution to exercise a federal sovereignty complementary to the sovereignty that the then thirteen states had been exercising since Independence. Given the existence of state sovereignty and the fact that the Constitution would be establishing a federal government to exercise a comparable sovereignty, it was necessary that the Constitution deal specifically with the states and with the relationship between federal power and state power. The Constitution did so in a number of ways.

141. The first thing that the Constitution did was to recognize and confirm the sovereignty of the states and to provide for the formation of new states. Article IV, section 3 gives Congress the authority to admit new states into the Union. However, Congress cannot form a new state from the territory of any existing state, nor can it combine parts of two or more states to form a new state without the consent of the

175. The Supreme Court has said that, "The Constitution, in all its provisions, looks to an indestructible Union, composed of indestructible states." *Texas v. White*, 74 U.S. 700, 725 (1869). Because this is so, the Supreme Court held in that case that during the American civil war, the Confederate states were still a part of the Union, although they were trying to secede from it.

legislatures of all the involved states. As settlement increased in the late eighteenth and early nineteenth centuries, the inhabitants of the settled territories petitioned Congress for admission to the Union, and a number of new states were admitted, beginning with Vermont in 1791. Some of these new states, such as Kentucky, admitted in 1792, were formed out of territory belonging to existing states, with the consent of the legislatures of those states. More new states came into the Union as the American west was settled at various times throughout the nineteenth century. With the admission of Alaska and Hawaii as the 49th and 50th states in 1959, the Union that we call the United States of America emerged in its present form. As each new state was admitted to the Union, it automatically became entitled to exercise the same state sovereignty that was exercised by the original thirteen states at the time of the adoption of the Constitution.[176]

Closely related to the "equal footing" doctrine and finding its source in the same constitutional values is the "equal sovereignty" doctrine, which embodies the principle that Congress must treat all states equally. The Court upheld a departure from the "equal sovereignty" doctrine when it upheld "preclearance provisions" of sections 4 and 5 of the Voting Rights Act of 1965. [177] These provisions required certain states that had a long history of voting discrimination against their African-American citizens—Alabama, Georgia, Louisiana, Mississippi, South Carolina, and Virginia—to obtain preclearance from the United States Attorney-General or a special federal court for any change in voting procedures by proving that the change had neither the purpose or effect of denying or abridging the right to vote on account of race or color. In all the other states, a change in voting procedures could go into effect unless the change was successfully challenged under section 2 as "result[ing] in a denial or abridgment of the right to vote on account of race or color." The mechanism for triggering the preclearance requirement for a covered jurisdiction was that it had maintained a test or device as a prerequisite for voting as of November 1, 1964, and had less than 50% voter registration or turnout in the 1964 Presidential election. The Supreme Court upheld the application of the preclearance requirement to these states despite the departure from the "equal sovereignty" doctrine on the ground that its

---

176. Under the "equal footing" doctrine, all states are admitted to the Union with the same attributes of sovereignty as were possessed by the original thirteen states. This doctrine thus prevents the federal government from impairing any fundamental attributes of state sovereignty when it admits a new state into the Union. In *Minnesota v. Mille Lacs Band of Chippewa Indians*, 526 U.S. 172 (1999), the Court held that recognition of Indian rights to hunt, fish and gather on state land, provided for under a treaty between an Indian tribe and the federal government, was not irreconcilable with a state's sovereignty over the natural resources in the state, and so the treaty was not abrogated upon admission of the state to the Union.

Under the "equal footing" doctrine, upon statehood, a state gains title within its borders to beds of water then navigable. The United States retains title vested in it before statehood to land beneath waters not then navigable. To be navigable for purposes of title under the "equal footing" doctrine, the rivers must be "navigable in fact" in that they are used or are susceptible of being used as highways for commerce. To determine navigability, the Court considers the river on a segment- by- segment basis. In *PPL Montana, LLC v. Montana*, 132 S.Ct. 1215 (2012), the Court held that certain segments of three rivers running through Montana were not navigable at the time of statehood.

177. 42 U.S.C. sec. 1973.

Congress needed to address entrenched discrimination in voting that had been "perpetuated in certain parts of our country through unremitting and ingenious defiance of the Constitution."[178] The Voting Rights Act of 1965 was to expire in five years, but it has been extended by Congress numerous times. In 1975, Congress extended its coverage to deal with language discrimination, with the result that three more states—Alaska, Arizona and Texas—and several counties in six other states became covered jurisdictions. In 1982, Congress reauthorized the Act for twenty-five years, but did not alter its coverage formula. There have been many changes in voting practices in the years since 1965, most particularly, there has been a much higher level voting by African-Americans in the covered jurisdictions. It is conceded by all sides that much of the voting discrimination that the 1965 Voting Rights Act was designed to prevent has ceased to exist, although there is still disagreement over the need for the preclearance provisions of sections 4 and 5. Recently, a sharply divided Supreme Court held 5-4, that Congress' basing the coverage formula on the situation as it existed in 1965 was unconstitutional, because it was not based on current conditions, and so no longer could justify a departure from the "equal sovereignty" doctrine.[179]

142. We cannot emphasize strongly enough the fundamental principle of state sovereignty in the American constitutional system. As a constitutional matter, all of the American states can exercise full sovereignty over domestic matters except to the extent that the Constitution prohibits or restricts a particular exercise of such sovereignty. With this in mind, we can now consider precisely how the Constitution restricts state sovereignty.

143. In terms of allocation of power, the Constitution restricts state sovereignty in essentially three ways.[180] First, it provides that certain powers, relatively few in number, are exclusive federal powers, in the sense that they cannot be exercised by the states at all, such as the power to enter into a treaty or the power to coin money, or cannot be exercised without the consent of Congress, such as the power to impose a duty of tonnage or to enter into a compact with another state or foreign government. However, in order for a power to be an exclusive federal power, it must be affirmatively granted to Congress in Article I, section 8, and either expressly denied to the states in Article I, section 10, or be of such a nature that the exercise of that power by the states would be incompatible with its exercise by Congress.[181]

Second, and more significantly, the Constitution provides for federal supremacy in the event of a conflict between the exercise of federal power and the exercise of

---

178. *South Carolina v. Katzenbach*, 383 U.S. 301 (1966).

179. *Shelby County v. Holder*, 133 Sup.Ct. 2612 (2013).

180. As we will *see* in Part IV, the Constitution restricts both state and federal sovereignty to the extent that it imposes limitations on governmental power in order to protect individual rights.

181. Research has disclosed no case where the Supreme Court has specifically held that a particular power is an exclusive federal power by necessary implication, and the Court has held that certain federal powers, such as the power over bankruptcy and the power over copyright, are not exclusive federal powers. Certain examples of powers that are exclusively federal powers by necessary implication, however, come readily to mind, such as the naturalization and immigration power and the power to fix the standard of weights and measures.

state power.[182] So, where a state law, for example, conflicts with a law of Congress, the operation of the state law is preempted to the extent of that conflict. We will discuss preemption in Chapter 3, §3.

Third, as we will discuss in Chapter 3, §§4 and 5, the Supreme Court has held that the affirmative grant of the power to regulate interstate and foreign commerce to Congress under Article I, section 8, has a negative implication as well, and imposes some limitations on the power of the states to regulate and tax interstate and foreign commerce.

144. However, since state sovereignty is a "given" in the American constitutional system, and since there are very few exclusively federal powers, it follows that the American states have enormous power over all activity that takes place within their boundaries. While this power is always subject to federal preemption, we will see that on the whole, Congress has exercised caution in preempting state regulatory power, and that in practice federal preemption is only a modest restriction on the exercise of state power. Since state power is so extensive and since, as we have discussed previously, the powers of Congress have been construed very broadly, so as to reach virtually every activity, no matter how "local," it follows that the overriding feature of the American federal system as regards domestic matters is *concurrent power*. Just as the federal government can exercise its power throughout the United States, each state, in the absence of federal preemption, can exercise comparable power within the boundaries of that state. What this all adds up to is a large amount of sometimes overlapping governmental regulation in the United States, but this is because the American federal system is comprised of two sets of independent sovereigns that usually have concurrent power over the same matter.

182. The Supremacy Clause, Art. VI, s. 2, provides: "The Constitution, and the Laws of the United States which shall be made in Pursuance thereof, and all Treaties made, or which shall be made, under the Authority of the United States, shall be the supreme Law of the Land; and the Judges in every State shall be bound thereby, any Thing in the Constitution or Laws of any State to the Contrary notwithstanding."

Chapter 2. State and Municipal Government

145. Since each state is a sovereign entity, the federal Constitution does not regulate the governmental structure and internal organization of the states. Each state has its own constitution, which regulates the governmental structure and internal organization of that state, and which provides for municipal government. While the governmental structure and internal organization of each state differ in some detail, all of the states have the same basic governmental structure, which in turn is the same basic governmental structure as that of the federal government. Thus, each state government consists of a Legislative Branch, an Executive Branch, and a Judicial Branch.[183] Like the Congress, the legislative branch of the state government consists of two houses,[184] and like the Presidency, each state has a Chief Executive called the Governor. The members of the Legislature and the Governor, of course, are elected by the voters. The allocation of powers between the Legislature and the Governor varies somewhat among the different states. In some states, the Governor has more power in relation to the Legislature than the President has in relation to the Congress, and in some states the Governor has less. All the states have essentially the same legislative process as that of the national government, with legislation being a collaborative effort between the legislature and the Governor: proposed legislation must pass both houses, and must be approved by the Governor or passed again by both houses over his veto. A number of state constitutions also provide that legislation may be enacted or existing legislation repealed directly by the people by means of voter initiative,[185] and that legislation enacted by the legislature may be subject to voter approval by referendum before it takes effect. Because the principle of state sovereignty necessarily gives the state legislature the general regulatory and taxation power, it is not necessary that state constitutions enumerate the specific powers of the legislature, as the federal Constitution does for the Congress. However, state constitutions typically set forth a number of areas in which the legislature is directed to enact legislation, and impose some limitations on the exercise of legislative power.

146. Perhaps the most important power exercised by the states in the American constitutional system is the power over education.[186] Every state constitution directs the legislature to provide for a system of elementary and secondary education and for a system of public colleges and universities. While the structure and organization of public colleges and universities differs considerably from state to state, the system of

183. The state courts have been discussed in paras. 90–92, *supra* .

184. Except for Nebraska, which has only one house, the members of which are elected on a nonpartisan basis.

185. Typically, proposed legislation gets on the ballot by way of a petition containing a specified number of voter signatures.

186. Congress is not given the power over education, and the power over education traditionally has been exercised only by the states. However, Congress is much involved in education through the appropriation of funds to the states, and with such appropriation often comes the imposition of conditions. There is a Secretary of Education in the President's Cabinet, and the federal government has substantial influence over education in the United States. Nonetheless, only the states exercise direct power over education.

elementary and secondary education is generally entrusted to local school districts. Although the local school districts are organized pursuant to state law and are subject to state regulation, there is a great deal of local control over elementary and secondary education. The governing body of the local school district is usually elected by the voters, the local school district has a good deal of discretion in the operation of the school system, and a substantial amount of its revenue comes from taxes on land located in the school district. The state legislatures, however, also appropriate funds for use by local school districts, and in varying degrees, the states exercise some direct control over elementary and secondary education as well.

147. Within each state, there is a system of municipal government, specified by the state constitution. However, units of municipal government are considered "creatures of the state," and are subject to complete control by the state legislature. That is, they can only exercise the regulatory and taxation powers given to them by the state legislature. The structure and organization of the system of municipal government varies somewhat among the different states, but generally operates along the following lines. The basic unit of municipal government is the county, and every state is divided into a number of counties of varying size. The county government exercises the state-authorized regulatory authority within the county and provides basic services, such as police and fire protection, except in those areas of the county where such services are provided by another unit of municipal government. The other units of municipal government are variously denominated cities, townships, villages and towns, and are incorporated as such pursuant to state law. In most states, the form of incorporation is related to population size, with cities being the largest unit of municipal government. Each unit of municipal government exercises the powers authorized for that unit of municipal government under state law, with cities usually having the most extensive powers. The internal organization of a unit of municipal government generally consists of a legislative body, variously denominated as a "council," "commission," or "board," and an executive officer, usually denominated as "county executive" for counties, "mayor" for cities, and by many different terms for other units of local government. These officials are almost invariably elected by the voters.

148. The above discussion of state and municipal government is obviously very generalized, and the specific features of state and municipal governmental organization vary considerably from state to state. Nonetheless, there is substantial similarity in the organization and structure of state and municipal government in all of the states.

Chapter 3. The Interaction Between Federal and State Power

§1. Federal Power over Foreign Affairs

149. In foreign affairs, federal power dominates over state power. For a discussion of the interrelationship between this principle and the principle of state sovereignty, *see* Part V, Chapter 1, §3.

§2. Intergovernmental Immunities and Cooperative Arrangements

150. Because both the federal government and the states are sovereign in the American federal system, it follows that the Constitution imposes certain limits on the ability of each sovereign to interfere with the operations of the other. However, this concept of intergovernmental immunity operates in relation to the principle of federal supremacy. What this means in the final analysis is that the states cannot in any way interfere with the operations of the federal government, but that the federal government may, to a very considerable degree, apply its laws to the "states as states."

151. It was very early decided that the states cannot impose a tax on any instrumentality of the federal government, such as a federally chartered bank, or otherwise directly interfere with the operations of the federal government.[187] For a period of time thereafter the Court extended this principle and held that neither sovereign could impose a tax on the officials or employees of the other sovereign. However, in the late 1930s, the Court moved away from this position and held that each sovereign had the constitutional power to impose nondiscriminatory income taxes on the employees of the other sovereign.[188] In response to the Court's decisions, Congress enacted a law specifically extending the federal income tax to state and local governmental employees and specifically authorizing the states to impose nondiscriminatory taxes on federal employees. Thus, both as a matter of constitutional interpretation and Congressional legislation, the operative principle today is that the employees of each sovereign are subject to the imposition of nondiscriminatory taxes by the other sovereign.[189]

---

187. *McCulloch v. Maryland*, 17 U.S. 316 (1819).

188. *Helvering v. Gerhardt*, 304 U.S. 405 (1938) (federal government taxation of state governmental employees); *Graves v. New York ex rel.* O'Keefe, 306 U.S. 466 (1939) (state government taxation of federal governmental employees). *See also Jefferson County, Alabama v. Acker*, 527 U.S. 423 (1999), where the Court held that an "occupational tax," calculated on a percentage of the income of persons working within a county, was a nondiscriminatory tax that could be levied on federal judges.

189. In *Davis v. Michigan Department of Treasury*, 489 U.S. 803 (1989), the Court relied on the principle of intergovernmental tax immunity to invalidate a Michigan taxation scheme that excluded the retirement pay of state and local governmental employees, but not federal employees, from the state income tax.

152. When it comes to the imposition of federal taxes on activities operated by the state governments, the constitutional situation is not as clear. It is not disputed that the federal government could not constitutionally impose a tax on state revenues or on an "instrumentality" of state government. However, state governments carry on a large number of activities, including some of a proprietary nature that are no different from activities carried on by private entities. The Supreme Court has upheld the imposition of federal taxes on revenue-generating activities of the state that are of the same nature as those traditionally engaged in by private entities, such as the imposition of a federal excise tax on a state's sale of mineral waters bottled and sold by the state to provide funds for a state health resort.[190] The Court has also upheld the application to airplanes owned by the state police force of a federal registration tax on all civil aircraft, imposed to defray the cost of federal air navigational facilities and services.[191] For the most part, however, Congress has not sought to apply federal tax law to activities operated by the state governments, and it is recognized that power of Congress to do so is clearly subject to some constitutional limitations.

153. The more controversial constitutional question concerns the power of Congress to apply federal regulatory laws to state and municipal governmental operations.[192] This question has arisen primarily when Congress seeks to apply general laws, such as a federal wage and hour law, to the operations of state and municipal governments. The states have contended that the Constitution embodies a "state sovereignty" principle that limits the power of Congress to regulate the "states as states," and so precludes Congress from directly regulating the operations of state and municipal governments.[193] The Supreme Court has been sharply divided over this question and has reached conflicting results in cases decided within just a few years of the other, overruling earlier decisions in the process. However, its latest decision on this question, rendered in 1985, holds that the "state sovereignty" principle does not operate as an independent limitation on Congress' power to regulate interstate commerce. So, since Congress, under the interstate commerce power, can impose wage and hour regulations on employees of a private business within a state, it can

---

190. *New York v. United States*, 326 U.S. 572 (1946).

191. *Massachusetts v. United States*, 435 U.S. 444 (1978).

192. For constitutional purposes, municipal governments are considered a part of the state government, since they are established by the state and derive their powers solely from the state. *See* para. 147, *supra* .

193. The state sovereignty argument has been based primarily on the Tenth Amendment, which provides that, "The powers not delegated to the United States by the Constitution, nor prohibited to it by the States, are reserved to the States respectively, or to the people." The Supreme Court has said that the Tenth Amendment merely states a truism: since the states possess the general sovereignty, as discussed previously, and since Congress theoretically has only the powers specifically enumerated in Art. I, s. 8, it would follow, even in the absence of the Tenth Amendment, that any power not granted to Congress nor denied to the states would be "reserved" to the states. Under this view, the Tenth Amendment would not independently limit the power of Congress to regulate the "states as states." The contrary argument is that the Tenth Amendment reinforces the notion that Congress must respect state sovereignty, so that the Constitution by its own force imposes some limits on the power of Congress to regulate the "states as states."

likewise impose wage and hour regulations with respect to employees of state and local governments.[194]

154. The question of Congress' power to apply federal regulatory laws to state and municipal governments ties in with Congress' use of the spending power to engage in cooperative ventures with state and municipal governments. Congress, in the exercise of its spending power, has established a large number of grant-in-aid programs by which it provides funds to state and municipal governments for specific purposes. Congress sometimes imposes restrictions on the state and municipal governments as a condition for the receipt of the federal funds. Here, of course, the states theoretically have a choice: they can give up the funds rather than comply with the conditions, although they are extremely reluctant to give up the funds. The Supreme Court has held that while there may be some limits on the conditions that Congress can impose on the states, Congress has broad authority to condition the receipt of federal funds on compliance with federal policies. Thus, the Court has upheld, for example, a provision in a federal highway program withholding 5% of the allocated highway funds from any state that did not prohibit the purchase of alcoholic beverages by persons under the age of 21.[195]

However, in its most recent decision on the power of Congress to impose conditions on the states, *National Federation of Independent Business v. Sebelius*,[196] the Court held that Congress could not condition a state's continued participation in the Medicaid program, which is financed jointly by the United States and the states, on a state's agreement to expand Medicaid coverage under the Patient Protection and Affordable Act. Under the Act, a state would be barred from receiving any Medicaid funds unless it agreed to expand Medicaid coverage under the Act. The Court held that as a constitutional matter, Congress must give a state the choice whether or not to participate in Medicaid expansion and could not try to "coerce" that choice by denying a state any Medicaid funds unless the state agreed to participate in the Medicaid expansion.

155. The difference between Congress' attempting to influence the actions of the states by means of financial inducements and attempting to regulate the "states as states" directly surfaced in a Supreme Court case involving a federal law regulating the disposal of low-level radioactive waste. The law imposed upon the states the obligation to deal with the disposal of low-level radioactive waste generated within their borders and provided a number of financial incentives for the states to do so, such as allowing a state to impose a surcharge on radioactive waste received from other states. But the law also contained a provision to the effect that if a state failed to provide for the disposal of all radioactive waste by a given date, the state would become the owner of the waste and would be liable for all harm caused by the state's failure to take prompt possession of the waste.

194. *Garcia v. San Antonio Metropolitan Transit Authority*, 469 U.S. 528 (1985). Note, however, that the federal government itself must enforce these wage and hour regulations against the state governments, since suits by the affected employees against the state governments (but against not the local governments) are precluded by the Eleventh Amendment. *See* para. 125, *supra* .

195. *South Dakota v. Dole*, 483 U.S. 203 (1987).

196. 132 Sup.Ct. 2566 (2012).

The Court, while upholding Congress' power to encourage the states to regulate the disposal of radioactive waste by means of financial incentives, held that Congress did not have the constitutional power to compel the states to become the owners of the waste. This, said the Court, "crosses the line distinguishing encouragement from coercion," because it would force the states either to accept ownership of the waste or to regulate its disposal according to instructions from Congress. The Court held that Congress lacked the constitutional power to "commandeer state governments into the service of federal regulatory purposes," and that for Congress to do so would be "inconsistent with the Constitution's division of authority between federal and state governments."[197]

156. The constitutional controversy over Congress' power to regulate the states as states' may be expected to continue. As things now stand, Congress may regulate state operations in the same manner as it regulates private entities and may provide financial encouragement to the states to take a particular course of action, but it cannot directly require them to assume a regulatory function as a part of Congress' overall regulatory scheme.[198]

157. Congress is also involved in cooperative arrangements with the states to the extent that it exercises its power under Article I, section 10, to approve interstate compacts, into which the states may not enter without Congressional approval. The Supreme Court has held that this provision applies only to agreements which may increase the political power of the involved states or encroach upon or interfere with federal supremacy. Thus, the consent of Congress is not required, for example, for an agreement between states to promote regional banking.[199] Where Congressional consent is required, it may take any form, and may be given before or after the states have entered into the compact. And where Congressional consent has been given, whether or not required, the federal courts have jurisdiction to interpret the provisions of the compact.[200]

§3. Federal Preemption

158. The matter of federal preemption of state law is very important in practice, and is the subject of considerable litigation. The question arises quite frequently because

---

197. *New York v. United States*, 505 U.S. 144 (1992). *See also Printz v. United States*, 521 U.S. 898 (1997), holding that Congress lacked the power to require state and local law enforcement officers to conduct background checks on prospective handgun purchasers as a part of a detailed federal scheme governing the distribution of handguns. Congress, however, may impose regulations on the states that interfere with state sovereignty, such as prohibiting the states from disclosing or selling information obtained from motor vehicle registration, since Congress is not thereby "commandeering state regulation." *Reno v. Condon*, 528 U.S. 141 (2000).
198. For cases where the Court found that Congress was "encouraging" rather than "compelling" state regulation, *see Federal Energy Commission v. Mississippi*, 456 U.S. 742 (1982) (states' utility regulation would not be preempted if they considered adopting proposed federal standards in such regulation); *South Carolina v. Baker*, 485 U.S. 505 (1988) (state wishing to enact regulation in field where state regulation could be preempted must comply with federal standards).
199. *Northeast Bancorp, Inc. v. Board of Governors of Federal Reserve System*, 472 U.S. 159 (1985).
200. *Cuyler v. Adams*, 449 U.S. 433 (1981).

of the fact, as has been emphasized repeatedly, that as regards domestic matters, the overriding feature of the American federal system is concurrent power. Since there is a great deal of overlapping state and federal governmental regulation, the objects of state regulation will often try to avoid it by asserting federal preemption of the state regulation in question. In order to assert federal preemption, they must as a preliminary matter identify a particular federal law that arguably has preempted the challenged state regulation.

159. As the above discussion indicates, federal preemption necessarily involves a conflict and interaction between the principle of federal supremacy and the principle of state sovereignty. On the one hand, as a matter of federal supremacy, Congress can preempt any or all state regulation affecting an area in which Congress has legislated. In this sense, preemption depends entirely on Congressional intent, and analytically the question is whether Congress intended, expressly or impliedly, to preempt all or some state regulation in the relevant area. On the other hand, a strong respect for the principle of state sovereignty contributes to a reluctance on the part of Congress to preempt state regulation and correspondingly to a reluctance on the part of the Supreme Court to find that Congress intended to do so. In this section, we will try to analyze the structural bases of federal preemption and explain the operation of preemption in practice in the American federal system.

160. Congress may expressly deal with the matter of preemption in the legislation it enacts, and in recent years, it has increasingly done so. One way for Congress to deal with the matter is to expressly disclaim any intention to preempt state regulation by including a "savings clause" in the legislation. The "savings clause" will typically authorize state regulation that does not conflict with the provisions of the federal law, and depending on the area involved, the "savings clause" may have the effect of authorizing the states to impose even more extensive regulation than has been provided under federal law.[201] It was on this basis that the Supreme Court upheld an Arizona law providing that the licenses of employers that knowingly employ illegal aliens may be, and in certain circumstances, must be suspended or revoked and requiring that employers use a federal electronic verification system to confirm that the workers they employ are legally authorized workers, as coming within the "savings" clause of the federal law that does not preempt state "licensing" laws imposing sanctions on those who employ illegal aliens.[202]

161. The other way that Congress may expressly deal with the matter is to establish a standard of federal preemption in the legislation. When Congress has done

---

201. An example of a "savings clause" is that contained in the Securities Exchange Act of 1934, which provides that, "Nothing in this chapter shall affect the jurisdiction of the securities commissioner of any State over any security or any person so far as it does not conflict with the provisions of this chapter or the rules and regulations thereunder." 15 U.S.C. sec. 78bb(a). A similar example is contained in the Civil Rights Act of 1964, which was designed to prevent preemption of state civil rights laws: "Nothing contained in any title of this Act shall be construed as indicating an intent on the part of Congress to occupy the field in which any such title operates to the exclusion of State laws on the same subject matter, nor shall any provision of this Act be construed as invalidating any provision of State law unless such provision is inconsistent with any of the purposes of this Act, or any provision thereof." 42 U.S.C. sec. 2000h-4.

202. *Chamber of Commerce of the United States v. Whiting*, 563 U.S. 582 (2011).

so, the courts must apply that standard according to its terms in order to determine whether a particular state regulation that affects the area in which Congress has legislated has been preempted. For example, in the Employee Retirement Income Security Act of 1974 (ERISA), Congress comprehensively regulated employee benefit plans, imposing participation, funding and vesting requirements. As a part of this regulatory scheme, it included a broad preemption provision, which provides that, subject to limited exceptions, ERISA "shall supersede any and all State laws insofar as they may now or hereafter relate to any employee benefit plan described [in the law]."[203] Whenever a state law is challenged as being preempted by ERISA, the question to be determined is whether the state law "relate[s] to any employee benefit plan" as defined in ERISA. Applying that standard, the Supreme Court has held that ERISA preempted a state common law rule that would impose liability on an employer for discharging an employee in order to prevent him from receiving benefits under a plan covered by ERISA.[204] The Court has also found ERISA preemption in the following cases: ERISA preempted a provision of a state community property law, allowing a spouse to make a testamentary transfer of her interest in the other spouse's undistributed pension plan benefits,[205] a state law providing for automatic revocation upon divorce of any designation of the divorced spouse as beneficiary of an asset that was not subject to probate,[206] and a state law allowing a suit for damages against a health maintenance organization that provided benefits under an employer's health insurance plan.[207] ERISA does not preempt state laws "regulating insurance." Applying this exception to ERISA preemption, the Court held that a state's "notice-prejudice" rule, under which an insurer must show that it was prejudiced by an untimely proof of claim before it can avoid liability, was a law "regulating insurance" within the meaning of the ERISA exception, and so was not preempted.[208] The Court also held, however, that another state rule allowing the employer to be deemed an agent in administering a group

---

203. 42 U.S.C. sec. 1144(a).

204. *Ingersoll-Rand Co. v. McClendon*, 498 U.S. 133 (1990). To the same effect, *see District of Columbia v. Greater Washington Board of Trade*, 506 U.S. 125 (1993), holding that ERISA preempted a state law requiring employers who purchased health insurance for their employees to provide equivalent health insurance coverage for injured employees eligible for worker's compensation benefits. In contrast, the Court has held that ERISA did not preempt a state law setting wage rates for apprentices employed on public works projects, because this area was quite remote from the areas with which ERISA was expressly concerned, and there was no indication that Congress intended for ERISA to reach this area. *California Division of Labor Standards Enforcement v. Dillingham Construction, NA., Inc.*, 519 U.S. 316 (1997).

205. *Boggs v. Boggs*, 520 U.S. 833 (1997).

206. *Egelhoff v. Egelhoff*, 532 U.S. 141 (2001),

207. *Aetna Health, Inc. v. Davila*, 542 U.S. 200 (2004).

208. *Unum Life Insurance Co. of America v. Ward*, 526 U.S. 358 (1999). The Court also held, however, that another state rule allowing the employer to be deemed an agent in administering a group insurance policy was a rule "relating to an employee benefit plan" rather than a rule "regulating insurance," and so was preempted. In *Rush Prudential HMO v. Moran*, 536 U.S. 355 (2002), the Court held that an Illinois law requiring health maintenance organizations to provide an independent review of disputes between the primary care physician and the health maintenance organization and to cover services deemed medically necessary by the independent reviewer was a law "regulating insurance" within the meaning of the ERISA exemption.

insurance policy was a rule "relating to an employee benefit plan" rather than a rule "regulating insurance," and so was preempted.[209]

Most recently the Court that ERISA preempted a state law requiring the disclosure of payments relating to health care claims and other health care services as it applied to ERISA plans.[210]

Likewise, the Court has held that a provision in the Airline Deregulation Act of 1978,[211] prohibiting the states from enforcing any law "relating to rates, routes or services of [any air carrier]," preempted the states from regulating allegedly deceptive airline fare advertisements through enforcement of their general consumer protection laws.[212] The Court has also held that the Act preempted frequent flyer claims against airlines under state consumer fraud laws, because this would be a state-imposed regulation of air carriers, but did not preempt frequent flyer claims for breach of contract, because here the state would be enforcing contract terms set by the parties themselves.[213] However, the Act did preempt a claim for breach of an implied covenant of good faith, because state law prohibited the parties from contracting out of this covenant.[214]

162. The operation of a standard of federal preemption is also illustrated by the Public Health Cigarette Smoking Act of 1969,[215] which requires that all cigarette packages carry the warning, "Caution: Cigarette Smoking is Dangerous to Your Health," and further provides that: "No requirement or prohibition based on smoking and health shall be imposed under State law with respect to the advertising or promotion of any cigarette, the packages of which are labeled in conformity with the provisions of this Act." The first case involving this standard dealt with state tort law claims brought by cigarette smokers against the tobacco companies. A person who claimed that she had contracted lung cancer as a result of smoking cigarettes for many years brought a state tort law action against the tobacco company that manufactured the brand of cigarettes

---

209. In *Rush Prudential HMO v. Moran*, 536 U.S. 355 (2002), the Court held that an Illinois law requiring health maintenance organizations to provide an independent review of disputes between the primary care physician and the health maintenance organization and to cover services deemed medically necessary by the independent reviewer was a law "regulating insurance" within the meaning of the ERISA exemption.

210. *Gobeille v. Liberty Mutual Insurance Co.*, 136 S.Ct. 936 (2016).

211. 49 U.S.C.App. sec. 1305(a)(1).

212. *Morales, Attorney-General of Texas v. Trans World Airlines, Inc.*, 504 U.S. 374 (1992).

213. *American Airlines, Inc. v. Wolens*, 513 U.S. 219 (1995).

214. *Northwest, Inc. v. Ginsberg*, 134 S.Ct. 1422 (2014). This preemption provision was included in a 1994 law deregulating trucking, and the Court held that this provision preempted state laws regulating the delivery of tobacco within the state. *Rowe v. New Hampshire Motor Transport Ass'n.*, 552 U.S. 364 (2008). However, this provision did not preempt state law claims for damages stemming from the storage and disposal of a towed vehicle, since once the towing is ended, transportation is no longer involved. *Dan's City Used Cars, Inc. v. Pelkey*, 133 Sup.Ct. 1769 (2013). Conversely, the Court has held that it preempts the provisions of a municipal port concession agreement that trucking companies had to sign before they could transport cargo at a city's port, which required that the companies develop off-street parking plans and display designated placards on their vehicles. *American Trucking Association, Inc. v. City of Los Angeles*, 133 Sup.Ct. 2096 (2013).

215. 15 U.S.C. secs. 1331–1340.

she had smoked, alleging a number of theories of liability. The tobacco company argued that the federal law preempted all state tort law claims for harm suffered after the federal "warning" requirement went into effect. The Supreme Court held that the federal law preempted some state tort law claims, but not others. Focusing on the operative language, "requirement or prohibition ... with respect to ... advertising or promotion," the Court held that the federal law did not preempt liability for breach of an express warranty, since liability for this claim would be based on what the company expressly warranted rather than on the requirements of state law. It also held that the federal law did not preempt claims based on intentional fraud and misrepresentation or on a conspiracy theory. However, it held that the federal law did preempt claims based on a failure to adequately warn of the dangers of smoking and on advertising that allegedly "neutralized the effect of the federally mandated warning labels."[216]

The second case involved an effort by a state to prohibit cigarette advertising directed at children. The state law prohibited any outdoor advertising of tobacco products that was directed toward or visible in any location within a 1,000 foot radius of any public playground, playground area in a public park, elementary school or secondary school and also regulated advertising in retail stores selling cigarettes. Here the Court found that Congress intended to preempt all state cigarette advertising regulations motivated by concerns about smoking and health, including those regulating only the location of the advertisement. The decision dealt a severe blow to state efforts to regulate cigarette advertising directed at children.[217]

In practice, there are a substantial number of cases involving the operation of an express standard of preemption, and the result depends on the Court's application of the particular statutory standard to the state law in question. The Court has held that federal regulations establishing terms under which states could use federal funds to eliminate hazards at railroad grade crossings did not preempt state tort law requirements regarding a railroad's duty to maintain warning devices at railroad crossings.[218] The Court also held, however, that federal regulations regarding the maximum speeds at which trains were to operate along certain types of tracks did preempt any tort claim against railroad for negligence in operating train within those limits. In a similar case, it held that where federal funds were used in the installation of warning devices at railroad crossings, once the devices were installed, the federal standard for adequacy of the warnings preempted state law.[219]

In *Medtronic, Inc. v. Lohr*,[220] the Court held that state common law liability rules for defective medical device products that were at issue in the particular case were not preempted by a federal law providing that no state may establish or maintain "any requirement that is different from, or in a addition to," "any requirement that is different from, or in addition to," any requirement of the federal Food, Drug and Cosmetic Act,[221] and which relates to the safety or effectiveness of the device under the Act. The Court emphasized that application of preemption should be informed by "the assumption

216. *Cipollone v. Liggett Group*, Inc., 505 U.S. 504 (1992).
217. *Lorillard Tobacco Co. v. Reilly*, 533 U.S. 525 (2001).
218. *CSX Transportation, Inc. v. Easterwood*, 507 U.S. 658 (1993).
219. *Norfolk Southern Railway Co. v. Shanklin*, 529 U.S. 344 (2000).
220. 518 U.S. 470 (1996).
221. 21 U.S.C. secs. 301 et seq.

that the historic police powers of the States were not to be superseded by the Federal Act unless that was the clear and manifest purpose of Congress." It was significant in that case that the federal Food and Drug Administration had not issued manufacturing and labeling requirements that were specific to the device in question. In a later case involving a medical device to which the Food and Drug Administration had given premarket approval, including an evaluation of the device's safety and effectiveness under the conditions of use set forth on the label, the Court held that the preemption provision operated to preempt state common law tort claims imposing liability on the basis of a different standard than used by the Food and Drug Administration in its approval process.[222] The Court has also held that the National Childhood Vaccine Injury Act of 1986,[223] providing that: "No vaccine manufacturer shall be liable in a civil action for damages resulting from a vaccine-related injury or death associated with the administration of a vaccine if the injury or death resulted from side effects that were unavoidable even though the vaccine was properly prepared and was accompanied by proper directions and warnings," preempted a state law design defect claim where the vaccine resulted in the death of a child.[224]

In other cases involving an express standard of preemption, the Court has held that the preemption clause of the Federal Boat Safety Act referring to "state law or regulation,"[225] did not preempt state common law tort claims arising out of the failure to install propeller guards on a boat engine.[226] It has also held that a provision of the federal Telecommunications Act preempting state laws prohibiting the ability of "any entity to provide telecommunications services,"[227] did not preempt a state law barring political subdivisions of a state, such as municipalities from providing telecommunications services[228] and that a provision of the federal Insecticide, Fungicide, and Rodenticide Act, providing that no state "shall impose or continue in effect any requirements for labeling in addition to or different from those required in this subchapter,"[229] did not preempt state law claims for defective design, defective manufacture, negligent testing, and breach of express warranty brought by farmers whose crops had been severely damaged by the application of a pesticide.[230]

Conversely, the Court has held that the provision of the federal Clean Air Act,[231] which prohibits the adoption of any state or local "standard relating to the control of emissions from new motor vehicles" preempted state laws prohibiting the purchase by fleet operators of vehicles that did not comply with the state's stricter emission requirements.[232] It has also held that the Federal Meat Inspection Act (FMIA),[233] which

---

222. *Riegel v. Medtronic, Inc.*, 552 U.S. 312 (2008).
223. 42 U.S.C. sec. 300aa-22(b)(1).
224. *Bruesewitz v. Wyeth, Inc.*, 562 U.S. 223 (2011).
225. 46 U.S.C. secs. 4301 et seq.
226. *Sprietsma v. Mercury Marine*, 537 U.S. 51 (2002).
227. 47 U.S.C. sec. 253.
228. *Nixon v. Missouri Municipal League*, 541 U.S. 125 (2004).
229. 7 U.S.C. sec. 136(v)(b).
230. *Bates v. Dow Agrisciences LLC*, 544 U.S. 431 (2005).
231. 42 U.S.C. sec. 7543.
232. *Engine Manufacturers Association v. South Coast Air Quality Management District*. 541 U.S. 246 (2004).
233. 21 U.S.C. secs. 601 et seq.

precludes states from imposing requirements that are "within the scope" of FMIA, relate to slaughterhouse "premises, facilities and operations," and are "in addition to, or different than those made under FMIA", preempted a California law prohibiting slaughterhouses from processing non-ambulatory animals.[234] The Court has also recently held that the National Voter Registration Act of 1993 (NVRA),[235] which requires the states to "accept and use" a uniform federal election form to register voters for federal elections, preempts a state law requiring the applicants for registration must provide documentary evidence of citizenship.[236] Most recently it held that a statute, 42 U.S.C. sec. 9658, that preempted state "statutes of limitation," which are procedural statutes barring suit after a period of time has elapsed, state did not preempt state "statues of repose," which are substantive statutes immunizing actors from tort liability after a period of time has elapsed following the commission of the tort.[237]

163. Where Congress has not expressly dealt with the matter of preemption in the federal law relied on by the party asserting preemption, the question becomes whether Congress impliedly intended to preempt the state regulation in question. Congress is deemed to have intended to preempt state law whenever there is a direct conflict between state law and federal law. A direct conflict occurs whenever compliance with both the state law and the federal law is a physical impossibility, or whenever the state law stands as an obstacle to the implementation of the full purposes of the federal law.[238]

The following are a few examples of cases where the Court has found a direct conflict. Where a product was labeled in a manner that complied with federal labeling requirements, but compliance with the federal requirements would cause the product to be mislabeled under state law, the state could not impose its labeling requirements.[239] Where a federal law providing retirement benefits explicitly stated that the benefits would not be subject to legal attachment, a state could not apply its marital property

234. *National Meat Association v. Harris*, 132 S.Ct. 965 (2012).
235. 42 U.S.C. sec. 1973gg-4(a)(1).
236. *Arizona v. Inter Tribal Council of Arizona*, 133 S.Ct. 2247 (2013).
237. *CTS Corporation v. Waldburger*, 134 S.Ct. 2175 (2014).
238. In a recent case, the Court rejected the claim of implied preemption due to a direct conflict between state and federal law. A state court action was brought against a drug manufacturer, alleging that the manufacturer had failed to provide an adequate warning about the significant risks of administering the drug by a certain method. The manufacturer asserted implied preemption on the ground that the drug's labeling had been approved by the federal Food and Drug Administration. The Court found that the federal agency's approval of the drug's labeling would not have prevented the manufacturer from adding a stronger warning about the risks of administering the drug by this method, so that it was not impossible for the manufacturer to comply both with both the state law duties underlying the claims and its federal labeling duties. The Court also found that requiring the manufacturer to comply with the state law duty to provide a stronger warning would not stand as an obstacle to the implementation of federal law, because Congress had not expressly authorized the federal agency to preempt state law failure to warn actions. *Wyeth v. Levine*, 555 U.S. 555 (2009).
239. *McDermott v. Wisconsin*, 228 U.S. 115 (1913).

law to require that a share of these benefits go to the other spouse upon divorce.[240] So too, where a federal agency regulating federally chartered savings and loan associations authorized them to include a certain kind of provision in the mortgages that they issued, this had the effect of preempting state law making such mortgage provisions unenforceable.[241] A state law that attempts to regulate a national bank operating subsidiary is preempted, because it interferes with the scheme of regulation contained in federal banking law.[242] The Court has recently held that the federal Medicaid statute's anti-lien provision, 42 U.S.C. sec. 1396(a)(1), which preempts attempts by a state to claim any portion of a Medicaid beneficiary's tort judgment or settlement not "designated as payments for medical care" preempts a state law providing that one-third of a tort recovery is attributable to medical expenses.[243] And most recently it has held that the Federal Power Act[244] preempted a state program requiring load servicing entities to enter into a twenty-year pricing contract at a rate set by an independent power generator, because it had the effect of setting an interstate wholesale rate.[245]

164. The following examples illustrate the situation where state law stands as an obstacle to the implementation of the full purposes of the federal law. Since under federal law, the Federal Aviation Agency has the responsibility to ensure aircraft safety and the efficient utilization of airspace, a state law controlling the timing of takeoffs and landing at airports would limit the flexibility of the agency in controlling air traffic flow, and so is preempted.[246] In another case, the Court found that a state regulation of the labeling of packaged flour sold in the state would probably cause national flour manufacturers seeking to meet that standard to "overpack" in order to prevent moisture loss during distribution from bringing the weight of the flour packages below the weight stated on the labels. It also found that local manufacturers and national manufacturers distributing in states following only the federal standard would not "overpack." The result would be to frustrate a major purpose of the relevant federal law, to facilitate value comparisons among similar products, because consumers throughout the country who compared the value of identically labeled packages of flour would not be comparing packages containing identical amounts of solid flour. Thus, the state labeling law was preempted.[247] In a third case, the Court held that

---

240. *Hisquierdo v. Hisquierdo*, 439 U.S. 572 (1979). *See also Hillman v. Maretta*, 133 Sup.Ct. 1943 (2013), holding that the federal law establishing an insurance program for federal employees, the purpose of which was to ensure that a federal employee's named beneficiary receives the insurance proceeds, preempted a provision of Virginia law addressing the situation in which the employee's marital status has changed, but the employee did not change the beneficiary, and taking the insurance proceeds away from the named beneficiary.
241. *Fidelity Federal Savings & Loan Assn. v. de la Cuesta*, 458 U.S. 141 (1982). When a regulation promulgated by a federal agency is asserted as the basis for preemption, the question is whether the federal agency intended to preempt state regulation and if so, whether the agency's action is within the scope of the authority granted to the agency by Congress.
242. *Watters v. Wachovia Bank*, 550 U.S. 1 (2007).
243. *Wos v. E.M.A. ex rel. Johnson*, 133 S.Ct. 1391 (2013).
244. 16 U.S.C. secs. 791a et seq.
245. *Hughes v. Talen Energy Marketing, LLC.*, 136 S.Ct. 1288 (2016).
246. *City of Burbank v. Lockheed Air Terminal, Inc.*, 411 U.S. 624 (1973).
247. *Jones v. Rath Packing Co.*, 439 U.S. 519 (1977). *See also Geier v. American Honda Motor Co., Inc.*, 529 U.S. 861(2000).

federal laws regulating oil tankers preempted state laws relating to oil tanker design, equipment and operating requirements, The Court found that enforcement of state requirements would frustrate the congressional intention of establishing a uniform federal law governing the design and operation of all tankers.[248] In other cases preempting state law on this basis, the Court has held that a federal law allowing automobile manufacturers to select from several passive restraint alternatives, including airbags, as a means of complying with federal vehicle standards for the 1987 model year preempted a claim under state law that the manufacturer was negligent in not equipping a 1987 model with airbags,[249] and that the federal Food, Drug and Cosmetic Act preempted state law claims based on "fraud on the federal Food and Drug Administration."[250] In two recent cases, the Court has found federal preemption of state laws that imposed requirements on manufacturers that conflicted with their obligations under federal law. Since the federal Food and Drug Administration requires that the warning labels of a brand-name drug and its generic copy must always be the same, the states could not require the manufacturers of generic drugs to provide different and allegedly more accurate warning labels.[251] The preemption rationale also preempted a state law that required the manufacturer of a generic drug to change the label or to stop selling the drug.[252] The Court has held that since the Federal Arbitration Act, 9 U.S.C. secs. 2 et seq. is assigned to promote arbitration of individual disputes, it preempts a state law that in certain circumstances requires class-wide arbitration.[253] Finally, the Court has invalidated a number of provisions of an Arizona law targeted at illegal aliens as creating "obstacles" to "Congress" objectives in enacting immigration statutes. The preempted provisions of state law: (1) imposed stiffer penalties than federal law for failing to carry federal registration documents; (2) made it a crime for illegal aliens to work when Congress had imposed criminal prohibitions on employers but not employees; (3) gave broader authority to Arizona law enforcement personnel than federal law gives to federal officials to make warrantless arrests of suspected deportable aliens.[254]

165. Where there is no direct conflict between state law and federal law, the question becomes one of "implied field preemption," that is, whether Congress impliedly intended to "occupy the field," so as to leave no scope for state regulation at all, even if the state regulation is not inconsistent with and may actually supplement the federal

248. *United States v. Locke*, 529 U.S. 89 (2000).

249. *Geier v. American Honda Motor Co., Inc.*, 529 U.S. 861 (2000). However, when a subsequent statute also gave manufacturers a choice, but giving them the choice was not a significant regulatory objective of the statute, the Court held that the statute did not preempt a claim under state law that the manufacturer was negligent in equipping the vehicle's rear-aisle seats with lap belts instead of with lap-and-shoulder belts. *Williamson v. Mazda Motor of America, Inc.*, 562 U.S. 323 (2011).

250. *Buckman Co. v. Plaintiffs' Legal Committee*, 531 U.S. 341 (2001).

251. *PLIVA, Inc. v. Mensing*, 564 U.S. 604 (2011).

252. *Mutual Pharmaceutical Co. v. Bartlett*, 133 Sup.Ct. 2466 (2013).

253. *AT&T Mobility LLC v. Concepcion*, 563 U.S. 333 *(2011). See also* DIRECTV *v. Imburgia*, 136 Sup.Ct. 463 (2015), holding that the Act preempted a state court interpretation of state law that did not place arbitration contracts on an equal footing with other contracts.

254. *Arizona v. United States*, 132 Sup.Ct. 2492 (2012).

regulation. It is here that respect for the principle of state sovereignty comes into play most strongly.

Where the matter in issue involves a field that the states have traditionally regulated, the Court has stated that the presumption is against preemption, and that, "[w]e start with the assumption that the historic police powers of the states were not to be superseded [by federal law] unless that was the clear and manifest purpose of Congress."[255]

In order for the Court to find implied field preemption, there must be a "scheme of federal regulation so pervasive as to make reasonable the inference that Congress left no room for the states to supplement it." This will occur only when: (1) the federal law "touche[s] a field in which the federal interest is so dominant that the federal system will be assumed to preclude enforcement of state laws on the same subject;" or (2) "the object sought to be obtained by the federal law and the character of obligations imposed by it may reveal the same purpose."[256]

166. While it is difficult to state general principles here, because implied field preemption depends on Congressional intent with respect to the particular scheme of federal regulation, it is possible to identify some factors that the Court takes into account in resolving this kind of preemption question.

167. The most significant factor leading to a finding of implied field preemption is that of dominant federal interest. This is most likely to be found where the federal law is based on a power other than the commerce power, such as the power over immigration and naturalization or the power over national security. Thus, the Court has held that the federal law dealing with the registration of aliens preempts all state alien registration laws,[257] and that federal laws against sedition preempt all state laws in this area.[258]

168. Once we get beyond matters such as these, where the federal government clearly has the dominant interest, the Court is reluctant to find implied field preemption. The Court focuses not only on the comprehensiveness of the scheme of federal regulation, but also on whether the particular state regulation would actually interfere with the objectives of the federal regulatory scheme. So, even where the Court has found that the federal law was intended to impose a comprehensive scheme of federal regulation, it has also typically found that the federal law was not intended to preempt all elements of state regulation. For example, the Court has held that the comprehensive federal regulation of nuclear energy preempts all state nuclear safety regulation, but

---

255. *Pacific Gas & Electric Co. v. State Energy Resources Conservation & Development Comm'n.*, 461 U.S. 190, 206 (1983).
256. *Ibid.*, at 204.
257. *Hines v. Davidowitz*, 312 U.S. 52 (1941).
258. *Pennsylvania v. Nelson*, 350 U.S. 497 (1956).

does not preempt the states from regulating the economic aspects of nuclear power,[259] or allowing tort recovery of compensatory and punitive damages for the harm caused by the escape of hazardous nuclear energy materials.[260]

169. In a similar vein, the Court has held that while federal labor relations law reflects a comprehensive scheme of federal regulation, it does not preempt state law with respect to all matters that may affect the employers, employees, and labor unions who are generally subject to the provisions of federal labor relations law. Federal labor relations law preempts state law with respect to questions of unfair labor practices and employee rights that are within the jurisdiction of the National Labor Relations Board,[261] with respect to matters that could alter the balance of power between labor unions and employers,[262] and with respect to the interpretation and construction of collective bargaining agreements.[263]

However, the Court has held that federal labor relations law does not prohibit the states from awarding damages to an employee who was subject to a retaliatory

---

259. *Pacific Gas & Electric Co. v. State Energy Resources Conservation & Development Comm'n.*, 461 U.S. 190, 206 (1983). In that case, the Court upheld California's authority to refuse to license a nuclear facility until the facility had a federally approved plan for the permanent disposition of high-level nuclear waste. The state agency concluded that in the absence of such a plan, the facility would not be economically viable. In finding that this action was not preempted by federal law, the Court concluded that Congress had intended that the federal government should regulate the radiological safety aspects involved in the construction and operation of a nuclear plant, but that the states should retain their traditional regulatory responsibility for determining questions of need, reliability and cost.

However, in a recent case, the Court, basing its decision on an older case, held that in the Locomotive Inspection Act (LIA), 49 U.S.C. secs. 20701 et seq., Congress intended to occupy the field and preempt all state regulation, here a railroad employee's state law claim that he suffered from mesothelioma due to negligent exposure to asbestos. *Kerns v. Railroad Friction Products Corporation*, 132 Sup.Ct. 1261 (2012).

260. *Silkwood v. Kerr-McGee Corp.*, 464 U.S. 238 (1984). *See also Freightliner Corporation v. Myrick*, 514 U.S. 280 (1995), holding that the National Traffic and Motor Vehicle Safety Act of 1966, 15 U.S.C. secs. 1381 et seq. and implementing regulations did not preempt state common law tort claims against tractor-trailer manufacturers; *American Dredging Co. v. Miller*, 510 U.S. 443 (1994), holding that a federal law permitting seamen injured in the course of their employment to bring their claims in state courts did not preempt state law barring the application of the forum non conveniens doctrine in such cases.

261. *San Diego Building Trades Council v. Garmon*, 359 U.S. 236 (1959). All such claims must be brought before the National Labor Relations Board, and so cannot be brought in the federal courts either.

262. Lodge 76, *Intern. Assn of Machinists and Aerospace Workers, AFL-CIO v. Wisconsin Employment Relations Commission*, 427 U.S. 132 (1976). In that case, a labor union was pressing its economic demands on an employer by refusing to work overtime. The National Labor Relations Board refused to act on the employer's complaint that the union was engaging in an unfair labor practice, but a state agency and a state court found the action to be violative of state law and enjoined it. The Supreme Court held that federal law preempted state law in this situation, on the basis that the state's adding to obligations between employers and unions would frustrate federal labor policy.

263. *Charles Dowd Box Co. v. Courtney*, 368 U.S. 502 (1962).

discharge for filing a worker's compensation claim,[264] or to a union member claiming damages against a union for emotional harm caused by the union's discrimination against him.[265] The Court has likewise held that federal labor relations law does not preempt a state law requiring employers to provide a one-time severance payment to employees in the event of a plant closing,[266] or a state's grant of unemployment compensation to striking workers.[267]

170. Where the federal scheme of regulation is less comprehensive, the Court is correspondingly less likely to find any implied field preemption.[268] This is especially true where the federal government has not regulated the particular activity, so that a finding of preemption would leave a regulatory vacuum.[269] The Court is also not disposed to find implied field preemption where the challenged state regulation supplements the federal regulation and does not interfere with its operation.[270]

171. In summary, in resolving questions of implied field preemption, the most significant factor leading to a finding of preemption is that the matter in issue is one in which there is a dominant federal interest, such as matters of immigration and naturalization. If there is no dominant federal interest, the crucial question is whether there is a comprehensive scheme of federal regulation. Where such a scheme of federal regulation exists, the Court is likely to find implied field preemption with respect to those elements of state regulation that would actually interfere with the objectives of

---

264. *Lingle v. Norge Division of Magic Chef, Inc.*, 486 U.S. 399 (1988). Similarly, the Court has held that federal labor relations law does not preempt an employee's state law claims against the employer for wrongful discharge. *Hawaiian Airlines, Inc. v. Norris*, 512 U.S. 246 (1994).
265. *Farmer v. United Brotherhood of Carpenters and Joiners*, 430 U.S. 290 (1977).
266. *Fort Halifax Packing Co., Inc. v. Coyne*, 482 U.S. 1 (1987).
267. *New York Telephone Co. v. New York State Department of Labor*, 440 U.S. 519 (1979).
268. *See* e.g., *Itel Containers International Corporation v. Huddleston*, 507 U.S. 60 (1993), where the Court held that a federal treaty permitting foreign cargo containers to enter the United States "free of import duties and taxes" referred only to customs duties, and was not intended to occupy the field of container regulation and taxation. This being so, it did not preempt the states from imposing a tax on the income derived from leasing the containers within the state. And the Court has very recently held that the Natural Gas Act, 52 Stat. 821 did not preempt the states from regulating the retail sale of natural gas, so that purchasers of natural gas directly from interstate pipelines could sue the pipelines under state antitrust laws. *Oneok, Inc. v. Learjet, Inc.*, 135 S.Ct. 1591 (2015).
269. *See* e.g., *Maurer v. Hamilton*, 309 U.S. 598 (1940) (where the Interstate Commerce Commission had not promulgated regulations dealing with carrying of automobiles over the cab of automobile transportation vehicle, although it had the authority to do so, state regulation prohibiting this practice was not preempted); *Arkansas Electric Cooperative Corp. v. Arkansas Public Service Commission*, 461 U.S. 375 (1983) (where federal agencies having jurisdiction over the matter had not regulated rates charged by rural electric cooperative to local members, state regulation of such rates was not preempted by federal law).
270. *See* e.g., *California v. Zook*, 336 U.S. 725 (1949) (state prohibition of transportation not licensed by federal Interstate Commerce Commission); *Colorado Anti-Discrimination Commission v. Continental Air Lines*, 372 U.S. 714 (1963) (state application of employment discrimination law to federally regulated air carrier); *California Coastal Commission v. Granite Rock Co.*, 480 U.S. 572 (1987) (state requirement that mining company apply for state permit not preempted as applied to company that was mining in national forest pursuant to permit granted by a federal agency).

the federal scheme, but not with respect to other elements of state regulation. Where the federal scheme of regulation is less comprehensive, the Court is correspondingly less likely to find implied field regulation at all, especially when this would result in a regulatory vacuum, and when the state regulation supplements and does not interfere with the effective operation of the federal regulation.

§4. State Regulation of Interstate and Foreign Commerce

172. The Supreme Court has held that the affirmative grant of the power to Congress under Article I, section 8, to regulate interstate and foreign commerce has a negative implication as well, and by its own force, imposes some limitations on the power of the states to regulate interstate and foreign commerce. This means that in the absence of Congressional legislation authorizing or prohibiting state regulation of interstate and foreign commerce, the Court will hold that some state regulation of interstate and foreign commerce is beyond the states' constitutional power. The Court has stated that this constitutional restriction on state power is either predicated on the "implications of the commerce clause itself" or on the "implied intention of Congress" that the states not impose certain kinds of regulation on interstate commerce.[271] While academic commentators, including the present author,[272] have questioned this kind of conceptual justification for a negative aspect to the commerce clause, the Court has consistently adhered to it, and the negative aspect of the commerce clause is a focused, but significant, limitation on the exercise of state power in this area.

173. The negative aspect of the commerce clause comes into play only in the absence of Congressional legislation specifically authorizing the challenged regulation. Since Congress has the affirmative power to regulate interstate and foreign commerce, it may decide to exercise this power in such a way as to authorize state regulation that would violate the negative aspect of the commerce clause in the absence of such authorization. The negative aspect of the commerce clause, by definition, is a limitation only on the exercise of state power, so if Congress has authorized the states to act,

271. *Southern Pacific Co. v. Arizona*, 325 U.S. 761, 769 (1945).

272. Sedler, *The Negative Commerce Clause as a Restriction on State Regulation and Taxation: An Analysis in Terms of Constitutional Structure*, 31 Wayne L. Rev. 885, 968–982 (1985).

such action cannot be challenged as violative of the negative aspect of the commerce clause.[273]

174. The Court's current articulated approach to the negative aspect of the commerce clause contains both a "nondiscrimination" and an "undue burden" component.[274] As we will see, however, in practice, the Court has invariably invalidated any regulation that it has found to be "discriminatory," but, with few exceptions it has upheld against "undue burden" challenge any regulation that it found to be truly nondiscriminatory. Most of the cases that arise, as might be expected, involve interstate commerce, but the same constitutional doctrine applies to state regulation of foreign commerce as well.[275]

175. The reason why the Court has invariably invalidated regulation that it has found to be "discriminatory" goes to the fact that a major historic purpose for the affirmative grant of the commerce power to Congress was to prevent the "protectionism" that had existed on the part of the states during the period between the end of the Revolutionary War and the adoption of the Constitution. The states, exercising the sovereignty over domestic matters to which they had succeeded upon Independence, were imposing duties on goods coming in from other states and were trying to promote their own economic well-being at the expense of the sister states. The affirmative grant of the commerce power to Congress was designed to end this "protectionism," and the Court has relied on the negative aspect of the commerce clause to strike down state

---

273. *See* e.g., *Prudential Ins. Co. v. Benjamin*, 328 U.S. 408 (1946); *Northeast Bankcorp, Inc. v. Board of Governors of Federal Reserve System*, 472 U.S. 159 (1985). In these cases, the Court relied on federal legislation authorizing state regulation of insurance and interstate banking respectively to uphold discrimination against out-of-state insurance companies and interstate banks that would otherwise be violative of the negative aspect of the commerce clause. However, in *American Insurance Association v. Garamendi*, 539 U.S. 396 (2003), the Court held that federal legislation authorizing state regulation of insurance did not authorize a state to require insurance companies to disclose information about all insurance policies sold in Europe between 1920 and 1945 by the company or one related to it. The law was in conflict with federal control over foreign relations. *See also Hillside Dairy, Inc. v. Lyons*, 539 U.S. 59 (2003), where the Court held a federal law permitting the State of California to regulate the percentage of milk solids in fluid milk products sold or marketed in the state did not insulate the state's milk pricing laws from negative commerce clause challenge.

274. In the author's view, the only proper conceptual justification for a negative aspect to the commerce clause is the nondiscrimination principle, which the author finds embodied in the internal inferences of the Constitution, in particular the historic purpose for the grant of the affirmative commerce power to Congress. Under this view, all discriminatory regulation would be unconstitutional, but all nondiscriminatory regulation would be constitutional, and there would be no concern with an "undue burden" on interstate or foreign commerce. Sedler, *The Negative Commerce Clause as a Restriction on State Regulation and Taxation: An Analysis in Terms of Constitutional Structure, supra,* para. 172, n. 272 at 991–999.

275. As discussed in para. 454, *infra* , certain state regulation of foreign commerce may be found to be an improper interference with federal power over foreign affairs. *See Japan Line, Ltd. v. Los Angeles County*, 441 U.S. 434 (1979).

"protectionism," even in the absence of Congressional action.[276] Thus, the Court has stated that, "Where simple economic protectionism is effected by state legislation, a virtually per se rule of invalidity has been erected."[277]

176. The "economic protectionism" against which the negative aspect of the commerce clause is directed may be found to exist in the express language of the state regulation or it may result from its practical operation. In other words, the negative aspect of the commerce clause reaches both state regulation that discriminates against interstate commerce on its face and state regulation that in practical operation has a discriminatory effect.[278] The author has described the results of the Court's "discrimination against interstate commerce" cases as follows:

> Where the essential effect of the regulation is to discriminate against interstate commerce or out-of-state interests in favor of local commerce or in-state interests because of the interstate nature of that commerce or the out-of-state nature of those interests, the regulation is violative of the negative commerce clause.[279]

The key elements in this analysis are "essential effect" and "because of."

177. The "essential effect" of the regulation will be to discriminate against interstate commerce or out-of-state interests in favor of local commerce or in-state interests when it: (1) prohibits or restricts the entry of out-of-state products into the state; (2) prevents local products from leaving the state; or (3) otherwise provides an advantage to local commerce over interstate commerce.

---

276. The Court has stated that: "[A] chief occasion of the commerce clause was the mutual jealousies and aggressions of the States, taking form in customs barriers and economic retaliation," and that, "What is ultimate is the principle that one state in its dealings with another may not place itself in a position of economic isolation ... [by] establishing an economic barrier against competition with the products of another state or the labor of its residents." *Baldwin v. G.A.F. Seelig, Inc.*, 294 U.S. 511, 522, 527 (1935).

277. *Philadelphia v. New Jersey*, 437 U.S. 617, 624 (1978).

278. Where the challenged regulation is neutral on its face, but has a discriminatory effect in practical operation, the Court has stated that it is unconstitutional "if reasonable non-discriminatory alternatives adequate to conserve legitimate local interests are available." *Dean Milk Co. v. City of Madison*, 340 U.S. 349, 354 (1951). In practice, "reasonable non-discriminatory alternatives" will always be available. They were not used precisely because the state wanted to discriminate against interstate commerce or out-of-state interests in favor of local commerce or in-state interests.

279. Sedler, *The Negative Commerce Clause as a Restriction on State Regulation and Taxation: An Analysis in Terms of Constitutional Structure*, *supra* , para. 172, n. 272 at 898.

The law is discriminatory where by its terms or in practical effect it prevents entry of out-of-state products into the state,[280] or where it disadvantages out-of-state products by treating them differently from local products.[281] In this connection, it should be noted that a unit of local government within a state cannot justify discrimination against interstate commerce or out-of-state interests on the ground that it also discriminates against commerce originating in other parts of the state.[282] Nor can a state justify discrimination against products coming in from another state on the ground that it is retaliating against discrimination against its own products by the other state. In this circumstance, both states are violating the negative aspect of the commerce clause, and can be prevented from doing so.[283] However, in *United Haulers Ass'n., Inc. v. Oneida-Herkimer Solid Waste Management Auth,*[284] a sharply divided Court upheld the constitutionality of county ordinances requiring that all solid waste generated in the counties be delivered to publicly owned waste processing facilities. Four Justices held that the ordinances were non-discriminatory for negative commerce clause purposes because: (1) the facilities were owned by the government, which had the responsibility to protect the health, safety and welfare of its citizens, and (2) the ordinances treated in-state private businesses the same way as they treated out-of-state businesses. Two Justices took the position that there should be no negative aspect to the commerce clause and so voted to uphold the ordinances. Three Justices took the position that the ordinances were discriminatory and so dissented.[285] The law is discriminatory again where by its terms or in practical effect, it prevents local products

---

280. For illustrative cases *see* : *Baldwin v. GA.F. Seelig, Inc.*, 294 U.S. 511, 522, 527 (1935) (prohibition of sale in New York of milk purchased from farmers in other states at lower prices than the New York minimum price); *Lewis v. B.T. Investment Managers*, Inc., 447 U.S. 27 (1980) (prohibition against out-of-state banking institutions controlling in-state investment advisory firms); *Philadelphia v. New Jersey*, 437 U.S. 617, 624 (1978) (prohibition on private landfills in state receiving out-of-state waste); *Dean Milk Co. v. Madison*, 340 U.S. 349, 354 (1951) (municipal law prohibiting sale of milk in city that was not processed at approved facility located within 5 miles of the municipality); *Granholm v. Heald*, 544 U.S. 460 (2005) (state regulatory scheme allowing in-state wineries to make direct sales to consumers, but prohibiting out-of-state wineries from doing so).

281. For illustrative cases, *see Chemical Waste Management, Inc. v. Hunt*, 504 U.S. 334 (1992), or a state law prohibiting private landfill operators from accepting solid waste generated in another state or another county within the state unless expressly authorized by the receiving county, *Fort Gratiot Sanitary Landfill, Inc. v. Michigan Department of Natural Resources*, 504 U.S. 353 (1992), or a local law requiring that all nonrecyclable solid waste generated within a town be processed at a facility owned by the town. *C & A Carbone, Inc. v. Clarkstown*, 511 U.S. 383 (1994).

282. *See Fort Gratiot* and *Clarkstown, supra* , n. 281.

283. *Great A & P. Tea Co. v.* Cottrell, 424 U.S. 366 (1976).

284. 550 U.S. 330 (2007).

285. Under the 'quarantine and inspection" rule, a state may bar "harmful" products from another state, such as cattle suffering from a particular bovine disease, *Mintz v. Baldwin*, 289 U.S. 346 (1933), or live baitfish that could not be shown to be free of parasites that could endanger local species of fish. *Maine v. Taylor*, 477 U.S. 131 (1986).

from leaving the state.[286] The Court has also held that laws are discriminatory where they otherwise provide an advantage to local commerce over interstate commerce. One example is *Hunt v. Washington State Apple Advertising Commission*.[287] There, North Carolina required that all apples sold in closed containers in the state either use the grading system approved by the United States Department of Agriculture or carry a "non-graded" label. The State of Washington had developed a grading system that was considered in the industry to be superior to the Department of Agriculture grading system, and this being so, the application of the rule to apple containers coming from Washington deprived these containers of a competitive advantage they enjoyed because of their out-of-state origin.

Another example of such a situation is *Pike v. Bruce Church*,[288] where the Court held unconstitutional an Arizona regulation requiring cantaloupe growers in Arizona to package the cantaloupes picked there in containers bearing the Arizona name and address of the packer. A packer having a packing facility across the border in California challenged the regulation, and the Court held it unconstitutional as imposing an "undue burden" on interstate commerce. The regulation more properly should have been invalidated on "discriminatory effect" grounds, because its effect was to divert to Arizona employment and business from California. The packer necessarily would be more likely to employ Arizona workers and use Arizona suppliers if it had to maintain the packing facility in Arizona than it would if it could retain its California facility. So, the effect of the regulation was to favor in-state interests—here Arizona employees and suppliers—over out-of-state interests.[289]

On the other hand, if the regulation affects local commerce and in-state interests in the same way that it affects interstate commerce and out-of-state interests, it does not have a "discriminatory effect" for negative commerce clause purposes, although it regulates a product that is primarily destined for the interstate market.[290]

178. In addition, in order for the regulation to have a "discriminatory effect" for negative commerce clause purposes, the "discriminatory effect" must be "because of" the interstate nature of that commerce or the out-of-state nature of those interests. What this means is that the discrimination effected by the regulation must be between

286. For illustrative cases *see New England Power Co. v. New Hampshire*, 455 U.S. 331 (1982) (ban on exportation of hydroelectric power produced by privately owned facilities in the state); *Hughes v. Oklahoma*, 441 U.S. 332 (1979) (ban on exportation of small fish caught in waters within the state); *Sporhase v. Nebraska*, 458 U.S. 941 (1982((ban on exportation of ground water to adjoining states that do not grant reciprocal rights with respect to exportation of water to the state); *H.P.Hood & Sons v. Du*Mond, 335 U.S. 808 (1948) (refusal to license milk processing facility on express ground that the facility would divert local milk supplies to other states).

287. 432 U.S. 333 (1977).

288. 397 U.S. 137 (1970).

289. To the same effect is *Toomer v. Witsell*, 334 U.S. 385 (1948), where the Court held unconstitutional a state law requiring that owners of shrimp boats licensed to fish in the state's waters unload and pack their catch in the state before shipping it to another state.

290. On this basis, the Court has held that state price-fixing laws do not violate the negative aspect of the commerce clause, although they apply to products that are primarily destined for shipment in interstate commerce. *See Parker v. Brown*, 317 U.S. 341 (1943); *Cities Service Gas Co. v. Peerless Oil & Gas Co.*, 340 U.S. 179 (1950).

groups that are similarly situated except for their in-state and out-of-state location. The fact that the regulation benefits one kind of economic interest at the expense of a different kind of economic interest does not make it "discriminatory" for negative commerce clause purposes, even though the economic interest benefited is primarily local while the economic interest disadvantaged is primarily interstate. So, a ban on door-to-door solicitation does not violate the negative aspect of the commerce clause when it is applied to prohibit door-to-door solicitation for national magazines. The effect of the ban is to favor local retail merchants over magazine solicitors, both local and interstate, and the favored and disfavored groups are not similarly situated except for their in-state and out-of-state location.[291] In the same vein, a rule prohibiting oil companies from also owning retail service stations does not violate the negative aspect of the commerce clause, although it favors retail service stations, most of which are local, over oil companies, all of which are interstate.[292] And a regulation barring the use of plastic nonrefillable milk containers, but permitting the use of paperboard nonrefillable milk containers, likewise does not violate the negative aspect of the commerce clause, although all the producers of plastic resin are from out-of-state, while pulpwood, which is the source of paperboard nonrefillable milk containers, is a major in-state industry.[293] The Court more recently affirmed this principle when it upheld the State of Maine's prescription drug rebate program, under which enrollees could purchase prescription drugs from participating Maine pharmacies at a discounted price, with the discount reimbursed from participating drug manufacturers, and under which any drug manufactured by a nonparticipating manufacturer could not be dispensed under the state program providing medical assistance to lower-income people without specific approval of the program administrator.[294]

179. The nondiscrimination component of the negative aspect of the commerce clause is very important in practice. States have continued to try to promote local commerce and in-state interests over interstate commerce and out-of-state interests by cloaking the discrimination as an "environmental measure" or the like. The Court, however, has consistently invalidated all such efforts, and when the essential effect of the regulation is to discriminate against interstate commerce or out-of-state interests because of the interstate nature of that commerce or the out-of-state nature of those interests, it will be found to violate the negative aspect of the commerce clause.

180. In contrast, where the effect of the regulation is truly nondiscriminatory, it is not likely to be invalidated as an "undue burden" on interstate commerce. While some relatively older cases found that particular regulations imposed an "undue burden"

---

291. *Breard v. City of Alexandria*, 341 U.S. 622 (1951).
292. *EXXON Corp. v. Maryland*, 437 U.S. 117 (1978).
293. *Minnesota v. Clover Leaf Creamery Co.*, 449 U.S. 456 (1981).
294. *Pharmaceutical Research and Manufacturers of America v. Walsh*, 538 U.S. 644 (2003). The program benefited local pharmacists and allegedly disadvantaged manufacturers. The Court noted that the benefits to local pharmacists provided no special benefit to competitors of rebate paying manufacturers.

on interstate transportation,[295] for the most part in more recent years, the Court has rejected the "undue burden" challenge to nondiscriminatory state regulation affecting interstate commerce. The exception to this practice has been when the state regulation was found to have an "extraterritorial effect" in that it would control the conduct of entities engaged in interstate commerce in another state. The Court has held that this kind of regulation is unconstitutional as imposing an "undue burden" on interstate commerce.[296]

181. The constraints of the negative commerce clause do not apply when the state is acting as a "market participant." Thus, when the state purchases goods from suppliers or sells goods produced at state-owned facilities, it can give preference to its own residents.[297] However, once the state disposes of a state-owned resource, the constraints of the negative commerce clause do apply, and the state cannot impose conditions on the purchaser of the resource that would require preferential access to state residents or otherwise discriminate against interstate commerce or out-of-state interests in favor of local commerce or in-state interests.[298]

182. As the above discussion indicates, the negative aspect of the commerce clause imposes some limitations on the power of the states to regulate interstate and foreign commerce. The primary restriction is that the states cannot engage in discrimination against interstate commerce or out-of-state interests in favor of local commerce or in-state interests. While, in theory, the negative commerce clause also invalidates state regulations that impose an "undue burden" on interstate commerce, in practice, a truly nondiscriminatory regulation will be invalidated only when it has an "extraterritorial

---

295. *Southern Pacific Co. v. Arizona*, 325 U.S. 761 (1945) (state law limiting the size of railroad trains); *Bibb v. Navajo Freight Lines*, 359 U.S. 520 (1959) (state law requiring that trucks be equipped with a specific kind of mudflap instead of a different kind of mudflap that was permitted in virtually all other states and required in a neighboring state). In more recent cases where the Court has invalidated state regulations affecting interstate transportation on "undue burden" grounds, the invalidated regulations also contained exemptions favoring local interests and so could have been invalidated under the "non-discrimination" principle. The "protectionism" effected by the regulations was significant in the Court's balancing analysis in those cases. *See Raymond Motor Transp., Inc. v. Rice*, 434 U.S. 429 (1978); *Kassell v. Consolidated Freightways*, 450 U.S. 662 (1981).

296. The cases have involved attempts to control wholesale prices at which alcoholic beverages can be sold in the state by tying the in-state prices to the wholesale prices at which the distiller sells alcoholic beverages in neighboring states. *See Brown-Foreman Distillers Corp. v. New York State Liquor Authority*, 476 U.S. 573 (1986); *Healy v. Beer Institute, Inc.*, 491 U.S. 324 (1989).

297. *Hughes v. Alexandria Scrap Corp.*, 426 U.S. 794 (1976) (eligibility requirements for state subsidy for recycling automobile hulks favoring state residents); *Reeves, Inc. v. Stake*, 447 U.S. 429 (1980) (resident preference for cement produced by state-owned cement plant). *See also White v. Massachusetts Council of Construction Employers, Inc.*, 460 U.S. 204 (1982), where the Court upheld against negative commerce clause challenge a municipality's rule requiring that contractors on municipally funded projects employ at least 50% municipality residents in their work force. Similarly, the citizens-only provision of the Virginia Freedom of Information Act does not violate the negative commerce clause. *McBurney v. Young*, 133 S.Ct. 1709 (2013).

298. *South-Central Timber Development, Inc. v. Wunnicke*, 467 U.S. 82 (1984) (requirement that purchaser of state-owned timber must saw timber in state before shipping it in interstate commerce violated negative aspect of the commerce clause).

effect" in that it controls the conduct of an entity engaged in interstate commerce in another state.

§5. State Taxation of Interstate and Foreign Commerce

183. Limitations on the power of the states to tax interstate and foreign commerce derive from both the negative aspect of the commerce clause and from the Fourteenth Amendment's due process clause. In *Complete Auto Transit, Inc. v. Brady*,[299] the Supreme Court adopted a combined negative commerce clause-due process approach to the constitutional permissibility of such taxation, now referred to as the "*Complete Auto* four-part test." This approach is a pragmatic one, designed to take into account the realities of interstate and international business operations and the legitimate needs of the states to obtain revenue from multistate and multinational corporations that do business within their boundaries. Under the "*Complete Auto* four-part test," state taxation of interstate and foreign commerce is constitutionally permissible if: (1) the tax is applied to an activity having a substantial nexus with the taxing state; (2) the tax is fairly apportioned to that activity; (3) the tax does not discriminate against interstate or foreign commerce; (4) the tax is fairly related to services provided by the state. If any of these elements is not satisfied with respect to the particular tax, the imposition of the tax was held to be unconstitutional.

184. The first element of the test precludes the states from imposing taxes on an out-of-state enterprise that does not have some tangible physical connection with the state, although that enterprise may derive economic benefit from business activity within the state. The Supreme Court applied this element of the test to hold unconstitutional a state's effort to compel an interstate mail order company to collect a "use tax" from its customers in the state. The Court said that while requiring the mail order company to collect the tax would not violate the due process clause, it would impose an "undue burden" on interstate commerce, and so was violative of the negative aspect of the commerce clause. The Court concluded that the concern for the free flow of commerce across state lines required a "bright line" rule by which interstate sellers would know when their sales could be subject to the state's taxing power, and that this "bright line" rule should take the form of a requirement of physical presence, however slight, in the taxing state.[300]

The third element of the test, discrimination against interstate or foreign commerce, is determined by the same standard that is used to determine when state regulation of interstate or foreign commerce is impermissibly discriminatory. Where a state taxation scheme, expressly or in practical operation, has the effect of discriminating against

299. 430 U.S. 274 (1977).

300. *Quill Corp. v. North Dakota By and Through Heitkamp*, 504 U.S. 298 (1992). The Court reaffirmed an earlier decision to the same effect, *National Bellas Hess, Inc. v. Department of Revenue of Illinois*, 386 U.S. 753 (1967), which the state Supreme Court in *Quill* and many commentators thought had been superseded by the "*Complete Auto* four-part test" and the Court's subsequent decisions in this area. *Compare Scripto, Inc. v. Carson*, 362 U.S. 207 (1960), where the Court upheld the state's power to require the out-of-state seller to collect the use tax despite the fact that all the seller's in-state solicitation was performed by independent contractors.

interstate or foreign commerce or out-of-state interests in favor of local commerce or in-state interests because of the interstate or foreign nature of that commerce or the out-of-state nature of those interests, it violates the negative aspect of the commerce clause. The Court has invalidated a number of state taxation schemes on this basis.[301] They include the following:[302]

However, as with state regulation affecting interstate commerce, if the tax applies equally to in-state and out-of-state consumers of the product, it is not discriminatory, although most of the product is shipped out of state.[303]

185. Where the state taxation scheme is nondiscriminatory and the enterprise subject to the tax has some physical connection to the taxing state, the Court has taken a very pragmatic approach to the permissibility of state taxation of that enterprise. The general principle here is that the state may fully tax such enterprise, so long as it does not tax "value earned outside its borders." Under this principle, the Court has upheld the application of state taxes to enterprises engaged in interstate commerce where the

301. *Corp. v. Tracy*, 519 U.S. 278 (1997) (sales and use taxes on natural gas purchases except for purchases from in-state regulated utilities); *South Central Bell Telephone Co. v. Alabama*, 526 U.S. 160 (1999) (franchise tax based on corporation's capital, but allowing in-state corporation to pay tax based on par value of stock, which can be set by corporation, while requiring out-of-state corporation to pay tax based upon the value of the actual amount of capital it employs in the state).

302. But *compare Department of Revenue of Kentucky v. Davis*, 489 U.S. 803 (2008), where the Court upheld a state income tax law that exempted from the tax interest on bonds issued by the state and local governments, but not on bonds issued by other states or their local governments. The Court emphasized that the tax was imposed on all bonds issued by private entities and that the state as a public entity did not have to treat itself as being "substantially similar" to all the other bond issuers in the market. *Maryland v. Louisiana*, 451 U.S. 725 (1981).

303. *Commonwealth Edison Co. v. Montana*, 453 U.S. 609 (1981). There the state had imposed a severance tax on all coal mined in the state, 90% of which was shipped out-of-state. Similarly, in *American Trucking Ass'n., Inc. v. Michigan Public Service Commission*, 545 U.S. 434 (2005), the Court held that Michigan's imposition of a flat annual fee on all trucks hauling goods between one point in Michigan and another could constitutionally be applied to trucking companies engaged in interstate commerce.

However, as with state regulation affecting interstate commerce, if the tax applies equally to in-state and out-of-state consumers of the product, it is not discriminatory, although most of the product is shipped out of state.

state has succeeded in isolating the local activity and imposing the tax only on that activity.[304]

186. More significantly, the Court has allowed the states to impose taxes on the gross receipts or net income of out-of-state corporations doing business within the state, so long as the state uses a reasonable apportionment formula that apportions the total gross receipts or net income of the corporation to its proportionate business activity within the state. The premise of this approach is that the corporation is a "unitary business," one part of which consists of its activities in the taxing state, so that the taxing state may apportion the total income of the "unitary business" between the taxing state and the "rest of the world," taking into account objective measures of the corporation's activities within and without the taxing state. Although no particular apportionment formula is constitutionally required, many states use a "three-factor" formula, which is based in equal parts on the proportion of a unitary business' total payroll, property, and sales which are located in the taxing state. The Supreme Court has said that the state's apportionment formula must be internally consistent in the sense that, if applied by every state, it would result in no more than all of the corporation's gross receipts or net income being taxed. It must also be externally consistent in the sense that the factor or factors used in the apportionment formula must actually reflect a reasonable sense of how the corporation's income is generated. With these considerations in mind, the Court has emphasized, nonetheless, that an apportionment formula will be upheld unless the income that it attributes to the taxing state is in fact "out of all appropriate proportion to the business that the corporation actually transacts within the state."[305] In practice, the Court has generally upheld the state's application of its apportionment formula to tax the gross receipts or net income of an out-of-state corporation doing business in the state.[306]

---

304. For illustrative cases *see* : *General Motors Corp. v. Washington*, 377 U.S. 436 (1964) (sales tax measured by gross receipts on sales of goods delivered within the state); *Standard Pressed Steel Co. v. Washington*, 419 U.S. 560 (1975) (sales tax applied to sales of product shipped from out-of-state to single manufacturer within the state); *Limbach v. Hooven & Allison Co.*, 466 U.S. 353 (1984) (property tax on foreign-imported goods held for use in the importer's factory), *Department of Revenue of State of Washington v. Association of Washington Stevedoring Companies*, 435 U.S. 734 (1978) (tax on gross receipts of stevedoring, as applied to the loading and unloading of ships engaged in interstate and foreign commerce); *Tyler Pipe Industries, Inc. v. Washington State Department of Revenue*, 483 U.S. 232 (1987) (tax on wholesaling measured by gross receipts on sale to buyers within state by out-of-state manufacturer working through a sales agent); *Itel Containers International Corporation v. Huddleston*, 507 U.S. 60 (1993) (tax on proceeds from lease in state of cargo container used in international shipping); *Oklahoma Tax Commission v. Jefferson Lines, Inc.*, 514 U.S. 175 (1995) (sales tax on full price of bus ticket sold in state for transportation to another state).

305. *See* generally the discussion in *Container Corporation of America v. Franchise Tax Board*, 463 U.S. 159,169–170 (1983).

306. For illustrative cases *see* : *Container Corporation of America v. Franchise Tax Board*, 463 U.S. 159 (1983) (three-factor apportionment); *Moorman Manufacturing Co. v. Bair*, 437 U.S. 267 (1978) (single factor apportionment based on the ratio of in-state sales to total gross sales); *EXXON Corp. v. Wisconsin Department of Revenue*, 447 U.S. 207 (1980) (apportioned income tax on total net income, although corporation only conducted marketing activities in taxing state).

187. The most difficult problem in this regard concerns the efforts of the states to include the foreign subsidiaries of an American corporation as part of the "unitary business" that is subject to the apportionment formula. Where the state taxing authority could reasonably conclude that there is "substantial mutual interdependence" between the American corporation and its foreign subsidiaries, so that they constitute a "functionally integrated enterprise," the foreign subsidiaries can be included in the apportionment formula.[307] However, when the control exercised by the American corporation over its foreign subsidiary is rather loose, so that the foreign subsidiary can be considered to be engaged in "unrelated business activity," the foreign subsidiary cannot constitutionally be included in the apportionment formula.[308] The Court has also held that a state, in determining an out-of-state corporation's apportionable tax base, cannot authorize a deduction for interest expense only to the extent that the amount exceeded certain out-of-state income arising from the unrelated business activity of a discrete business enterprise.[309] With this exception, the states have a considerable degree of discretion in adopting an apportionment formula that will enable them to tax the gross receipts or net income of an out-of-state corporation doing business in the state.[310]

307. *See Container Corporation of America v. Franchise Tax Board*, 463 U.S. 159 (1983); *Mobil Oil Corp. v. Commissioner of Taxes of Vermont*, 445 U.S. 425 (1980).
308. *See ASARCO v. Idaho State Tax Commission*, 458 U.S. 307 (1982) (American corporation had partial ownership in foreign subsidiary, but exercised no voting control and made no operational or management decisions); *F.W. Woolworth Co. v. Taxation and Revenue Department of State of New. Mexico*, 458 U.S. 354 (1982) (although American retailing corporation owned foreign retailing subsidiaries, there was no integration of business activities or centralized management and purchasing). *See also Allied-Signal, Inc. v. Director*, Division of Taxation, 504 U.S. 768 (1992), where a closely divided Court held that a state could not include in an out-of-state corporation's apportionable tax base the income realized by the corporation from the sale of stock in other corporations.
309. *Hunt-Wesson, Inc. v. Franchise Tax Board of California*, 528 U.S. 458 (2000). And where the businesses are not "unitary," the state may not impose an apportioned tax on the out-of-state income of an out-of-state subsidiary of a domestic corporation, even if the out-of-state subsidiary served an "operational function" in the business of the in-state corporation. *MeadWestvaco Corp. v. Illinois Department of Revenue*, 553 U.S. 16 (2008).
310. *See also Barclays Bank v. Franchise Tax Board of California*, 512 U.S. 298 (1994), where the Court upheld a state's use of a "worldwide combined reporting method," under which a corporation was required to aggregate the income of all corporate entities comprising the corporation's unitary business enterprise, including affiliates operating abroad and those operating within the United States, and pay a tax on a percentage of the corporation's worldwide income equal to the average of the percentages of worldwide payroll, property and sales located within the state.

Chapter 4. The States and "National Unity"

188. A primary motivating force behind the promulgation of the Constitution in 1787 was to transform the loose confederation of sovereign states into a nation, an "indestructible union composed of indestructible states," and to "constitute the citizens of the United States as one people." The provisions of Article IV, sections 1 and 2, are directed toward the accomplishment of this objective.

189. The "privileges and immunities" clause of Article IV, section 2, clause 1, provides that, "The citizens of each State shall be entitled to all Privileges and Immunities of Citizens of the several States."[311] The Supreme Court has said that the clause prohibits a state from discriminating against residents of other states with respect to "basic rights"—rights that "bear on the vitality of the Nation as a single entity," interference with which would "frustrate the purposes of the formation of the Union."[312] However, most rights would be considered "basic rights" for privileges and immunities purposes, such as the right to work within a state, the right to own property, and the right of access to courts. With respect to these "basic rights," the privileges and immunities clause prohibits the states from discriminating against nonresidents unless the state can justify the differential treatment because of differences between residents and nonresidents with respect to the matter in issue. For example, a requirement that a nonresident plaintiff bringing a lawsuit in a state court post security for costs would be reasonable in view of the fact that the state might not otherwise be able to collect costs against a nonresident. But a rule requiring private employers to give preference to local residents in employment in all oil and gas operations somehow connected to state-owned oil and gas reserves violates the privileges and immunities clause.[313] So does the imposition of a "commuters tax" applicable only to nonresidents,[314] and a prohibition against the admission of nonresidents to the practice of law in the state.[315]

190. The privileges and immunities clause does not prevent the state from giving preferential treatment to its residents with respect to benefits directly provided by the state that involve the expenditure of state funds or the utilization of state resources. Such preference is justified by considerations of state sovereignty, in that each state is entitled to use the collective wealth of the state for the benefit of its own residents,

311. This clause protects only individuals, so a corporation is not a "citizen" for purposes of the clause. The negative aspect of the commerce clause, by contrast, protects entities engaged in interstate commerce, which necessarily include out-of-state corporations.

312. *Baldwin v. Fish & Game Commission of Montana*, 436 U.S. 371, 383 (1978). In that case, the Court held that denial of access to elk hunting, a sporting activity, was not a "basic right," and so upheld a state's rule imposing a substantially higher hunting license fee for nonresidents. The Court has also recently held that citizens-only provision of the Virginia Freedom of Information Act does not violate the Privileges and Immunities Clause. *McBurney v. Young*, 133 Sup.Ct. 1709 (2013).

313. *Hicklin v. Orbeck*, 437 U.S. 518 (1978).

314. *Austin v. New Hampshire*, 420 U.S. 656 (1975). *See also Lunding v. New York*, 522 U.S. 287 (1998), holding violative of the privileges and immunities clause a state law that effectively denied nonresident taxpayers a state income tax deduction for alimony payments that was available to resident taxpayers.

315. *Supreme Court of New Hampshire v. Piper*, 470 U.S. 274 (1985).

whose welfare is the state's primary concern. So, a state can limit state employment and attendance at a public university to state residents, or can charge nonresident students higher tuition in order to attend a public university. It can also give state residents preference with respect to access to state-owned resources.[316] And while discrimination against nonresidents with respect to employment by a private contractor on a state-funded public works project must be independently justified, such justification may be found in the state's need to provide employment for disadvantaged segments of its work force.[317] Finally, the state may limit requests for public information under its freedom of information act to state residents.[318]

191. The privileges and immunities clause is an important limitation on state power, prohibiting discrimination against nonresidents solely because they are nonresidents, and ensuring that Americans are generally free to carry on their activities within the boundaries of any state on an equal footing with residents of that state.[319]

192. The full faith and credit clause of Article IV, section 1, was adopted to deal with a specific concern of the Framers, namely that a party against whom a state court judgment had been rendered should not be able to avoid that judgment by fleeing to another state. The Framers also wanted to ensure that the legal proceedings of one state be recognized in other states. So, the full faith and credit clause provides that, "Full Faith and Credit shall be given in each State to the public Acts, Records and judicial proceedings of every other State." The primary effect of the full faith and credit clause, in light of its historical purpose, has been to require maximum recognition of state court judgments in the courts of other American states, and these judgments must be recognized in circumstances where principles of private international law

316. *See* e.g., *McCready v. Virginia*, 94 U.S. 391 (1877), upholding a state's exclusion of nonresidents from planting oysters in state-owned tidelands.
317. *See United Building and Construction Trades Council v. City of Camden*, 465 U.S. 208 (1984).
318. *McBurney v. Young*, 133 S.Ct. 1709 (2013).
319. The protections provided by the privileges and immunities clause and the protections provided by the nondiscrimination principle of the negative aspect of the commerce clause overlap where there is express discrimination against nonresident individuals with respect to commercial activity in a state. Such discrimination is violative of both provisions.

would not require recognition of foreign court judgments.[320] In addition, the "federal interest in national unity," embodied in the full faith and credit clause, requires that certain kinds of legal issues be determined by the law of a single state.[321]

Finally, the "interstate rendition clause" of Article IV, section 2, provides that when a person charged with a crime in one state moves to another state, the Governor of the state from which the person has fled may demand that the person be apprehended and returned to the state for trial. The demand is addressed to the Governor of the state where the person has fled, and the authorities there must arrest the person and arrange

---

320. An American court could not, for example, refuse to recognize a judgment of sister state court on "public policy" grounds. *Faunterloy v. Lum*, 210 U.S. 230 (1908). A final judgment on the merits rendered by an American state court or federal court must be recognized by another state court or federal court with only three exceptions: (1) The court that rendered the judgment could not constitutionally exercise jurisdiction over the defendant, and the defendant did not appear in the first action to litigate the jurisdictional question. *Durfee v. Duke*, 375 U.S. 106 (1963). (2) The judgment is subject to collateral attack under the law of the state where it was rendered. *Thompson v. Whitman*, 85 U.S. 457 (1873). (3) Enforcement of the judgment is barred by the nondiscriminatory statute of limitations of the state where enforcement is sought. *Watkins v. Conway*, 385 U.S. 188 (1966). *See also Baker v. General Motors Corp.*, 522 U.S. 222 (1998), holding that an injunction issued by a state court prohibiting one party from testifying against the other party in another case could not be applied to bar the testimony of that party in a case brought by another person in another state court. The first court was held to lack jurisdiction to bar a party from testifying in a case brought in another state court. The Court has recently held that a court judgment of adoption is a judgment for purposes of the full faith and credit clause, so that a state must recognize a judgment of adoption by another state. *V.L. v. E.L.*, 136 S.Ct. 1017 (2016).

321. The primary application of this principle has involved matters going to the internal affairs of a corporation, which the Supreme Court has indicated must be determined by the law of the state of incorporation or the law of the state where the corporation has its principal place of business. *See* e.g., *Supreme Council of the Royal Arcanum v. Green*, 237 U.S. 531 (1915), involving the now obsolete matter of deficiency assessments. In *Edgar v. MITE Corporation*, 457 U.S. 624 (1982), the Court held that a state that was neither the state of incorporation nor the principal place of business could not constitutionally apply its "anti-takeover" law to takeover efforts directed at the corporation. While the Court based its decision on the "undue burden" element of the negative aspect of the commerce clause, the decision more appropriately could have been based on the full faith and credit clause. Despite the "burden" this may place on interstate commerce, there is no constitutional objection to the state of incorporation's applying its "anti-takeover" law to such efforts. *CTS Corporation v. Dynamics Corporation*, 481 U.S. 69 (1987).

The full faith and credit clause does not require a state to give full faith and credit to the law of another state giving that state's governmental agencies immunity from suit. So, where Nevada did not confer immunity on its state agencies for liability for intentional torts committed by state employees in the course of its employment, Nevada could apply its own law to a claim for liability for intentional torts brought against a California state agency in Nevada, although California law provided for such immunity. *Franchise Tax Board of California v. Hyatt*, 538 U.S. 488 (2003). But the full faith and credit clause does prohibit a state from applying a rule of law that allows a higher award of damages in suits against officials of sister states than it allows in suits against its own officials. *Franchise Tax Board of California v. Hyatt*, 136 Sup. Ct. 1277 (2016).

for his return. There is no discretion to refuse to return the person, and if the Governor of that state refuses to do so, the federal courts will order that the person be returned.[322]

322. *Puerto Rico v. Branstad*, 483 U.S. 219 (1987).

Part IV. Citizenship and the Administration of Justice

Chapter 1. Citizenship and the Relevance of Citizenship

§1. The Constitutional Basis of American Citizenship

193. The concept of citizenship in American constitutional law is related to the American federal system in which both the federal government and the states exercise sovereignty. Thus, American constitutional law recognizes both national citizenship and state citizenship. The Fourteenth Amendment, section 1, specifically provides that, "ll persons born or naturalized in the United States and subject to the jurisdiction thereof are citizens of the United States and of the State wherein they reside." Birth or naturalization within the United States makes a person a citizen of the United States, and so gives that person rights and imposes obligations with respect to the United States. Residence within a state makes a person a citizen of that state and likewise gives that person rights and imposes obligations with respect to that state. United States citizenship and state citizenship are distinct in the sense that state citizenship depends on residence within a state, so if, for example, an American citizen leaves the United States to take up permanent residence in a foreign country, that person retains United States citizenship, but is no longer a citizen of any state.[323]

However, since state citizenship is linked to United States citizenship, if a person loses United States citizenship, that person loses state citizenship as well.

194. The right to vote for Members of Congress and the President is dependent on state citizenship rather than United States citizenship. This is because Members of Congress are elected from each state, and the President is elected by electors from each state who are chosen by voters in that state. So, an American citizen residing abroad who wishes to vote for Members of Congress and the President must retain at least a mailing address in the state of former residence and attempt to vote by absentee

323. As the Supreme Court stated in *In re Slaughter-House* Cases, 83 U.S. 36, 74 (1873): "[T]he distinction between citizenship of the United States and citizenship of a state is clearly recognized and established. Not only may a man be a citizen of the United States without being a citizen of a state, but an important element is necessary to convert the former into the latter. He must reside within the state to make him a citizen of it, but it is only necessary that he should be born or naturalized in the United States to be a citizen of the Union."

ballot.[324] And because the right to vote for President is dependent on state citizenship, residents of American territories, who have been made United States citizens by Act of Congress, cannot vote for President, and the Twenty-Third Amendment was necessary to give residents of the District of Columbia the right to vote for President.

195. Having explained the dual nature of American citizenship under the Constitution, we will now use the term "American citizenship" in the more conventional sense to refer to United States citizenship.

196. American citizenship connotes membership in the American political society and permanent allegiance to that society. While Americans have the right to renounce American citizenship, so long as they have not done so, this duty of permanent allegiance remains,[325] and they are subject to the obligations of American citizenship even when residing abroad.[326] Conversely, so long as they are American citizens, they have an absolute right to remain in the United States and to return to the United States from abroad, and cannot be expelled or barred from the United States.

197. In the United States, as elsewhere, the distinction between aliens and citizens is that aliens are not part of the political society and do not owe permanent allegiance to the United States. In theory, their only obligation is to comply with American laws while residing in the United States. However, the United States is a "nation of immigrants," and has always been somewhat solicitous of aliens who have been admitted to the United States for permanent residence.[327] It is not difficult for aliens admitted to the United States for permanent residence to acquire American citizenship by naturalization after residing in the United States for a period of time. However, they are not required to do so, and as long as they do not engage in conduct that would subject them to deportation, they can remain in the United States for as long as they wish. Under federal law, they are entitled to receive certain governmental benefits, and are subject to certain obligations, such as compulsory military service when this was required in the United States. Moreover, as we will see, resident aliens are entitled to procedural due process if deportation proceedings are brought against them, and the state governments are generally precluded from discriminating against them because of their status as aliens.

---

324. Federal employees and military personnel stationed abroad are required to designate a "home state of record," and are citizens of that state for constitutional purposes.

325. *See Tomoya Kawakita v. United States*, 343 U.S. 717 (1952), where an American citizen who also had Japanese citizenship, was convicted of treason for acts performed against the United States in Japan during World War II. Since he had not renounced his American citizenship by any of the methods prescribed under federal law, he remained an American citizen for constitutional purposes and could be punished for treason against the United States.

326. Certain American laws apply to American citizens who engage in prohibited acts in foreign countries, such as bribing foreign officials or having sex with children.

327. Aliens seeking admission to the United States for permanent residence must qualify for an immigrant visa. There are two broad categories of immigrant visas, those that are not subject to numerical limitations and those that are. Visas not subject to numerical limitations are primarily those granted to close relatives of American citizens. Visas subject to numerical limitations are those limited both by the total that can be granted in a given year and by country of origin. There are preferences in the granting of these visas, designed to achieve the goals of family reunification and United States employment needs.

Federal law lists a large number of grounds for exclusion of aliens. These include: a communicable disease of public health significance; a physical or mental disorder and resulting behavior that poses a threat to the welfare of others; conviction of a crime involving moral turpitude or a controlled substance; two or more criminal convictions with sentences aggregating five years; prostitution; terrorist activity and activity having serious foreign policy consequences; participation in Nazi persecutions or genocide; the likeliness of becoming a public charge; permanent ineligibility for citizenship; and polygamy.[328]

§2. Acquisition and Loss of Citizenship

I. Acquisition of Citizenship

198. As pointed out above, under the Fourteenth Amendment, United States citizenship is acquired by birth within the United States or by naturalization. The principle of citizenship by birth, *jus soli*, was a part of the English common law that was received in the United States and was given constitutional status by the Fourteenth Amendment in order to confer automatic citizenship upon newly emancipated blacks, who were not citizens during the time of slavery. The Fourteenth Amendment's incorporation of the *jus soli* principle also ensured that the children of the large number of immigrants who arrived in the United States during the middle and latter part of the nineteenth century and early part of the twentieth century would become American citizens upon birth even if their parents were still aliens.[329]

199. The United States follows the principle of *jus sanguinis* to a limited degree in that under federal law, children born abroad to United States citizens can become citizens upon birth. There have been a series of such laws, going back to 1790, differing somewhat in their terms. The current law, effective for persons born abroad after December 23, 1952, distinguishes between the situation where both parents are American citizens and the situation where only one is a citizen. If both parents are citizens, the child becomes an American citizen upon birth so long as one citizen parent had previously resided in the United States or its possessions at any time. But if one parent is a citizen and the other parent is an alien, the citizen parent must have been physically

328. 8 U.S.C. sec. 1182.

329. In *United States v. Wong Kim Ark*, 169 U.S. 649 (1898), the Court made it absolutely clear that children born in the United States to alien parents were American citizens upon birth. The phrase in s. 1 of the Fourteenth Amendment, "and subject to the jurisdiction thereof," means that children born in the United States of parents in the diplomatic service of a foreign government or children born on foreign public vessels in the territorial waters of the United States are not American citizens upon birth. However, children born of foreign parents who are temporarily in the United States are American citizens upon birth, even though their parents have not been admitted to permanent residence or in fact are in the United States illegally.

present in the United States or its possessions for five years, at least two of which were after attaining the age of 14.[330]

200. The premise of citizenship by naturalization in the United States is that aliens admitted to the United States for permanent residence should be able to acquire United States citizenship after living in the United States for a reasonable period of time and becoming a part of the American political community. The requirements for naturalization are stated in terms of: (1) residence and physical presence; (2) age; (3) literacy and knowledge; (4) good moral character; (5) attachment to constitutional principles; (6) an oath of allegiance.[331]

201. An applicant for naturalization must have resided continuously in the United States for five years as a lawfully admitted permanent resident, must have been physically present in the United States for at least half of the time during the five years immediately prior to filing the naturalization petition, and must have resided for at least three months in the state where the naturalization petition has been filed.[332] The five years continuous residence requirement is reduced to three years for spouses of American citizens, and aliens who have served honorably in the Armed Forces for periods aggregating three years may apply for naturalization without meeting the continuous residence and physical presence requirements. The applicant must be 18 years or older, but a citizen parent can file the application on behalf of a minor child residing with the parent. Unless the applicant is unable to do so because of blindness or deafness, the applicant must be able to speak, read, write, and understand the English language.[333] The applicant must also pass an examination demonstrating "a knowledge and understanding of the fundamentals of the history, principles and form of government of the United States." In practice, this requirement is applied rather leniently, in light of the applicant's age, education and length of residence in the United States, and the applicant has three chances to pass the examination.

202. The statute requires that the applicant show that the applicant "has been and still is a person of good moral character," and sets forth a number of factors that preclude a finding that the applicant is "of good moral character."[334] These factors are

330. 8 U.S.C. sec. 1401. For these purposes, overseas service as a federal employee, or in military service, or as an employee of an international organization of which the United States is a member, counts toward the requisite physical presence within the United States or its territories.

331. The current requirements for naturalization are set forth in 8 U.S.C. sec. 1427.

332. This refers to maintaining the United States as the applicant's legal residence. Temporary absences from the United States for up to six months will not break the continuity of residence, but an absence from the United States for one year or more will do so. An absence of between six months and one year presumptively breaks the continuity of residence, but the presumption can be overcome.

333. This requirement is waived for applicants who are over 50 years of age at the time of the filing of the petition and who have been admitted for permanent residence for periods totaling twenty years. For persons over 55 years of age, the period is fifteen years.

334. These include the following: (1) being a habitual drunkard; (2) committing polygamy; (3) being illegally connected with prostitution, narcotics or the unlawful entry of other aliens; (4) criminal conviction for murder, or a crime involving moral turpitude, or two gambling offenses, or two crimes for which the actual sentences imposed were five years or more, or a single crime for which the applicant served at least six months in jail; (5) giving false testimony for purposes of obtaining benefits under the immigration and naturalization law.

not exclusive, and in the determination of "good moral character," the court passing on the naturalization application may consider the applicant's conduct at any time preceding the filing of the application. The applicant must show "attachment to constitutional principles," in the sense of a belief in representative democracy and acceptance of the principle that change can be effected only in a peaceful manner. Finally, the applicant must take an oath of renunciation of existing citizenship and allegiance to the United States in open court. Upon executing the oath of allegiance, the applicant becomes a naturalized citizen. The naturalization of both parents or of the surviving or custodial parent will confer American citizenship on children who were born outside of the United States, and so did not acquire American citizenship upon birth.

II. Loss of Citizenship

203. Once acquired, American citizenship can be lost only by a voluntary act of expatriation or by the denaturalization of a naturalized citizen. The Supreme Court has held that as a constitutional matter, expatriation requires a specific intent to renounce American citizenship. So, while Congress can provide that certain acts may result in expatriation, these acts must be accompanied with the intention to relinquish American citizenship thereby.[335] Congress has provided that an American citizen can lose that citizenship by "performing any of the following acts with the intention of relinquishing United States nationality: (1) obtaining naturalization in a foreign country; (2) taking an oath or other formal declaration of allegiance to a foreign country; (3) serving in the government of a foreign country; (4) entering the armed forces of a foreign country that are engaged in hostilities with the United States or serving as a commissioned or noncommissioned officer in the armed forces of a foreign country; (5) making a formal renunciation of nationality before a diplomatic or consular officer of the United States in a foreign country; (6) conviction of treason, of attempt to overthrow the government, or of conspiracy to incite insurrection."[336] Again, these acts must be accompanied by a specific intent to renounce American citizenship, and the burden is on the government to prove by a "preponderance of the evidence" that such specific intent existed at the time the act relied on to establish expatriation occurred.[337] The constitutional requirements relating to expatriation apply equally to native-born and naturalized citizens, and Congress cannot constitutionally distinguish between American citizens with respect to voluntary expatriation, such as by providing that a naturalized citizen can be expatriated for three years continuous residence in the country of the naturalized citizen's former nationality.[338]

204. The denaturalization of a naturalized citizen is constitutionally permissible only on the basis that the naturalization itself "was procured by concealment of a

335. *Afroyim v. Rusk*, 387 U.S. 253 (1967). In that case, the Court held that Congress had no general power to force expatriation because of an act that a citizen performed, such as voting in a foreign country election.

336. 8 U.S.C. sec. 1481.

337. *Vance v. Terrazas*, 444 U.S. 252 (1980).

338. *Schneider v. Rusk*, 377 U.S. 163 (1964).

material fact or by willful misrepresentation," or was "illegally procured."[339] For this purpose, facts are "material" if they "have a natural tendency to produce the conclusion that the applicant was qualified for citizenship."[340] Examples would include concealment of criminal convictions, false statements concerning marital or family status, and as has appeared in some recent cases, concealment of atrocities committed by Nazi concentration camp guards during World War II.[341] "Illegal procurement" of naturalization refers to matters connected with the naturalization proceeding itself, such as giving false testimony in that proceeding. The government has a very heavy burden of proof in denaturalization cases, and must prove by clear, unequivocal and convincing evidence that the person was not entitled to naturalization at the time it was granted.[342]

339. 8 U.S.C. sec. 1451. The same improper conduct that led to the revocation of the certificate of naturalization is likely to be a basis for deportation as well.

340. *Kungys v. United States*, 485 U.S. 759, 772 (1988).

341. The statute also provides that if a naturalized citizen takes up permanent residence in a foreign country within one year after naturalization, this shall be considered prima facie evidence of a lack of intention to establish a permanent residence in the United States at the time of the petition for naturalization. This presumption may be rebutted by testimony that the person intended in good faith to establish a permanent residence in the United States, but if no such testimony is forthcoming, the presumption is sufficient to justify revocation of the naturalization as having been obtained by concealment of a material fact or by willful misrepresentation.

342. *Schneiderman v. United States*, 320 U.S. 118 (1943).

Chapter 2. Fundamental Rights and Liberties

§1. The Structural Basis of Constitutional Protection of Individual Rights

205. From the very beginning of the Nation's constitutional history, it was recognized that the power of the government must be limited in order to protect individual rights. The Framers of the Constitution were very familiar with the violations of individual rights that had occurred during the Colonial era and were seriously concerned about abuse of governmental power, even by a government that had been democratically elected. Moreover, they believed that certain important individual rights should be protected from governmental action, and that there were certain things that no government, no matter how democratically elected, should be able to do to those whom it governed. The original Constitution contained a few "individual rights" provisions. These provisions were directed against certain specific abuses that had occurred in Great Britain and the Colonies during the Colonial era, and their restrictions were imposed both against the federal government under Article I, section 9, and against the states under Article I, section 10. These provisions prohibited suspension of the writ of habeas corpus (a judicial proceeding challenging the illegal detention of a person by the government),[343] the enactment of an ex post facto law (a criminal law that retroactively punished conduct that was lawful when performed),[344] and the

343. Very recently, the Court had the occasion to consider the prohibition against suspension of the writ of habeas corpus. Congress enacted a law which purported to strip all federal courts of habeas corpus jurisdiction over all detainees held by the United States military at the prison in Guantanamo, Cuba. As a substitute for habeas corpus—the traditional method by which courts have ruled on the lawfulness of executive detentions of persons not convicted of crimes by civilian courts—Congress provided a very limited form of review by the United States Court of Appeals for the District of Columbia over decisions of a review committee that had been set up by the Department of Defense pursuant to statutory authorization. The Court held that the constitutional prohibition against suspension of the writ of habeas corpus rendered the withdrawal of habeas corpus jurisdiction for the Guantanamo detainees unconstitutional. *Boumediene v. Bush*, 553 U.S. 723 (2008).

344. The ex post facto clause has been invoked successfully in some recent cases to challenge state laws designed to make it easier to for the state to obtain criminal convictions. *See Carmell v. Texas*, 529 U.S. 513 (2000) (state law authorizing conviction of certain sexual offenses on victim's testimony alone where previous law required other corroborating testimony was ex post facto law and could not be applied to acts occurring prior to change in the law). The retroactive application of laws eliminating or restricting parole to prisoners currently serving their sentences raises ex post facto law questions, since the ex post facto clause prohibits increasing the punishment for a crime after its commission. *See Garner v. Jones*, 529 U.S. 244 (2000). In *Stogner v. Superior Court of Contra County*, California, 539 U.S. 607 (2003), the Court held that a state law reviving time-barred criminal prosecutions against persons charged with sex crimes against children that was enacted after the time for initiating such prosecutions under previously applicable law had expired was an unconstitutional ex post facto law.

enactment of a bill of attainder (punishment by the legislature instead of by the courts).[345] Because these prohibitions were directed against specific abuses, their meaning is fairly clear, and their scope is correspondingly limited. Only on very rare occasions has the government done something that the courts have held to be violative of these provisions.[346]

It is in the Bill of Rights that the historical concern for the constitutional protection of individual rights achieved full realization.[347] In the Bill of Rights, the Framers imposed numerous, and sometimes in sweeping terms, limitations on governmental power designed to protect individual rights. The First Amendment protects freedom of religion and freedom of expression, the Fourth Amendment prohibits unreasonable searches and seizures, the due process clause of the Fifth Amendment protects liberty and property interests, the Fifth and Sixth Amendments provide many procedural protections for persons accused of crime, and the Eighth Amendment prohibits excessive bail and the imposition of "cruel and unusual punishment."[348]

Looking to the Bill of Rights, it can fairly be said that the overriding principle in the structure of constitutional governance established by the Constitution is that the power of the government must be limited in order to protect individual rights.

---

345. *See Ex parte Garland,* 71 U.S. 333 (1866) (law that required lawyers as a condition to practicing law in federal court to take an oath that they had not participated in the rebellion during the American Civil War was unconstitutional as an ex post facto law and bill of attainder); *United States v. Lovett*, 328 U.S. 303 (1946) (law prohibiting payment of salaries to three named federal employees because Congress believed they were "subversives" is an unconstitutional bill of attainder); *United States v. Brown*, 381 U.S. 437 (1965) (law prohibiting Communist Party members from serving as labor union officers is an unconstitutional bill of attainder).

346. In addition, the Framers, concerned that the states would enact laws enabling debtors to avoid payments of their debts, prohibited the states from enacting any law "impairing the obligations of contracts. " The "Contracts Clause," as this provision is called, will be discussed in paras. 398–402.

347. As discussed earlier, General Introduction, §1, the original Constitution did not contain a Bill of Rights. The absence of a Bill of Rights figured prominently in the debates in the state ratifying conventions, and the proponents of the Constitution promised that a Bill of Rights would be promulgated soon after the ratification of the Constitution. The Bill of Rights was approved by Congress in September 1789, and was ratified in December 1791. The Bill of Rights is considered a part of the original Constitution because it was promulgated "practically contemporaneous with the adoption of the original." In re Slaughter-House Cases, 83 U.S. 36, 67 (1873).

348. Because the constitutional protections afforded persons accused of crime in the United States are so extensive, they form a major part of the administration of criminal law, and are typically dealt with in texts on Criminal Law and Criminal Procedure rather than in texts on Constitutional Law. For this reason, in the International Encyclopedia of Laws, they will be covered in the monograph on Criminal Law, along with constitutional protection against unreasonable searches and seizures and against the imposition of excessive bail and cruel and unusual punishment.

Some of the guarantees of the Bill of Rights, such as the Third Amendment's guarantee against the quartering of soldiers in private homes, and the Seventh Amendment's guarantee of the right to trial by jury in civil cases, were enacted in reaction to specific conditions that existed during the Colonial era. The Ninth Amendment is a "savings" clause, saying that the enumeration of the rights in the Bill of Rights "shall not be construed to deny or disparage others retained by the people." It has not served as an independent source of limitation on governmental power. The Tenth Amendment, reaffirming state sovereignty, has been discussed in paras. 152–155.

206. The Bill of Rights, by its terms, applies only to the actions of the federal government, and prior to the American Civil War, the federal Constitution did not serve as a significant limitation on the exercise of state governmental action interfering with individual rights. The American Civil War and the defeat of the eleven southern states seeking to secede from the Union changed all this. In the "Reconstruction" period following the Civil War, the Thirteenth, Fourteenth, and Fifteenth Amendments were adopted. The Thirteenth, adopted in 1865, prohibited slavery or involuntary servitude in the United States, and the Fifteenth, adopted in 1870, prohibited racial discrimination in voting. The Fourteenth Amendment, adopted in 1868, contained broad provisions designed to protect individual rights against state governmental action and has become the primary textual basis of constitutional protection of individual rights against the states. The due process clause of the Fourteenth Amendment tracks the Fifth Amendment's due process clause, and as we will see, the Fourteenth Amendment's due process clause has been held to incorporate the principal guarantees of the Bill of Rights, so as to make them binding on the states as well as on the federal government. In addition, since the primary historical purpose of the Fourteenth Amendment was to prevent discrimination against the newly emancipated black citizens, the Fourteenth Amendment contains an "equal protection" clause, providing that no state shall "deny to any person within its jurisdiction the equal protection of the laws." As we will see, the equal protection clause has proved to be very important not only in prohibiting racial discrimination, but also in prohibiting gender discrimination and other kinds of discrimination on the basis of identifiable group membership.

207. The Bill of Rights and the Fourteenth Amendment, taken together, provide a strong structural basis of constitutional protection of individual rights, and support the proposition that the overriding principle in the structure of constitutional governance established by the Constitution is that the power of the government must be limited in order to protect individual rights. Our primary focus in this Part will be on equality, freedom of expression, freedom of religion, and liberty and property rights.

I. Comparability of Protection Against Federal and State Governmental Action

208. As stated above, the Bill of Rights by its own terms applies only to the federal government, and the Fourteenth Amendment applies only to the states. However, in the areas of equality, freedom of expression, freedom of religion, and liberty and property rights, the nature and extent of constitutional protection afforded to individual rights against action by the federal government and action by the state governments is substantially comparable. The primary reason why this is so is that the Supreme Court has held that the Fourteenth Amendment's due process clause incorporates the principal guarantees of the Bill of Rights, and so makes them directly binding on the states. The Court has said that the "liberty" protected by the Fourteenth Amendment's "due process" clause includes those guarantees of the Bill of Rights that are "implicit in the concept of ordered liberty,"[349] which include freedom of expression, freedom of religion, the right to be free from unreasonable searches and seizures, most of the

349. *Palko v. Connecticut*, 302 U.S. 319, 325 (1937).

protections of the Bill of Rights afforded persons accused of crime,[350] and freedom from excessive bail and cruel and unusual punishment.[351]

209. On the other side of the equation, the Bill of Rights contains no equivalent of the Fourteenth Amendment's equal protection clause. However, the Supreme Court has held that the Fifth Amendment's due process clause also has an "equal protection" component,[352] and under the Court's current doctrine, whatever is a denial of equal protection on the part of the states is also a violation of due process on the part of the federal government. The only exception to "Fifth Amendment equal protection" is where there is a federal interest that can be relied on to justify the challenged discrimination and no corresponding state interest.[353]

210. As a result of the Supreme Court's "incorporation" of the principal guarantees of the Bill of Rights into the due process clause of the Fourteenth Amendment and its finding an "equal protection" component in the Fifth Amendment's due process clause, the nature and extent of constitutional protection afforded to individual rights against the actions of the federal and state governments in the United States is substantially comparable. Thus, we routinely speak, for example, of a First Amendment challenge to state governmental action affecting freedom of expression or freedom of religion, and of an equal protection challenge to discrimination by the federal government, and we assume that the Constitution protects against federal and state governmental action affecting individual rights in substantially equal measure.

II. Standards of Review

211. The major provisions of the Constitution protecting individual rights—the First Amendment and the due process and equal protection clauses—are very general and broadly phrased, and so must be interpreted and applied by the Supreme Court to determine the constitutionality of a large and varied number of governmental actions affecting individual rights. Constitutional doctrine with respect to the meaning of these provisions has developed in part with reference to differing articulated standards of review. The essence of different standards of review relates to the degree of scrutiny that the Court applies under each articulated standard in order to determine the validity of a challenged law or governmental action, both in terms of the permissibility of the asserted purpose for which the law was enacted or the action undertaken, and in terms

350. Such as the privilege against self-incrimination, the protection against double jeopardy, the right to a speedy and public trial, the right to trial by jury, the right to compulsory process for securing the attendance of witnesses, the right to confrontation, and the right to the assistance of counsel.

351. The only operational guarantees of the Bill of Rights that have not been incorporated into the Fourteenth Amendment's due process clause, and so are binding only on the federal government and not the states, are the Fifth Amendment's guarantee of indictment by grand jury, and the Seventh Amendment's guarantee of a jury trial in civil cases.

352. "[D]iscrimination may be so unjustifiable as to be violative of due process." *Bolling v. Sharpe*, 347 U.S. 497, 499 (1954).

353. As we will *see* in paras. 434–436, *infra* , this exception has been applied only with respect to discrimination against aliens, which brings into play the strong federal interest in regulating immigration and naturalization.

of appropriateness of the particular law or action as a means of advancing the asserted purpose. The higher the degree of scrutiny, of course, the more likely the Court is to invalidate the challenged law or governmental action.

212. The differing articulated standards of review that the Court has developed depend on: (1) the nature of the constitutional provision involved; (2) the importance of the individual interest affected by the challenged law or governmental action; (3) the societal position of the individual or group toward which the challenged law or action has been directed. Because of the significance of freedom of expression and freedom of religion in the American constitutional system—as reflected by the fact that these freedoms are protected by the "First" Amendment—the Court has applied very careful scrutiny to any interference with these freedoms and has demanded a strong showing of justification for the particular restriction. As a result, as we will see, these freedoms receive a very high level of constitutional protection.

213. Outside of the First Amendment area, and primarily in regard to due process and equal protection challenges, the Court has held that certain individual interests are so important as to be ranked as "fundamental." Four individual interests have been held to be "fundamental" for purposes of due process and equal protection analysis. These are: (1) interests relating to marriage and the family; (2) reproductive rights; (3) the right to interstate travel; (4) the right to vote. Whenever the challenged law or governmental action is found to impose an "undue burden" on a "fundamental right," the articulated compelling governmental interest standard applies. This means that the governmental interest asserted to justify the interference with the individual interest must be found by the Court to be "compelling," and that the challenged governmental action must be the "least drastic means" of advancing the asserted interest. With respect to other or "non-fundamental" interests, the articulated rational basis standard of review applies. This means that the asserted governmental interest need only be "legitimate," and that the challenged law or governmental action need only be "rationally related" to advancing the asserted interest. Although, as we will see, there are a number of factors influencing the application of the articulated standard of review in particular circumstances, and the articulated standard of review is not always dispositive of the result, the fact remains that laws or governmental action evaluated under the articulated compelling governmental interest standard of review are more likely to be invalidated, while laws or governmental action evaluated under the articulated rational basis standard of review are more likely to be upheld against constitutional challenge.

214. In the United States, there has been a long history of governmental racial discrimination and discrimination against other identifiable groups, such as women, aliens, and out-of-wedlock children. This discrimination has been challenged as violative of equal protection, and in the process of determining the constitutionality of such discrimination, the Court has articulated different standards of review, depending in part on the "invidiousness" or "suspectness" of the particular kind of discrimination. The "invidiousness" or "suspectness" of the particular kind of discrimination has, in turn, related to the societal position of the group toward which the discrimination is directed. Because the primary historical purpose of the Fourteenth Amendment was to prevent discrimination against the newly emancipated black citizens, and because such discrimination on the part of the states and the federal governments continued long after the adoption of the Fourteenth Amendment, the Court has held that all racial discrimination is "suspect," and so is subject to "strict scrutiny." The articulated standard of review is "compelling governmental interest," but that standard is applied here with even greater scrutiny than it is applied in other areas. Where the use of race-conscious criteria has resulted in racial discrimination, not only must the asserted governmental interest be "compelling," but the particular form that the use of race-conscious criteria takes must be "precisely tailored" to the advancement of that asserted interest. As we will see, today it is only in rare circumstances that laws or governmental action resulting in racial discrimination will be upheld, and this appears to be limited to some actions designed to benefit racial minorities in an effort to overcome the present consequences of prior racial discrimination. The Court has also held that most discrimination against resident aliens by state governments is "suspect," and so is evaluated under the "compelling governmental interest" standard.

215. The next level of scrutiny applied to discrimination on the basis of identifiable group membership is the "important and substantial relationship" standard. Under this standard, the governmental interest asserted to justify the discrimination must be "important," and the particular form of discrimination must be "substantially related" to the advancement of the asserted governmental interest. This articulated standard of review applies to discrimination on the basis of gender and discrimination on the basis of illegitimacy. As we will see, this standard also involves a high degree of scrutiny and frequently results in the invalidation of the challenged law or governmental action. All other forms of group discrimination—either against identifiable groups, such as discrimination on the basis of age, or group discrimination resulting from general classifications contained in legislation—are evaluated under the less restrictive rational basis standard: the particular group discrimination need only be rationally related to the advancement of a legitimate governmental interest. As we will see, and as would be expected under this less restrictive standard, most other forms of group discrimination are likely to be upheld against constitutional challenge.

216. The operation of the differing articulated standards of review will be discussed in the material that follows, particularly in §4 (Equality) and §5 ("Liberty" and "Property" Rights).

III. The Problem of "State Action"

217. By definition, the provisions of the Constitution protecting individual rights run only against the actions of the federal and state governments, and so do not apply to the actions of private entities.[354] The problem of "state action" arises when the conduct of a private entity directly impinges on an adversely affected individual interest, but the adversely affected individual asserts that, notwithstanding, the actions of this private entity in the circumstances presented, are subject to constitutional constraints.

354. Strictly speaking, the Thirteenth Amendment, prohibiting slavery and involuntary servitude throughout the United States, does apply to the actions of private entities. This means that s. 2, which gives Congress the power to implement the provisions of the Thirteenth Amendment, authorizes Congress to prohibit private entities from engaging in peonage and to prohibit racial discrimination by private entities as constituting a "badge of servitude." *Jones v. Alfred H. Mayer Co.*, 392 U.S. 409 (1968).

The "state action" doctrine promulgated by the Supreme Court over the years has recognized that in certain circumstances, action directly taken by a private entity can constitute "state action" for constitutional purposes. Under the Court's "state action" doctrine, however, there must always be governmental responsibility with respect to the action of the private entity. In certain circumstances, because of the nature of the activity of the private entity, in relation to governmental activity, the government may have the affirmative duty to take action with respect to the activity of the private entity, and its failure to take such action itself violates the Constitution. Otherwise, "state action" will be found to exist only when the government itself is directly involved in the challenged activity of the private entity.

218. The government has the affirmative duty to take action with respect to the activity of a private entity when the government has acted in such a way as to delegate a governmental function to that private entity, such as fixing the qualifications to vote in an election,[355] or performing the function of municipal governance.[356] The government also has the affirmative duty to take action with respect to certain activities of a private entity when it permits that entity to make use of public property under its control. Thus, the government cannot permit the operator of a restaurant located in a public facility to discriminate against its customers on the basis of race,[357] nor can the government assist private entities in practicing racial discrimination, such as by providing textbooks for students in racially segregated schools or by giving these schools the exclusive use of public facilities to carry out their athletic program.[358] Finally, the government is responsible for the operation of its legal system, so it cannot

355. It will be recalled that candidates for political office are often chosen in a party primary election. If the government allows a political party to fix the qualifications for voting in a primary election, it must at the same time ensure that in those elections, there will be no abridgment of the right to vote on the basis of race, in violation of the Fifteenth Amendment, or on the basis of sex, in violation of the Nineteenth Amendment, or on the basis of being over 18 years of age, in violation the Twenty-Sixth Amendment. So, in times past, where political parties in some southern states prohibited blacks from voting in party primary elections, there was impermissible "state action" for constitutional purposes. *Smith v. Allwright*, 321 U.S. 649 (1944); *Terry v. Adams*, 345 U.S. 461 (1953).

356. In times past, some states allowed private entities to operate "company towns" on their property, where their employees lived and worked. Since these "company towns" in effect performed the function of municipal governance, the state had the affirmative duty to prevent the "company town" from doing anything that an ordinary municipality could not constitutionally do, such as to prohibit the distribution of literature on the streets of the town, in violation of the First Amendment. *Marsh v. Alabama*, 326 U.S. 501 (1946).

357. *Burton v. Wilmington Parking Authority*, 365 U.S. 715 (1961).

358. *Norwood v. Harrison*, 413 U.S. 455 (1973); *Gilmore v. City of Montgomery*, 417 U.S. 556 (1974).

adopt rules, for example, that permit private litigants to engage in racial discrimination in selecting the persons who will be serving on the juries hearing their cases.[359]

219. In this connection, it will be recalled that the "law" of an American state not only includes legislation, but also includes the "common law," that has been promulgated by the courts in judicial decisions. Thus, "common law" rules are "state action" for constitutional purposes, even though they are invoked by private litigants to enforce their private rights.[360]

220. When there is no affirmative duty on the part of the government to take action with respect to the activity of a private entity, "state action" will be found to exist only when the government itself is involved with the challenged activity of the private entity.[361] The Court has rejected the contention that "state action" exists where the private entity taking the challenged action is heavily regulated by the government or where it is performing a "public function," such as providing electricity service, under a governmentally granted monopoly,[362] or where it receives substantial governmental funding to perform a "public function" that the government would otherwise have to perform itself.[363] So long as the government itself is not involved with the challenged

---

359. *Edmonson v. Leesville Concrete Co.*, 500 U.S. 614 (1991) (litigants in civil cases); *Georgia v. McCollum*, 505 U.S. 42 (1992) (criminal defendant). The rules in question permitted each side in the case to exercise a number of "peremptory" challenges to exclude otherwise qualified persons from serving on the jury. While the use of peremptory challenges is a well-recognized feature of the American jury system, the Supreme Court has held that the systematic use of "peremptory" challenges to exclude persons from serving on a jury on racial grounds is unconstitutional. Since the state is responsible for the operation of its legal system, it cannot permit private litigants to exercise peremptory challenges in such a way as to systematically exclude persons from serving on the jury because of their race.

360. In *Shelley v. Kraemer*, 334 U.S. 1 (1948), the Court held unconstitutional judicial enforcement of a "restrictive covenant" that prohibited the sale of land to a black person. In effect, the state common law rule recognizing and enforcing "restrictive covenants" was unconstitutional insofar as it would recognize and enforce a "restrictive covenant" that was based on the buyer's race.
The Court has held, however, that state laws authorizing private creditors to repossess goods from the debtor do not constitute "state action" for constitutional purposes unless the creditor invokes the assistance of a state officer in effecting the repossession. *See Lugar v. Edmonson Oil Co.*, 457 U.S. 922 (1982).

361. *Moose Lodge No. 107 v. Irvis*, 407 U.S. 163 (1972) (private entity held a liquor license from the government).

362. *Jackson v. Metropolitan Edison Co.*, 419 U.S. 345 (1974).

363. *Rendell-Baker v. Kohn*, 457 U.S. 830 (1982) (private entity operating a school for "problem students"); *American Manufacturers Mutual Insurance Co. v. Sullivan*, 526 U.S. 40 (1999) (private insurer's decision pursuant to statutory scheme to withhold payment and seek utilization review by state agency of the reasonableness and necessity of particular medical treatments). However, when a law establishes a governmental agency for the furtherance of governmental objectives, that agency is a governmental actor for constitutional purposes, although the law establishing the agency expressly provides that it is not a governmental actor. *Lebron v. National R.R. Passenger Corp.*, 513 U.S. 374 (1995). *See also Brentwood Academy v. Tennessee Secondary School Athletic Association*, 531 U.S. 288 (2001), where the Court found that there was "pervasive entwinement" of state officials in the structure of the state secondary school athletic association, which included both public and private schools, so that the association was a state actor for constitutional purposes.

activity of the private entity, its involvement with that entity in other respects, no matter how extensive, does not satisfy the "state action" requirement, and the action of the private entity is not "state action" for constitutional purposes.

§2. Freedom of Expression and Association

I. Introduction

221. The First Amendment provides that, "Congress shall make no law ... abridging the freedom of speech, or of the press, or the right of the people peaceably to assemble, and to petition the Government for a redress of grievances." While the language of the First Amendment would indicate that it protects separate interests in freedom of speech, freedom of the press, freedom of assembly, and freedom of petition, the Supreme Court has treated the separate freedoms denominated in the First Amendment as an integrated whole, designed to protect a comprehensive freedom of expression. The comprehensive freedom of expression protected by the First Amendment includes both the speech and writing of individual persons and the institutional expression of the media. It not only includes words and writings, but also includes expressive acts, such as the burning of a flag to protest governmental policies, and includes concerted expression, such as demonstrations and parades. The Court has also held that the First Amendment protects freedom of association, which is related to, but somewhat different from freedom of expression, and we will discuss freedom of association separately.

222. The Supreme Court has interpreted the First Amendment's guarantee of freedom of expression very expansively, and the constitutional protection afforded to freedom of expression is perhaps the strongest protection afforded to any individual right under the Constitution.[364] It is also fair to say that the constitutional protection afforded to freedom of expression in the United States is seemingly unparalleled in

364. In practice, laws or governmental action that clearly would be upheld when challenged under other constitutional provisions are more likely to be invalidated when they also implicate the interest in freedom of expression. For example, while a public school system or public university can refuse to renew the contract of a nontenured teacher on seemingly "arbitrary" grounds, it cannot do so on the ground that the teacher has engaged in activity that is protected by the First Amendment, such as criticizing American foreign policy. *See* e.g., *Perry v. Sindermann*, 408 U.S. 593 (1972). Likewise, governmental economic regulation, which, as we will *see*, is virtually immune from constitutional challenge under the due process or equal protection clause, becomes subject to serious constitutional challenge and possible invalidation when the regulation reaches advertising, because advertising is expression for First Amendment purposes. *See* e.g., *Central Hudson Gas & Electric Corp. v. Public Service Commission*, 447 U.S. 557 (1980) (ban on promotional advertising by regulated public utility, purportedly designed to advance government's interest in energy conservation, violates First Amendment).

other constitutional systems, and that in the United States, as a constitutional matter, the value of freedom of expression generally prevails over other democratic values.[365]

223. Our analysis of constitutional protection to freedom of expression will take place under what I have referred to as the "Law of the First Amendment."[366] The "Law of the First Amendment" consists in large part of concepts, principles, specific doctrines, and precedents in particular areas of First Amendment activity that the Supreme Court has developed and applied over the years in the process of deciding First Amendment cases. Thus, in practice, the constitutional protection of freedom of expression is very much a matter of identification and application. In many cases, once the appropriate concept, principle, specific doctrine or precedent has been identified and applied, the parameters for the resolution of the First Amendment issue have been established, and the result is often fairly clear.[367]

224. The content and line of growth of the "Law of the First Amendment" has been strongly influenced by the context in which it has developed. The "Law of the First Amendment" has been developing for nearly 100 years,[368] and the primary context in which it developed for many of those years was in response to governmental repression of dissent and the expression of unpopular ideas. As the Supreme Court extended protection to freedom of expression in this context, it promulgated concepts, principles and specific doctrines designed to ensure that dissent may occur and unpopular ideas may be expressed. These concepts, principles and specific doctrines apply "across the board," so to speak, to any interference with freedom of expression, and they are

365. For example, while Art. 19 of the International Covenant on Civil and Political Rights generally protects freedom of expression, Art. 20 requires that any propaganda for war and any advocacy of national, racial or religious hatred that constitutes incitement to discrimination, hostility or violence, be prohibited by law. War propaganda and "hate speech" are in most circumstances protected by the First Amendment, so when the United States Senate ratified the International Covenant on Civil and Political Rights, the resolution of ratification contained a reservation to the effect that, "Art. 20 does not authorize or require legislation or other action by the United States that would restrict the right of free speech and association protected by the Constitution and laws of the United States." *See* generally Sedler, *Essay on Freedom of Speech: The United States Versus the Rest of the World*, 2006 Michigan State L. Rev. 377 (2006).

366. *See* generally Sedler, *The First Amendment in Litigation: The "Law of the First Amendment,"* 48 Washington & Lee L. Rev. 457 (1991); *The "Law of the First Amendment" Revisited*, 58 Wayne L.Rev. 1003 (2013).

367. The First Amendment does not apply to the government's own speech. The government may use its funds or public property to convey a message, and it is entitled to decide what message it will convey. *See* e.g., *Pleasant Grove City v. Summum*, 555 U.S. 460(2009) (since display of donated monuments in a city-owned public park is a form of government speech, the city could choose to accept a monument donated by one group and reject a monument proposed to be donated by another group); *Walker v. Texas Division, Sons of Confederate Veterans*, 135 S.Ct. 2239 (2015)(where the state-authorized automobile owners to choose a specialty license plate with the owner's design or message, the license plates were governmental speech and the state could reject a design or message that it found to be objectionable).

368. The development of the modem "Law of the First Amendment" is generally considered to have begun with First Amendment challenges to espionage and sedition prosecutions brought against opponents of American involvement in World War I, and to sedition and "criminal anarchy" prosecutions brought against "left-wing" activists in the "red scare" that followed in the United States after the 1917 "Bolshevik Revolution" in the former Soviet Union.

the principal vehicles by which the very strong protection to freedom of expression is achieved under the First Amendment.

225. The most fundamental and pervasive concept in the "Law of the First Amendment" is that of chilling effect.[369] Precisely because the "Law of the First Amendment" developed initially in response to governmental repression of dissent and the expression of unpopular ideas, there has always been a strong concern with the existence of a chilling effect on expression that could result from laws and governmental action regulating or applicable to acts of expression. The chilling effect concept has been the basis of a number of principles and specific doctrines of the "Law of the First Amendment," and the possibility of a serious chilling effect on expression is an analytical basis for invalidating any regulation of expression.[370] In II *infra*, we will discuss some of the more important First Amendment principles and specific doctrines, focusing primarily on how their application frequently results in the invalidation of laws or governmental action interfering with freedom of expression.

226. Not all activity that somehow involves speech or writing constitutes freedom of expression for First Amendment purposes. For example, certain crimes such as perjury, bribery and illegal solicitation, are carried out by means of words, but this does not make them crimes any less, and the punishment of those crimes is in no way constrained by the First Amendment. This is equally true of other unlawful acts, such as racial or gender discrimination. In addition, the Supreme Court has held that certain forms of speech, such as a portrayal of sexual activity that amounts to "obscenity," and "child pornography" likewise do not constitute freedom of expression for First Amendment purposes. Finally, the Supreme Court has upheld various restrictions on expression against First Amendment challenge. In III *infra*, we will attempt to explain the nature of permissible restrictions on expression under the First Amendment. A different kind of analysis comes into play when the First Amendment is asserted to obtain access to governmentally controlled information, and with respect to acts of expression that take place on or seek access to public property. In IV *infra*, we will discuss access to governmental-controlled information, both as a constitutional matter and as provided under the federal Freedom of Information Act (FOIA), and in V *infra*, we will discuss the application of the First Amendment to expression that takes place on or seeks access to public property. In VI, *infra*, we will discuss the constitutional protection of freedom of association.

369. At this point in time, it is the only clear First Amendment concept that I have been able to identify.

370. *See* e.g., *Miami Herald Publishing Co. v. Tornillo*, 418 U.S. 241 (1974) (state law requiring a newspaper to give a right of reply in the newspaper to a political candidate that it has attacked in print violates the First Amendment, because it could have a chilling effect on political commentary); *Lamont v. Postmaster-General*, 381 U.S. 301 (1965) (federal law permitting mail delivery of "communist political propaganda" only if addressee specifically requests delivery in writing violates First Amendment because of possible chilling effect on willingness of identified recipients to receive "communist political propaganda").

II. Principles, Specific Doctrines, and Precedents

A. First Amendment Principles

227. Here we will discuss three important First Amendment principles: the principle of narrow specificity; the principle of content neutrality; and the principle of protection of offensive speech.

1. Narrow Specificity

228. The principle of narrow specificity derives from the chilling effect concept. As the Supreme Court has stated: "Because First Amendment freedoms need breathing space to survive, government may regulate in this area only with narrow specificity."[371] This being so, any regulation of expression is always subject to challenge on the ground that it "sweeps more broadly than is necessary to advance the legitimate governmental interests at stake."[372] Under the principle of narrow specificity, absolute prohibitions on expressive activity will frequently be found to be unconstitutional, since the asserted governmental interest could be advanced by "less drastic means" than an absolute prohibition.[373]

2. Content Neutrality

229. Perhaps the most important principle in terms of its applicability in actual litigation is the principle of content neutrality. Under this principle, the government may not proscribe any expression because of its content, and an otherwise valid regulation will violate the First Amendment if it discriminates between different types of expression based on their content. Analytically, there are two aspects to the principle of content neutrality: viewpoint neutrality and category neutrality. Under the viewpoint neutrality aspect of the principle, to which the Supreme Court has recognized no

---

371. *NAACP v. Button*, 371 U.S. 415, 433 (1963).
372. *See* e.g., *Shelton v. Tucker*, 364 U.S. 479 (1960). In that case, the Court invalidated a requirement that public school teachers list all of the organizations to which they had belonged or had contributed money during the preceding five years.
373. For illustrative cases, *see* : *Butterworth v. Smith*, 494 U.S. 624 (1990) (absolute ban on witnesses' disclosing testimony given before grand jury, even after grand jury's term has been completed); *Globe Newspaper Co. v. Superior Court*, 457 U.S. 596 (1982) (routine exclusion of press and public during testimony of minor victim of sex offense); *Schad v. Borough of Mt. Ephraim*, 452 U.S. 61 (1981) (prohibition of all live entertainment in city's small commercial zone); *Martin v. City of Struthers*, 319 U.S. 141 (1943) (absolute ban on knocking of door or ringing doorbell of resident in order to deliver handbills); *Schneider v. New Jersey*, 308 U.S. 147 (1939) (absolute ban on distribution of leaflets in public streets or other public places). In the recent case of *United States v. Alvarez*, 132 S.Ct. 2357 (2012), where the Court held unconstitutional a federal law prohibiting any person from making a false statement that the person had been awarded a military medal, two of the Justices based their decision on the narrow specificity principle, saying that the law swept far too broadly by prohibiting all false representations, as opposed to prohibiting only false representations that were likely to cause harm, and so violated the narrow specificity principle.

exceptions, the government cannot regulate expression in such a way as to favor one viewpoint over another viewpoint. Thus, a law prohibiting the display of any sign in front of a foreign embassy that "tends to bring the foreign government into public odium or public dispute" violates the First Amendment, since it only prohibits displays that are critical of the foreign government and not display that are favorable to it.[374] So does a federal law that allowed the wearing of American military uniforms in a portrayal only if that portrayal did not "tend to discredit the military."[375] The viewpoint neutrality aspect of the principle was the basis of the Court's invalidation of state and federal laws prohibiting the burning of the American flag. Since the laws authorized burning as a proper means of disposing of a torn or soiled flag, the thrust of the ban was directed toward the "content of the message" conveyed by the burning, and so was unconstitutional.[376] The Court has also invalidated as a content-based restriction on political speech a judicial conduct rule in a state where judges are elected by popular vote that prohibited candidates for judicial office from announcing their views on "disputed legal or political issues."[377] In another case, the Court held that a regulation of the federal agency funding local legal assistance programs that prohibited those programs from engaging in representation involving efforts to amend or challenge the validity of existing welfare laws was impermissible viewpoint discrimination.[378]

The Court has also held that the viewpoint neutrality aspect of the principle applies to governmental regulation of expression that is not itself constitutionally protected, such as "fighting words." Thus, a law that prohibited only "fighting words" expressing a message of "racial hatred," but did not prohibit "fighting words" expressing a message of "racial tolerance," violated the First Amendment.[379] The Court more recently dealt with the constitutionality of a state law that prohibited the burning of a cross "with the intent to intimidate a person or group" and further provided that any burning of a cross was prima facie evidence of "intent to intimidate." In the United States, cross-burning has been inextricably linked with the history of the Ku Klux Klan, which had engaged in acts of violence and intimidation against African-Americans and which used cross-burning both as a means of threatening African-Americans and as a means of communicating its racist ideology. The Court was sharply divided and the Members issued a number of opinions. A majority of the Justices took the position that since a "true threat" is an unprotected verbal act (*see* paragraphs 255, 256, *infra*), and since cross-burning done with the intent to intimidate was a "particularly virulent form of intimidation," the content neutrality principle did not preclude the state from "regulating this subset of intimidating messages in light of cross burning's long and pernicious history as a signal of impending violence." However, a majority of Justices also took the position that making cross-burning prima facie evidence of intent to discriminate violated the First Amendment, because it could result in a conviction for cross-burning without proof of intent to intimidate and so could have a chilling effect

374. *Boos v. Barry*, 485 U.S. 312 (1988).
375. *Schacht v. United States*, 398 U.S. 58 (1970).
376. *See Texas v. Johnson*, 491 U.S. 397 (1989); *United States v. Eichman*, 496 U.S. 310 (1990).
377. *Republican Party of Minnesota v. White*, 536 U.S. 765 (2002).
378. *Legal Services Corporation v. Velazquez*, 531 U.S. 533 (2001).
379. *R.A.V. v. City of St. Paul*, Minnesota, 505 U.S. 377 (1992).

on constitutionally protected cross-burning.[380] The principle of content neutrality does not apply when the government imposes conditions on the expression of recipients of federal funds that are related to advancing government policy objectives. Thus, since federal law prohibits the use of federal funds to subsidize abortion, the government may require that recipients of federal funds for family planning purposes not provide counseling concerning the use of abortion as a means of family planning or make referrals for abortion as a method of family planning. The Court emphasized that the government may selectively fund a program to encourage certain activities it believes to be in the public interest, here pregnancy, without at the same time funding an alternative program that seeks to deal with the problem in another way.[381] The government may also set advisory guidelines relating to content of artistic programs that the government is funding, such as a guideline that the funding agency take into account "general standards of decency and respect for the diverse beliefs and values of the American public."[382] And recently, the Court has held that a public university's policy requiring student groups seeking official recognition and benefits to open their membership and leadership positions to all students, including those who do not share their core beliefs about religion and sexual orientation, is a reasonable, viewpoint neutral condition that does not impair the group's First Amendment rights.[383]

230. Under the category neutrality aspect of the principle, to which the Court has recognized only limited exceptions, the government cannot regulate in such a way as to discriminate between different categories of expression, and an otherwise valid regulation will be found to violate the First Amendment if it discriminates on this basis. Thus, a ban on picketing within 100 feet of a school building while school was in session, which could otherwise be sustained as a reasonable time, place and manner regulation of expression, was unconstitutional, because it contained an exception for picketing in connection with a labor dispute.[384] Other examples of laws invalidated under the category neutrality aspect of the principle include a law prohibiting drive-in movie theatres from showing films containing nudity when the screen was visible from the highway, since the law singled out one kind of film for differential treatment based on its content,[385] a law imposing a tax on general interest magazines, but not on religious, professional, trade and sports journals,[386] and a sign regulation that imposed more stringent regulations on "temporary directional signs" directing the public to a meeting of a nonprofit organization than it did on signs conveying other messages.[387]

---

380. *Virginia v. Black*, 538 U.S. 343 (2003).
381. *Rust v. Sullivan*, 500 U.S. 173 (1991).
382. *National Endowment for the Arts v. Finley*, 524 U.S. 569 (1998).
383. *Christian Legal Society Chapter of Hastings College of Law v. Martinez*, 561 U.S. 661 (2010).
384. *Chicago Police Department v. Mosley*, 408 U.S. 92 (1972).
385. *Erznoznik v. City of Jacksonville*, 422 U.S. 205 (1975).
386. *Arkansas Writers' Project, Inc. v. Ragland*, 481 U.S. 221 (1987). The Court has also invoked the category neutrality aspect of the principle to invalidate laws that discriminate between expression and other activity, and so held unconstitutional a law requiring that proceeds from a book written by a criminal about the crime be used to compensate crime victims, but not providing compensation from the criminal's other assets. *Simon & Schuster, Inc. v. Members of New York State Crime Victims Board*, 502 U.S. 105 (1992).
387. *Reed v. Town of Gilbert*, 135 Sup.Ct. 2218 (2015).

231. The Court has recognized two limited exceptions to the category neutrality aspect of the principle, both involving the regulation of particular "lower level" speech. First, in order to deal with the secondary consequences resulting from the concentration of businesses purveying sexually explicit materials, the government can enact zoning regulations requiring that such businesses be located at some distance from each other.[388] Second, because commercial speech is considered to receive less constitutional protection than noncommercial speech, the Court has held that a billboard regulation does not violate the First Amendment when it exempts some commercial billboards from the regulation, although it does violate the First Amendment when it exempts some noncommercial billboards from the regulation.[389]

It should be noted that the Court itself has not expressly distinguished between what I have called "viewpoint neutrality" and what I have called "content neutrality." I have made the distinction only for the purpose of showing that there are two aspects to the content neutrality principle, and that the Court has allowed limited exceptions to the category aspect of the principle. In the context of actual First Amendment litigation, all that matters is that the law contains content-based restrictions. When the law does contain content-based restrictions, the content neutrality principle applies, and it is very likely that the law will be invalidated.

In a recent application of the content neutrality principle, the Court held unconstitutional a Vermont law that prohibited pharmacies from selling or disclosing pharmacy records that revealed the prescribing practices of individual doctors and that prohibited the use of this information by pharmaceutical manufacturers. Since the law did not prohibit the disclosure of this kind of information to those who wished to engage in certain "educational communications," such as academic organizations for "use in countering the messages of brand-name pharmaceutical manufacturers and in promoting the prescription of generic drugs," the Court found that "[o]n its face the law enact[ed] content-and speaker-based restrictions, and so was unconstitutional."[390] In another recent decision, the Court held unconstitutional a federal law prohibiting any person from making a false statement that the person had been awarded a military medal. Four of the Justices based their decision on the ground that this was a content-based restriction that prohibited only a certain kind of false representation.[391]

3. Protection of Offensive Speech

232. Another important First Amendment principle is the principle of protection of offensive speech. Under this principle, the government cannot prohibit the expression

---

388. *See Young v. American Mini Theatres, Inc.*, 427 U.S. 50 (1976).

389. *Metromedia, Inc. v. City of San Diego*, 453 U.S. 490 (1981). And since, as we will *see* subsequently, the government may reserve public property that is not a "public forum" for its intended purposes, communicative or otherwise, it may impose category-type restrictions on access to such property that are appropriate to the purpose for which particular property is being used.

390. *Sorrell v. IMS Health, Inc.*, 562 U.S. 443 (2011).

391. *United States v. Alvarez*, 132 S.Ct. 2537 (2012). Two other Justices found that the law swept far too broadly by prohibiting all false representations, and so violated the narrow specificity principle. *See* para. 228, n. 373, *supra* .

of an idea on the ground that the idea itself or the manner in which the idea is expressed is highly offensive to many people.[392] Thus, any time the government tries to justify a restriction on expression on the grounds of the offensiveness of the expression, that justification is necessarily improper. A public university, for example, cannot constitutionally justify a ban on "racist speech" on the ground that it expresses a highly offensive idea or that it is very offensive to the "victim groups,"[393] nor can a city with a large Jewish population, including many Holocaust survivors, ban a march by self-styled "Nazis" with Nazi uniforms and swastikas.[394] The Court has recently held that the First Amendment protects the right of members of a Fundamentalist Church to picket on a public street near the site of a military funeral with the message that the death of American soldiers in combat is God's punishment for America's tolerance of homosexuality.[395]

B. Specific Doctrines

233. A number of specific First Amendment doctrines have emerged from the Supreme Court's decisions in First Amendment cases, reflecting the Court's efforts to balance the interest in freedom of expression against other societal interests. Some of these doctrines, such as the void on its face doctrine, are applicable to any regulation of expression, while others are designed to deal with the regulation of particular kinds of expression. Whenever a specific doctrine is applicable to a challenged regulation of expression, the application of that doctrine determines the constitutionality of the regulation. We will now discuss a number of these specific doctrines, and in V *infra*, we will discuss the specific doctrines that are applicable to expression that takes place on or seeks access to public property.

392. As the Supreme Court has stated: "If there is a bedrock principle underlying the First Amendment, it is that the government may not prohibit the expression of an idea simply because society itself finds the idea itself offensive or disagreeable." *Texas v. Johnson*, 491 U.S. 397, 414 (1989). In that case, where the Court held unconstitutional a state law prohibiting the burning of the American flag, the Court noted that there was no exception to this principle "even where our flag has been involved." *See also Cohen v. California*, 403 U.S. 15 (1971), where the Court applied this principle to the public display of a jacket containing an "unseemly expletive" ("fuck the draft"). The principle of protection of offensive speech also applies to commercial speech, so the government cannot prohibit product advertising, such as an advertisement for contraceptives, on the ground that such advertising would be offensive to many persons. *Bolger v. Youngs Drug Products Corp.*, 463 U.S. 60 (1983).

393. *See* e.g., *Doe v. University of Michigan*, 721 F.Supp. 852 (E.D. Mich. 1989). *See also R.A.V. v. City of St. Paul, Minnesota, supra* , para. 229, n. 379.

394. *See Collin v. Smith*, 578 F.2d 1197 (7th Cir.), *cert. denied*, 439 U.S. 916 (1978). In the same vein, the government cannot restrict expression on the ground that its offensiveness to the audience toward which it is directed creates a danger of violent reaction against the speaker from the hostile audience. In such circumstances, the police have a constitutionally imposed duty to protect the speaker from the hostile audience. *See* e.g., *Edwards v. South Carolina*, 372 U.S. 229 (1963); *Terminiello v. Chicago*, 337 U.S. 1 (1949).

395. *Snyder v. Phelps,* 562 U.S. 443 (2011).

1. The Void on Its Face Doctrine

234. The void on its face doctrine finds its source in the chilling effect concept. In order to prevent a chilling effect on expression resulting from the existence and threatened enforcement of overbroad and vague laws regulating or applicable to acts of expression, such laws may be challenged on their face for substantial overbreadth or vagueness without regard to whether the activity of the party challenging the law is itself constitutionally protected. The void on its face doctrine is very important in practice, not only because it permits a law to be invalidated on its face without regard to whether the activity of the party challenging the law is itself constitutionally protected,[396] but also because the constitutional analysis does not go beyond the terms of the law itself. Moreover, once a law is held void on its face, the law literally ceases to exist: it cannot be enforced against any person in any circumstance. In applying the void on its face doctrine, a court must look to the terms of the law and must determine whether the law includes or reasonably could be interpreted to include within its prohibitions a substantial amount of protected expression. The more sweeping the terms of the law, the more likely it is to include within its prohibitions protected expression, and so the more likely it is to be found to be void on its face.

Applying the void on its face doctrine, the Court has struck down, for example, a law imposing an absolute ban on peaceful picketing,[397] a law making it unlawful for a person to "in any manner oppose, molest, abuse or interrupt any policeman in the execution of his duty,"[398] a law forbidding the use of "opprobrious words or abusive language tending to cause a breach of the peace,"[399] a law forbidding individuals to "assemble on the sidewalk and conduct themselves in a manner annoying to persons passing by,"[400] a federal law banning "indecent" interstate commercial telephone messages,[401] and a federal law criminalizing the commercial creation, sale or possession of certain depictions of animal cruelty.[402] However, the void on its face doctrine will not be applied to invalidate a law unless there is a showing of substantial overbreadth.

---

396. In effect, all persons have a substantive First Amendment right, grounded in a concern for preventing a chilling effect on expression, not to be subject to sanction under a law that is "void on its face." Where a party is not subject to sanction under a challenged law, the party cannot assert a void on its face challenge on the ground that the law violates the First Amendment rights of third parties. *Los Angeles Police Department v. United Reporting Publishing Corp.*, 528 U.S. 32 (1999) (party who wanted to obtain governmental information for purposes not authorized by statute could not assert facial challenge to statutory requirements).
397. *See Thornhill v. Alabama*, 310 U.S. 88 (1940).
398. *City of Houston v. Hill*, 482 U.S. 451 (1987).
399. *Gooding v. Wilson*, 405 U.S. 518 (1972).
400. *Coates v. City of Cincinnati*, 402 U.S. 611 (1971).
401. *Sable Communications of California, Inc. v. Federal Communications Commission*, 492 U.S. 115 (1989).
402. *United States v. Stevens*, 559 U.S. 460 (2010).

The overbreadth must be "real and substantial in relation to the law's plainly legitimate sweep."[403]

2. The Prior Restraint Doctrine

235. Any effort by the government to obtain an injunction or otherwise to impose an advance prohibition against expression brings into play the prior restraint doctrine. Since a prior restraint directly interferes with the ability of the public to receive the information, it creates a "freezing effect" on expression. A prior restraint thus is presumptively unconstitutional, and requires a very heavy burden of justification on the part of the government. Applying the prior restraint doctrine, the Supreme Court has held that the United States government could not obtain an injunction against the publication of the "Pentagon Papers," a series of "secret" governmental documents detailing the events that led up to American military involvement in Vietnam, which had been illegally disclosed to the press by disaffected governmental officials.[404] The Court has also held that under the prior restraint doctrine, injunctions against the media, prohibiting the publication of facts connected with criminal prosecutions, and issued for the purpose of preventing "prejudicial publicity" against the accused, are generally unconstitutional.[405]

236. Any system of governmental licensing of expression analytically involves a prior restraint, and the Court has dealt with governmental licensing of expression by imposing specific requirements on any form of licensing. As a general proposition,

403. *Broadrick v. Oklahoma*, 413 U.S. 601 (1973). That case involved a challenge to a state law prohibiting partisan political activity on the part of state civil service employees. The Court upheld the law on the ground that partisan political activity on the part of state civil service employees could interfere with the impartial and efficient operation of the civil service, and emphasized that the ban on such activity did not interfere with the ability of civil service employees to express political views outside the context of a partisan political campaign. The civil service employees challenging the law, who had engaged in soliciting contributions from their subordinates, argued that the law could be interpreted as applying to activities such as wearing campaign buttons or placing campaign signs on the bumpers of their automobiles. The Court held that if the law ever were applied to such activities, it could be challenged as unconstitutional as applied to such activities, but that this possible overbreadth was not substantial in relation to the law's plainly legitimate sweep. *See also Virginia v. Hicks*, 539 U.S. 113 (2003), where the Court, in upholding a municipal law closing to public use streets adjacent to a municipal housing development for low-income residents in an effort to combat rampant crime and drug dealing there, rejected an overbreadth challenge to the law despite the possibility that it could be applied to bar a person seeking to come to the development for expressive purposes.

404. *New York Times v. United States* (The "Pentagon Papers" Case), 403 U.S. 713 (1971). The Court there refused to recognize a so-called national security exception to the prior restraint doctrine, and in the particular case, the United States could not sustain the heavy burden of justification required under the doctrine. The heavy burden of justification might be sustained in a case where the government sought an injunction against a publication that would disclose the names of CIA agents engaged in covert activities in foreign countries. *C.f. Haig v. Agee*, 453 U.S. 280 (1981), upholding against First Amendment challenge the revocation of the passport of an American citizen and former CIA employee who had announced his intention to "expose CIA officers and drive them out of the countries where they are operating."

405. *See Nebraska Press Association v. Stuart*, 427 U.S. 539 (1976).

any law licensing expression must be content neutral and must contain narrow, objective and definite standards that control the discretion of the licensing official. If the law fails to contain such standards, it is invalidated "on its face," and a party subject to the law is not required to apply for a license as a condition for challenging its constitutionality.[406] In addition, the First Amendment imposes procedural requirements on the operation of licensing systems, which are designed to ensure that expression will not be delayed or "chilled" due to the licensing requirement.[407]

3. The Clear and Present Danger Doctrine

237. As stated previously, the primary context in which the "Law of the First Amendment" developed for many years was in response to governmental repression of dissent and the expression of unpopular ideas. The Supreme Court very early promulgated the "clear and present danger" test as the basis for determining when the government could constitutionally prohibit advocacy of unlawful action, such as the violent overthrow of the government. While the Court's application of this test was not always consistent, especially during the early "cold war" period, when the Court applied the test rather loosely to sustain the constitutionality of laws directed against the Communist Party (which was widely believed in this country to be controlled by the then Soviet Union and to be a part of an international conspiracy directed toward bringing about violent revolution in the United States), the Court has now reformulated the test to provide strong constitutional protection to advocacy of unlawful action. Under the Court's current formulation of the clear and present danger test, advocacy of unlawful action is constitutionally protected "except where such advocacy is directed toward inciting imminent lawless action and is likely to incite or produce such action."[408]

---

406. For illustrative cases invalidating licensing laws on this basis, *see* : *Lovell v. City of Griffin*, 303 U.S. 444 (1938); *Staub v. City of Baxley*, 355 U.S. 313 (1958); *Hynes v. Mayor and Council of Borough of Oradell*, 425 U.S. 610 (1976). *See also Watchtower Bible & Tract Society of New York v. Village of Stratton*, 536 U.S. 150 (2002), where the Court held unconstitutional a municipal law that required individuals to obtain a permit prior to engaging in door-to-door advocacy, and to display on demand the permit containing the individual's name. The Court found that the law was not narrowly tailored to advancing the asserted interests in protecting the privacy of the residents and preventing fraud and crime.

The licensing of expression involving access to public property, such as that reflected in parade permit laws, will be discussed in V *infra* . As we will *see* , the constitutional requirements for such licensing laws are the same as those for laws licensing expression generally.

407. For example, as we will *see* in III *infra* , certain sexually explicit expression is deemed to constitute "obscenity," and is not entitled to First Amendment protection. If a state seeks to enjoin the publication of a work or the distribution of a film on the ground that it is "obscene," the state must initiate a judicial proceeding in which the alleged "obscenity" of the work or film will be expeditiously determined. It is only after the judicial determination of the "obscenity" of the work or film in an adversarial proceeding that an injunction can be issued against its publication or distribution. *See Freedman v. Maryland*, 380 U.S. 51 (1965). Likewise, laws requiring the licensing of charitable solicitors must provide that if the license is not issued within a specified brief period of time, the government will initiate a judicial proceeding to seek a determination that the applicant does not meet the constitutionally permissible licensing criteria. *See Riley v. National Federation of the Blind*, 487 U.S. 781 (1988).

408. *Brandenburg v. Ohio*, 395 U.S. 444 (1969).

This formulation effectively protects virtually any expression directed toward dissent and social change effort despite the government's claim that the expression advocates unlawful action.[409] The Court has also applied the clear and present danger test to efforts by judges to punish individual or media criticism as "contempt of court," and has found all such efforts to be unconstitutional.[410]

4. The New York Times Rule

238. The *New York Times* rule, promulgated in *New York Times Co. v. Sullivan*,[411] is derived from the "chilling effect" concept, and imposes stringent requirements in defamation and other "personal tort" actions brought by public officials and public figures. In order to avoid a "chilling effect" on the discussion of issues of public interest, the *New York Times* rule mandates there can be no recovery for false statements about public officials or public figures, unless the plaintiff can prove with "convincing clarity" that the statement was knowingly false, or was made with "reckless disregard" for its truth or falsity. The *New York Times* rule also applies to actions for invasion of privacy and for the infliction of emotional distress.[412] Moreover, it imposes certain limitations on defamation actions brought by private figure plaintiffs against newspapers when the newspaper has "publishe[d] speech of public concern." In such a case, the plaintiff must prove the falsity of the statements at issue,[413] and there can be no award of punitive damages unless the test of "knowing falsity or reckless disregard for truth" has been satisfied.[414]

5. The Commercial Speech Doctrine

239. The Supreme Court has held that purely commercial speech, that is, speech involving the exchange of goods or services for a profit, such as product advertising, as distinct from speech involving the production or exchange of ideas, is protected by the First Amendment, and the Court has promulgated the commercial speech doctrine to determine the constitutional permissibility of governmental regulation of commercial speech. The application of the commercial speech doctrine, referred to as the *Central*

409. *See* e.g., *Hess v. Indiana*, 414 U.S. 105 (1973), where the Court found that threats of violence made by university students during an anti-war demonstration did not reach the point of "likely to incite or produce imminent lawless action."

410. The Court has said that the criticism must be of such a nature as to present an extremely high danger of an actual obstruction of the administration of justice, and has never found this rigorous test to be satisfied. *See* e.g., *Pennekamp v. Florida*, 328 U.S. 331 (1946); *Wood v. Georgia*, 370 U.S. 375 (1962).

411. 376 U.S. 254 (1964).

412. *See Time, Inc. v. Hill*, 385 U.S. 374 (1967); *Hustler Magazine v. Falwell*, 485 U.S. 46 (1988). In *Bartnicki v. Vopper*, 532 U.S. 514 (2001), the Court held that the federal wiretap law, prohibiting the illegal interception of telephone communications, could not constitutionally be applied to impose liability against a newspaper for broadcasting an illegally intercepted communication concerning a matter of public interest, notwithstanding that the newspaper had reason to know that the communication had been illegally intercepted.

413. *See Philadelphia Newspapers, Inc. v. Hepps*, 475 U.S. 767 (1986).

414. *See Gertz v. Robert Welch, Inc.*, 418 U.S. 323 (1974).

Hudson test,[415] requires a four-part analysis. First, the commercial speech must concern lawful activity and must not be misleading.[416] Assuming that the commercial speech in question meets this requirement, three factors must be evaluated to determine the constitutionality of the particular regulation of commercial speech: (1) the governmental interest asserted to justify the regulation must be substantial; (2) the regulation must directly advance the asserted governmental interest; (3) the regulation may not be more extensive than is necessary to serve that interest.

240. Applying the commercial speech doctrine, the Court has invalidated a number of restrictions on commercial speech, such as bans on advertising by lawyers and other professionals,[417] bans on promotional advertising by regulated public utilities,[418] bans on advertising contraceptives,[419] bans on placing "for sale" signs on the lawns of private homes,[420] bans on display of alcoholic content of beverages on product label,[421] bans on advertising the retail price of alcoholic beverages,[422] location prohibitions and point-of-sale restrictions on tobacco advertising directed at children,[423] and a provision of federal regulation that exempted certain drugs from standard federal agency approval requirements, on condition that the providers refrain from advertising or promoting

415. *Central Hudson Gas & Electric Corp. v. Public Service Commission,* 447 U.S. 557 (1980). The "no more extensive than is necessary" element incorporates the narrow specificity principle into the commercial speech doctrine.

416. An advertisement for illegal activity constitutes an unprotected "verbal act." *See* the discussion, paras. 255–256, *infra* . And under this element of the commercial speech doctrine, the First Amendment does not preclude governmental regulation of false or misleading advertising.

417. *See Virginia State Board of Pharmacy v. Virginia Citizens Consumer Council,* 425 U.S. 748 (1976) (ban on pharmacists' advertising prices of prescription drugs); *Bates v. State Bar of Arizona,* 433 U.S. 350 (1977) (absolute ban on lawyer advertising); *Edenfield v. Fane,* 507 U.S. 761 (1993) (ban on certified public accountants' direct in-person solicitation of prospective business clients).

418. *Central Hudson Gas & Electric Corp. v. Public Service Commission, supra* , para. 222, n. 364 and para. 239, n. 415.

419. *See Bolger v. Youngs Drug Products Corp., supra* , para. 232, n. 392. The government's attempt to justify the ban on the ground that such advertising would be offensive to many persons ran afoul of the principle of protection of offensive speech. *Ibid.*

420. *Linmark Associates, Inc. v. Willingboro Twp.,* 431 U.S. 85 (1977).

421. *Rubin v. Coors Brewing Co.,* 514 U.S. 476 (1995).

422. *44 Liquormart, Inc. v. Rhode Island,* 517 U.S. 484 (1996).

423. *Lorillard Tobacco Co. v. Reilly,* 533 U.S. 525 (2001). The state law prohibited any outdoor advertising of tobacco products that was directed toward or visible in any location within a 1,000 foot radius of any public playground, playground area in a public park, elementary school or secondary school, and also regulated advertising in retail stores selling tobacco and located within a 1,000 foot radius of the above playgrounds and schools by requiring that point-of-sale advertising be placed at least five feet above the floor. The Court had held that the law was preempted with respect to cigarette advertising by federal law, *see* para. 162, *supra* , then considered whether the law violated the First Amendment as applied to the advertising of cigars and smokeless tobacco. Applying the commercial speech doctrine, a Court majority held that the prohibition of outdoor advertising was more restrictive than necessary to advance the state's interest in preventing underage tobacco use, and that the regulation of on-site advertising did not directly advance the asserted interest in preventing underage tobacco use and was more extensive than necessary to advance this interest.

these drugs.[424] Although lawyer advertising is generally protected, the state may prohibit lawyers from engaging in direct-in-person solicitation of prospective clients for remunerative employment, although not for the purpose of litigating "public interest" issues without any compensation to the lawyer.[425] The justification for the ban on a lawyer's in-person solicitation of prospective clients for remunerative employment is that it is a necessary prophylactic rule because of the inherent danger of overreaching in direct solicitation by lawyers. This danger is not present where a lawyer is soliciting clients to litigate public interest issues, usually on behalf of a "public interest" organization, or where a certified public accounting is soliciting business clients for accounting services. The state may also prohibit targeted direct-mail solicitations by personal injury lawyers to accident victims and their relatives for thirty days following an accident.[426]

However, in some cases, the Court, emphasizing that commercial speech does not receive as much protection as noncommercial speech, has upheld the challenged regulation under the *Central Hudson* test. These have included a ban on commercial billboards, in order to advance governmental interests in aesthetics and traffic safety,[427] and a public university's ban on sales presentations in student residences.[428] The Court has also held that at least in some circumstances the government may limit advertising about the availability of activities that are illegal in some states, such as lotteries or

424. *Thompson v. Western States Medical Center*, 535 U.S. 357 (2002). Again, the Court found that the regulation was more extensive than necessary to advance the state's asserted interest in preventing large-scale manufacturing of drugs that had been exempted from the standard drug approval requirements. In *Sorrell v. IMS Health, Inc.* 562 U.S. 443 (2011), the Court, after holding that a Vermont law prohibiting pharmacies from selling or disclosing pharmacy records that revealed the prescribing practices of individual doctors was unconstitutional, addressed the state's argument that a lesser standard of scrutiny should apply, because the speech at issue was commercial speech, and concluded that the law was unconstitutional under the commercial speech doctrine, because the state could not have a substantial interest in suppressing a disfavored message.

425. *Ohralik v. Ohio State Bar Association*, 436 U.S. 447 (1978); In re Primus, 436 U.S. 412 (1978).

426. *Florida Bar v. Went-for-It*, 515 U.S. 618 (1995). But the state may not otherwise prohibit lawyer advertising containing truthful information. *See Ibanez v. Florida Department of Business and Professional Regulation*, 512 U.S. 136 (1994) (lawyer's references in advertising to her credentials as an accountant and certified financial planner); *Peel v. Attorney Registration and Disciplinary Commission*, 496 U.S. 91 (1990) (reference on letterhead to prestigious certification).

427. *Metromedia, Inc. v. City of San Diego*, 453 U.S. 490 (1981). In that case, the Court also recognized an exception to the category neutrality aspect of the principle of content neutrality, holding that the government could exempt some commercial billboards from the regulation, although it could not constitutionally exempt some noncommercial billboards from the regulation. *See* the discussion in para. 230, *supra* . *Compare City of Cincinnati v. Discovery Network, Inc.*, 507 U.S. 410 (1993), where the Court held that where a city permitted newsracks containing newspapers to be placed on public sidewalks, it could not exclude newsracks containing advertising and promotional materials. The Court found that there was no valid basis for distinguishing between newsracks in terms of the content of the material contained in the newsrack.

428. *Board of Trustees v. Fox*, 492 U.S. 469 (1989).

casino gambling.[429] It has also been assumed that the First Amendment does not prevent the government from requiring that commercial advertising contain additional information, such as the "cigarette smoking is harmful to your health" warning that the federal government requires be carried on all cigarette advertising.[430]

Older cases, decided before the Court had promulgated the commercial speech doctrine, have upheld certain bans on commercial speech, such as bans on the distribution of advertising leaflets in the public streets, and bans on door-to-door solicitation, which the Court had held were unconstitutional as applied to noncommercial speech. Today, the constitutionality of such restrictions on commercial speech would be evaluated under the commercial speech doctrine, and they would not as readily be upheld.

6. The Symbolic Speech Doctrine

241. The constitutionality of governmental regulation of activity that combines "speech" and "nonspeech" elements is determined under the symbolic speech doctrine. Under this doctrine, a sufficiently important governmental interest in regulating the "non-speech" elements of the activity may justify "incidental" restrictions on expression.[431] In order to be sustained, the challenged regulation must satisfy four requirements: (1) the regulation must be within the constitutional power of the government; (2) the regulation must further a substantial governmental interest; (3) the governmental interest must be unrelated to the suppression of free expression;[432] (4) the "incidental" restriction on expression must be no greater than is essential to the furtherance of that interest.[433] Applying the symbolic speech doctrine, the Court has upheld a Congressional ban on the destruction of "draft registration" cards, which men subject to the military draft were required to carry in their possession,[434] but has held that a public high school

429. *See Federal Communications Commission v. Edge Broadcasting Co.*, 509 U.S. 418 (1993), where the Court upheld a federal law prohibiting the broadcasting of lottery advertisements in states where lotteries are illegal. However, in *Greater New Orleans Broadcasting Association, Inc. v. United States*, 527 U.S. 173 (1999), the Court held that the law was unconstitutional as applied to prohibit the broadcasting of advertisements for casino gambling in states where casino gambling was legal, notwithstanding that the broadcast signals could under certain conditions be heard in neighboring states where casino gambling was illegal.

430. The additional information advances the public information function of the First Amendment. And since advertisers must advertise, there is no concern that the requirement that the advertiser provide additional information will "chill" the advertising. In *Zauderer v. Office of Disciplinary Counsel*, 471 U.S. 626 (1985), the Court held that in order to prevent the advertisement from being misleading, the state could require that lawyers advertising their availability on a contingent fee basis, under which the lawyer receives no fee unless the suit is successful, must disclose in the advertisement that the client would be liable for court costs if the suit were unsuccessful.

431. The symbolic speech doctrine was first promulgated in *United States v. O'Brien*, 391 U.S. 367 (1968).

432. This requirement incorporates the viewpoint neutrality aspect of the content neutrality principle into the symbolic speech doctrine. In the flag burning cases (*Texas v. Johnson*, 491 U.S. 397 (1989); *United States v. Eichman*, 496 U.S. 310 (1990)) the Court found that the ban was directed to the "content of the message" conveyed by the burning. The ban thus violated the content neutrality principle and likewise failed the third requirement of the symbolic speech doctrine.

433. This element incorporates the principle of narrow specificity.

434. *O'Brien v. United States, supra*, n. 431.

could not constitutionally prohibit a student from wearing a black armband to school to protest the Vietnam War.[435] Although many cases involve "symbolic speech" in the sense that the activity in issue combines "speech" and "non-speech" elements, relatively few cases see the Court actually invoking the symbolic speech doctrine to resolve the constitutional issue presented in the particular case. It may be that in practice the Court is likely to invoke the symbolic speech doctrine only when the government specifically asserts an interest in regulating the "non-speech" element of the activity, as it did with respect to the destruction of "draft registration" cards.

C. *The Precedents*

242. Where the result in a First Amendment case is not controlled by the application of a principle or specific doctrine, it usually will depend on the Court's application of its precedents dealing with a particular kind of restriction or interference with freedom of expression. We will now discuss the application of the Court's precedents in a number of the more important areas of First Amendment activity.

1. Restrictions on Expression Relating to the Administration of Justice

243. The Court has generally rejected governmental efforts to justify restrictions on freedom of expression on the ground that they are necessary to promote the fair and efficient administration of justice or to protect the privacy interests of persons involved in legal proceedings. The Court has sometimes invoked the narrow specificity principle to find that the particular challenged restriction is broader than necessary to advance the asserted "fairness and efficiency" or "protection of privacy" interest. Other times, it has found the asserted governmental interest insufficient to justify the restriction on expression in the circumstances presented. In any event, the Court has held unconstitutional the following restrictions on expression relating to the administration of justice: an absolute ban on witnesses' disclosing their testimony before a grand jury after the grand jury's term has been completed,[436] a state law prohibiting the publishing or broadcasting of the name of a victim of a sexual offense, as applied to a newspaper that obtained the name from an inadvertently released police report;[437] a law prohibiting newspapers from publishing the name of a youth charged as a juvenile offender, as applied to information that the newspaper lawfully obtained from private sources;[438] a law prohibiting the publication of information in confidential legal proceedings, as applied to a nonparticipant who had lawfully obtained the information;[439] a law imposing liability for public dissemination of the name of a rape victim where the name had been obtained from public court documents;[440] an order prohibiting the press from publishing the name or picture of an 11-year-old boy accused of murder, when the reporter had been lawfully present at a public court hearing and had photographed the

435. *Tinker v. Des Moines School District*, 393 U.S. 503 (1969).
436. *Butterworth v. Smith*, 494 U.S. 624 (1990).
437. *Florida Star v. B.I.F.*, 491 U.S. 524 (1989).
438. *Smith v. Daily Mail Publishing Co.*, 443 U.S. 97 (1979).
439. *Landmark Communications, Inc. v. Virginia*, 435 U.S. 829 (1978).
440. *Cox Broadcasting Corp. v. Cohn*, 420 U.S. 469 (1975).

boy en route from the courthouse.[441] A court, however, can prohibit lawyers and parties from making public statements about pending legal proceedings where the statements could create a "substantial likelihood of material prejudice" in the case.[442]

2. Campaign Financing Regulation

244. The Court has held the expenditure of funds in support of political candidates and public issues involves freedom of expression for First Amendment purposes, so that the First Amendment imposes constraints on governmental campaign financing regulation. These constraints are the strongest whenever the government attempts to regulate political expenditures by individuals and nonprofit organizations. They are not as strong when the government attempts to regulate political contributions to candidates and political parties. The Court has upheld the provisions of the federal campaign financing law that limit the amount of money that can be contributed to a candidate but has held unconstitutional those provisions that limit the amount of money that a candidate could spend on his or her own behalf and the amount of money that an individual could spend independently in support of a candidate.[443]

The Court also held that limits on the amount that state candidates could spend on their own campaigns were unconstitutional. Conversely, the Court has held that Congress could not constitutionally increase the contribution limits for a candidate whose opponent had achieved a specified advantage in spending by virtue of the opponent's personal funds.[444] So, the Court has held unconstitutional a limitation on independent expenditures made by political parties.[445] However, the Court has also held that it is constitutionally permissible to limit the expenditures of a political party that were coordinated with the campaign of the party's candidate.[446]

In 2002, Congress enacted the Bipartisan Campaign Reform Act of 2002, which amended and supplemented the federal campaign financing law that had been in effect

---

441. *Oklahoma Publishing Co. v. District Court*, 430 U.S. 308 (1977).

442. *Gentile v. State Bar of Nevada*, 501 U.S. 1030 (1991).

443. *Buckley v. Valeo*, 424 U.S. 1 (1976). The Court has more recently reaffirmed the holding in this case that the government can constitutionally limit the amount of money that can be contributed to a candidate, and that it does not matter that the limits were lower in current dollar value than those upheld in Buckley. *Nixon v. Shrink Missouri Government PAC*, 528 U.S. 377 (2000). However, in *Randall v. Sorrell*, 548 U.S. 230 (2006), the Court held that very low limits on contributions imposed by a state law, here slightly more than 1/20th of the limit on contributions to federal office upheld in *Buckley*, and the lowest per election limit in the nation, were unconstitutional.

444. *Davis v. Federal Election Commission*, 554 U.S. 724 (2008) Similarly, the Court has held unconstitutional a state campaign financing scheme in which candidates who accepted public financing in exchange for foregoing private contributions were receiving matching funds virtually dollar for dollar when their opponents in conjunction with their independent supporters spent beyond the public financing cap. *Arizona Free Enterprise Clubs Freedom Club PAC v. Bennett*, 564 U.S. 721(2011).

445. *Colorado Republican Federal Campaign Committee v. Federal Election Committee*, 518 U.S. 604 (1996).

446. *Federal Election Commission v. Colorado Republican Campaign Committee*, 533 U.S. 431 (2001).

for the preceding thirty years.[447] Among other provisions, the law prohibited corporations and labor unions from making expenditures for any "electioneering communication" within sixty days before a general election or thirty days before a primary election, imposed limitations on so-called soft money contributions by corporations and labor unions to political parties, prohibited all contributions by persons under the age of 18, required disclosures by persons who expend more than USD 10,000 in any year for "electioneering communications," limited the source and amount of disbursements that are "coordinated" with a federal candidate or a national, state or local party committee, and severely restricted any national, state or local political party committee from soliciting, receiving or transferring "soft money" funds that are not subject to federal regulation, but that are subject to state regulation. When the constitutionality of this law came before the Supreme Court in *McConnell v. Federal Election Commission*,[448] the Court was sharply divided on the different constitutional issues presented by the law but a majority of the Justices ended up by holding that all the provisions, except for the ban on contributions by persons under 18 years of age, did not violate the First Amendment. The recurring theme in the different opinions upholding the constitutionality of these provisions was that the governmental interest in preventing actual or apparent corruption of federal candidates was sufficiently important to justify limits on political contributions and efforts to circumvent those limits, and on independent expenditures by corporations and labor unions.

However, in the more recent case of *Citizens United v. Federal Election Commission*,[449] a sharply divided Court held that the First Amendment protected the right of corporations and labor unions to use corporate and union funds to make *expenditures* on behalf of political candidates.[450] This being so, the Court overruled that part of the *McConnell* decision, upholding the ban on using corporate and union funds for any "electioneering communication" within sixty days before a general election or thirty days before a primary election. The effect of this part of *Citizens United* is that corporations or unions can use their general funds without restraint to make independent expenditures on behalf of political candidates. In *Citizens United*, the Court specifically upheld the disclosure and disclaimer and the noncoordination provisions of the Act as applied to corporations and labor unions, and did not question the constitutionality of the bans on the use of general funds to make direct contributions to candidates and political parties.[451] Under the present state of the law, therefore, the government can prohibit corporations and labor unions from using their general funds to make direct contributions, but cannot prohibit them from using their general funds to make independent expenditures on behalf of candidates and political parties, although

447. 2 U.S.C. secs. 431 et seq.
448. 540 U.S. 93 (2003).
449. 558 U.S. 310 (2010).
450. The Court had previously held unconstitutional a law prohibiting a non-profit corporation from expending its general funds in connection with an election for public office, *Federal Election Commission v. Massachusetts Citizens for Life*, 479 U.S. 238 (1986), and a law barring corporations from expending its general funds to influence a voter referendum on a proposed progressive income tax on corporations. *First National Bank of Boston v. Bellotti*, 435 U.S. 765 (1978).
451. In *Federal Election Commission v. Beaumont*, 539 U.S. 146 (2003).

it can apply disclosure and disclaimer and noncoordination requirements to those expenditures.[452]

The Court has also held in a very recent decision that the First Amendment imposes some limitations on the power of Congress to limit the contributions that an individual could make to political candidates. While the Court has upheld the constitutionality of the law limiting the amount of money that an individual could contribute to one political candidate, it has held unconstitutional a law limiting the aggregate amount that an individual to contribute to all the candidates during an election cycle. Again, the Court was divided in the same way as it was in *Citizens United*, but the Court majority concluded that there was no connection between the limit on aggregate amounts to all candidates and the asserted governmental interest in preventing corruption or the appearance of corruption. It took the position that since the interest in preventing corruption or the appearance of corruption was advanced by limiting the amount of money that an individual could contribute to one political candidate, the additional limit on aggregate contributions did not serve a compelling governmental interest and so violated the First Amendment.[453]

In many states judges, including appellate court judges are elected by the voters. The states have greater leeway in limiting judges from soliciting political contributions in order to prevent corruption or the appearance of corruption in the administration of justice. On this basis, the Court held that a state law that prohibited candidates in judicial elections from personally soliciting campaign funds advanced the compelling governmental interest in protecting the integrity of the judiciary and maintaining the public's confidence in an impartial judiciary, and so did not violate the First Amendment.[454]

3. "The Right to Refrain from Speaking"

245. The Court has held that the First Amendment protects the "right to refrain from speaking." There are two aspects to the First Amendment "right to refrain from speaking." First, the First Amendment generally prohibits the government from requiring disclosure of a person's beliefs or associations. For example, a governmental body investigating "subversion" cannot require witnesses to testify as to their past membership in allegedly "subversive" organizations,[455] nor can it require a civil rights organization to turn over its membership list to the committee.[456] A school board cannot require that teachers list all the organizations to which they belonged or had contributed money for the preceding five years,[457] and a state cannot require that applicants for admission

---

452. For the same reasons that it is unconstitutional for Congress to limit independent expenditures by corporations and labor unions, it is unconstitutional for Congress to impose a limit on contributions that an individual could make to an organization that itself made only independent expenditures on behalf of political candidates. *Speech Now.org. v. Federal Election Commission*, 599 F.3d 686 (D.C.Cir.2010).
453. *McCutheon v. Federal Election Commission*, 134 S.Ct. 1434 (2014).
454. *Williams-Yulee v. Florida Bar*, 135 S.Ct. 1656 (2015).
455. *DeGregory v. Attorney General of New Hampshire*, 383 U.S. 825 (1966).
456. *Gibson v. Florida Legislative Investigation Committee*, 372 U.S. 539 (1963).
457. *Shelton v. Tucker*, 364 U.S. 479 (1960).

to the practice of law disclose their political beliefs and organizational memberships.[458] The First Amendment does not prevent the government from requiring that political contributors report their contributions to or expenditures on behalf of a candidate, or that campaign committees disclose a list of their contributors.[459] However, the Court has held that a state law requiring political parties to report the names of their campaign contributors and recipients of campaign disbursements could not constitutionally be applied to a minor political party, where the party showed a "reasonable probability" that such disclosure would subject the contributors to "threats, harassment, or reprisals" from government officials or private parties.[460] Finally, the First Amendment generally prohibits the government from requiring that government employees take "loyalty oaths," except for an affirmative oath to support the constitutional system of government.[461]

246. Second, the "right to refrain from speaking" includes the "right not to be associated with particular ideas." This means that the government cannot force a person to express an idea with which that person disagrees, such as compelling public school children to participate in a salute to the American flag,[462] or compelling a person to display an automobile license plate containing an ideological message with which that person disagrees.[463] Likewise, the Court has held unconstitutional a directive of a state regulatory agency that a public utility included in its billing envelopes messages from

458. *Law Students Civil Rights Research Council, Inc. v. Wadmond*, 401 U.S. 154 (1971); *Baird v. State Bar of Arizona*, 401 U.S. 1 (1971). The state, however, can make inquiry into an applicant's "knowing membership in an illegal organization with intent to further the organization's illegal purpose" in order to determine the applicant's "character and fitness" to practice law.

459. *Buckley v. Valeo*, 424 U.S. 1 (1976).

460. *Brown v. Socialist Workers 74 Campaign Committee*, 459 U.S. 87 (1982). However, the public disclosure of petitions supporting a referendum on a state law, with the names and addresses of the signers, on its face, does not violate the First Amendment. *Doe v. Reed*, 561 U.S. 186. (2010).

461. *See Cole v. Richardson*, 405 U.S. 676 (1972), upholding an affirmative oath. Most loyalty oath requirements have been held to be unconstitutional because they were not limited to an affirmative oath. *See* e.g., *Keyishian v. Board of Regents of University of State of N.Y.*, 385 U.S. 589 (1967).

462. *West Virginia State Board of Education v. Barnette*, 319 U.S. 624 (1943). The "right to refrain from speaking" protects the ability of sponsors of a parade to exclude from the parade groups expressing ideas with which the sponsors disagree. *Hurley v. Irish-American Gay, Lesbian and Bisexual Group of Boston,* 515 U.S. 557 (1995). In that case, the Court held unconstitutional the application of a state public accommodations law that would have required a veterans group sponsoring a parade to permit a gay, lesbian and bisexual group to march in the parade.

463. *Wooley v. Maynard*, 430 U.S. 705 (1977). In that case, a Jehovah's Witness covered up that portion of the state-issued automobile license plate containing the state's motto, "Live Free or Die," which he contended was inconsistent with the Jehovah's Witnesses' beliefs in "eternal life."

a group that opposed the utility's position on utility rates.[464] The Court has also held that the "right not to be associated with particular ideas" is violated when a labor union uses fees imposed by law on nonunion members of the bargaining unit to advance ideological purposes unrelated to the union's function as collective bargaining representative.[465] The same is true when the state requires all lawyers to pay dues to the state bar association under what is called an "integrated bar" arrangement; objecting lawyers are entitled to a pro rata refund of that portion of the compulsory dues that are used by the bar association for ideological purposes.[466]

---

464. *Pacific Gas & Electric Co. v. Public Utilities Commission*, 475 U.S. 1 (1986). *Compare Pruneyard Shopping Center v. Robins*, 447 U.S. 74 (1980). There, under state law, a privately owned shopping center was compelled to allow expressive activities to take place in the central courtyard of the shopping center, such as the solicitation of signatures on a petition. The shopping center contended that the requirement violated its "right not to be associated with particular ideas," but the Court disagreed. The Court found that there was no danger that public would associate the shopping center with the expressive activity taking place in the courtyard, so that the requirement did not violate the shopping center's "right not to be associated with particular ideas."

465. *Abood v. Detroit Board of Education*, 431 U.S. 209 (1977).

466. *Keller v. State Bar of California*, 496 U.S. 1 (1990). However, the "right to refrain from speaking" is not violated by governmentally authorized assessments for generic advertising imposed on members of an association of agricultural producers. This is because the generic advertisements did not promote any particular message, but merely urged consumers to buy the agricultural products. *Glickman v. Wileman Brothers & Elliot, Inc.*, 521 U.S. 457 (1997). But it is violated by a mushroom marketing scheme under which a federally established Mushroom Council could impose mandatory assessments on handlers of fresh mushrooms for generic advertising to promote mushroom sales. Here the Court concluded that the assessment was not germane to a purpose of the association independent of the speech itself and so compelled support only for speech, thereby violating "the right to refrain from speaking." *United States Department of Agriculture v. United Foods, Inc.*, 533 U.S. 405 (2001). However the First Amendment is not violated by a university's use of a mandatory student activity fee to provide grants to student organizations on the basis of viewpoint neutral criteria. *Board of Regents of the University of Wisconsin System v. Southworth*, 529 U.S. 217 (2000).

In Rumsfeld v. Forum v. Academic and Institutional Rights, 547 U.S. 47 (2006), the Court upheld the constitutionality of a federal law that provided that if any part of a university denied military recruiters access equal to that afforded to other recruiters (as a number of law schools were doing in order to protest a rule barring openly gay and lesbian persons from serving in the military, the so-called don't ask, don't tell rule), the entire university would be deprived of federal funds. The Court held that the law did not require the university to support the policy, and that the university was free to oppose the policy, so long as the university did not deny access to military recruiters.

However, in *Agency for International Development v. Alliance for an Open Society,* 133 S.Ct. 2321 (2013), the Court held unconstitutional a provision in a federal funding law requiring that organizations receiving federal funding to combat AIDS and other diseases have an express policy opposing prostitution. Because the condition related to speech that was outside of the contours of the federal program itself, it was an unconstitutional condition and violated the First Amendment.

4. Governmental Broadcast, Cable and Internet Regulation

247. Governmental regulation of broadcasting in the United States has traditionally taken place in connection with the allocation of radio and television frequencies by the Federal Communications Commission. The Supreme Court has held that such regulation can proceed on the assumption of "public ownership of the airwaves," and that the Federal Communications Commission can require that broadcasters operate "in the public interest." This being so, the Court has upheld against First Amendment challenge the Federal Communication Commission's now-repealed "fairness doctrine," which required that broadcasters provide for a balanced presentation of viewpoints, allocate a reasonable percentage of broadcast time for the discussion of public issues, and in certain circumstances allow other persons to have access to broadcasting facilities in order to respond to positions taken by the broadcasters.[467] The Court has also held that Congress may constitutionally provide that candidates for federal office have a legally enforceable right to purchase a reasonable amount of broadcast time.[468] Finally, the Federal Communications Commission may impose certain limited restrictions on programming that might be objectionable to children during the time of the day when children are likely to be viewing or listening.[469] Nonetheless, the First Amendment does apply to governmental regulation of broadcasting, and certain broadcasting

467. *Red Lion Broadcasting Co. v. Federal Communications Commission*, 395 U.S. 367 (1969). The government's imposition of such a requirement on newspapers would be unconstitutional because of the chilling effect it could have on the newspapers' discussion of public issues. *See Miami Herald Publishing Co. v. Tornillo*, 418 U.S. 241 (1974). While the imposition of this requirement could have the same chilling effect on the discussion of public issues by broadcasters, the Court has held that this possible chilling effect was justified because of the "public interest" considerations that followed from the allocation of scarce radio and television frequencies to the broadcasters. In repealing the "fairness doctrine" in 1987, the Federal Communications Commission took the position that there had been a marked increase in the availability of information services to the public since *Red Lion*, most particularly, the advent of cable television, and that enforcement of the "fairness doctrine" was no longer in the public interest.

468. *CBS, Inc. v. Federal Communications Commission*, 453 U.S. 367 (1981). *Compare CBS, Inc. v. Democratic National Committee*, 412 U.S. 94 (1973). There the television network had refused to accept any public issue advertising. Parties seeking to purchase such advertising challenged the ban, and the Supreme Court held that there was no First Amendment requirement that the network accept such advertising. While the television network was not a "state actor" for constitutional purposes, the contention was that the First Amendment imposed the obligation on the Federal Communications Commission to make the airwaves open for such advertising. The contrary contention was that for the Federal Communications Commission to make the networks accept such advertising would itself violate the networks' First Amendment rights. While the Court's decision did not rest on the latter ground, it was a consideration in the Court's determination that the First Amendment did not impose the obligation on the Federal Communications Commission to require broadcasters to accept public issue advertising.

469. *See* e.g., *Federal Communications Commission v. Pacifica Foundation*, 438 U.S. 726 (1978). In *Federal Communications Commission v. Fox Television Stations, Inc.*, 132 Sup.Ct. 2307 (2012), the Court dealt with the constitutionality of a Federal Communications Commission rule prohibiting "fleeting expletives" or "partial nudity," but avoided the First Amendment question by finding that the policy was unconstitutionally vague as applied to the particular incidents with which the broadcaster was charged.

regulations may be found to violate the First Amendment, such as a complete ban on editorializing by public broadcasting stations that receive grants from the federal government.[470]

The advent of cable television and its regulation by the federal government and local municipalities has given rise to a number of First Amendment questions that cannot be fitted neatly into the doctrine that the Court has developed to deal with broadcast regulation. Conventional cablecasting involves placing cable wires under or on municipally owned streets and utility poles, and municipalities generally enter into a franchise agreement with a particular cable operator to serve the city, thereby giving that operator an effective monopoly on conventional cablecasting. These franchise agreements typically require the cable operator to reserve some channels for public, educational, and governmental access ("public access channels" or "pegs").

Congress was concerned about the monopolistic character of cablecasting in most municipalities, and in the Cable Television and Consumer Protection and Competition Act of 1992, Congress required cable operators to devote a portion of their channels to carrying the programs of local broadcasters. A sharply divided Court upheld the constitutionality of these "must carry" provisions.[471] Federal law generally prevents cable operators from exercising any editorial control over the content of leased access or public access channels. In the 1992 Act, however, Congress permitted cable operators to prohibit the broadcast of material that the cable operator "reasonably believes describes or depicts sexual or excretory activities or organs in a patently offensive manner" on leased access and public access channels. The Act further provided that if the cable operator did not prohibit such material from being broadcast on leased access channels, the cable operator was required to provide a separate channel for the material, to scramble or otherwise block its presentation, and to permit viewing only upon written request of the subscriber. Congress also imposed these "block and segregate" requirements for channels primarily dedicated to sexual programming and required cable operators to honor a subscriber's request to block any undesired programs. The Court, again sharply divided, upheld against First Amendment challenge the provision giving cable operators the authority to prohibit the broadcast of "patently offensive," material, but held unconstitutional all "block and segregate" requirements.[472]

---

470. *See Federal Communications Commission v. League of Women Voters*, 468 U.S. 364 (1984). Compare *Arkansas Educational Television Commission v. Forbes*, 523 U.S. 666 (1998), holding that a state-owned public television broadcaster sponsoring a candidate debate, could exclude from that debate an independent candidate having little popular support.

471. *Turner Broadcasting System, Inc. v. Federal Communications Commission*, 520 U.S. 180 (1997). The majority took the position that in this area, it was appropriate for the Court to defer to Congressional judgment so long as Congress "had drawn reasonable inferences based upon substantial evidence." The majority found that the legislation was narrowly tailored to preserve the benefits of local broadcast television, to promote widespread dissemination from a multiplicity of sources, and to promote fair competition. The dissenting Justices contended that the record in the case did not support the conclusion that cable television posed a significant threat to local broadcast markets or that the law was narrowly tailored to deal with anticompetitive conduct.

472. *Denver Area Educational Telecommunications Consortium, Inc. v. Federal Communications Commission*, 518 U.S. 727 (1996). The majority took the position that the "block and segregate" requirements did not "properly accommodate the speech restrictions they impose and the legitimate objective they seek to attain."

There is much concern in the United States today about protecting minors from harmful material on the Internet. In response to this concern, Congress enacted a law that prohibited the "transmission of indecent messages to any recipient under 18 years of age," and the "knowing sending or displaying of patently offensive messages in a manner that is available to a person under 18 years of age." The Court, this time with little dissent, invalidated both provisions as being too vague and overbroad to withstand First Amendment scrutiny.[473] However, the Court has held that when Congress provides assistance to public libraries for internet access, it can impose as a condition a requirement that libraries install filtering software that blocks access to visual depictions that constitute "obscenity or pornography" and visual depictions that are "harmful to minors." The law was held not to violate the First Amendment because it permitted the libraries to disable the filter at the request of an adult patron and to disable it for use by minors for "bona fide research or other lawful purposes."[474]

5. Expression in Special Environments

248. While the First Amendment clearly applies to expression that takes place in special environments, such as the public schools, prisons, and the military, the Court has recognized that the government has a legitimate interest in regulating expression in these environments precisely because of the special function that they are established to perform. Thus, the Court has been disposed to uphold restrictions on expression in the school environment that can be shown to be related to valid educational objectives, restrictions in the prison environment that can be shown to be related to prison discipline, and restrictions in the military environment that can be shown to be related to efficient military operation.

249. In the public school environment, the Court has held that a school may discipline a student for delivering a speech at a school assembly that contained a number of sexual innuendos, emphasizing the broad authority of school officials to prohibit "inappropriate" student speech at a school assembly.[475] In a similar vein, the Court has held that a school may discipline a student for displaying a banner at a school-sponsored event that was reasonably viewed as promoting illegal drug use.[476] The Court has also held that where the publication of a school newspaper was part of

473. *Reno v. American Civil Liberties Union*, 521 U.S. 844 (1997). A major problem with this kind of legislation is that it could suppress the dissemination of sexually oriented material to adults, since existing technology does not include any effective method for a sender to prevent minors from obtaining access to its internet communications without also denying access to adults. *See also United States v. Playboy Entertainment Group*, 529 U.S. 903 (2000), invalidating "blocking" restrictions on cable channels that were primarily transmitting sexually oriented programming. The Court emphasized that less restrictive means, such as the use of a technological solution that was available to parents who chose to implement it, were available to protect minors from exposure to sexually oriented materials. In *Ashcroft v. American Civil Liberties Union*, 542 U.S. 656 (2004), the Court indicated that efforts to regulate the internet dissemination of sexually oriented materials to minors would probably violate the First Amendment, since filtering software could be used to block such material at the receiving end.

474. *United States v. American Library Association, Inc.*, 539 U.S. 194 (2003).

475. *Bethel School District No. 403 v. Fraser*, 478 U.S. 675 (1986).

476. *Morse v. Frederick*, 549 U.S. 1263 (2007).

a regular course for which academic credit was given, the faculty advisor could exercise editorial control over the content of the student work that would be published in the newspaper.[477] However, the Court held that a public school could not, consistent with the First Amendment, prohibit a student from wearing a black armband to school to protest the Vietnam War.[478]

250. In the prison context, the Court has held that the First Amendment permits the prison authorities to exercise extensive control over prisoner correspondence and over the publications that the prisoners may receive from the outside. The test is whether the regulation is "reasonably related to legitimate penological interests," and applying this test, the Court has held that the prison authorities may exclude incoming publications found to be "detrimental to security, good order, or discipline of the institution," or that "might facilitate criminal activity."[479] The prison authorities have less discretion to regulate outgoing correspondence, which does not pose the same kind of danger to "prison security," and the Court has held unconstitutional prison regulations that prohibited outgoing correspondence which "unduly complained" of prison conditions or "expressed inflammatory views or beliefs."[480] However, precisely because prisoners may communicate with the media by mail, they cannot claim a First Amendment right to face-to-face interviews with the media in prison.[481]

251. The First Amendment rights of persons in military service are subject to the exigencies of efficient military operation, and can be severely restricted while the persons are on base or in military uniform.[482] The Court, for example, has upheld a military regulation prohibiting a serviceperson while on base or in uniform or in a foreign country, from soliciting signatures on a petition or from distributing material on base without authorization from the post commander. Permission could be denied if the commander determined that the solicitation or distribution would result in a "clear danger to the loyalty," discipline or morale of members of the Armed Forces, or material interference with the accomplishment of a military mission.[483] The Court

477. *Hazelwood School District v. Kuhlmeier*, 484 U.S. 260 (1988).

478. *Tinker v. Des Moines School District*, 393 U.S. 503 (1969). *See also Board of Education v. Pico*, 457 U.S. 853 (1982), where the Court indicated that the First Amendment may impose some limitations on the power of school authorities to remove "objectionable" books from a public school library.

479. *Thornburgh v. Abbott*, 490 U.S. 401 (1989). The Court has also upheld a regulation that in effect prohibited inmates from writing to nonrelative inmates at other institutions, *Turner v. Safley*, 482 U.S. 78 (1987), and a ban on the receipt of hardcover books (which could be used to smuggle in contraband) unless mailed directly from the publisher, a bookstore or a book club. *Bell v. Wolfish*, 441 U.S. 520 (1979). In addition, the Court has held that an inmate does not have a First Amendment right to provide legal assistance to fellow inmates. *Shaw v. Murphy*, 532 U.S. 223 (2001).

480. *Procunier v. Martinez*, 416 U.S. 396 (1974).

481. *Pell v. Procunier*, 417 U.S. 817 (1974). As we will *see* in para. 264, *infra* , the denial of face-to-face interviews with prisoners does not violate the media's First Amendment rights.

482. As we will *see* in para. 284, *infra* , the military also has broad discretion to deny non-service persons access to military bases for purposes of expression.

483. *Brown v. Glines*, 444 U.S. 348 (1980).

has also held that the military may constitutionally punish as "conduct unbecoming an officer" an officer's urging black soldiers to refuse orders to serve in Vietnam.[484]

6. Government Employment and Contracting

252. The Supreme Court has held that the First Amendment applies to actions taken by the government in its capacity as employer and contractor. The general principle in determining the First Amendment rights of government employees and contractors is that there must be a balance between the interest of the employee or contractor as a citizen in commenting on matter of public concern and the interest of the government in promoting the efficiency of the public services it performs through its employers and contractors.[485] Applying this principle, the Court has held that a school board violated the First Amendment rights of a teacher by terminating the teacher for sending a letter to a newspaper that was critical of the way that the school had handled past proposals to raise new revenues for the schools;[486] that a government agency violated the First Amendment rights of a lower level employee by terminating that employee for expressing to another employee, in private conversation, the hope that the President would be assassinated;[487] and that a county violated the First Amendment rights of a contractor by preventing the renewal of the contractor's trash hauling contract with the county because of his criticism of the county board of commissioners.[488]

On the other hand, when an employee took what the governmental employer considered to be inappropriate action to protest a personal office grievance, her discharge for doing so did not violate her First Amendment rights.[489] The First Amendment also does not protect statements made by public employees in the course of their official duties.[490]

The government does not violate the First Amendment rights of civil service employees by prohibiting them from engaging in partisan political activity.[491] The other side of the coin, so to speak, is that even in the absence of a civil service, state

---

484. *Parker v. Levy*, 417 U.S. 733 (1974).

485. *Connick v. Myers*, 461 U.S. 138, 140 (1983); *Pickering v. Board of Education*, 391 U.S. 563, 568 (1968).

486. *Pickering v. Board of Education, supra,* n. 485. A community college violated the First Amendment rights of an employee when it fired the employee after he investigated a state legislator who was employed by the college, and testified as a witness in two prosecutions that the federal government initiated against the legislator, claiming that she committed mail fraud and theft with respect to a program receiving federal funds. *Lane v. Franks*, 134 S.Ct. 2369 (2014).

487. *Rankin v. McPherson,* 483 U.S. 378 (1987).

488. *Board of County Commissioners, Wabaunsee County, Kansas v. Umbehr,* 518 U.S. 668 (1996).

489. *Connick v. Myers, supra.* In order to come within the protection of the First Amendment, the employee must be speaking on a matter of public concern and not simply airing a personal grievance. *Pickering v. Board of Education, supra* ; *Borough of Duryea v. Guarnieri* 564 U.S. 379 (2011).

490. *Garcetti v. Ceballos*, 547 U.S. 410 (2006).

491. *See United States Civil Service Commission v. National Association of Letter Carriers,* 1. U.S. 548 (1973).

and local governments cannot deny governmental employment on the basis of political party membership.[492]

III. Permissible Restrictions on Expression

253. From a structural standpoint, permissible restrictions on expression may be analyzed in terms of the following categories:

(1) unprotected "verbal acts;"
(2) "obscenity" and child pornography;
(3) restrictions that are permissible under the application of specific doctrines and precedent;
(4) restrictions relating to government-controlled information and expression that takes place on or seeks access to public property;
(5) other restrictions that have been sustained under a residually applicable "balancing" approach.

254. In Part II we discussed the application of a number of specific First Amendment doctrines and precedents. This discussion demonstrated that while the application of these specific doctrines and precedents has frequently resulted in the invalidation of the challenged law or governmental action as violative of the First Amendment, some laws and governmental actions, however, have been sustained against First Amendment challenge.[493] In Parts IV and V *infra*, we will see that certain restrictions relating to government-controlled information and to expression that takes place on or seeks access to public property likewise have been sustained against First Amendment challenge.

255. In this section, our focus will be on the other permissible restrictions on expression. We will first discuss two permissible restrictions on expression that are premised on the fact that the particular expression in issue does not constitute freedom of expression for First Amendment purposes: (A) unprotected "verbal acts," and (B) "obscenity" and child pornography. We will then discuss some restrictions on expression that have been upheld under a residually applicable "balancing" approach.

A. Unprotected "Verbal Acts"

256. Not all activity that somehow involves speech or writing constitutes freedom of expression for First Amendment purposes. The fact that certain crimes such as perjury, bribery or illegal solicitation are carried out by means of words does not make them any less "criminal," and the punishment of these crimes is in no way constrained by the First Amendment. As the Supreme Court has stated: "[i]t has never been deemed an abridgment of freedom of speech or press to make a course of conduct illegal merely because the conduct was in part initiated, evidenced or carried out by means of

492. *See Elrod v. Burns*, 427 U.S. 347 (1976), and the discussion, *infra* , para. 288.
493. We also saw that laws and governmental action are more likely to be sustained against First Amendment challenge under some specific doctrines and precedents than under others.

language."[494] In other words, conduct that the government may otherwise make unlawful does not cease to be unlawful merely because it is carried out by means of speech or writing. We will use the term "verbal acts" to refer to such conduct.

257. In addition to crimes, such as perjury, bribery and illegal solicitation, unprotected "verbal acts" include acts of discrimination that are carried out by means of speech or writing, such as a newspaper's carrying sex-designated "help-wanted" advertisements,[495] or an employer's sexual harassment of an employee by threatening to discharge her if she does not submit to his sexual advances. Again, what is being prohibited here is an act of discrimination, and it is irrelevant for constitutional purposes how the act of discrimination is being carried out.[496] The Court has also held that "fighting words" addressed by one person to another are not protected by the First Amendment, because they are "likely to provoke the average person to retaliation and thereby cause a breach of the peace."[497] Another example of an unprotected "verbal act" is the classic "false cry of fire in a crowded theater." The "false cry of fire in a crowded theater" is not protected expression for First Amendment purposes because the speaker is not trying to convey an idea. Instead, the speaker is trying to induce panic as an automatic response to the statement, and the government may constitutionally prohibit a person from trying to induce panic in this manner.[498]

258. However, the concept of unlawful "verbal act" may be applied only to activity that is otherwise unlawful and does not involve the expression of an idea or the discussion of matters of public interest. The government may not avoid the

494. *Giboney v. Empire Storage & Ice Co.*, 336 U.S. 490, 502 (1949).

495. *See Pittsburgh Press Co. v. Pittsburgh Commission on Human Relations*, 413 U.S. 376 (1973). This principle is incorporated into the "concerns lawful activity" element of the commercial speech doctrine. A newspaper's carrying sex-designated help-wanted advertisements itself amounts to an act of sex discrimination, and so is not protected by the First Amendment. Likewise, an advertisement for an illegal activity is not protected expression for First Amendment purposes.

496. *See also Wisconsin v. Mitchell*, 508 U.S. 476 (1993), holding that the First Amendment does not preclude a state from imposing additional punishment for an assault that was racially motivated. The basis for the imposition of additional punishment is not the actor's beliefs, but the actor's discriminatory conduct taken pursuant to those beliefs.

497. *Chaplinsky v. New Hampshire*, 315 U.S. 568, 574 (1942). "Fighting words" for these purposes appear to be limited to one-to-one insults uttered in such circumstances as to amount to an invitation to a fight. The Court has resisted any effort to expand the notion of "fighting words" to include highly offensive speech designed to cause emotional distress to the recipient. It has also held that the content neutrality principle applies to any governmental prohibition of "fighting words," and so has held unconstitutional a law that prohibited only "fighting words" that expressed a message of "racial hatred." *R.A.V. v. City of St. Paul*, Minnesota, 505 U.S. 377 (1992).

498. Contrast the situation where there is in fact a fire in a multistoried building, and someone says: "Ignore the 'In case of fire, don't take the elevator, take the stairs' signs. Let's take the elevator, or we'll all be burned to death." Here the speaker is expressing an idea. The speaker is invoking the listener's cognition and is trying to persuade the listener to take certain action. The idea that the speaker is expressing may be an unsound idea, but, unlike the "false cry of fue in a crowded theater," it is an idea and not a "verbal act." Thus, it involves freedom of expression for First Amendment purposes, and any governmental effort to sanction it must be justified under the "Law of the First Amendment."

constraints of the First Amendment simply by making the expression of a particular idea or the discussion of particular matters of public interest "unlawful" because of the purported harm that such expression or discussion is deemed to cause to individuals or to the public at large. For example, material contained in a book or newspaper article may injure a person's reputation or privacy or may cause a person to suffer emotional distress, and the government may seek to redress that injury by the imposition of tort liability, such as in an action for defamation, invasion of privacy or the intentional infliction of emotional distress. But the injury that the government seeks to redress by the imposition of tort liability has resulted from the expression of an idea or the discussion of matters of public interest. This being so, the concept of unlawful "verbal act" cannot be invoked to take the purportedly harmful expression out of the protection of the First Amendment, and the government's imposition of tort liability for the harm caused by the expression must be justified under the "Law of the First Amendment."[499]

B. Obscenity and Child Pornography

259. Pornography, in the sense of the depiction or description of sexual activity in books, magazines, motion pictures and the like, is fully protected by the First Amendment, and the government cannot prohibit pornographic expression on the ground that it is considered to be "immoral" or "degrading to women." However, the Supreme Court has carved out an "obscenity" exception to the constitutional protection otherwise afforded to pornographic expression. In an unusual "historical context" interpretation of the First Amendment, the Court held that the Framers of the First Amendment did not intend to include "obscenity" within its protections, because they considered "obscenity" to be "utterly without redeeming social importance."[500] A work is "obscene" for First Amendment purposes if, taken as a whole: (1) the dominant theme of the work appeals to a "prurient" interest in sex;[501] (2) it is patently offensive

499. As we have seen, there are First Amendment limitations on actions for defamation, invasion of privacy and the infliction of emotional distress. *See* the discussion of the *New York Times* rule in para. 238, *supra* .

500. *Roth v. United States*, 354 U.S. 476, 484–85 (1957).

501. "Prurient" means a "shameful or morbid interest in nudity, sex or excretion."

to contemporary community standards relating to the description or depiction of sexual activity;[502] (3) it lacks serious literary, artistic, political or scientific value.[503]

260. The constitutional test for "obscenity" makes it clear that serious books and motion pictures describing and depicting sexual activity, even in a very graphic way, are fully protected by the First Amendment. "Obscenity" is limited to "hard core" books, motion pictures, and video cassettes that contain nothing more than graphic description or depiction of sexual activity and that are typically purveyed in "adult bookstores" and "adult theaters."[504] Nudity, of course, is not synonymous with "obscenity," and the fact that performers appear in the nude on stage or in motion pictures does not deprive the performance of First Amendment protection.[505]

---

502. Under this element, standards for "obscenity" may vary from one community to another. Material that may be "acceptable" in a large city, for example, may be "unacceptable" in a rural area.

503. *Miller v. California*, 413 U.S. 15 (1973). In the years between *Roth* and *Miller*, the Court had difficulty in agreeing on the precise test for "obscenity," although it usually found that the particular work was not "obscene." This difficulty was resolved in *Miller*.

"Anti-obscenity" laws must very precisely define the sexual activity that cannot be described or depicted, and any law that fails to do so or that goes beyond the Court's definition of "obscenity" in *Miller* will be found to be void on its face.

In the recent case of *Brown v. Entertainment Merchants Association*, 564 U.S. 786 (2011), the Court rejected the argument that "violent video games" should be added to the category of unprotected speech. It noted that the "obscenity" exception applied only to depictions of sexual conduct and did not permit the legislature to ban whatever it found to be "shocking." Thus, the Court held violative of the First Amendment, a state law prohibiting the sale of "violent video games" to minors.

504. In practice, there is relatively little enforcement of "anti-obscenity" laws. The focus instead has been on the containment of the "commercial sex" industry, such as by requiring "adult entertainment" establishments, massage parlors and the like either to concentrate in certain locations or conversely to be located at some distance from each other. As discussed earlier, para. 229, *supra* , the Court has recognized an exception to the category neutrality aspect of the content neutrality principle to hold that the government may enact zoning regulations specifically applicable to businesses purveying sexually explicit materials.

505. Nude dancing, even of the "striptease" variety, also involves freedom of expression for First Amendment purposes, since it conveys the idea of sexuality. However, the Court has upheld the constitutionality of a ban on totally nude dancing in "adult entertainment" establishments on the ground that the state may find that there are harmful "secondary effects" associated with totally nude dancing in this kind of establishment, such as a higher incidence of sexual assaults and prostitution. *Barnes v. Glen Theatre, Inc.*, 501 U.S. 560 (1991); *City of Erie v. Pap's A.M.*, 529 277 (2000). In *California v. LaRue*, 409 U.S. 109 (1972), the Court held that the Twenty-First Amendment, which gives the states plenary control over the regulation of alcoholic beverages, qualifies the First Amendment to the extent of permitting the states to ban nude dancing in establishments serving alcoholic beverages. In *44 Liquormart, Inc., v. Rhode Island*, para. 240, n. 422 *supra* , the Court appeared to reject the notion that the Twenty-First Amendment qualified the First Amendment. Since *LaRue* involved nude dancing in an adult entertainment establishment, the result in that case can be upheld and explained under the rationale of *Barnes*. And it may be that certain restrictions on First Amendment activity can be justified because of the state's interest in regulating alcoholic beverages. But as a general proposition, the Twenty-First Amendment should no longer be seen as qualifying the First Amendment.

261. Since "obscenity" is not protected by the First Amendment, the government may constitutionally prohibit the dissemination of "obscenity" to persons wishing to receive it,[506] and may obtain an injunction against such dissemination. However, in order to prevent a chilling effect on the dissemination of constitutionally protected pornography resulting from the government's efforts to suppress constitutionally unprotected "obscenity," the First Amendment requires that the government establish procedures that will minimize this possible chilling effect and ensure that there will be no actual suppression of constitutionally protected pornography. The most significant constitutionally required procedure is that there can be no advance prohibition of the dissemination of a work alleged to be "obscene" until there has been a judicial determination of "obscenity" in an adversary proceeding initiated by the government.[507]

262. The participation of children in the depiction of sexual activity, which is referred to as child pornography, is deemed to cause serious harm to the children. The government's interest in preventing such harm thus "constitutes a governmental objective of surpassing importance." For this reason, the Court has held that child pornography does not constitute freedom of expression for First Amendment purposes, and that the government may prohibit the dissemination of all child pornography without regard to whether the work itself is legally "obscene."[508] However, because the unprotected nature of child pornography is based on the harm it causes to children, the government may not constitutionally prohibit the depiction of children engaging in sexual activity that does not involve actual children, such as the use of adults who look like children, or virtual child pornography, involving the use of computer-generated images of children engaging in sexual activity.[509]

C. Permissible Restrictions on Expression under the "Balancing Approach"

263. In most of the First Amendment cases arising in practice, the result will depend on the Court's application of First Amendment principles, specific doctrines, and precedents. In the relatively few cases that are decided solely under the residually applicable "balancing approach," the Court is more likely to uphold the challenged law or governmental action.

264. Applying the residually applicable "balancing" approach, the Court has upheld against First Amendment challenge federal and state laws prohibiting partisan political activity on the part of federal and state civil service employees. The Court concluded that partisan political activity by civil service employees could interfere with the impartial and efficient operation of the civil service system, and emphasized that the ban on such activity did not interfere with the ability of civil service employees

---

506. *See* e.g., *Paris Adult Theatre v. Slaton*, 413 U.S. 49 (1973). The government may not, however, make it a criminal offense for an individual to read or view "obscenity" in the privacy of the individual's home. *Stanley v. Georgia*, 394 U.S. 557 (1969).

507. *See* e.g., *Kingsley Books v. Brown*, 354 U.S. 436 (1957); *Freedman v. Maryland*, 380 U.S. 51 (1965).

508. *New York v. Farber*, 458 U.S. 747 (1982).

509. *Ashcroft v. The Free Speech Coalition*, 535 U.S. 234 (2002).

to express political views outside the context of a partisan political campaign.[510] The Court has also held that the "fair use" provisions in the federal copyright law have struck the proper balance between the competing interests in the free communication of information and the protection of the author's creative work, and so has rejected First Amendment challenges to the enforcement of copyright infringement claims.[511] In another "balancing" case, the Court balanced a reporter's asserted need to maintain confidentiality of sources against the need of a governmental body investigating criminal conduct to obtain the information that the reporter had derived from a confidential source, and held that the balance would be struck against the reporter's First Amendment claim.[512]

IV. Access to Government-Controlled Information

A. Constitutional Access

265. As a general proposition, there is no First Amendment right of access to information possessed by the government or sources of information within the government's control.[513] Thus, as a constitutional matter, the government may refuse to release information within its control and may deny access to governmental facilities in which governmental functions and operations are taking place.[514] The Court has held, however, that the public does have a First Amendment right of access to criminal

510. *United States Civil Service Commission v. National Association of Letter Carriers*, 413 U.S. 548 (1973); *Broadrick v. Oklahoma*, 413 U.S. 601 (1973).
511. *See* e.g., *Harper & Row, Inc. v. Nation Enterprises*, 471 U.S. 539 (1985); *San Francisco Arts & Athletics, Inc v. United States Olympic Committee*, 483 U.S. 522 (1987). The alleged infringer can always assert that the use of the copyrighted work comes within the statutory "fair use" exception. In *Eldred v. Ashcroft*, 537 U.S. 186 (2003), the Court held that Congress' extension of existing and future copyrights did not violate the First Amendment. And in *Golan v. Holder*, 132 Sup.Ct. 873 (2012), the Court held that the First Amendment did not preclude Congress from granting protection to certain works of Berne Convention member countries that were protected in their country of origin, but lacked protection in the United States.
512. *Branzburg v. Hayes*, 408 U.S. 665 (1972). The Court also concluded that the requirement that the reporter testify and reveal information derived from confidential sources would not have a substantial chilling effect on the reporter's ability to make use of confidential sources. Likewise, the Court has held that the First Amendment does not prevent the government from imposing liability for damages on a newspaper that voluntarily violated a promise of confidentiality given by a reporter to a news source. *Cohen v. Cowles Media Co.*, 501 U.S. 663 (1991).
513. *See* the discussion in *Houchins v. KQED*, 438 U.S. 1, 9–12 (1978). Since the media has no greater First Amendment rights than are enjoyed by the public at large, the media likewise cannot claim a constitutional right of access to government-controlled information.
514. The cases establishing this proposition have involved unsuccessful efforts by the media to obtain face-to-face interviews with prison inmates and to challenge restrictions on media access to prisons. *See* e.g., *Pell v. Procunier*, 417 U.S. 817 (1974); *Houchins v. KQED*, 438 U.S. 1, 9–12 (1978).

trials.[515] This includes access to all stages of the criminal process, such as a preliminary hearing to determine whether the accused will be held over for trial.[516] Because of this constitutional right of access to criminal trials, any restriction on such access is subject to a strong burden of justification. Thus, the routine exclusion of the public from the courtroom during the testimony of the minor victim of a sexual offense is unconstitutional. Such exclusion would be permissible only upon a finding that the particular victim would be inhibited from testifying unless the public was excluded, and the making of a transcript of the victim's testimony immediately available to the public.[517]

B. The Freedom of Information Act

266. In 1976, Congress enacted the FOIA,[518] which provides very broad access to information within the control of the executive branch of the federal government. The basic concept of the Act, referred to as FOIA, is that all records of federal agencies and all information within their control must be available to the public unless specifically exempt from disclosure. Under FOIA, any person has a right to request any record held by a federal agency on proper identification and request to the appropriate agency, according to rules established by the agency. No reason need be given for an FOIA request, and unless the requested materials fall within one of FOIA's enumerated exceptions, the agency must make the records promptly available to the requester. If an agency refuses to furnish the requested records, the requester may file suit in federal court and obtain an injunction ordering the production of any agency records improperly withheld.[519] While in practice, the focus is on what information may be withheld, the Supreme Court has emphasized that disclosure, not secrecy, is the dominant objective of the FOIA.[520] Any member of the public can obtain any nonexempt information. Most states have enacted equivalents of FOIA, so that in the United States today, there is in practice broad access to government-controlled information, although the legal basis of that access is primarily statutory rather than constitutional.

In addition, FOIA requires federal agencies to publish in the official Federal Register information relating to agency procedures, and "substantive rules of general applicability adopted as authorized by law, and statements of general policy or interpretations of general applicability formulated and adopted by the agency." It also

---

515. *Richmond Newspapers, Inc. v. Virginia*, 448 U.S. 555 (1980). In finding this right of access, the Court relied on the historical evidence showing the openness of criminal trials in England and in the United States at the time the First Amendment was adopted. As the Court stated, a trial courtroom is a "public place where the people generally—and representatives of the media—have a right to be present, and where their presence historically has been thought to enhance the integrity and quality of what takes place." In that case, the Court held unconstitutional a state law allowing closure of the trial to the public upon the unopposed request of the defendant.

516. *Press-Enterprise Co. v. Superior Court*, 478 U.S. I (1986).

517. *See Globe Newspaper Co. v. Superior Court*, 457 U.S. 596 (1982). It is assumed that the court may exclude television cameras from the courtroom because of their potentially disruptive effect on the trial. However, permitting television cameras in the courtroom is not considered to violate the accused's fair trial rights. *Chandler v. Florida*, 449 U.S. 560 (1981).

518. 5 U.S.C. sec. 552.

519. *See Taylor v. Sturgell*, 553 U.S. 880 (2008).

520. *See Department of Air Force v. Rose*, 425 U.S. 352 (1976).

requires federal agencies to make available for public inspection and copying final opinions in cases adjudicated by the agency, statements of policy and adopted interpretations that are not published in the Federal Register, and administrative manuals and staff manuals that are applicable in the agency's dealings with the public, unless these manuals are promptly published and offered for sale. In certain circumstances, the failure of an agency to comply with the publication or public availability requirements of the FOIA will result in the invalidation of agency action. [521]

267. The FOIA contains nine exemptions to the information required to be disclosed to the public upon request, and most of the litigation under FOIA has involved the question of what information is exempt from disclosure. These exemptions are to be interpreted narrowly, and the government has the burden of proving that the requested document falls within one of these exemptions.[522] They are also discretionary, in the sense that the FOIA permits, but does not require, the agency to refuse to disclose a document covered by the exemption. The refusal of the FOIA to disclose information is subject to judicial review for an abuse of discretion under the Administrative Procedures Act, and it is in such a proceeding that questions of what information is exempt are determined.

268. We will briefly review the major categories of information that are exempt from disclosure under FOIA.

1. Classified Information

269. The FOIA exempts from disclosure national defense or foreign policy information properly classified pursuant to an executive order issued by or under the authority of the President. The current executive order exempts information pertaining to military plans, weapons or operations, information pertaining to the vulnerabilities or capabilities of national security systems, installations, plans or projects, information pertaining to foreign governments and foreign relations, information about scientific, technological or economic matters that relate to national security, information pertaining to programs for safeguarding nuclear materials or facilities, cryptology information, confidential source information, and other categories of national security information ordered classified by the President.

In reviewing an agency's claim of classified information exemption, a court must determine whether the classification of the requested document conforms to the procedural and substantive requirements of the executive order and may examine the requested document in camera to determine whether the claimed exemption is permissible.

521. *See* e.g., *Morton v. Ruiz*, 415 U.S. 199 (1974) (provisions in the Bureau of Indian Affairs manual establishing the eligibility of Indians for certain welfare programs invalidated because not published in the Federal Register).

522. In limited circumstances, an agency may also refuse to confirm, or deny the existence of certain information, such as that contained in records concerning an ongoing criminal investigation, that which would identify an informant, and that contained in classified records relating to foreign intelligence.

2. Internal Personnel Rules and Practices

270. The FOIA exempts from disclosure matters related solely to an agency's personnel rules and internal practices. This exemption applies, however, only to matters in which the public could not reasonably be expected to have an interest, and so does not include, for example, case summaries of hearings concerning honor code violations at a military academy,[523] nor does it include data and maps used to help store explosives at a naval base.[524]

3. Statutory Exemptions

271. The FOIA exempts from disclosure any information that is specifically exempted from disclosure by another statute, provided that the statute either unequivocally requires that the information be withheld or establishes particular criteria for withholding. Applying this standard, the Supreme Court has held that federal laws relating to the taking of the decennial census preclude the disclosure of any information furnished to the government during the census.[525] Lower courts have found certain information to be exempt from disclosure under a number of statutes, such as those governing the operations of the CIA and the Internal Revenue Service, and given the existence of a very large number of federal statutes, it should not be surprising that some of them will be interpreted as authorizing the withholding of certain information. Nonetheless, the agency resisting disclosure has the burden of showing specifically and clearly that the requested information has been exempted from disclosure under the particular statute, and in practice this showing can be made for only a limited number of statutes.

4. Business Information

272. The FOIA exempts from disclosure trade secrets and privileged or confidential commercial or financial information that has been obtained by the government from individuals or private entities. There is some dispute among the lower courts over the meaning of "trade secret" for these purposes, which has not yet been resolved by the Supreme Court. The term, "commercial or financial information," has been given its ordinary meaning. Information is "privileged" for these purposes if it is generally privileged from disclosure in legal proceedings, and it is "confidential" for these purposes if its disclosure is likely to impair the government's ability to obtain the necessary information in the future or cause substantial harm to the competitive position of the person or entity from whom the information was obtained. The existence of this exemption has given rise to what are called "reverse FOIA" actions, in which the person or private entity from whom the information has been obtained sues the government to restrain the disclosure of the information. The Supreme Court has held that "reverse FOIA" actions may be maintained for the purpose of determining whether the information is exempt from disclosure. However, since the agency has the discretion to disclose exempt information, the private party cannot prevent the agency from

---

523. *Department of Air Force v. Rose*, 425 U.S. 352 (1976).
524. *Milner v. Department of the Navy*, 562 U.S. 562 (2011).
525. *Baldridge v. Shapiro*, 455 U.S. 345 (1982).

disclosing the information if the agency chooses to do so, unless disclosure is otherwise prohibited by law.[526]

5. Interagency and Intra-agency Memoranda

273. Internal memoranda within an agency and communications between agencies are exempt from disclosure under FOIA if they would not be subject to disclosure to a private party engaged in litigation with the agency. The purpose of this exemption is to incorporate into FOIA the discovery privileges the government enjoys in litigation with private parties. These privileges include the "executive privilege," which protects from disclosure advice, recommendations and opinions that are a part of the governmental decision-making process. The "executive privilege" part of this exemption, however, only protects pre-decisional documents, so the National Labor Relations Board, for example, could not rely on "executive privilege" to refuse to disclose memoranda which explained its General Counsel's final decisions not to file unfair labor practices complaints.[527] An attorney's "work product" reflected in documents prepared by a government attorney in connection with or in anticipation of litigation is protected from disclosure under this exemption, since it would be protected from discovery in litigation. The same is true of confidential communications to a government attorney that would be protected from disclosure under the attorney-client privilege. There is also a qualified privilege to withhold confidential commercial information that is generated by the government itself in the process leading up to the award of a government contract.[528] However, the Supreme Court has held that presentence reports in criminal cases must be disclosed to the person who is the subject of the report.[529] Finally, any claim of privilege under this exemption is waived if the agency itself has disclosed the requested information to third parties or nonfederal agencies.

6. Personal Privacy

274. The FOIA exempts from disclosure personnel, medical and similar files the disclosure of which would constitute "a clearly unwarranted invasion of personal privacy." The application of this exemption requires a balancing between the individual's interest in shielding private affairs from unnecessary public scrutiny and the public's right of access to government information. The Supreme Court has held that under this exemption, Federal Bureau of Investigation "rap sheets" containing information

---

526. *See* generally *Chrysler Corp. v. Brown*, 441 U.S. 281 (1979).
527. *NLRB v. Sears, Roebuck & Co.*, 421 U.S. 132 (1975). Moreover, facts contained in pre-decisional documents generally must be disclosed. *See also Department of the Interior and Bureau of Indian Affairs v. Klamath Water Users Protective Association*, 532 U.S. 1 (2001), where the Court held that documents exchanged between the Bureau of Indian Affairs and Indian tribes relating to the tribes' water allocation planning effort were not inter-agency or intra-agency documents exempt from disclosure.
528. *See Federal Open Market Committee of Federal Reserve System v. Merrill*, 443 U.S. 340 (1979).
529. *Julian v. United States Department of Justice*, 486 U.S. 1 (1988).

about individuals suspected of committing crimes are exempt from disclosure.[530] Lower court cases interpreting this exemption have held that it exempted from disclosure matters such as the property location, identity of the lender, and loan amounts of home loans guaranteed by the federal government, marital status of governmental employees, and names and addresses of American citizens incarcerated in foreign prisons. In some cases, the requested material may be released after identifying details have been eliminated.[531]

7. Law Enforcement Records

275. As might be expected, the most extensive of the exemptions relates to law enforcement records. Records or information compiled for law enforcement purposes are exempt to the extent that the disclosure of such records: (1) could reasonably be expected to interfere with law enforcement proceedings; (2) would deprive a person of the right to a fair trial; (3) could reasonably be expected to constitute an unwarranted invasion of personal privacy; (4) could reasonably be expected to disclose the identity of a confidential source;[532] (5) would disclose techniques and procedures for law enforcement investigations or prosecutions; or (6) could reasonably be expected to endanger an individual's life or physical safety. The threshold test for the application of this exemption is whether the records have been "compiled for law enforcement purposes," and the Supreme Court has held that it is sufficient if the records are used for law enforcement purposes at a later time, although they were originally compiled for a different purpose.[533] When the exemption is invoked on the ground that disclosure could reasonably be expected to interfere with law enforcement proceedings, the government must demonstrate that the information relates to a pending or prospective case in court.[534] While there are numerous lower court cases involving this exemption, with the result generally turning on the particular facts, it is fair to say that the

---

530. *United States Department of Justice v. Reporters Committee for Freedom of Press*, 489 U.S. 749 (1989).

531. More recent Supreme Court cases applying this exemption are: *United States Department of State v. Ray*, 502 U.S. 164 (1991) (names and identifying information of Haitian nationals returned to Haiti after attempting illegal emigration were exempt from disclosure); *Department of Defense v. Federal Labor Relations Authority*, 510 U.S. 487 (1994) (home addresses of federal employees who were in bargaining units represented by labor unions were exempt from unions' request for disclosure). *National Archives and Records Administration v. Favish*, 541 U.S. 157 (2004) (privacy interest of family of President's deputy counsel who died of apparent suicide precluded disclosure of death scene photographs taken by police investigators). The Court has recently held that this exemption did not include corporations as well as individuals. *Federal Communications Commission v. AT&T, Inc.*, 562 U.S. 397 (2011).

532. Not all "sources" supplying information to the Federal Bureau of Investigation in the course of a criminal investigation are "confidential sources" for this purpose. A "source" is deemed "confidential" only if the "source" furnished the information with the understanding that the Bureau would not divulge the communication except to the extent that the Bureau thought was necessary for law enforcement purposes. *United States Department of Justice v. Landano*, 508 U.S. 165 (1993).

533. *John Doe Agency v. John Doe Corp.*, 493 U.S. 146 (1989).

534. *NLRB v. Robbins Tire & Rubber Co.*, 437 U.S. 214 (1978).

government's refusal to disclose the information under this exemption frequently stands a good chance of being sustained.[535]

The final exemption is for oil well information that oil companies must provide to the federal government in order to lease government-owned land for exploration.

276. The above discussion of FOIA is somewhat general and is designed to demonstrate that in the United States, FOIA and its state law counterparts are an effective vehicle for providing substantial access to government-controlled information. In practice, there is extensive litigation over the scope of FOIA, and a detailed discussion of the details of the operation of the FOIA is obviously beyond the scope of the present writing.[536]

V. Expression on Public Property

A. Introduction

277. The protections of the First Amendment apply to acts of expression that take place on or seek access to public property. However, precisely because public property is involved, the government may, consistent with the First Amendment, impose some restrictions on the expression that takes place on public property that would not be permissible in other contexts, and may in some circumstances limit access to public property for expressive purposes. The public forum doctrine and the doctrine of reasonable time, place and manner regulation interact with each other to determine the constitutional permissibility of governmental regulation of expression that takes place on or seeks access to public property.[537]

278. Under the public forum doctrine, the permissible scope of regulation or restriction of expression that takes place on or seeks access to public property depends on whether or not the public property in question constitutes a public forum. The public forum doctrine thus distinguishes between public property that is a public forum and all other public property that is capable of being used for expressive purposes. If the

---

535. Another exemption is provided for matters contained in reports prepared by or for the use of the federal agencies that regulate financial institutions, such as banks. This exemption is designed to protect the security and integrity of the regulated financial institutions and indeed of the banking system, on the theory that the disclosure of the information that the government collects about these institutions could cause harm to the banking system if indiscriminately disclosed.

536. A companion law, the Government in the Sunshine Act of 1976, 5 U.S.C. sec. 552b, requires most government agencies to open their meetings to the public. The exemptions to the public meetings requirement parallel most of the FOIA exemptions. Also exempted from the public meetings requirement are agency discussions that involve accusing a person of a crime or censuring a person, meetings that may result in the premature disclosure of certain information, and meetings involving the agency's participation in legal proceedings. Many states have also adopted "open meetings" acts with similar provisions.

537. The government may decide to use public property to convey its own message. When it does so, the government controls the message conveyed, and is not required to allow the property to be used to convey a different message. *See* e.g., *Pleasant Grove City v. Summum*, 555 U.S. 460 (2009) (permanent monuments in city park constituted government speech, and city could refuse to accept the offer of a private organization to donate a monument to the park).

public property constitutes a public forum, there must be universal access to that property for purposes of expression by all persons and groups, subject only to reasonable time, place and manner regulations. Universal access is not required with respect to public property that is not a public forum, and the permissibility of any restriction on access to or use of such property for expressive purposes is determined under a general "reasonableness" test. The government may "reserve the [property] for its intended purposes, communicative or otherwise, as long as the regulation on speech is reasonable and not an effort to suppress expression merely because public officials oppose the speaker's views."[538] This means that the government may constitutionally impose category-type restrictions on access to public property that does not constitute a public forum, so long as the particular category-type restriction is reasonably related to the purpose for which the property is being used.[539] However, the category neutrality aspect of the principle does apply to invalidate a category-type restriction that is not reasonably related to the purpose for which the property is being used. In *Chicago Police Department v. Mosley*,[540] a municipal law prohibited picketing within 150 feet of a school building while the school was in session. Such a restriction would be upheld as a reasonable time, place and manner regulation, even as applied to the sidewalk adjoining the school, which would constitute a public forum, and so clearly would be upheld as a reasonable restriction on access to the school grounds, which are not a public forum. However, the law contained an exception for "the peaceful picketing of any school involved in a labor dispute." This category distinction was not related to the purpose for which the property in question was being used—picketing in connection with a labor dispute would disrupt the functioning of the school in the same manner as any other picketing—so the law violated the category neutrality aspect of the content neutrality principle and was unconstitutional. The viewpoint neutrality aspect of the content neutrality principle applies fully to the non-public forum as well as to the public forum. This is the meaning of "[no] effort to suppress expression merely because public officials oppose the speaker's views' language" in the *Perry* case.[541]

279. We will see that under the Court's application of the reasonable time, place and manner regulation doctrine to the regulation of expression in the public forum, the focus is on the reasonableness of the regulation in relation to the nature of the expression and the particular property involved. We will also see that the Court had been very disposed to find that most time, place and manner regulations are "reasonable." This means that in practice there is not much difference between the Court's application of the general "reasonableness" test to determine the validity of a restriction imposed on expression in a "physically open" nonpublic forum, such as an airport terminal, and its application of the reasonable time, place and manner regulation doctrine to determine the validity of a restriction imposed on expression in a public forum.

---

538. *Perry Education Association v. Perry Local Educators Association*, 460 U.S. 37, 46 (1983).

539. Thus, in *Perry*, *supra* , n. 538, the Court held that a school district could limit access to the interschool mail system to the exclusive bargaining representative of its teachers. To this extent, the category neutrality aspect of the content neutrality principle does not apply unreservedly to access to public property that does not constitute a public forum.

540. 408 U.S. 92 (1972).

541. *Supra*, n. 538.

B. The Public Forum

280. The public streets and parks are traditional public forums, which, "have immemorially been held in trust for the use of the public and time out of mind, have been used for purposes of assembly, communicating thoughts between citizens, and discussing public questions."[542] Any other public property may be designated as a public forum by the government's opening it up for use by the public as a place for expressive activity.[543] Where the public property in question is either a traditional or designated public forum, the government cannot deny access to or prohibit expression on the property, but can only impose reasonable and content neutral regulations with respect to the time, place and manner in which expression may occur on the property. In order for a particular regulation to be sustained as a reasonable time, place and manner regulation, it must: (1) serve a significant governmental interest;[544] (2) leave open ample alternative channels of communication.

281. The application of the reasonable time, place and manner regulation doctrine may be illustrated by consideration of a case where the Supreme Court upheld a regulation requiring that the sale or distribution of merchandise, including written materials, at a state fair take place only from a booth on the fairground, and not on the fairground itself. Any person or group wishing to sell merchandise or materials could rent a booth on a first-come, first-served basis with the rental charge based on the size and location of the booth. In upholding the rule, the Court emphasized the state's interest in maintaining crowd movement within the relatively small area of the fairground, and noted that a fairground presented crowd control problems that were absent on a city street. The Court also emphasized that the rule did not prohibit any expression on the fairground other than that involving sale or distribution. Thus, the

542. *Hague v. Committee for Industrial Organization*, 307 U.S. 496, 515 (1939).

543. The designated public forum may be created for a limited purpose, such as for use by certain groups. *See* e.g., *Widmar v. Vincent*, 454 U.S. 263 (1981) (facilities of state university available for use by student groups); *Madison School District v. Wisconsin Employment Relations Commission*, 429 U.S. 167 (1976) (school board meetings open to public). Since the reasonable time, place and manner regulation doctrine applies to both traditional and designated public forums, the university's attempt to exclude a student group wishing to use the facilities for religious worship and discussion was held unconstitutional in *Widmar*, and in *Madison*, the school board could not constitutionally deny a nonunion teacher the opportunity to speak on pending labor negotiations at a school board meeting. The distinction between the different groups or persons seeking access to the public forum violates the content neutrality requirement. *See also Lamb's Chapel v. Center Moriches Union Free School District*, 508 U.S. 384 (1993), holding that where a school district permitted after-hours use of school facilities for "social, civic and recreational purposes" by private organizations, it could not prohibit such use of school facilities by a private organization seeking to show a religious film.

544. In this regard, *see Schneider v. Irvington*, 308 U.S. 147 (1939), where the Court held that a city's interest in preventing littering was not of sufficient importance to justify a ban on distributing leaflets on the public streets.

Court concluded the rule served a significant governmental interest while leaving open ample alternative channels of communication.[545]

282. As stated previously, the Court has been disposed to uphold most restrictions on expression in the public forum on the ground that can be brought within the ambit of the reasonable time, place and manner regulation doctrine. In some cases, the Court has given the challenged regulation a narrowing construction, so that it could be sustained as "reasonable." In this vein, the Court has upheld as a reasonable time, place and manner regulation a law prohibiting the congregation of persons within 500 feet of a foreign embassy "when the police reasonably believe that such congregation poses a threat to the security or peace of the embassy,"[546] a law prohibiting voter solicitation and the display or distribution of campaign materials within 100 feet of the voting place,[547] a ban on "focused picketing" in front of a person's home,[548] a rule of the federal park service prohibiting overnight sleeping in a small public park near the White House, as applied to prohibit "tenting" in connection with a demonstration intended to call attention to the plight of the homeless,[549] an "anti-noise" regulation prohibiting the making of "any noise or diversion on school grounds while school is in session which tends to disturb the peace or good order of such school session," as applied to a public sidewalk adjacent to the school,[550] and a municipal noise regulation requiring that musical performances in a bandshell in a public park make use of the sound system and sound technician provided by the city.[551] However, the Court has

---

545. *Heffron v. International Society for Krishna Consciousness, Inc.*, 452 U.S. 640 (1981). If the state had tried to advance the interest in maintaining crowd control by prohibiting any crowd mingling not involving sale or distribution, or had not provided the booths on a first-come, first served basis and at a reasonable cost, the rule would not have been found to be "reasonable," and so would be constitutionally invalid.

546. *Boos v. Barry*, 485 U.S. 312 (1988).

547. *Burson v. Freeman*, 504 U.S. 191 (1992).

548. *Frisby v. Schultz*, 487 U.S. 474 (1988). In that case, in response to picketing by antiabortion protestors in front of the home of a physician who performed abortions, a city enacted a law that by its terms prohibited "engag[ing] in picketing before or about the residence or dwelling of any individual." The Court gave the law a narrowing construction, so as to be limited to "focused picketing," directed at a particular residence. As narrowed, the law did not reach walking through residential neighborhoods or even walking a route in front of an entire block of houses. Thus, it would advance the asserted interest in promoting residential privacy without substantially interfering with the ability of the protestors to convey their message to the general public and even to the doctor who was target of their protest, and so could be upheld as a reasonable time, place and manner regulation.

In *Madsen v. Women's Health Center*, 512 U.S. 753 (1994), the Court held unconstitutional an injunction creating a 300 foot buffer zone around the homes of those who worked in an abortion clinic. The Court noted that the zone around the residence was much larger than the zone approved in *Frisby* and that a limitation on the time, duration of picketing, and the number of pickets outside a smaller zone would advance the asserted interest in protecting residential privacy.

549. *Clark v. Community for Creative Non-violence*, 468 U.S. 288 (1984).

550. *Grayned v. City of Rockford*, 408 U.S. 104 (1972).

551. *Ward v. Rock Against Racism*, 491 U.S. 781 (1989).

held unconstitutional a law prohibiting all displays and leafletting on a sidewalk in front of the Supreme Court building.[552]

283. There is no First Amendment requirement that the government permit concerted expression in the form of demonstrations or parades, to take place in a public forum, such as the public streets or parks. However, if the government chooses to permit concerted expression to take place in a public forum, as for example, by opening up the public streets for parades, the First Amendment comes into play and imposes significant limits on how the government can regulate access to a public forum for purposes of concerted expression. Most fundamental in this regard is the principle of content neutrality. The government cannot distinguish between different kinds of concerted expression based on the content of that expression. If, for example, the government sponsors or allows a private group to hold a parade celebrating a national holiday, it has thereby opened up the public streets for concerted expression, and it must allow other groups to use the public streets for other parades or demonstrations, such as one to protest government policy.

284. Any "parade permit" law, therefore, must be content neutral and must satisfy the requirements of a reasonable, time, place and manner regulation. The Supreme Court has emphasized that such a law must not give the governmental officials enforcing it any discretion to deny the permit based on the content of the expression, and so must contain "narrow, objective and definite standards," controlling the discretion of the licensing official.[553] If the "parade permit" law fails to contain such standards, it is invalidated "on its face," and a party seeking to hold a parade is not required to

552. *United States v. Grace*, 461 U.S. 171 (1983). *Compare Cox v. Louisiana*, 379 U.S. 559 (1965), where the Court upheld a ban against picketing "in or near a courthouse with the intent of interfering with, obstructing or impeding the administration of justice." *See also Schenck v. Pro-Choice Network of Western New York*, 519 U.S. 357 (1997), holding unconstitutional an injunction ordering antiabortion protestors to refrain from attempting to "counsel women entering abortion clinics who indicated that they did not wish to be counseled." In *Madsen v. Women's Health Center*, *supra* , the Court upheld a provision of an injunction establishing a buffer zone around abortion clinics, but held unconstitutional those provisions, prohibiting antiabortion protestors from making uninvited approaches and displaying "observable images" of aborted fetuses and the like. In *Hill v. Colorado*, 120 U.S. 2480 (2000), the Court upheld a state law prohibiting antiabortion protestors, within 100 feet of the abortion clinic, from coming within 8 feet of a person going to the clinic, without that person's consent, in an effort to persuade her against having an abortion. However, in *McCullen v. Coakley*, 134 Sup.Ct. 2518 (2014), the Court held unconstitutional a state law prohibiting antiabortion protestors, to knowingly stand on a public way or sidewalk within 35 feet of an entrance to an abortion clinic, because the zone impaired the protestors' ability to engage in "sidewalk counseling" and to distribute literature to arriving patients.

553. *See City of Lakewood v. Plain Dealer Publishing Co.*, 486 U.S. 750 (1988). In that case, the Court applied this principle to invalidate a municipal permit law regulating the placing of newsracks on public property. It was irrelevant in this regard that the city was not required to permit newsracks on public property at all, since the city had established a procedure for allowing some newsracks to be placed on public property.

apply for a permit in order to challenge the law's constitutionality.[554] The government may impose a reasonable licensing fee to cover the costs of the licensing system, but it may not charge "controversial" speakers for the costs of police protection.[555]

C. *The Nonpublic Forum*

285. In practice, it is fairly rare that public property will be found to have been designated as a public forum, so except for the traditional public forums of the public streets and parks, most public property constitutes a nonpublic forum for purposes of the public forum doctrine. This means, as stated previously, that the constitutional permissibility of any restrictions on access to or use of such public property for expressive purposes is determined under a general "reasonableness" test, which recognizes the government's entitlement to "reserve the property for its intended purposes, communicative or otherwise." Thus, the government may impose category-type restrictions on access to the nonpublic forum, so long as they are reasonably related to the purpose for which the property is being used. Applying this standard, the Court has held that a school district may limit access to the interschool mail system to the exclusive bargaining representative of its teachers,[556] that the military may exclude all partisan political activity from military bases,[557] and that the federal government may exclude legal defense and political advocacy groups from a charity drive aimed at federal employees and conducted in a federal workplace during working hours under governmental regulation.[558]

---

554. *See Shuttlesworth v. City of Birmingham*, 394 U.S. 147 (1969). As the above discussion indicates, the constitutional requirements for the licensing of expression involving access to public property are the same as those for the licensing of expression generally. *See* the discussion para. 236, *supra* . For an example of a permissible "parade permit" law, *see Thomas v. Chicago Park District*, 534 U.S. 316 (2002), upholding a municipal "parade permit" law requiring individuals to obtain a permit before conducting large scale events in public parks. The law contained neutral standards, a requirement that an application be processed within twenty-eight days, a provision for an explanation of the reasons for denial of the application, and provisions for administrative and judicial review.

555. *See Forsyth County, Georgia v. Nationalist Movement*, 505 U.S. 123 (1992). As discussed in II.A.3, *supra* , the First Amendment requires that the government protect the rights of controversial speakers against interference from a hostile crowd. *See* e.g., *Edwards v. South Carolina*, 372 U.S. 229 (1963).

556. *Perry Education Association v. Perry Local Educators Association*, 460 U.S. 37 (1983).

557. *Greer v. Spock*, 424 U.S. 828 (1976). The reasonableness of this category-type restriction relates to the fact that the United States has had a long tradition of a politically neutral military establishment. This being so, the military could properly exclude partisan political activity from the base, although it allowed other activity, such as charitable solicitation, to take place there. Note again, however, that the government must maintain strict viewpoint neutrality in regard to access to the nonpublic forum. If, for example, the military allowed the President to speak on a military base during a political campaign, it could not refuse to allow a speech by a candidate of the opposite party.

558. *Cornelius v. NAACP Legal Defense and Educational Fund, Inc.*, 473 U.S. 788 (1985). The Court found that the exclusion was reasonable because it advanced governmental interests in avoiding the appearance of political favoritism, in avoiding controversy, and in maximizing support of agencies that provide direct aid to the poor.

286. In addition to imposing category-type restrictions on access to certain kinds of public property, the government, in an effort to "reserve the property for its intended purposes," may prohibit any expressive activity that is "basically incompatible with the normal activity of a particular place at a particular time."[559] Under this test, except for permissible category-type restrictions on access, the government may not declare the nonpublic forum "off-limits" for expression, but may only impose reasonable restrictions related to preventing interference with the "normal activity of a particular place at a particular time." For example, the government could prohibit making a speech in the reading room of a public library, but could not prohibit a silent vigil where persons sat on the floor of the reading room to protest the library's policies.[560] Likewise, the government can prohibit a demonstration on the grounds of a school while the school is in session, but not after the school day has ended. The Court has also held that the government may prohibit the posting of signs on public property such as utility poles and lamp posts, in order to prevent "visual clutter,"[561] that the United States Postal Service may prohibit the deposit of unstamped materials in a Postal Service-approved letter box,[562] and that the military may generally prohibit protest activity at military bases.[563]

287. As a practical matter, where the nonpublic forum is "physically open," such as an airport terminal, the Court's application of the general "reasonableness" test does not appear to differ significantly from its application of the reasonable time, place and manner regulation doctrine to the public forum. So, although the Court has held that an airport terminal is not a public forum, it has held unconstitutional an absolute ban against "all First Amendment activity" at the terminal.[564] It has also held

559. *See Grayned v. City of Rockford*, 408 U.S. 104, 116–117 (1972).

560. *See Brown v. Louisiana*, 383 U.S. 131 (1965), where the Court held that the government could not prohibit a silent "sit-in" at a public library to protest its policy of racial segregation.

561. *Los Angeles City Council v. Taxpayers for Vincent*, 466 U.S. 789 (1984).

562. *United States Postal Service v. Council of Greenburgh Civic Associations*, 453 U.S. 114 (1981). The ban was on the deposit of unstamped mailable matter in a Postal Service-approved letterbox, and the purpose was to ensure that only material on which postage has been paid could be deposited in letterboxes.

563. *See United States v. Albertini*, 472 U.S. 675 (1985).

564. *Board of Airport Commissioners v. Jews for Jesus*, 482 U.S. 569 (1987).

unconstitutional a ban on the distribution of literature in an airport terminal, but has upheld a ban on the solicitation and receipt of funds in the terminal.[565]

288. As the above discussion indicates, the First Amendment applies to governmental efforts to restrict expression that takes place on or seeks to access to public property. The Court's application of the public forum doctrine and the reasonable time, place and manner regulation doctrine recognizes the government's legitimate interests in imposing some controls on such expression precisely because public property is involved, but at the same time extends significant protection to expression that takes place on or seeks access to public property.

VI. Freedom of Association

289. The freedom of association protected by the First Amendment focuses on the right of people to belong to groups and organizations and to engage in concerted organizational activity. As a general proposition, the government cannot impose sanctions on people because they belong to organizations, and this includes membership in organizations advocating illegal conduct.[566] Likewise, people generally cannot be denied or discriminated against with respect to governmental employment because of their membership in particular organizations. This principle has been extended to the denial of governmental employment on the basis of political party membership. Under traditional "political patronage" practices prevailing in many states and local governmental

---

565. *International Society for Krishna Consciousness, Inc. v. Lee*, 505 U.S. 672 (1992). In that case, four Justices took the position that the interior area of an airport terminal was a public forum for purposes of the public forum doctrine, and that neither the ban on distribution nor the ban on "solicitation and receipt of funds" could be sustained as a reasonable time, place and manner regulation. A fifth Justice, whose vote provided a majority on all the issues in the case, took the position that the interior area of an airport terminal did not constitute a public forum, and applying the general "reasonableness" test, concluded that the ban on distribution was not reasonable, but that the ban on "solicitation and receipt of funds" was. In a similar vein, in *United States v. Kokinda*, 497 U.S. 720 (1990), the Court upheld the Postal Service's ban on solicitation on postal premises, as applied to a sidewalk near the entrance of a postal building. Four Justices took the position that the postal sidewalk was not a public forum, and that the ban on solicitation could be sustained under the general "reasonableness" test. A fifth Justice took the position that the postal sidewalk was a public forum, but concluded that the ban on solicitation there could be sustained as a reasonable time, place and manner regulation.

566. In *Schware v. Board of Bar Examiners of State of N.M.*, 353 U.S. 232 (1957), the Court held that a state could not refuse to license a person as a lawyer because of the person's past membership in the Communist Party. And in *United States v. Robel*, 389 U.S. 258 (1967), the Court held that the federal government could not deny employment in defense facilities to members of designated "communist action" groups, at least in the absence of a showing that the individual was a member of a "subversive" organization, with knowledge of the organization's illegal purpose and a specific intent to further that illegal purpose. However, in the recent case of *Holder v. Humanitarian Law Project*, 561 U.S. 1 (2010), the Court held that a federal law making it a crime to knowingly provide material support or resources to a "foreign terrorist organization" prohibited a group from providing educational programs designed to persuade such an organization to pursue its aims through peaceful means, and that such prohibition did not violate the group's freedom of association.

units, all governmental employment was dependent on political party membership. If the Democratic Party was in power in a particular state or locality, for example, only members of the Democratic Party could obtain governmental employment. If the Republican Party won the next election, all of the existing governmental employees who were Democrats would be terminated, and replaced by Republicans. The Supreme Court has held that these traditional "political patronage" practices violate the First Amendment's guarantee of freedom of association, and that non-policymaking and nonconfidential state and local governmental employees cannot be dismissed solely on the ground that they were not affiliated with or sponsored by the political party in power.[567] Nor can hiring, promotion, transfer and recall decisions in governmental employment be made on this basis.[568]

290. Because organizational membership is protected by the First Amendment, the government cannot, in the exercise of its regulatory power over organizations, compel an organization to turn over its membership lists to the government.[569] Likewise, since organizations have a protected First Amendment right to engage in concerted organizational activity, an organization that sponsors a consumer boycott for the purpose of achieving political change, cannot be held liable in damages for the economic losses suffered by businesses against which the boycott is directed.[570] And the government cannot, in the guise of regulating the practice of law, prohibit an organization from soliciting parties to bring litigation to advance organizational objectives,[571] or prohibit an organization from arranging for lawyers to represent the organization's members in private litigation.[572]

291. The First Amendment guarantee of freedom of association also restricts governmental efforts to regulate political party primary elections, at which the voters of each political party select the party's candidate to run in the general election. Each party must be able to determine for itself who will participate in the party's primary election, so if a party chooses to open the party primary to nonparty members, the

---

567. *Elrod v. Burns*, 427 U.S. 347 (1976).

568. *Rutan v. Republican Party of Illinois*, 497 U.S. 62 (1990). The Court has also held that a city could not deny governmental contracts to independent contractors who supported the incumbent mayor's opponent in the last election. *O'Hare Truck Service v. City of Northlake*, 518 U.S. 712 (1996).

569. *NAACP v. Alabama ex rei. Patterson*, 357 U.S. 449 (1958).

570. *NAACP v. Claiborne Hardware Co.*, 458 U.S. 886 (1982). In that case a civil rights organization had organized a consumer boycott against local businesses for the purpose of forcing them to put pressure on the local governmental body to accede to the organization's political demands.

571. *NAACP v. Button*, 371 U.S. 415 (1963).

572. *See* e.g., *United Transportation Union v. Michigan State Bar*, 401 U.S. 576 (1971).

state cannot prevent it from doing so by requiring that only voters who have declared party membership can vote in the party primary.[573]

292. The First Amendment's guarantee of freedom of association cannot be asserted, however, by large private membership organizations and "private business clubs" to avoid the application of state antidiscrimination laws to their discriminatory membership practices that deny membership to racial minorities and women. The Supreme Court has held that because these organizations are large and are relatively unselective in their membership, a requirement that they admit racial minorities and women to membership will not impede the organizations' ability to carry out their organizational activity or "unduly burden" the associational interests of their members.[574] The only limitation on the government's power to prohibit discrimination is that it cannot act in such a way that would destroy the structural integrity of the particular organization and prevent it from carrying out the purpose for which it was formed, such as by prohibiting an avowedly religious or ethnic organization from limiting its membership to persons of that religious or ethnic group.[575]

§3. Freedom of Religion

I. General Principles: The Twofold Protection to Freedom of Religion

293. The First Amendment provides twofold protection to freedom of religion by means of an "Establishment Clause" and a "Free Exercise Clause."[576] The Establishment Clause protects against the "establishment" of an official church by the government and against governmental action "establishing" religion, while the Free Exercise Clause is a textual guarantee of peoples' right to practice their religion and to hold and act on

573. *Tashjian v. Republican Party of Connecticut*, 479 U.S. 208 (1986). The state also violates a political party's First Amendment rights by requiring that the candidates of all parties run in a "blanket primary" in which voters could vote for any candidate regardless of the candidate's party affiliation, and the candidate of each party who receives the highest number of votes is the party's nominee at the general election. *California Democratic Party v. Jones*, 530 U.S. 567 (2000). The state, however, may prohibit "fusion" candidacies, by which a candidate appears on the ballot as a candidate for more than one party. *Timmons v. Twin Cities Area New Party*, 520 U.S. 351 (1997).

574. *Roberts v. United States Jaycees*, 468 U.S. 609 (1984); *New York State Club Association, Inc. v. New York City*, 487 U.S. 1 (1988).

575. In *Boy Scouts of America v. Dale*, 530 U.S. 640 (2000), the Court held that the state could not apply its antidiscrimination law to require the Boy Scouts of America, a nonprofit organization engaged in instilling its own system of values in young people, which included opposition to homosexuality, to accept homosexuals as members. The organization has since changed its policy and now accepts homosexuals as members.

576. The First Amendment states that: "Congress shall make no law respecting an establishment of religion, or prohibiting the free exercise thereof."

religious beliefs, free from governmental interference.[577] It is thus common to speak of the "religion clauses" of the Constitution,[578] and these clauses are considered to constitutionalize the value of religious freedom.[579]

294. The religion clauses were adopted against the background of an Established Church in Great Britain during the colonial period and the official persecution of religious dissenters in Great Britain and in Colonial America. Despite the relationship between the two clauses, the mode of analysis differs for each clause, and we may properly refer to an Establishment Clause challenge and a Free Exercise Clause challenge. In practice, an Establishment Clause challenge is easier to sustain than a Free Exercise Clause challenge, because, as the Supreme Court has stated, "[a] violation of the Free Exercise Clause is predicated on coercion while the Establishment Clause violation need not be so attended."[580] For example, compulsory Bible reading in the public schools can adversely affect the free exercise of religion by children who are members of a religious minority, such as children who do not believe in the existence of a Supreme Being. If these children ask to be excused from class during Bible reading, their relationships with teachers and classmates could be adversely affected, and so these children will have suffered harm because of their religious beliefs. To sustain a Free Exercise Clause challenge to compulsory Bible reading in the schools, this harm to the children as a result of the compulsory Bible reading would have to be demonstrated.[581] The demonstrated harm to the children, however, is completely irrelevant with respect to an Establishment Clause claim. The issue in regard to the Establishment Clause claim is simply whether compulsory Bible reading in the schools amounts to an "establishment of religion." The focus is on the governmental action itself and not on any resulting interference with an individual's free exercise of religion. Because of the Establishment Clause then, all persons have a constitutionally protected right to be free from governmental action "establishing religion."[582]

---

577. As the Supreme Court has stated: "The structure of our government has, for the preservation of religious liberty, rescued the temporal institutions from religious interference. On the other hand, it has secured religious liberty from the invasion of the civil authority." *Everson v. Board of Education*, 330 U.S. 1, 15 (1947).
578. The Fourteenth Amendment's due process clause incorporates both the "establishment clause" and the "free exercise" clause, and so makes these clauses binding on state and local governments as well.
579. Religious freedom means freedom with respect to religious belief: the belief in the existence or nonexistence of a Supreme Being, and the nature and manifestation of such existence. In this sense, all people, atheists and agnostics as well as religious adherents, have religious beliefs, and the religion clauses protect peoples' freedom with respect to those beliefs.
580. *School District of Abington Township v. Schempp*, 374 U.S. 203, 223 (1963).
581. Again as the Supreme Court stated in *Schempp, ibid.*, "The Free Exercise Clause'[s] purpose is to secure religious liberty in the individual by prohibiting any invasions thereof by civil authority. Hence it is necessary in a free exercise case for one to show the coercive effect of the enactment as it operates against him in the practice of his religion."
582. Any law or governmental action that by its terms interferes with a person's freedom to practice religion or to hold religious beliefs would have the effect of "disfavoring" that religion and implicitly favoring another religion, and so would amount to a prohibited "establishment of religion." Thus, it does not matter that it would also be a violation of the Free Exercise Clause.

295. A Free Exercise Clause claim is most frequently asserted when a facially neutral law—that is, a law that cannot be challenged as a violation of the Establishment Clause—impacts on a person's religious beliefs and practices. One example of a Free Exercise claim would be a challenge to a law that compels people to do something that their religion forbids, such as a requirement of compulsory school attendance applied to a religious group whose religion forbids children from attending school beyond a certain age. Another example would be challenge to a law that forbids people from doing something that their religion requires, such as a law forbidding the use of illegal drugs as applied to a religious group whose religion requires the use of an illegal drug in religious services. Still another example would be a challenge to a law that imposes a burden on a person because of that person's adherence to religious beliefs, such as a law denying unemployment compensation to persons who will not work on Saturday, as applied to a person who observes Saturday rather than Sunday as the sabbath.

296. We will discuss the Establishment Clause in Part V, Chapter 4. In this section, we will discuss the Free Exercise Clause. We will see that the Establishment Clause has been interpreted to invalidate a large number of governmental practices that have the purpose or effect of favoring religion, including most forms of governmental financial aid to religiously oriented or "parochial" schools. We will also see that while some facially neutral laws have been invalidated in their application to particular persons or groups on Free Exercise Clause grounds, Free Exercise challenges have become increasingly difficult to sustain. Thus, in practice, at least as regards laws and governmental action now being challenged as being violative of the "religion clauses," the success of the challenge frequently depends on whether it can be brought within the scope of the Establishment Clause.

II. The Free Exercise Clause

297. Because the Supreme Court's expansive interpretation of the Establishment Clause has made it the primary method of protecting religious freedom in the American constitutional system, the Free Exercise Clause has necessarily come to play a subsidiary role in the protection of this important constitutional right. To the extent that the interests protected by the two clauses may overlap, the Free Exercise Clause has become supplanted by the Establishment Clause, because, as pointed out previously, a Free Exercise Clause challenge is more difficult to sustain in that it requires a showing of governmental coercion, while an Establishment Clause challenge does not. And the Supreme Court's apparent reluctance to expand the scope of the Free Exercise Clause may be due in no small part to the fact that freedom of religion is so strongly protected in the United States by the Establishment Clause.

298. A law that expressly discriminates against religion, such as a law disqualifying members of the clergy from serving as legislators,[583] or a law that interferes with religious beliefs, such as a law requiring a declaration of a belief in the existence of

583. *McDaniel v. Paty*, 435 U.S. 618 (1978).

God as a test for holding public office, clearly violates the Free Exercise Clause.[584] But such laws are very rare.[585]

Typically, a Free Exercise Clause challenge is asserted against a facially neutral law on the ground that: (1) the law compels people to do something that their religion forbids, or prohibits people from doing something that their religion requires; or that (2) compliance with the requirements of the law imposes a burden on a person because of that person's adherence to religious beliefs; or (3) the law interferes with the operations of a religious organization.

299. The Court has stated that the Free Exercise Clause embraces two concepts, freedom to believe and freedom to act on the basis of religious beliefs, and that while freedom to believe is "absolute,"[586] freedom to act "in the nature of things cannot be," and so "must have appropriate definition to preserve the enforcement of that protection." However, as the Court went on to say: "In every case the power to regulate must be so exercised as not, in attaining a permissible end, unduly to infringe the protected freedom."[587] The Court's analysis of the constitutionality of governmental action interfering with an individual's freedom to act in the compulsion/prohibition and burden situations discussed above has generally seen the Court employing a balancing approach. That is, the Court has balanced the individual's interest in acting on the basis of religious beliefs against the governmental interest that is advanced by the challenged law or governmental action in the circumstances presented. Sometimes, but not always, the Court has imposed a strong burden of justification on the government, stating that the asserted governmental interest must be "compelling," and that, "[O]

---

584. *Torasco v. Watkins*, 367 U.S. 488 (1961). Art. VI, cl. 3 of the Constitution specifically prohibits a religious test as a qualification for holding federal office.

585. In Church of the *Lukumi Babaluaye v. City of Hialeah*, 508 U.S. 520 (1993), the Court found that a city's enactment of a number of laws prohibiting "animal sacrifice" was directed against the Santeria religion, which practices "animal sacrifice" as an essential part of its religious beliefs. The Court then held that the challenged laws violated the Free Exercise Clause, because they had the impermissible purpose of interfering with the religious freedom of the Santerian adherents and could not be justified as being "narrowly tailored" to advance a "compelling" governmental interest.

In *Locke v. Davey*, 540 U.S. 712 (2004), the Court held that an American state did not violate the Free Exercise Clause when, pursuant to the state constitution, it excluded theology study from a university scholarship program. Although the Establishment Clause would not prohibit the inclusion of theology in university scholarship programs, *see* para. 471, *infra* , the Court held that what a state was permitted to do by the Establishment Clause was not coextensive with what a state was required to do by the Free Exercise Clause. The state could choose not to fund this category of instruction in order to maintain its view of religious neutrality.

586. As stated above, it is highly unlikely that a law or governmental action will interfere with a person's freedom to believe as opposed to a person's freedom to act on the basis of religious beliefs. The only case that appears to involve a direct interference with a person's freedom to believe is *Torasco v. Watkins*, 367 U.S. 488 (1961), *supra* , para. 297, n. 584. The Free Exercise Clause also precludes the government from inquiring into the truth or falsity of an asserted religious belief. So, when a person was charged with fraudulent use of the mails for claiming that he was a "divine messenger," and had the "divine power" to cure incurable diseases, there could be no inquiry into the truth or falsity of those assertions. *United States v. Ballard*, 322 U.S. 78 (1944).

587. *Cantwell v. Connecticut*, 310 U.S. 296, 304 (1940).

nly those interests of the highest order and those not otherwise served can overbalance legitimate claims of the free exercise of religion."[588] However, more recently the Court has held that the Free Exercise Clause does not require that the government exempt religiously motivated conduct from neutral and generally applicable criminal laws, and that in this circumstance no "balancing" takes place.[589] The majority opinion in that case also cast doubt on the appropriateness of the "compelling governmental interest" test to resolve Free Exercise challenges in other contexts, although a minority of Justices insisted that this test was still appropriate.[590] Be that as it may, it may be assumed that apart from the matter of an exemption of religiously motivated conduct from neutral and generally applicable criminal laws, the Court will continue to follow a "balancing" approach in the resolution of Free Exercise challenges. However, the nature of the governmental interest asserted to justify the interference with the freedom to act on the basis of religious beliefs may not have to reach the level of "compelling."

300. Congress attempted to restore the compelling governmental interest test by the enactment of the Religious Freedom Restoration Act of 1993.[591] Under the Act, "government shall not substantially burden a person's exercise of religion even if the burden results from a rule of general applicability [unless] it demonstrates that the application of the burden to the person: (1) is in the furtherance of a compelling governmental interest, and (2) is the least restrictive means of furthering that compelling interest.". The Act was declared unconstitutional in its application to the states, as not being a permissible exercise of Congress's enforcement power under section 5 of the Fourteenth Amendment.[592] The Act can be applied to federal laws as a Congressional direction that federal laws be interpreted by the courts in a certain way, here as being subject to the "compelling governmental interest test" when they "substantially burden a person's free exercise of religion."[593] The Court has recently applied the Act to hold that the owners of a closely held corporation (a corporation which all the stock is

588. *Wisconsin v. Yoder*, 406 U.S. 205, 215 (1972).

589. *Employment Division, Department of Human Resources of Oregon v. Smith*, 494 U.S. 872 (1990). In that case, the Court held that the state could constitutionally apply its general prohibition against the use of illegal substances, here peyote, in a religious ceremony. The same result was reached in what may have been the very first case to present a Free Exercise Clause challenge, *Reynolds v. United States*, 98 U.S. 145 (1879), where the Court held that a law prohibiting polygamy could constitutionally be applied to members of the Mormon religion, whose faith at that time commanded that its members engage in that practice. The Court has also held that the Free Exercise Clause does not require an exemption of religious goods and literature from a general sales or use tax. *Jimmy Swaggart Ministries v. Board of Equalization*, 493 U.S. 378 (1990).

590. In *Church of the Lukumi Babaluaye v. City of Hialeah, supra*, para. 297, n. 585, the Court held that the "compelling governmental interest" test was applicable when the challenged law had the impermissible purpose of interfering with the religious freedom of a particular religious group.

591. 42 U.S.C. sec. 2000bb.

592. *Boerne v. Flores*, 521 U.S. 507 (1997).

593. *See Gonzales v. O Centro Espirita Beneficente Uniao Do Vegetal*, 546 U.S. 418 (2006), where the Act applied the Act to hold that the government could not apply its substance abuse laws to the drinking of hoasca, a tea brewed from plants unique to the Amazon rainforest, by members of a religion who received communion by drinking that tea.

owned by an individual or by a family) could not be made subject to a federal law requiring employers to provide health insurance coverage for contraceptive methods that violated the owners' sincerely held religious beliefs. The Court found that this requirement substantially burdened the owners' exercise of religion and that there were less restrictive means of ensuring that all of their women employees had cost-free access to those contraceptive methods.[594]

301. In any event, there are a large number of cases, especially those arising in more recent years, where the Court, applying some form of a "balancing" approach, has rejected a Free Exercise Clause challenge to the application of facially neutral laws that compel people to do something that their religion forbids or prohibit people from doing something that their religion requires. The Court has upheld the following laws against Free Exercise challenge: a law requiring the payment of social security taxes as applied to members of a traditional religious community whose religion prohibited both the payment of social security taxes and the receipt of social security benefits;[595] a law denying a tax exemption to private schools that practice racial discrimination on the basis of sincerely held religious beliefs;[596] a law requiring military service by persons who oppose a particular war on the basis of conscience and religion;[597] the governmental assignment of a social security number to a child, contrary to her parents' religious beliefs;[598] a law prohibiting children from selling merchandise as applied to a child who was distributing religious literature with her guardian;[599] and a military regulation prohibiting an Orthodox Jewish officer from wearing a skullcap, in accordance with his religious beliefs.[600] However, in a decision that seems limited to its particular facts, the Court held that a state could not constitutionally apply its compulsory school attendance law to require secondary school attendance by children of a traditional religious community whose religion forbade education beyond the primary level. The Court found that compliance with the requirement would seriously interfere with the community's religiously based way of life, and that education beyond the primary level was not necessary to enable the children to function within that way of life.[601]

302. Some religious groups in the United States object to blood transfusions and have refused to give their consent to their children having blood transfusions. When this occurs, the courts have asserted the state's interest in protecting the welfare of the children to override the parents' religiously based objection, and there is no doubt that the Supreme Court would hold, as all the lower courts have done, that this does not violate the parents' rights under the Free Exercise Clause.

---

594. *Burwell v. Hobby Lobby Stores, Inc.*, 134 S.Ct. 2751 (2014).
595. *United States v. Lee*, 455 U.S. 252 (1982).
596. *Bob Jones University v. United States*, 461 U.S. 574 (1983).
597. *Gillette v. United States*, 401 U.S. 437 (1971). The now-repealed compulsory military service law provided a conscientious objector exemption for persons who opposed all wars on the basis of conscience and religion. The exemption extended to those whose opposition to war was based on "ethical and moral" as well as on conventional religious beliefs.
598. *Bowen v. Roy*, 476 U.S. 693 (1986).
599. *Prince v. Massachusetts*, 321 U.S. 158 (1944).
600. *Goldman v. Weinberger*, 475 U.S. 503 (1986).
601. *Wisconsin v. Yoder*, 406 U.S. 205 (1972).

303. As the above discussion demonstrates, the Free Exercise Clause has not provided a high degree of protection against compliance with facially neutral laws that compel people to do something that their religion forbids or prohibit people from doing something that their religion requires.

304. A Free Exercise Clause challenge has had a better chance of being sustained when the claim is that compliance with the requirements of a facially neutral law imposes a burden on a person because of that person's adherence to religious beliefs. In a series of cases, the Court has held that the government cannot constitutionally condition the availability of unemployment compensation upon a person's willingness to work under conditions forbidden by that person's religion, such as requiring a person who observes the sabbath on Saturday to accept a job entailing Saturday work,[602] or denying unemployment compensation to a person who was discharged for refusing to work in weapons production, contrary to his religious beliefs.[603] The Court has also held that a state could not constitutionally deny welfare benefits to a family that had refused on religious grounds to furnish their child's governmentally assigned social security number to the welfare officials.[604]

305. However, the Court has upheld against Free Exercise Clause challenge a requirement that a person who observed the sabbath on Saturday and thus closed his place of business on that day, comply with the state's Sunday Closing law, designed to achieve a uniform day of rest for all employees.[605] It has also rejected a Free Exercise Clause challenge to the refusal of prison officials to excuse inmates from work requirements so that they could attend religious services,[606] and has held that the Free Exercise Clause did not preclude the federal government from carrying out logging and road construction in a national forest, although this would seriously interfere with the use of the forest for religious purposes by Native-American groups.[607]

306. The third category of Free Exercise challenge has involved claims by religious organizations that subjecting them to governmental regulation improperly interferes with their religious operations. This category of Free Exercise challenge may raise some questions about the interaction between the Establishment Clause and the Free Exercise Clause in that to the extent that the government exempts religious organizations from the requirements of otherwise applicable laws, it may be "favoring religion" in violation of the Establishment Clause. However, to the extent that such an exemption is required by the Free Exercise Clause, or at least prevents an interference with religious activity, it would not seem to constitute a prohibited "favoring of religion" for purposes of the Establishment Clause. This proposition is illustrated by the Court's upholding a provision in the federal civil rights law exempting religious organizations

---

602. *Sherbert v. Verner*, 374 U.S. 398 (1963); *Hobbie v. Unemployment Appeals Commission of Florida*, 480 U.S. 136 (1987).
603. *Thomas v. Review Board of Indiana Employment Security Division*, 450 U.S. 707 (1981).
604. *Bowen v. Roy*, 476 U.S. 693 (1986). The Court noted that the welfare officials could require other forms of identification from the family.
605. *Braunfeld v. Brown*, 366 U.S. 599 (1961).
606. *O'Lone v. Estate of Shabazz*, 482 U.S. 342 (1987). However, federal law may require the prison officials to make some provision for the inmates to conduct or attend religious services. *See* para. 306, *infra* .
607. *Lyng v. Northwest Indian Cemetery Protective Association*, 485 U.S. 439 (1988).

from the prohibitions against religious discrimination in employment in all of the organization's nonprofit activities.[608] The exemption was challenged as violative of the Establishment Clause insofar as it went beyond the purely religious activities of the organization and embraced all nonprofit activities. In upholding the exemption against Establishment Clause challenge, the Supreme Court indicated that for the government to require a religious organization to employ non-adherents in its religious activities would violate the Free Exercise Clause. The Court went on to say that to require the organization to distinguish between "religious" and "nonreligious" nonprofit activities could interfere with the organization's ability to carry on "religious" activities, and that for this reason, the government could, consistent with the Establishment Clause, extend the exemption to all nonprofit activities.

The Court has more recently held that Congress does not violate the Establishment Clause when it requires that states, as a condition to receiving federal funds, not impose a substantial burden on the religious exercise of a purpose residing in a state institution, such as a prison or a mental hospital, unless that burden is the least restrictive means of advancing a compelling governmental interest. The Court held that this requirement alleviates exceptional governmental-created burdens on private religious exercise, so that it represents a permissible government accommodation for religious freedom.[609]

307. At the same time, the Court has held that the Free Exercise Clause does not require an exemption of religious goods and literature from a general sales or use tax. This is because the tax is neutral in its operation and does not interfere with the ability of the religious organization to purvey its religious goods and literature. Its only effect is to reduce the amount of income that the organization will receive from its sales, and it does so in a nondiscriminatory way. Thus, it does not violate the Free Exercise Clause.[610] This being so, an exemption from the general sales tax for "periodicals that are published or distributed by a religious faith and that consist wholly of writings promulgating the teaching of the faith and books that consist wholly of writings sacred to a religious faith," does have the effect of favoring religious writings over other writings, and so violates the Establishment Clause.[611] The Court has also held that a provision in the federal income tax law denying a charitable deduction for payment to a charitable organization in exchange for goods and services, did not violate the Free Exercise Clause as applied to the denial of a charitable deduction for this kind of payment to a religious organization.[612]

308. As stated above, the Supreme Court has assumed that the Free Exercise Clause prohibits the government from requiring that a religious organization employ

---

608. *Corporation of the Presiding Bishop of the Church of Jesus Christ of Latter-Day Saints v. Amos*, 483 U.S. 327 (1987).

609. *Cutter v. Wilkinson*, 544 U.S. 709 (2005), upholding the constitutionality of the RLUIPA of 2000, 42 U.S.C. sec. 2000cc-1.

610. *Jimmy Swaggart Ministries v. Board of Equalization*, 493 U.S. 378 (1990). The government, however, may not apply a flat fee license tax on "soliciting" to persons distributing religious literature, *Murdock v. Pennsylvania*, 319 U.S. 105 (1943), nor may it apply a flat fee "bookseller" license tax to a preacher who earns his living by selling religious literature. *Follett v. McCormick*, 321 U.S. 573 (1944).

611. *Texas Monthly, Inc. v. Bullock*, 489 U.S. 1 (1989).

612. *Hernandez v. Commissioner of Internal Revenue*, 490 U.S. 680 (1989).

non-adherents in carrying out its religious activities. The Free Exercise Clause may also be implicated by the application to religious organizations of other laws regulating employment. The Supreme Court has held that Congress did not intend that the federal labor relations law apply to the unionization of lay faculty members at parochial schools, saying that such application would raise "serious constitutional questions."[613] However, the Court has also held that no constitutional problem was presented by the application of the federal wages and hours law to commercial businesses operated by a religious organization.[614]

In its most recent case dealing with the application of federal laws to the activities of a religious organization, the Court held that there was a "ministerial exception" to federal antidiscrimination laws, and that a religious organization's determination of who was a "minister" was binding on the federal courts.[615]

309. We see then that the Free Exercise Clause provides some protection against the application of facially neutral laws that interfere with or burden an individual's freedom to act on the basis of religious beliefs and against some applications of regulatory laws to religious organizations. On the whole, however, the protection provided to religious freedom by the Free Exercise Clause is considerably less than the protection provided by the Establishment Clause.

§4. Equality

310. The equal protection clause of the Fourteenth Amendment reflects a constitutional commitment to the value of equality and serves as the constitutional basis of protection for racial and other minorities against discriminatory governmental action. The primary historical purpose of the equal protection clause was to prevent racial discrimination against the newly emancipated black citizens by the states where slavery existed prior to the American Civil War. Unfortunately, there has been a long history of governmental and private racial discrimination against blacks and other racial minority groups in American society, and in times past the equal protection clause was only partially successful in providing a legal remedy against governmental racial discrimination. In American society, as elsewhere, there has also been a long history of legal discrimination against women and of legal rules classifying persons on the basis of gender. As American women began to assert a right to equality in the mid-1960s and thereafter, the equal protection clause was available as a constitutional

613. *National Labor Relations Board v. Catholic Bishop of Chicago*, 440 U.S. 490 (1979). The Court has also held that nonprofit church-affiliated schools are not subject to federal unemployment compensation laws. *St. Martin Evangelical Lutheran Church v. South Dakota*, 451 U.S. 772 (1981).

614. *Troy and Susan Alamo Foundation v. Secretary of Labor*, 471 U.S. 290 (1985).

615. *Hosanna-Tabor Evangelical Lutheran Church and School v. Equal Employment Opportunity Commission*, 132 S.Ct. 694 (2012). That case involved a teacher at a Lutheran parochial school, who had taken a course of religious instruction and was considered to have been "called" to her religious duties. The church held her out as a "minister," and she referred to herself as a minister in various ways. Her discrimination suit against the church was barred by the "ministerial exception." The decision was based on both the Free Exercise Clause and the Establishment Clause.

basis for challenging gender discrimination and gender-based classifications. The equal protection clause has also been used to challenge other forms of group discrimination, such as discrimination against out-of-wedlock children and discrimination against gay and lesbian persons.

311. It is race, however, that has been the paradigmatic form of group discrimination in American society, and for constitutional purposes, other forms of group discrimination have been likened to racial discrimination in terms of their "invidiousness" or "suspectness." As we have discussed previously, in the process of determining the constitutionality of different forms of group discrimination, the Supreme Court has articulated different standards of review, depending in part on the "invidiousness" or "suspectness" of the particular kind of group discrimination. Because the prevention of racial discrimination was the primary historical purpose of the equal protection clause, and because such discrimination continued long after the adoption of the Fourteenth Amendment, the Court has held that all racial discrimination is "suspect," and so is subject to "strict scrutiny" under the articulated "compelling governmental interest" standard of review. While no other form of group discrimination is subject in all respects to as high a degree of scrutiny as racial discrimination, we will see that the "important and substantial relationship" standard of review that is applicable to gender discrimination and discrimination against out-of-wedlock children also involves a considerable degree of judicial scrutiny. And while the Court has not stated that discrimination on the basis of sexual orientation is subject to heightened scrutiny, it has held unconstitutional all such discrimination in the cases coming before it, and very recently has held that the Constitution protects the right of same-sex couples to marry. All other forms of group discrimination, such as discrimination on the basis of age, are evaluated under the less restrictive "rational basis" standard of review, and so are more likely to be upheld against constitutional challenge.

312. In practice, both in terms of the articulated standard of review and in terms of the results that the Court reaches in the decided cases, we will see that the Court has developed a specific approach to determine the constitutionality of each different kind of discrimination on the basis of group membership. In effect, the Court has developed "subsidiary doctrine" for each kind of discrimination on the basis of group membership. The approach and "subsidiary doctrine" that the Court has developed to determine the constitutionality of one kind of group discrimination is not readily applicable to determine the constitutionality of another kind of group discrimination. In this section, we will divide our analysis into: (I) racial equality, (II) gender equality, and (III) other forms of group discrimination.

313. It should also be noted that Congress and many of the states have enacted civil rights laws, prohibiting racial and other forms of group discrimination in the areas of employment, education, housing, and public accommodations. These laws apply to governmental bodies as well as to private entities, and frequently provide greater protection against governmental discrimination than is provided by the Constitution.[616] Our discussion in this chapter will be limited to constitutional protection against discrimination.

I. Racial Equality

For constitutional purposes, racial discrimination refers to governmental action that disadvantages persons because of their race or ethnic origin.[617] While the primary historical purpose of the equal protection clause was to prevent discrimination against blacks and other racial minorities,[618] it is well-settled that the clause applies in the same measure to discrimination that is directed against whites or against blacks and whites equally.[619] However, the Court has not held, as it could have done, that the Constitution prohibits *all* racial discrimination. Rather, the Court has held that what the Constitution prohibits is *invidious racial discrimination*. Analytically, invidious racial discrimination is racial discrimination that cannot be justified when subject to "strict scrutiny" under the "compelling governmental interest" standard of review. This means that any form of racial discrimination will be held unconstitutional unless it can be shown to be "precisely tailored to advancing a compelling governmental interest."[620] Most racial discrimination, of course, particularly discrimination against

---

616. As we will see, the Constitution only prohibits intentional discrimination. Most civil rights laws also prohibit purportedly neutral action that in practice has a "disparate impact" or a "discriminatory effect" against racial minorities and other protected groups. *See* e.g., Texas Dept. of Housing and Community Affairs *v.* Inclusive Communities Project, Inc., 135 Sup.Ct. 2507 (2015) ("disparate impact" standard under federal Fair Housing law, 42 U.S.C. secs. 3601 et seq.). In addition, federal and many state civil rights laws prohibit discrimination on the basis of group characteristics such as age and physical or mental handicap, which are subject only to "rational basis" scrutiny for constitutional purposes.

617. Not every use of race by a governmental body disadvantages people. The government, for example, may and does keep racial statistics.

618. In the early years following the adoption of the Fourteenth Amendment, the Supreme Court used the equal protection clause to invalidate the blatant forms of racial discrimination that were being practiced against blacks, such as prohibiting blacks from serving on juries. *See Strauder v. West Virginia*, 100 U.S. 303 (1880). However, the Court refused to hold unconstitutional laws that required racially segregated public facilities, such as public schools or places of public accommodation. The Court held that as long as the separate facilities were tangibly equal, racial segregation did not amount to racial discrimination, and so was not unconstitutional. The "separate but equal doctrine" gave rise to the enactment of segregation laws in a number of American southern states. The "separate but equal" doctrine was finally overruled in the landmark case of *Brown v. Board of Education*, 347 U.S. 483 (1954), and it is indisputable that any form of governmentally imposed or sponsored racial segregation amounts to impermissible racial discrimination for constitutional purposes.

619. Thus, laws prohibiting interracial marriage are violative of equal protection. *Loving v. Virginia*, 388 U.S. 1 (1967).

620. *See* the discussion in *Loving v. Virginia, supra* , note 544. 388 U.S. at 1. As the Court has put it: "if [a] racial classification is ever to be upheld, [it] must be shown to be necessary to the accomplishment of some permissible state objective independent of the racial discrimination which it was the object of the Fourteenth Amendment to eliminate."

racial minorities, cannot be justified under this exacting standard of review, and so is unconstitutional. Thus, a state cannot require that a candidate's race be designated on an election ballot, since this would encourage racial prejudice in voting.[621] Nor can laws or governmental action that would benefit racial minorities receive disadvantageous treatment in the political process.[622] And a state cannot remove a child from the custody of an otherwise qualified divorced parent because the parent remarried a person of a different race, despite the claim that it is in the "best interests of the child" not to have a stepparent of a different race.[623] There has been only one case, now completely discredited, where the Supreme Court has upheld the constitutionality of governmental action that discriminated against racial minorities. This case, *Korematsu v. United States*,[624] involved the internment of Japanese-Americans living on the west coast during World War II. In the early days of the war, the military authorities said that they feared an invasion from Japan on the west coast, and that there was the danger that some Japanese-Americans were disloyal and would aid the Japanese invaders. They also said that it was not possible to expeditiously segregate the loyal Japanese from those who might be disloyal. The result was a military order requiring Japanese-Americans to be relocated from the west coast into internment camps in the interior United States. A sharply divided Supreme Court upheld the constitutionality of the internment order. The decision has been subject to extreme criticism on the ground that while the asserted interest in "military necessity" might be "compelling" for constitutional purposes, the blanket relocation order could not in any way be found to be "precisely tailored" to the advancement of that interest. The Court did not give any scrutiny at all to the contention of the military authorities that an invasion was imminent and that it was not possible to segregate the admittedly few disloyal Japanese-Americans from all the rest, who included a large number of older persons, women and children. The result in *Korematsu* can only be explained in the context of the anti-Japanese hysteria existing in the United States during World War II and the real fear of a Japanese invasion in the early days of the war. Congress has since issued an official apology for the internment and has made provision for the payment of compensation to the surviving Japanese-American internees.

Today, the major issue with respect to the constitutional permissibility of race-based governmental action involves "affirmative action" efforts that provide racial preference for minorities over whites in matters such as government employment and admission to public universities. While the purpose of this racial preference is not to injure whites as such, but to overcome the present consequences of the long and tragic

621. *Anderson v. Martin*, 375 U.S. 399 (1964).

622. *See Hunter v. Erickson*, 393 U.S. 385 (1969), holding unconstitutional a rule requiring that anti-discrimination laws be subject to advance voter approval in a referendum while other laws went into effect upon enactment unless overturned in a subsequent referendum. *See also Washington v. Seattle School District*, 458 U.S. 457 (1982), holding unconstitutional a state law that prohibited local school districts from transporting students to schools out of their residential neighborhoods for the purpose of achieving racial integration while allowing such transportation for a number of other purposes.

623. *Palmore v. Sidoti*, 466 U.S. 429 (1984). In that case, the Court emphasized that the government cannot take societal racial prejudice into account in official decision-making.

624. 323 U.S. 214 (1944).

history of racial discrimination in American society that has put blacks and other racial minorities in a societally subordinate position in comparison to whites, there is no doubt that such preference produces racial discrimination for constitutional purposes. The question is whether this discrimination can be justified when subject to "strict scrutiny," and the Supreme Court has held that in some circumstances it can be. The Court has held that when a governmental body has engaged in past discrimination against racial minorities in matters such as access to governmental employment, it has the constitutional obligation to remedy such discrimination, and so may provide a reasonable preference for minority persons with respect to such employment.[625] The Court has also held that the interest of a public university in achieving a "diverse" student body justifies giving some consideration to the minority race of an applicant in the admission process. The seminal case on this issue is *Regents of University of California v. Bakke*.[626] In that case, the Court held that a student's minority race could be considered as one of the factors in determining admission to the medical school of a public university, but that a strict "minimum quota" for minority students was not a constitutionally permissible method of achieving the "diversity" objective. The Court more recently reaffirmed this holding of *Bakke*, making it clear that a public university's interest in achieving "educational diversity" is a compelling governmental interest for constitutional purposes, so that the university may take race into account as one of the factors in determining admission. Applying this test, the Court upheld a university law school's race conscious admissions program under which race was one of a number of factors considered in determining admission.[627] However, the Court invalidated the university's undergraduate race-conscious admissions program that mechanically assigned a large number of points to an applicant's minority race and that did not

625. *See* e.g., *United States v. Paradise*, 480 U.S. 149 (1987), where the state had completely excluded blacks from serving on the state police force. In that case, the trial court had ordered the preference to remedy the identified past discrimination, and the Supreme Court held that the order was constitutionally permissible. The result would have been the same and the preference would be upheld as constitutional if the state had adopted the preference voluntarily to remedy its identified past discrimination. The preference must be reasonable and may not "unnecessarily trammel" the interests of the adversely affected whites. A typical constitutionally permissible preference designed to overcome the present consequences of past discrimination in governmental employment is the hiring of one minority applicant for each white applicant hired until the minority percentage of the governmental workforce reaches a specified reasonable level. The particular minority applicants given the preference need not themselves have been the identified victims of the prior discrimination, which may have occurred years before.

626. 438 U.S. 265 (1978).

627. *Grutter v. Bollinger* 539 U.S. 306 (2003).

provide for individual consideration of each applicant.[628] In *Parents Involved in Community Schools v. Seattle School District*,[629] the Court considered the constitutionality of race-conscious student assignment plans adopted by public school districts that had not engaged in unconstitutional racial segregation or had remedied such segregation. The assignment plans were designed to achieve racial integration and promote "racial diversity" in the schools. The Court was sharply divided over the issue. A Court majority held 5–4, that individual students could not be assigned to particular schools in the basis of their race in an effort to ensure that those schools were racially integrated. However, a different Court majority held 5–4, that the school district could try to achieve racial integration by other more general methods, such as drawing school district attendance zones with reference to the racial composition of the neighborhoods, strategic site selection designed to produce racially integrated schools, and tracking enrollments, performances, and other statistics by race.

Finally, the Court has held that a governmental body could not constitutionally "set aside" a fixed percentage of government contracts for minority-owned firms in the absence of a "strong showing in evidence" that it had engaged in past racial discrimination against minority-owned firms with respect to governmental contracting.[630]

314. As the above-discussion indicates, most racial discrimination on the part of the government will be found to be "invidious" and hence unconstitutional. But in certain limited circumstances, racial discrimination can be sustained as constitutional under the exacting "strict scrutiny" standard of review.

A current area of controversy involves the deliberate use of race in establishing Congressional and state legislative districts so that racial minorities will have a fair share of political power. The federal Voting Rights Act[631] prohibits establishing Congressional and state legislative districts in such a way as to "dilute" the political power of racial minorities. In order to avoid a possible violation of the Act as well as to affirmatively ensure that racial minorities will have a fair share of political power, states frequently establish these districts in such a way that racial minorities will constitute a majority of the voters in some districts. Typically, the percentage of "majority-minority" districts corresponds with the minority percentage of the state's

628. *Gratz v. Bollinger*, 539 U.S. 244 (2003). *See also Fisher v. University of Texas at Austin*, 136 Sup.Ct. 2198 (2016). In that case, a public university had a two-tiered admission process under which approximately 75% of the students were admitted based on their secondary school class rank, and the remaining 25% were admitted on the basis of personal characteristics, including race. Although a "critical mass" of minority students were admitted based on their secondary school class rank, the Court held that it was constitutional for the university to include race among the personal characteristics that it considered in admitting the remaining 25% of the students.

However, a voter-initiated state constitutional amendment prohibiting public universities from taking race into account in making admission and employment decisions was not shown to have a racially discriminatory purpose and so was not unconstitutional. *Schuette v. Coalition to Defend Affirmative Action*, 134 S.Ct. 1623 (2014).

629. 551 U.S. 701 (2007).

630. *See Richmond v. J.A. Crosson Co.*, 488 U.S. 469 (1989). *See also Adarand Construction Co. v. Pena*, 515 U.S. 200 (1995), holding that the "strong showing in evidence" requirement also applied to Congressionally authorized "set asides."

631. 42 U.S.C. sec. 1971.

total population. The Supreme Court has held that where it can be shown that race was the predominant factor motivating the drawing of a particular district, there has been unconstitutional racial discrimination unless the state in turn can demonstrate that the use of race in drawing the district was necessary to comply with the Voting Rights Act or was otherwise necessary to remedy identified past discrimination against minority voters.[632] Race is likely to be found to be the predominant factor motivating the drawing of the particular district where the state has ignored traditional districting criteria such as compactness, and has established an irregularly shaped "majority-minority" district, connecting by a narrow line separate concentrations of minority population.[633] However, the state may draw districts in such a way as to favor incumbents or political parties, and where the state can show, for example, that it equated a voter's race with a likelihood that the voter would vote for one of the political parties, the state's taking the racial composition of an area into account in the districting would not constitute the impermissible consideration of race.[634]

315. The racial discrimination that we have been discussing thus far is intentional racial discrimination that is expressly provided for by law or admittedly undertaken by the government. The Supreme Court has held that the equal protection clause only renders unconstitutional intentional racial discrimination, and that a facially neutral law is not violative of equal protection despite the fact that it may have a "disparate impact" or "discriminatory" effect on racial minorities.[635] So, in order to successfully challenge a facially neutral law or governmental action because of its "racially discriminatory effect," it is necessary to show that this "discriminatory effect" was intended by the governmental officials enacting or administering the law or undertaking the governmental action in question. The requisite "discriminatory intent" must be shown by direct or circumstantial evidence "with reference to the totality of the relevant

---

632. *Shaw v. Reno*, 509 U.S. 630 (1993); *Shaw v. Hunt,* 517 U.S. 899 (1596); *Miller v. Johnson,* 515 U.S. 900 (1995); *Bush v. Vera*, 517 U.S. 952 (1996) *Abrams v. Johnson*, 521 U.S. 74 (1997).

633. In the Shaw case, the "majority-minority" Congressional district was 160 miles long, and for much of its length was no wider than a highway.

634. *Hunt v. Cromartie*, 526 U.S. 541 (1999). *See also Easley v. Cromartie*, 532 U.S. 234 (2001), where the Court found that political rather than racial considerations were the predominant factor in the drawing of the districts. For a case involving a claim that the state had drawn legislative districts in such a way as to intentionally diminish black political power, *see Alabama Legislative Congress v. Alabama*, 135 Sup.Ct. 1257 (2015). The Supreme Court held that the lower should make factual findings on a district-by-district basis rather than on a statewide basis in order to determine whether black political power had been diminished.

635. *Washington v. Davis*, 426 U.S. 229 (1976). Because of the present consequences of past racial discrimination, the application of facially neutral laws or governmental action will often disadvantage racial minorities in comparison with whites. For example, a major consequence of this past racial discrimination is disproportionate racial poverty: blacks as a group, for example, have a substantially lower income level than whites as a group, and suffer disproportionately higher rates of unemployment and underemployment. So, the application of a facially neutral law or governmental action that disadvantages lower-income persons will also have a "racially discriminatory effect," but under the Court's current doctrine, this "racially discriminatory effect" does not render the law unconstitutional.

facts." In practice, this kind of showing usually will be difficult to make,[636] but when it has been made, the challenged law or governmental action is unconstitutional in the same manner as if the racial discrimination had been expressly contained in the text of the law. Following are some examples of intentional racial discrimination. A law requiring that laundries be operated in brick buildings was enforced only against Chinese launderers.[637] Where statistical evidence shows a significant statistical disparity between representation of racial minorities on list of persons eligible to serve on juries and their representation in the pool of persons selected for jury service, there has been a prima facie showing of intentional racial discrimination, and when, as usual, the government cannot provide a racially neutral explanation for the statistical disparity, there has been unconstitutional racial discrimination.[638] Prosecutor intentionally removed two black prospective jurors where proffered reasons for removing them applied to otherwise similar non-black jurors.[639] Expert testimony of historians showed that the purpose of adopting a provision in the state constitution barring persons who had been convicted of minor offenses involving "moral turpitude" from voting, was to exclude blacks from voting, so the provision was unconstitutional.[640] Evidence showed that city's purpose in retaining at-large system of electing members of city legislative body instead of electing members by district was to prevent black voters, who were concentrated in one area of city, from electing a member of the legislative body.[641]

316. Finally, where a governmental body has engaged in past unconstitutional racial discrimination, it has the affirmative duty to remedy the present consequences of that discrimination, and when an otherwise racially neutral action perpetuates the

---

636. *See* , for example, *United States v. Armstrong*, 517 U.S. 456 (1996), where a black defendant convicted in a "crack cocaine" case showed that all of the defendants in "crack cocaine" cases defended by the federal Public Defender in the previous year were black. This was held to be insufficient to show intentional racial discrimination in "crack cocaine" prosecutions in the absence of a showing that whites had also been involved in the sale or use of "crack cocaine" and were not prosecuted. *See also City of Cuyahoga Falls, Ohio v. Buckeye Community Hope Foundation*, 538 U.S. 188 (2003), where the Court found that the actions of a city in submitting to the voters a referendum calling for the repeal of an ordinance authorizing construction of a low-income housing project was not shown to have been motivated by an intent to discriminate against minority residents. It is sufficient, however, to show that intent to discriminate on the basis of race was one of the factors influencing the challenged governmental action. It need not be the sole or even the primary factor. When such intent is shown, the action is unconstitutional unless the governmental body can make the very difficult showing that it would have undertaken the same action in the absence of the discriminatory intent.
637. *Yick Wo v. Hopkins*, 118 U.S. 356 (1886).
638. *Castenada v. Partida*, 430 U.S. 482 (1977).
639. *Foster v. Chatman*, 136 Sup.Ct. 1737 (2016).
640. *Hunter v. Underwood*, 471 U.S. 222 (1985).
641. *Rogers v. Lodge*, 458 U.S. 613 (1982).

present consequences of past unconstitutional discrimination, that action itself is unconstitutional.[642]

II. Gender Equality

317. In the United States, as elsewhere, there has been a long history of legal discrimination against women and of legal classifications on the basis of gender. Indeed, gender-based classifications have been pervasive in American law, and proceeded on the basis of stereotyped assumptions about men and women and their respective societal roles. These gender-based classifications reinforced male domination and female subordination, but in many of their specific applications, they disadvantaged men as well as or instead of women.

318. The Supreme Court has held that gender-based classifications are subject to challenge under the equal protection clause,[643] and that such classifications are to be evaluated under an articulated "important and substantial relationship" standard of review. This standard involves a high degree of scrutiny, and its application means that a gender-based classification will be invalidated unless it can be shown to be substantially related to the advancement of an important governmental interest.[644]

319. Applying this standard, the Court has invalidated all of the traditional forms of discrimination against women, which were premised on stereotyped assumptions about men and women and their respective societal roles, such as that men were more competent than women to manage business affairs,[645] or that when both spouses were employed, the husband was the superior wage-earner,[646] or that men had the need for

---

642. For example, if a school district has engaged in unconstitutional racial segregation, it has the constitutional obligation to fully desegregate the school system, and until it does so, it cannot permit any school to become racially identifiable as a result of population changes, although in the absence of past unconstitutional segregation, the operation of a racially identifiable school would not be unconstitutional. *See Columbus Board of Education v. Penick*, 443 U.S. 449 (1979). So too, where a state university had previously refused to admit black students, it could not impose on a black student seeking admission a requirement that he obtain letters of recommendation from graduates of the university, all of whom would be white. *Meredith v. Fair*, 298 F.2d 696 (5th Cir.), *cert. denied*, 371 U.S. 828 (1962).

643. A proposed Equal Rights Amendment which provided that, "equality of rights under the law shall not be denied or abridged by the United States or by any State on account of sex," was submitted to the states for ratification in 1971, but failed to secure ratification by the necessary thirty-eight states when the time for ratification expired in 1982. The Supreme Court's interpretation of the equal protection clause, however, has achieved substantially the same constitutional objective as would have been achieved by the Equal Rights Amendment.

644. *See Craig v. Boren*, 429 U.S. 190 (1976).

645. *See Reed v. Reed*, 404 U.S. 71 (1971) (state law providing that when two persons are otherwise entitled to be the administrator of the estate of a deceased person, preference is given to the male); *Kirchberg v. Feenstra*, 450 U.S. 455 (1981) (in state following community property regime of marital property, state law made husband the manager of the community property).

646. *See Frontiero v. Richardson*, 411 U.S. 677 (1973) (federal law providing men in military service with an automatic "dependency allowance," but requiring women in military service to prove the actual dependency of their spouse in order to qualify for "dependency allowance."

more education than women.[647] It has also turned out that many of the gender-based classifications premised on such stereotyped assumptions disadvantaged men as well as or instead of women, and these too have been invalidated. The invalidated gender-based classifications disadvantaging men have included a law providing child support benefits to the surviving wife of a deceased male worker, but not to the surviving husband of a deceased female worker,[648] a requirement that divorced husbands, but not divorced wives, pay alimony to the former dependent spouse,[649] and a law providing survivors' benefits to all wives of deceased male workers without a showing of actual dependency on the deceased spouse, but providing such benefits to the husband of a deceased female worker only upon a showing of actual dependency.[650] The Court has also invalidated a law setting a lower age for women than for men with respect to entitlement to purchase alcoholic beverages,[651] and a state's effort to set aside one of the universities in the state's system of higher education exclusively for women.[652]

320. The Court has held, however, that the government may constitutionally employ gender-based classifications disadvantaging men where the actual purpose of the classification can be shown to be remedying the present consequences of past societal discrimination suffered by women as a group. On this basis, the Court has upheld a now-repealed provision in the social security law allowing women more

647. *See Stanton v. Stanton*, 421 U.S. 7 (1975) (state law imposing duty on parent to support male children until age 21, but imposing duty to support female children only until age 18).
648. *Weinberger v. Wiesenfeld*, 420 U.S. 636 (1975).
649. *Orr v. Orr*, 440 U.S. 268 (1979).
650. *Califano v. Goldfarb*, 430 U.S. 199 (1977).
651. *Craig v. Boren*, 429 U.S. 190 (1976). The age at which all persons could purchase alcoholic beverages was 21; the law made an exception that permitted women to purchase low-alcoholic content beer at age 18. The state tried to justify the distinction on the ground that empirical evidence showed that young men were more likely than young women to drive automobiles after they had been drinking. The empirical evidence, however, showed only that 2% of males in the 18–20 year old age group had been arrested for driving while intoxicated compared with virtually no women arrested for that offense. The Court held that this empirical evidence was insufficient to show that the gender-based classification was "substantially related" to the advancement of the assumedly important governmental interest in promoting traffic safety.
652. *Mississippi University for Women v. Hogan*, 458 U.S. 718 (1982). The state argued that since all the other universities in the higher education system were open to members of both sexes, it should be able to reserve one of the universities for single-sex education. The state's argument was that because of male domination generally, some women would benefit from attendance at a single sex university. The particular case, however, involved this university's nursing school. Since nursing is a field in which women predominate, the Court held that this asserted purpose would not be advanced by excluding males from the nursing school. The Court has also held unconstitutional the operation of state-supported male-only military academies. *United States v. Virginia*, 518 U.S. 515 (1996). There appear to be no remaining single-sex public universities in the United States today.

favorable treatment than men in calculating social security benefits,[653] and a state law providing a property tax exemption for widows but not for widowers.[654]

321. The Court has also been disposed to uphold legal distinctions between men and women that relate to what may be called sex-specific traits, that is, to biological and physical differences between men and women and their biologically different roles in the reproductive process. The Court has held, for example, that discrimination on the basis of pregnancy does not constitute discrimination on the basis of gender for constitutional purposes, and so as constitutional a state's exclusion of "disabilities connected with normal pregnancy and childbirth" from its disability insurance system for state employees.[655] The Court has also held that the state may constitutionally punish a teenage male for engaging in consensual sex with a teenage female without punishing the female. The Court said that this distinction was substantially related to advancing the state's interest in deterring teenage sex and unwanted pregnancy, since the state could conclude that a separate deterrent was necessary for males, who do not suffer the direct effects of pregnancy.[656] Likewise, because the mother of a child is identified by the birth process, the state may constitutionally permit the mother of an out-of-wedlock child to bring an action for the child's wrongful death, but deny that

653. *Califano v. Webster*, 430 U.S. 313 (1977). Social security benefits are determined in part by the beneficiary's earnings while employed. The Court held that Congress could reasonably conclude that virtually all women have suffered from discrimination in employment, either directly or because of "channeling" into lower-paid "women's jobs," so that allowing women workers more favorable treatment in calculating benefits (they could exclude more low-earning years from the base earnings on which benefits were calculated) would work directly to overcome some part of the past discrimination. Even with this favorable treatment, however, women beneficiaries on the average received substantially less benefits than male beneficiaries.

654. *Kahn v. Shevin*, 416 U.S. 351 (1974). The Court held that the state could conclude that the financial impact of spousal loss was much greater for widows as a group than for widowers as a group, since widows as a group were much more likely to have been financially dependent on their deceased spouses, and were much more likely than widowers to lack skills that would enable them to obtain employment.

655. *Geduldig v. Aiello*, 417 U.S. 484 (1974). Following this decision, the Court also held that employment discrimination on the basis of a woman's pregnancy did not constitute discrimination on the basis of sex within the meaning of the federal civil rights law. Congress responded with the enactment of the Pregnancy Discrimination Act, 42 U.S.C. sec. 2000e(k), which prohibits employment discrimination on the basis of pregnancy. It should be noted that allowing a woman to take "maternity leave" to recover from the effects of her pregnancy is permissible under federal civil rights laws, but that for an employer to provide "parenting leave" to only the mother would be illegal gender discrimination. *See California Federal Savings & Loan Assn. v. Guerra*, 479 U.S. 272 (1987).

656. *Michael M. v. Superior Court*, 450 U.S. 464 (1981).

right to the father unless the father has legitimated the child.[657] Similarly, the Court has upheld a provision of federal immigration law that drew a distinction between out-of-wedlock children born abroad to an American citizen parent and a noncitizen, depending on whether the child was claiming American citizenship through an American citizen father or through an American citizen mother. Automatic citizenship was conferred on the child claiming citizenship through an American citizen mother. However, where the child was claiming citizenship through an American citizen father, citizenship could be conferred only upon formal proof of paternity by age 18 through legitimation, written acknowledgment by the father under oath or adjudication by a competent court. In upholding the classification, the Court found that the distinction was based on "basic biological differences" between mothers and fathers and so was constitutionally permissible.[658] Finally the Court has upheld the constitutionality of

657. *Parham v. Hughes*, 441 U.S. 347 (1979). In *Caban v. Mohammed*, 441 U.S. 380 (1979), the Court dealt with the constitutionality of a state law that required the consent of the mother, but not the father, to the adoption of an out-of-wedlock child. Insofar as the law applied to consent for the adoption of a newborn out-of-wedlock child, the distinction could be said to relate to the different roles of men and women in the reproductive process: the mother is identified by the birth of the child while the biological father usually is unidentified or can be identified, if at all, only by the mother. In that context, the Court would likely hold that requiring the consent of only the mother would not be unconstitutional. (In practice, however, today the states require the consent of the father of the child where he can be identified.) But in this particular case, the law was applied to deprive the biological father of the right to object to the adoption of an older child with whom the father had established a substantial relationship when he was living with the mother. After they separated, the mother married and "consented" to the adoption of the child by her husband. The father, in an effort to preserve his relationship with the child, refused to consent, but the state court judge ordered the adoption as being in the child's "best interests." The Supreme Court held that in this circumstance, requiring the mother but not the father to consent to the child's adoption amounted to an unconstitutional gender-based classification.

658. *Nguyen v. Immigration and Naturalization Service*, 533 U.S. 53 (2001). These differences related to the fact that the mother was necessarily present at the birth of the child while this was not necessarily so for the father. The Court found that the classification served the important governmental interests of assuring that a biological parent-child relationship exists and assuring that the child and the parent through whom the child was claiming citizenship "have real everyday ties that provide a connection between the child and the citizen parent, and in turn, the United States." The dissenting Justices accused the majority of making "overbroad sex-based generalizations" that were constitutionally impermissible "even when they enjoy empirical support."

Congress' providing that if compulsory military service were required in the future, it could be limited to males.[659]

322. In summary, looking to the results of the decided cases, we see that the Court has invalidated all gender-based classifications disadvantaging women, and has likewise invalidated all gender-based classifications disadvantaging men except where the actual purpose of the classification was found to be overcoming the present consequences of past societal discrimination against women. The Court however, has been disposed to uphold legal distinctions between men and women when they relate to what are perceived as biological and physical differences between men and women and their different roles in the reproductive process. Because gender-based classifications are constitutionally disfavored, they have generally been eliminated in federal and state laws and replaced with gender-neutral criteria, such as "surviving spouse," "dependent spouse," "custodial parent," and the like.

III. Other Forms of Group Discrimination

323. The equal protection clause has been used to strike down most of the legal discrimination that had long existed against out-of-wedlock (the term "out-of-wedlock" replaces the former term "illegitimate") children in the United States. The assumption on which discrimination against out-of-wedlock children was premised was that rights dependent on or derived from family relationships could be accorded only to relationships based on marriage. All other relationships, including the parent-child relationship, that were formed outside of marriage were considered "illegitimate," and so were denied legal recognition.

324. The Supreme Court has held that the equality value embodied in the equal protection clause precludes the government from discriminating against out-of-wedlock children solely because of their status. As the Court has stated:

> The status of illegitimacy has expressed through the ages society's condemnation of irresponsible liaisons beyond the bounds of marriage. But visiting this

659. *Rostker v. Goldberg*, 453 U.S. 57 (1981). Compulsory military service has been abolished since 1972. However, federal law requires males to register for military service at age 18 in the event that compulsory military service should ever be reinstated. A male required to register under the law challenged the exemption of women from compulsory military service as unconstitutional. The purpose of compulsory military service in the past has been to supply troops for front-line combat. Congress has excluded women from front-line combat, and the constitutionality of that exclusion was not challenged by the male registrant in that case. The Court held that since women were excluded from front-line combat, it was not necessary for Congress to "draft" women for other forms of military service, and thus upheld the provision for "male only" compulsory military service. It is also difficult to believe that the Court would hold that the exclusion of women from front-line combat or from any other type of combat is unconstitutional. In all likelihood, the Court would defer to Congressional or military judgment in this regard, despite the clear discrimination between men and women. At the present time, all restrictions on women serving in combat have been removed. In the recent wars in Afghanistan and Iraq, the military went to great lengths to emphasize the important role that women played in the war.

> condemnation on the head of an infant is illogical and unjust. Moreover, imposing disabilities on the illegitimate child is contrary to the basic concept of our system that legal burdens should bear some relationship to individual responsibility or wrongdoing. Obviously, no child is responsible for his birth and penalizing the illegitimate child is an ineffectual – as well as an unjust – way of deterring the parent.[660]

In other words, the government must advance an independent justification for legitimacy-based classifications, which must be unrelated to discriminating against out-of-wedlock children solely because of their status. As with gender-based classifications, the articulated "important and substantial relationship" standard of review applies: the legitimacy-based classification must be substantially related to the advancement of an important governmental interest.

325. Applying this standard of review, the Court has held unconstitutional all of the traditional forms of discrimination against out-of-wedlock children, such as denying out-of-wedlock children the right to receive worker's compensation benefits or wrongful death recovery for the death of a parent,[661] denying welfare benefits to a family that includes an out-of-wedlock child,[662] and denying an identified out-of-wedlock child support from the natural father,[663] or the right to inherit from the father.[664] In addition, since in-wedlock children have the right to support from their fathers, the state must allow out-of-wedlock children a substantial period of time in which to establish paternity against the natural father, so that they will be able to claim support from him.[665] However, the Court has held that the state can constitutionally require that in order to inherit from a deceased natural father, paternity must be established in a judicial proceeding during the father's lifetime.[666] The Court has also held that with respect to the receipt of governmental benefits based on "actual dependency" on a deceased parent, it is not unconstitutional for the government to presume that in-

660. *Weber v. Aetna Casualty & Surety Co.*, 406 U.S. 164, 175 (1972).
661. *Weber v. Aetna Casualty & Surety Co.*, 406 U.S. 164, 175 (1972); *Levy v. Louisiana*, 391 U.S. 68 (1968). Nor may the state deny to the mother the right to recover damages for the wrongful death of an out-of-wedlock child. *Glona v. American Guarantee & Liability Insurance Co.*, 391 U.S. 73 (1968).
662. *New Jersey Welfare Rights Organization v. Cahill*, 411 U.S. 619 (1973).
663. *Gomez v. Perez*, 409 U.S. 535 (1973).
664. *Trimble v. Gordon*, 430 U.S. 762 (1977).
665. *See Clark v. Jeter*, 486 U.S. 456 (1988), holding that a six-year limitation on the time for filing a paternity action was constitutionally impermissible.
666. *Lalli v. Lalli*, 439 U.S. 259 (1978). With the ready availability of genetic testing to establish paternity today, this requirement will not impose a burden on the out-of-wedlock child. It also encourages the mother to bring a paternity action against the putative father, so that the child will be entitled to support during the father's lifetime.

wedlock children are dependent on the father, but to require out-of-wedlock children to establish actual dependency.[667]

326. The result of these constitutional decisions has been to substantially eliminate the pervasive discrimination against out-of-wedlock children that had previously existed in the United States.

327. As pointed out previously, the Court has not held that discrimination on the basis of sexual orientation is subject to heightened scrutiny. But without expressly discussing standards of review, the Court has held unconstitutional all forms of discrimination against gay and lesbian persons that have come before it. Sometimes, the Court has used equal protection as the doctrinal basis of its decision, sometimes it has used due process, and sometimes it has used both. In the first sexual orientation discrimination case coming before it, the Court held unconstitutional a state constitutional provision, adopted by voter initiative, prohibiting the inclusion of discrimination on the basis of sexual orientation in the state's antidiscrimination laws.[668] Next the Court struck down as violative of due process a state law prohibiting as "deviate sexual

---

667. *Mathews v. Lucas*, 427 U.S. 495 (1976). The law at issue provided benefits to the "dependent children" of the deceased wage-earner, and statutorily assumed that the deceased wage earner's in-wedlock children and some classes of out-of-wedlock children were dependent upon him. Certain classes of out-of-wedlock children were required to prove actual dependency as a condition for receiving the benefit. In this sense, the classification was "overinclusive," in that some in wedlock and some out-of-wedlock children who were not actually dependent on the deceased wage-earner would receive the benefit, while some out-of-wedlock children who were not actually dependent on the deceased wage-earner would not receive the benefit. But all out-of-wedlock children who were actually dependent on the deceased wage-earner would receive the benefit. It is unconstitutional to deny "dependency-based" benefits to any out-of-wedlock children who are actually dependent on the deceased wage-earner. *See Jiminez v. Weinberger*, 417 U.S. 628 (1974), holding unconstitutional a rule denying benefits to actually dependent out-of-wedlock children born after the onset of the wage-earner's disability. *Compare Califano v. Boles*, 443 U.S. 282 (1979), where the law, in addition to granting benefits to all the children, in wedlock and out-of-wedlock, of a deceased wage-earner, also granted separate "mother's benefits" to the deceased's widow or divorced wife, but not to the mother of his out-of-wedlock child. The Court held that it was reasonable for Congress to conclude that a woman who was never married to the deceased wage-earner was far less likely to have been dependent upon him at the time of his death than a woman who was or had been married to him. Again, the "children's benefits" could not constitutionally be denied to the deceased wage-earner's out-of-wedlock child.

668. *Romer v. Evans*, 517 U.S. 620 (1996). The Court noted that: "It [the state constitutional provision] identifies persons by a single trait and then denies them protection across the board. [It] is not within our constitutional tradition to enact laws of this sort. Central both to the idea of the rule of law and to our own Constitution's guarantee of equal protection is the principle that government and each of its parts remains open on impartial terms to all who seek its assistance. [Respect] for this principle explains why laws singling out a certain class of citizens for disfavored legal status or general hardships are rare. A law declaring that in general it shall be more difficult for one group of citizens than for all others to seek aid from the government itself is a denial of equal protection of the laws in the most literal sense."

intercourse" anal or oral sex by persons of the same sex.[669] The decision in this case coincided which a time when some state courts were striking down bans on marriage by same-sex couples as violative of the state constitution, and cases were initiated in some states challenging these bans as violative of federal due process and equal protection. The Court next held unconstitutional a federal law that denied federal "marriage benefits" to same-sex couples who had entered into legally valid marriages under the law of their home states.[670]

These cases set the stage for the landmark case of *Obergefell v. Hodges,* [671] where the Court held that same-sex couples have a constitutional right to have their marriages deemed lawful on the same terms and conditions as marriages between persons of the opposite sex. Marriage between persons of the opposite sex have long been held to constitute a fundamental right for purposes of the due process and equal protection clauses.[672] In *Obergefell* the Court held that the fundamental right to marry included marriages between same-sex couples, so that the marriage laws of many states that denied same-sex couples the right to marry violated due process. The Court went on to observe that the right of same-sex couples to marry was also derived from the Fourteenth Amendment's guarantee of equal protection of the laws, and that the equal protection clause, like the due process clause prohibited this unjustified infringement of the fundamental right to marry.

The Court sets forth four principles and traditions that demonstrated that the reasons marriage is fundamental under the Constitution apply with equal force to same-sex couples. One: The right to personal choice regarding marriage is inherent in the concept of individual autonomy. Two: The right to marry is fundamental because it supports a two-person union unlike any other in its importance to the committed individuals. Three: The right to marry safeguards children and families and thus draws meaning from related rights of childbearing, procreation, and education. Four: The Court's cases and the Nation's traditions make clear that marriage is the keystone of our social order.

For these reasons the right of same-sex couples to marry is protected as a fundamental right in the same manner as marriages between persons of the opposite sex. The states could not advance any valid reason for denying same-sex couples the right to marry, so all state law prohibiting same-sex couples from marrying *are now unconstitutional.* As a result of *Obergefell,* the institution of marriage in the United States means a union of two persons, whether they are persons of the same *sex or persons of the opposite sex.*

328. Equal protection challenges to other forms of group discrimination, such as age, are evaluated under the less restrictive "rational basis" standard. Applying this

---

669. *Lawrence v. Texas*, 539 U.S. 558 (2003). The Court noted that these laws prohibited homosexual persons from entering into intimate relationships, and stated that, "When homosexual conduct is made criminal by the law of the State, that declaration in and of itself is an invitation to subject homosexual persons to discrimination both in the public and in the private spheres and demeans the lives of homosexual persons."
670. *United States v. Windsor*, 133 S.Ct. 2675 (2013). In that case the effect of the federal law was to deny the validly married spouse of a same-sex couple the federal estate tax exemption.
671. 135 Sup.Ct. 2584 (2015).
672. *See* para. 338, *infra* .

standard, the Court has upheld the constitutionality of mandatory retirement of governmental employees.[673] However, even under this less restrictive standard, any form of group discrimination is subject to some scrutiny and must be justified. The Court, for example, has held unconstitutional a city's denial of a permit for the operation of a group home for mentally retarded persons, where the city could provide no justification for the denial of the permit other than the opposition of neighboring residents.[674]

329. There have been a number of cases involving equal protection challenges to governmental action that has the effect of discriminating against persons because of their poverty. The Court has not interpreted the equal protection clause as requiring the government affirmatively to take inequality of economic condition into account. To put it another way, the Court has made it clear that the equal protection clause will not be used to require the government to modify the essential class structure of American society. Thus, as a general proposition, facially neutral laws are not violative of equal protection on the ground that they have the effect of discriminating against or causing disadvantage to people because of their poverty or economic condition.[675] The Court

673. *See Massachusetts Board of Retirement v. Murgia*, 427 U.S. 307 (1976) (retirement of state police officers at age 50); *Vance v. Bradley*, 440 U.S. 93 (1979) (retirement of federal Foreign Service Personnel at age 60); *Gregory v. Ashcroft*, 501 U.S. 452 (1991) (retirement of state court judges at age 70). However, the federal Age Discrimination in Employment Act, 29 U.S.C. secs. 621–634, now prohibits most mandatory retirement on the part of governmental as well as private employers. Only governmental positions at the policymaking level are exempted from the requirements of the law.

674. *City of Cleburne v. Cleburne Living Center*, 473 U.S. 432 (1985). However, the Court has held 5-4, that a state did not violate the equal protection clause by establishing different standards for the involuntary commitment of mentally retarded persons and mentally ill persons. The applicable burden of proof for the commitment of mentally retarded persons was "clear and convincing evidence" as opposed to the more stringent "beyond a reasonable doubt" standard for mentally ill persons. In addition, the guardians and immediate family members of the subject of a mental retardation proceeding could participate as parties in those proceedings, with full legal rights, including that of an appeal, while the guardians and family members of the subject of a mental illness proceeding could not do so. The Court found that the legislature could reasonably conclude that the treatment of involuntarily committed mentally retarded persons was less "invasive" than the treatment of involuntarily committed mentally ill persons and that the guardians and family members of mentally retarded persons likely would have been involved with them at an early age and so could provide information relative to the need for commitment. *Heller v. Doe*, 509 U.S. 312 (1993).

675. *See* e.g., *United States v. Kras*, 409 U.S. 434 (1976) (federal law requiring all persons to pay a filing fee in order to file for bankruptcy is rationally related to the government's interest in making the bankruptcy system self-sustaining and paid for by those who use it, and thus is not violative of equal protection, even though some indigent persons may not be able to afford to pay the filing fee). *Compare Boddie v. Connecticut*, 401 U.S. 371 (1971), where the Court held that since divorce involves a "fundamental right," the due process clause precludes a state from imposing a filing fee on indigents in a divorce action. *See also San Antonio Independent School District v. Rodriguez*, 411 U.S. 1 (1973), holding that a state system of financing public elementary and secondary education that is based on the amount of taxable wealth within each school district and so results in substantial disparities in the amount of funds spent on education of children residing in different school districts, is not violative of equal protection.

has made an exception to this general proposition with respect to indigent persons accused of crime, and has held that the equal protection clause requires the state to provide financial assistance and to appoint counsel, so that indigent criminal defendants will have substantially the same opportunity to obtain meaningful review of their criminal conviction as is available to other criminal defendants.[676] And where the sentence imposed consists of a fine or a requirement that the defendant make restitution, the state cannot constitutionally imprison the defendant for inability to pay the fine or make restitution, but must provide alternative means for the defendant to do so.[677]

§5. Liberty and Property Rights

I. An Overview

330. The due process clauses of the Fifth and Fourteenth Amendments specifically provide constitutional protection to liberty and property rights.[678] It has long been established that the concept of due process of law embodies a substantive as well as a procedural component, and so provides a textual basis for challenging laws and governmental actions that substantively interfere with liberty and property interests. The Fourteenth Amendment's equal protection clause and the "equal protection" component of the Fifth Amendment's due process clause provide a textual basis for challenging classifications contained in legislation, and so furnish an additional basis for challenging laws that interfere with liberty and property interests.[679] Specialized protection to certain forms of property interests is provided by the "takings clause" of the Fifth Amendment, which is incorporated into the Fourteenth Amendment's due process clause, and, as regards the states, by the "contracts clause" of Article I, section 10.

---

676. This includes furnishing the indigent defendant with a free transcript of the trial proceedings and appointing counsel for an appeal as of right from the criminal conviction. For discretionary appeals and other forms of post-conviction review, the state is not constitutionally required to provide counsel for indigent defendants if the defendant has otherwise had an adequate opportunity to present his claims fairly in the state's appellate process. *See* generally *Ross v. Moffitt*, 417 U.S. 600 (1974). In an action to establish paternity, the state is constitutionally required to pay the cost of genetic blood grouping tests for indigent defendants. *Little v. Streater*, 452 U.S. 1 (1981).

677. *Tate v. Short*, 401 U.S. 395 (1971); *Bearden v. Georgia*, 461 U.S. 660 (1983).

678. In identical language, they provide that, "no person shall be deprived of life, liberty or property without due process of law."

679. We refer to classifications contained in laws that interfere with liberty and property interests as general classifications, so as to distinguish these kinds of classifications from classifications on the basis of identifiable group membership, such as race or gender. Part IV, Ch. 2, An act of discrimination can be violative of equal protection, even though the disfavored group is a "class of one." *See* *Village of Willowbrook v. Olech*, 528 U.S. 562 (2000) (homeowner could assert equal protection claim against municipality based on allegations that municipality imposed more onerous conditions on homeowner for connecting her property to municipal water supply than it imposed on other similarly situated homeowners).

331. A substantive due process challenge focuses on the underlying law or governmental action interfering with liberty and property interests, and the analytical question is whether the law or governmental action is an improper interference with those interests. The analysis of an equal protection challenge is somewhat more complicated. An equal protection challenge focuses on classifications that are contained in legislation rather than on the underlying legislation itself. It proceeds on the assumption that the underlying legislation is valid as a matter of due process,[680] and the claim is that the classification violates equal protection because it improperly discriminates between the different groups that have been established by the classification. We may refer to these groups as the favored group and the disfavored group. In a classification contained in a regulatory law, the favored group is the group that is exempted from the regulation, while the disfavored group is the group that remains subject to the regulation. In a classification contained in a law providing governmental benefits, the favored group is the group that is entitled to the benefit, while the disfavored group is the group that has been denied the benefit.

332. It is helpful to employ a three-part analysis in explaining how a court resolves the equal protection challenge to a general classification The first step is to identify the favored and disfavored groups established by the classification. The second step is to determine whether the favored and disfavored groups are similarly situated with respect to the purpose of the underlying legislation in which the classification is contained. If the court determines that they are not similarly situated in this regard, then the classification is necessarily nondiscriminatory, and the equal protection challenge will fail. If the court determines that the favored and disfavored groups are similarly situated with respect to the purpose of the underlying legislation, the court must then determine whether there is a sufficient independent justification for the differential treatment produced by the classification. If the court concludes that sufficient independent justification is lacking, then the classification is found to be violative of equal protection, but if sufficient independent justification has been shown, the classification is not violative of equal protection despite the differential treatment between the similarly situated groups.[681]

333. As has been discussed in Chapter 2, §1, II, constitutional doctrine with respect to challenges to interferences with liberty and property interests under the due process and equal protection clauses has developed in large part with reference to differing articulated standards of review. There are two articulated standards of review applicable to due process and equal protection challenges to interferences with liberty and property interests, and the Supreme Court's approach to such challenges is referred to as a "two-tier" approach. The significance of the differing standards of review relates to the different degree of scrutiny that the Court applies under each standard. The Court applies the degree of scrutiny called for under the applicable standard both to the determination of the permissibility of the asserted purpose for which the law was

---

680. Sometimes the same legislation is challenged both on due process and equal protection grounds. *See* the discussion of challenges to denial of the right to marry to same-sex couples, *supra* , para. 326.

681. While, as the above discussion indicates, due process and equal protection challenges are analytically different, in some circumstances the due process and equal protection challenges overlap, and the same result will obtain under either basis of constitutional challenge.

enacted or the action undertaken, or asserted purpose for which the classification was made, and to the appropriateness of the particular law or governmental action or classification as a means of advancing the asserted purpose. The higher the degree of scrutiny, of course, the more likely the Court is to invalidate the law or governmental action challenged as violative of due process, or the classification challenged as violative of equal protection.

334. The applicable articulated standard of review depends on whether the particular individual interest affected by the challenged law or governmental action or by the classification is of sufficient constitutional importance to be ranked as a *fundamental right.* There has been considerable disagreement on the Court over the appropriate method for determining whether a particular individual interest should be held to be a fundamental right, and there may not be any "objective" method by which the Court can make this determination.[682] Important individual interests, such as education, sexual freedom, and housing, have been held not to be fundamental rights for purposes of the two-tier standard of review.[683] Perhaps all that can be said in this regard is that the Court has concluded that certain individual interests are so important from a constitutional standpoint that any law or governmental action interfering with those interests should be subject to a higher degree of scrutiny. In any event, the Court has recognized four individual interests as having the status of fundamental rights: (1) interests relating to marriage and the family; (2) reproductive rights; (3) the right to interstate travel; (4) the right to vote.

335. With respect to laws or governmental action affecting "fundamental" rights, the articulated compelling governmental interest standard applies. This means that the governmental interest asserted to justify the interference with the individual interest must be found by the Court to be "compelling," and the challenged law or governmental action must be the "least drastic means" of advancing that interest. (In equal protection challenges, the reference is to the classification contained in the law rather than to the law itself.) With respect to laws or governmental action affecting all other interests, or "non-fundamental rights," the articulated rational basis standard of review applies. Under the rational basis standard, the asserted governmental interest need only be "legitimate," and the challenged law or governmental action need only be "rationally related" to advancing the asserted interest. Under this standard, there is considerably more deference to legislative judgment and discretion than under the compelling governmental interest standard. Although, as we will see, there are a number of factors influencing the application of the articulated standard of review in particular circumstances,

682. In *Washington v. Glucksberg*, 521 U.S. 702 (1997), Chief Justice Rehnquist, writing for the Court, stated that for purposes of the Due Process Clause, a fundamental right is one that is "deeply rooted in this Nation's history and tradition," and that is "implicit in the concept of ordered liberty." Justice Souter, in a concurring opinion, strongly disagreed with this formulation.

683. In *Washington v. Glucksberg*, n. 682, the Court held that the right to physician-assisted suicide, including the assertion of that right by persons who were terminally ill, was not a fundamental right for due process purposes. The Court then, applying the rational basis standard, upheld Washington's prohibition against physician-assisted suicide. There is likewise not a constitutionally protected "right to die," although the Constitution assumedly recognizes, as does the common law of every state, the right of a competent adult to refuse or discontinue medical treatment, including medical treatment necessary to save that person's life.

and although the articulated standard of review is not always dispositive of the result, as would be expected, laws or governmental action evaluated under the articulated compelling governmental interest standard of review are more likely to be invalidated than laws or governmental action evaluated under the articulated rational basis standard of review.

336. The difference between an analysis of constitutional challenges under the differing articulated standards of review is illustrated by two cases involving challenges to municipal zoning laws defining what constitutes a "single family" for purposes of residency in areas zoned for "single family residency." In one case, the law defined a "family" as "not more than two unrelated persons living together as a single housekeeping unit." This law was challenged by six unrelated university students who wanted to share a house together. The Court held that the right of unrelated individuals to share a household was not a "fundamental right" for purposes of due process and equal protection analysis, so the challenged restriction was analyzed under the rational basis standard of review. Applying that standard, the Court upheld the restriction as being rationally related to the municipality's legitimate interests in maintaining itself as a place for single-family living, in controlling population density, and in preventing noise and congestion.[684] In the other case, the zoning law defined "single family" in such a way as to prohibit a grandmother from sharing a household with her two grandchildren who were cousins rather than siblings. Since in this case the zoning law impacted on the "fundamental right" of family relationships (which includes the extended family) by prohibiting a grandmother from living with her grandchildren, this was analyzed under the compelling governmental interest standard of review. Applying that standard, the Court held that none of the interests asserted by the municipality to justify the restriction was sufficiently "compelling" to override the right of the grandmother and grandchildren to live together.[685]

337. We will first discuss constitutional challenges under the due process and equal protection clauses to laws and governmental actions interfering with "fundamental rights." We will then discuss constitutional challenges to economic and social regulation. In addition to discussing due process and equal protection challenges to economic and social regulation, which are evaluated under the rational basis standard of review, we will also discuss the specialized protection provided to certain forms of property interests under the "takings clause" and under the "contracts clause." Finally, we will discuss the procedural protections afforded to liberty and property interests by the concept of procedural due process.

II. Fundamental Rights

A. Marriage and Family Interests

338. Since marriage is a fundamental right, any legal restriction on a person's freedom to marry must be justified under the compelling governmental interest standard of review. Traditional restrictions on the freedom to marry, such as a prohibition on

684. *Village of Belle Terre v. Boraas*, 416 U.S. 1 (1974).
685. *Moore v. City of East Cleveland*, 431 U.S. 494 (1977).

plural marriage, age restrictions, and limitations on marriage between close relatives, assumedly would satisfy this standard. But most other restrictions on freedom to marry would not. Thus, a ban on marriage between persons of different races, in addition to being unconstitutional as amounting to invidious racial discrimination, is also violative of due process as improperly interfering with the freedom to marry.[686] It is also unconstitutional for the government to prohibit a prison inmate from marrying without the permission of the prison authorities.[687]

339. In another case, the Court held violative of equal protection a state law prohibiting the remarriage of a divorced parent under a duty of support to a child of a prior marriage unless the parent could demonstrate that he or she was in compliance with the existing support order and that the child was not likely to become a public charge. The effect of the law was to classify between persons with respect to the legal ability to enter into marriage and to deny this right to persons who were under a duty of support to a child of a prior marriage. The restriction could not satisfy the compelling governmental interest standard, both because it imposed too heavy a burden on the right to marry, and because it would not be effective in ensuring support of the child. In addition, there were less onerous means of enforcing the parent's support obligation, such as wage assignment and civil and criminal sanctions against the parent. As the Court concluded: "[I]n regulating the intimate human relationship of marriage, there is a limit beyond which the state may not constitutionally go."[688] Since a person may only be validly married to one person at one time, the right to marry includes the right to divorce. This being so, any law that interferes with the ability of a person to obtain a divorce is tested under the compelling governmental interest standard, and the Court has held that a state is constitutionally required to permit an indigent person to bring a divorce proceeding without having to pay court fees.[689]

340. In addition to marriage, the Court has recognized family autonomy as a fundamental right, and many years ago it held unconstitutional state laws that prohibited parents from sending their children to private schools.[690] Because the parent-child relationship involves a fundamental right, the due process clause requires that the state follow significant procedural safeguards in proceedings seeking to terminate the

686. *Loving v. Virginia*, 388 U.S. 1 (1967). And the Court has recently held that the state cannot deny the right to marry to a same-sex couple. *See* para. 326, *supra* .

687. *Turner v. Safley*, 482 U.S. 78 (1987). It is irrelevant in this regard that the prison inmate and the spouse may not be able to engage in sexual relations while the inmate is in prison, since they can still enjoy the other incidents of marriage.

688. *Zablocki v. Redhail*, 434 U.S. 374 (1978).

689. *Boddie v. Connecticut*, 401 U.S. 371 (1971).

690. *Pierce v. Society of Sisters*, 268 U.S. 510 (1925). *See also Meyer v. Nebraska*, 262 U.S. 390 (1923), where the Court invalidated a state law prohibiting the teaching of a foreign language in private schools on the ground that this interfered with the liberty of parents to make educational decisions concerning their children.

parent-child relationship, including a requirement that the state establish parental unfitness by "clear and convincing evidence."[691]

The right to parent was strongly affirmed in a more recent case involving a constitutional challenge to "grandparent visitation" laws, which had been enacted in most American states. Under these laws, courts were authorized to order the custodial parent to permit visitation with children by grandparents or other third parties, over the objection of the custodial parent, when a court finds such visitation to be in the "best interests of the child." The Court held that parents have a fundamental right to make decisions concerning the care, custody and control of their children, and that in deciding whether third party visitation can be permitted, the court must give special weight to the parent's views on whether and to what extent third party visitation should be permitted.[692]

341. The parent-child relationship, it should be noted, exists independently of the marriage relationship. Thus, the fathers of out-of-wedlock children have a constitutionally protected interest in their relationship with the child, and where the child has been living with the father, the state cannot take custody away without establishing in a judicial proceeding that the child's remaining with the father is not "in the child's best interests."[693] However, in some circumstances, the biological father of an out-of-wedlock child who has not taken steps to formalize his relationship with the child, may not be able to assert successfully parental rights with respect to that child. The Court has held that due process was not violated when the state permitted an adoption that was "in the child's best interests" by the man that the child's mother was about to marry, over the objection of the identified biological father, who could have legitimated the child, but did not do so. Had the biological father legitimated the child, the child could not have been adopted over his objection, and his failure to legitimate the child weakened his claim of parental rights with respect to the child.[694]

342. An interesting case involved a parental relationship claim of the biological father of a child born to a woman who was married to another man during the time of

---

691. *Santosky v. Kramer*, 455 U.S. 745 (1982). However, the Court has held that due process does not require the appointment of counsel in all parental termination proceedings involving indigent parents, but that it may impose such a requirement in particular cases where the appointment of counsel could make a determinative difference in the outcome of the proceedings. *Lassiter v. Department of Social Services*, 452 U.S. 18 (1981). The Court has also held that as a matter of equal protection, the state cannot deny an indigent parent the right to appeal from an order terminating parental rights because of the parent's inability to pay for the transcript, and that the state must provide a transcript of sufficient completeness to permit proper appellate consideration of the parent's claims. *M.L.B. v. S.L.J.*, 519 U.S. 102 (1996).

692. *Troxel v. Granville*, 530 U.S. 87 (2000).

693. *Stanley v. Illinois*, 405 U.S. 645 (1972). Conversely, when the state seeks a determination that a man is the biological father of a child, the man's interest in avoiding an incorrect determination of paternity is protected by the due process clause, and the Court has held that in such a proceeding the state is required to pay the cost of blood grouping tests for indigent defendants, since these tests could prove that the man is not the father of the child. *Little v. Streater*, 452 U.S. 1 (1981).

694. *Quilloin v. Walcott*, 434 U.S. 246 (1978). *See also Lehr v. Robertson*, 463 U.S. 248 (1983), holding that the state was not required to give notice of an adoption hearing to the putative father of a two-year old out-of-wedlock child, when the father had never sought to establish a substantial relationship with the child.

conception and birth of the child. The woman had left her husband to live with the child's biological father, who fathered the child while they were living together, but she later returned to her husband, and she and her husband wished to raise the child as their own. The biological father then sought a court order establishing his parental status with respect to the child and giving him visitation rights, which the child's mother and her husband resisted. State law established a virtually conclusive presumption that a child born to a married woman living with her husband was the child of the husband. The lower court denied the claim of the biological father, and its action was affirmed by the state Supreme Court. The United States Supreme Court came out highly fragmented on the issue of whether the biological father had a constitutionally protected liberty interest in his relationship with the child. Four Justices took the position that the biological father did not have such an interest. Four Justices took the position that the biological father did have such an interest, and that the lower court should have determined whether recognition of the father's parental status and the provision for visitation rights would be "in the child's best interests." The matter was not resolved definitively by the Court, because the Justice who cast the deciding vote to affirm the state court decision took the position that while the father probably did have such an interest, the lower court had not applied the "presumption of legitimacy" rule, but instead had determined that to recognize the relationship and to allow visitation rights would not be "in the child's best interests."[695]

343. As discussed previously, the fundamental right of family relationships includes the extended family, and for this reason, the Court has held that a zoning law that defined a "single family" in such a way as to preclude a grandmother from living with her grandchildren who were cousins rather than siblings, was unconstitutional.[696]

B. Reproductive Rights

344. The fundamental right of reproductive freedom includes the right to produce children and the right to avoid producing children by making use of contraception in sexual relations, by sterilization and by abortion. The Court first recognized reproductive freedom as a fundamental right over seventy years ago when it held unconstitutional a state law requiring the compulsory sterilization of persons who had been convicted of three serious criminal offenses. The Court based its decision on equal protection grounds, because the law expressly exempted certain "white collar" crimes from the sterilization requirement, but there is no doubt that if there had been no exemption,

---

695. *Michael H. v. Gerald D.*, 491 U.S. 110 (1989). Today most states have laws specifically dealing with the claim of a non-husband to be the father of the child of a married woman and with the husband of a married woman to assert a claim of non-paternity for a child born to the wife.

696. *Moore v. City of East Cleveland*, 431 U.S. 494 (1977).

the Court would have invalidated the requirement in its entirety on due process grounds.[697]

345. Some twenty years later, the Court again had occasion to deal with the right of reproductive freedom in the context of invalidating a state anti-contraception law that prohibited the use of contraceptives by married as well as by unmarried persons.[698] While the decision rested more on the interference with the fundamental right of marriage than on the interference with reproductive freedom, the Court held a few years later that since married persons had the right to use contraceptives, the state could not, as a matter of equal protection, prohibit unmarried persons from using contraceptives either.[699] The Court has also held that a state cannot constitutionally deny minors access to contraceptives.[700]

346. The Court's decisions on the constitutional entitlement of persons to use contraceptives set the stage for the Court's highly controversial 1973 abortion decision in *Roe v. Wade*.[701] The Court held that since a woman's decision to terminate a pregnancy by means of an abortion involved the fundamental right of reproductive freedom, any interference with the woman's decision had to be evaluated under the compelling governmental interest standard of review. Applying that standard, the Court held that the state's asserted interest in protecting potential human life did not become "compelling" until the pregnancy had reached the stage of viability, that is, the time in pregnancy in which the fetus could survive outside the uterus with the help of artificial life support. At that point, but not before, the state could prohibit abortion except where the abortion necessary to preserve the life or health of the woman. As a practical matter, the *Roe v. Wade* decision meant that the state could not prohibit abortion at all, since virtually every abortion is performed prior to the stage of viability, when abortion becomes extremely dangerous from a medical standpoint. In 1992, this essential part of the *Roe v. Wade* decision was affirmed by a divided Court in a 5-4 decision, *Planned Parenthood of Southeastern Pennsylvania v. Casey*.[702]

347. The *Casey* decision, however, modified another part of the *Roe v. Wade* decision that also imposed stringent constitutional limitations on the power of the state to regulate the abortion procedure. The Court in *Casey* held that the state could

---

697. *Skinner v. Oklahoma*, 316 U.S. 535 (1942). The Court had earlier upheld a law providing for the compulsory sterilization of mentally retarded persons confined to state institutions, so that they could be released to the outside world without the ability to procreate. The law was based on the then current and since discredited eugenics view that mental retardation was inheritable. *Buck v. Bell*, 274 U.S. 200 (1927). Today, such a law would have to satisfy the compelling governmental interest standard of review, and it is very possible that the law could be sustained under this standard on the ground that it was the "least drastic means" of protecting mentally retarded persons and the society at large from the harm that would be caused by their release from the institution with the ability to procreate. The argument would be that mentally retarded persons would not be able to understand how to avoid pregnancy by the use of contraception, and that sterilization would enable them to engage in sexual relations without the possibility of pregnancy, and thus to lead as normal a life as possible outside of the institution.
698. *Griswold v. Connecticut*, 381 U.S. 479 (1965).
699. *Eisenstadt v. Baird*, 405 U.S. 438 (1972).
700. *Carey v. Population Services Intern.*, 431 U.S. 678 (1977).
701. 410 U.S. 113 (1973).
702. 505 U.S. 833 (1992).

constitutionally regulate the abortion procedure, even to the point of trying to discourage the woman from having an abortion, so long as the regulation did not impose an "undue burden" on the woman's abortion decision. Applying the "undue burden" standard, the Court held that the state could require a woman to wait 24 hours after giving her written consent before having the abortion, and could require that the physician make available to her state-furnished information about abortion that was designed in part to influence her not to have the abortion. However, the Court held unconstitutional as an "undue burden" a requirement that the physician inform a married woman's husband of her decision to have an abortion.[703] The Court, recognizing that domestic violence is a serious problem in American society, reasoned that the notification requirement would cause some small number of married women to refrain from seeking an abortion because of fear of violence on the part of their husbands when notified that their wife wanted to have an abortion. Unreasonable regulations of the abortion procedure, such as a requirement that a post-first trimester abortion be performed in a hospital instead of in a properly equipped abortion clinic, would be found to impose an "undue burden" on the abortion decision, and so are unconstitutional.[704] The Court also held unconstitutional a state law prohibiting the use of a late-term abortion procedure, referred to as "partial birth abortion," because the law lacked any exception for the "health of the mother," and because it was drafted so vaguely that it could be construed as applying to another commonly used abortion procedure.[705] However, the Court upheld "on its face" a more narrowly drawn federal law that prohibited "partial birth abortions," notwithstanding that it did not contain an exception for the "health of the mother." Congress had made a factual finding that the prohibited procedure was never necessary to protect the "health of the mother," and the Court held that this finding was sufficient to enable the law to withstand a facial attack, but that the prohibition could be challenged as unconstitutional "as applied" in a particular case where it could be shown that the prohibited procedure was necessary to protect the "health of the mother."[706]

In a very recent decision, the Court more specifically defined "undue burden" to include unnecessary health regulations that had the purpose or effect of presenting a substantial obstacle to a woman seeking an abortion. It did not matter that after surmounting those substantial obstacles the woman could obtain an abortion. The Court held unconstitutional as an "undue burden" on the abortion decision state laws that required a doctor performing an abortion to have admitting privileges at a local hospital and required that an abortion facility meet the same standards as fully-equipped ambulatory surgical centers.[707]

348. The Court has also held that the state cannot interfere with a minor's right to have an abortion, such as by requiring parental consent to the abortion.[708] If the state wants to impose a parental consent requirement, it must also provide an expeditious judicial procedure by which a minor can obtain an abortion despite the refusal of the

703. The Court had previously held unconstitutional a law requiring that a married woman's husband consent to her abortion. *Planned Parenthood v. Danforth*, 428 U.S. 52 (1976).
704. *See Akron v. Akron Center for Reproductive Health, Inc.*, 462 U.S. 416 (1983).
705. *Stenberg v. Carhart*, 530 U.S. 914 (2000).
706. *Gonzales v. Carhart*, 550 U.S. 124 (2007).
707. *Whole Woman's Health v. Hellerstedt*, 136 S.Ct. 2292 (2016).
708. *Planned Parenthood v. Danforth*, 428 U.S. 52 (1976).

parents to consent. Under the constitutionally required procedure, the court must first determine whether the minor is sufficiently mature to make her own decision whether or not to have an abortion. If the court finds that the minor is sufficiently mature to make her own decision, she must be permitted to have the abortion. If the court finds that the minor is not sufficiently mature to make her own decision, the court must decide whether the abortion is in the "best interests of the minor," and if it finds that it is in her "best interests," she must be permitted to have the abortion.[709] In practice, the court will invariably find that it is in the "best interests" of the "immature" minor to have an abortion: precisely because she is "immature," it could not be in her "best interests" to continue with the pregnancy. So, in practice, a parental consent requirement will not operate to prevent a minor from having an abortion, so long as the minor is informed about and utilizes the "judicial by-pass" procedure.[710]

349. The United States does not yet have a system of universal health coverage, but there are special programs providing medical assistance for indigent persons. A number of states have excluded abortion from the coverage otherwise provided by medical assistance programs for indigents, and Congress, which partly funds state programs of medical assistance for indigents, has prohibited the use of federal funds for most abortions. The Supreme Court has upheld the constitutionality of the exclusion of abortion from programs of medical assistance for indigents. The Court held that when the state is acting as dispenser of benefits rather than as regulator, the rational basis standard of review rather than the compelling governmental interest standard applies. Applying the rational basis standard, the Court concluded that the ban on abortion coverage was rationally related to the state's legitimate interest in encouraging childbirth and in protecting potential human life.[711] In other words, while women have a fundamental right to an abortion, this fundamental right does not extend to having the government pay for the abortion even if the woman is indigent and otherwise eligible for medical assistance.

350. Just as a state cannot constitutionally prohibit a woman from having an abortion, it cannot, in any circumstance, constitutionally require that a woman have an abortion. Nor can a state impose any burdens on a woman because of her pregnancy. Thus, a school district cannot constitutionally require that a pregnant school teacher take a mandatory leave during the period of her pregnancy,[712] nor can a state deny a pregnant woman unemployment compensation when she becomes unemployed during

---

709. *Bellotti v. Baird*, 443 U.S. 622 (1979).

710. Alternatively, the state may require that the physician notify the parents of a minor before performing the abortion. However, if the requirement is that both parents be notified, there must be a "judicial by-pass" procedure, under which the requirement of notification to one of the parents can be avoided if this would be harmful to the minor. *Hodgson v. Minnesota*, 497 U.S. 417 (1990). The Court has not yet decided if a "judicial by-pass" procedure is constitutionally required if the state only requires notice to one of the parents.

It may be assumed that the state parental notification law must provide an "emergency" exception to the notice requirement where the pregnant minor needs an immediate abortion. However, if the law fails to include this requirement, but is otherwise valid, a court may issue an injunction against the enforcement of only the invalid provision. *Ayotte v. Planned Parenthood of Northern New England*, 546 U.S. 320 (2006).

711. *Maher v. Roe*, 432 U.S. 464 (1977); *Harris v. McRae*, 448 U.S. 297 (1980).

712. *Cleveland Board of Education v. LaFleur*, 414 U.S. 632 (1974).

her pregnancy.[713] In such cases, the state is constitutionally required to make an individual determination that pregnancy prevents the particular woman from continuing her employment, which is very unlikely. The Court has held, however, that a state disability insurance scheme for state employees that excluded from coverage disability due to normal pregnancy was not violative of equal protection. The Court based its decision on the fact that the inclusion of pregnancy in the program would substantially increase the costs because of the number of women who would voluntarily become pregnant.[714] Federal law now prohibits any discriminatory treatment of employees on the basis of pregnancy, so the Court's constitutional decision has in effect been superseded by federal law.[715]

C. *The Right of Interstate Travel*

351. The Supreme Court has long held that there is a fundamental right of interstate travel, and has stated that, "The right to travel from one State to another ... occupies a position fundamental to the concept of our Federal Union."[716] There are at least three components of the right of interstate travel.[717] First, the right of interstate travel protects the right of a citizen of one state to enter and to leave another state.[718] Second, it protects the right to be treated as a welcome visitor when a citizen of one state is temporarily present in another state.[719] Third, for those citizens who elect to become permanent residents of the state to which they have traveled, it protects the right to be treated like other citizens of that state.[720]

---

713. *Turner v. Department of Employment Security*, 423 U.S. 44 (1975).
714. *Geduldig v. Aiello*, 417 U.S. 484 (1974).
715. *See* the discussion, *supra* , para. 320, n. 655.
716. *United States v. Guest*, 383 U.S. 745, 757 (1966). The right of interstate travel was first recognized in *Crandall v. Nevada*, 73 U.S. 35 (1867), where the Court held unconstitutional a state's imposition of a head tax on the exit of all persons from the state. In *Edwards v. California*, 314 U.S. 160 (1941), the Court held unconstitutional as a "burden on interstate commerce" a state law that prohibited bringing an indigent person into the state. The law was also violative of the right of interstate travel, as some of the concurring Justices emphasized. While the right of interstate travel analytically is included in the "liberty" protected by the Fourteenth Amendment's due process clause, the Court has treated it as a "basic generic right inhering in the concept of the Federal Union that the Constitution was designed to establish." In this sense, the right of interstate travel is found in the internal inferences of the Constitution rather than in the text.
717. *See* the discussion in *Saenz v. Roe*, 526 U.S. 489, 500–503 (1999).
718. This component of the right of interstate travel was involved in *Crandall v. Nevada and Edwards v. California*, *supra* , para. 350, n. 716. In *Guest v. United States*, *supra* , para. 350, n. 716, the Court upheld the power of Congress to make it a crime to interfere with the right of interstate travel.
719. This component of the right of interstate travel is specifically protected by the "privileges and immunities" clause of Art. IV, s. 2, cl. 1, which prohibits state discrimination against nonresidents. *See* paras. 188–189, *supra* .
720. This component of the right of interstate travel is specifically protected as one of the "privileges and immunities" of United States citizenship by the "privileges and immunities" clause of the Fourteenth Amendment, s. 1, which provides that, "No State shall make or enforce any law which shall abridge the privileges or immunities of citizens of the United States." *Saenz v. Roe*, *supra* , n. 717.

352. Because the right of interstate travel is a fundamental right, the Court has held that laws interfering with or imposing a burden on interstate travel must be evaluated under the compelling governmental interest standard of review. Thus, laws imposing durational residency requirements on the receipt of governmental benefits, such as that a person reside in a state for a year before being eligible to receive welfare, are evaluated under the compelling governmental interest standard, even though the interest involved in receiving the underlying benefit does not itself constitute a fundamental right. A durational residency requirement for eligibility for a governmental benefit gives rise to an equal protection challenge because the effect of the requirement is to distinguish between two classes of residents: old residents, who are entitled to receive the benefit, and new residents, who are not entitled to receive the benefit until they have resided in the state for a year. The favored and disfavored groups are identically situated with respect to the need for and the statutorily defined entitlement to the benefit. Thus, the denial of benefits to the new residents under the durational residency requirement would be violative of equal protection unless the state could demonstrate a sufficiently "compelling" independent justification for the differential treatment. An asserted purpose to preserve the fiscal integrity of the welfare program by deterring indigents from other states from coming into the state either generally or to receive higher welfare benefits is a constitutionally impermissible purpose, because it is directed at discouraging the exercise of the fundamental right of interstate travel. Other asserted justifications, such as the prevention of fraudulent claims, have also been found wanting under the "less drastic means" aspect of the compelling governmental interest standard of review. Thus, the Court has held violative of equal protection durational residency requirements for eligibility for welfare benefits and for medical assistance to indigents.[721] And more recently, the Court held unconstitutional a state law limiting new residents during their first year of residency to the level of welfare benefits provided by the state from which they had moved.[722]

353. The Court has also held unconstitutional a one-year durational residency requirement for eligibility to vote. Such a requirement implicates the fundamental right to vote as well as the fundamental right of interstate travel. Again, none of the asserted justifications could justify a one-year durational residency requirement; the need for accurate voter records, for example, would justify only a limited time period for registration prior to the election.[723] However, the Court has upheld a one-year durational residency requirement for filing for a divorce in the state, although this requirement implicates the fundamental right of marriage as well as the fundamental

721. *Shapiro v. Thompson*, 394 U.S. 618 (1969); *Memorial Hospital v. Maricopa County*, 415 U.S. 250 (1974).

722. *Saenz v. Roe*, *supra* , n. 717. It did not matter that the new residents would be receiving the same level of benefits that they received in their former state, since they were still being treated differently from other residents of their new state. The Court noted that the "privileges and immunities" clause did not tolerate a "hierarchy of [s]ubclasses of similarly situated citizens based on the location of their prior residence." By the same token, the right to interstate travel also does not entitle a party to retain the same level of welfare benefits provided by the former state when the party moves to a new state. Upon making the move, the party is only entitled to the level of benefits provided by the new state. *Califano v. Torres*, 435 U.S. 1 (1978).

723. *Dunn v. Blumstein*, 405 U.S. 330 (1972).

right of interstate travel.[724] It is difficult to reconcile the result in this case with the results in Court's other durational residency requirement cases, as well as the results in the length of residency cases (*see* paragraph 353, *infra*), and it is highly unlikely that the Court would uphold any other durational residency requirement today.[725]

354. The third component of the right of interstate travel—for those citizens who elect to become permanent residents of the state to which they have traveled, it protects the right to be treated like other citizens of that state—precludes a state from imposing length of residency requirements that discriminate between "older" and "newer" residents. Thus, the Court has held unconstitutional a state law making the amount of a "windfall payment" from state revenues dependent on how long the person has lived in the state,[726] and provisions in state programs providing benefits for persons who had been in military service that limited the benefits to persons who were state residents at the time they entered into military service.[727]

355. The right of interstate travel must be distinguished from the right to travel abroad. While the right to travel abroad is part of the "liberty" protected by the Fourteenth Amendment's due process clause, the exercise of that right runs up against the federal government's power over foreign affairs. The Court has not held that the right to travel abroad is a fundamental right, and in particular contexts, the Court has balanced that right against the need for the federal government to control foreign travel in order to achieve foreign policy objectives. The Court has held that the federal government can restrict or prohibit travel to designated foreign countries, such as Cuba, with whom the United States did not have diplomatic relations at that time.[728] The Court has also held that the federal government can revoke the passport of an American residing abroad on the ground that his activities were likely to cause serious damage to national security or foreign policy interests, in this case, the passport of a former CIA employee who had announced his intention to disclose the identity of CIA

---

724. *Sosna v. Iowa*, 419 U.S. 393 (1975). It may be noted that this requirement is not very burdensome, since the new resident could file for divorce in the state of former residence, where the other spouse is likely to still reside. The requirement would also make the divorce decree less susceptible to challenge because of doubts as to the party's bona fide residence in the new state.

725. In an earlier case, the Court summarily affirmed a lower court case that upheld a one-year durational residency requirement for entitlement to lower resident tuition rates at public universities. *Starns v. Malkerson*, 401 U.S. 985 (1971), summarily affirming 326 F.Supp. 234 (D.Mino. 1970). In *Eastman v. University of Michigan*, 30 F.3d 670 (6th Cir. 1994), a federal appeals court took the position that a one-year durational residency requirement for entitlement to lower resident tuition at a public university, imposed upon a bona fide resident, would be unconstitutional.

The right to travel within a state is not a fundamental right for due process and equal protection purposes, so any interference with or burden on that right is evaluated under the rational basis standard of review. Applying that standard, the Court has upheld as constitutional a local residency requirement for municipal employees, *McCarthy v. Philadelphia Civil Service Commission*, 424 U.S. 645 (1976), and a requirement that children attend public school in the school district where their parents or guardian resides. *Martinez v. Bynum*, 461 U.S. 321 (1983).

726. *Zobel v. Williams*, 457 U.S. 55 (1982).

727. *See Attorney-General of New York v. Soto-Lopez*, 476 U.S. 898 (1986); *Hooper v. Bernalillo County Assessor*, 472 U.S. 612 (1985).

728. *Zemel v. Rusk*, 381 U.S. 1 (1965).

officials and agents operating in foreign countries.[729] However, the Court has held unconstitutional as "overbroad and indiscriminate" a law that prohibited any member of an organization under an order to register as a "subversive organization" from obtaining a passport.[730]

D. The Right to Vote

356. If there were no other basis for finding a right to vote in the Constitution, it could be said to be part of the "liberty" protected by the due process clauses of the Fifth and Fourteenth Amendments. However, the right to vote is more properly considered an attribute of United States and state citizenship recognized and protected by section 1 of the Fourteenth Amendment. The Twenty-Sixth Amendment also guarantees the right to vote to all persons 18 years or older, and the Fifteenth and Nineteenth Amendments prohibit abridgment of the right to vote on the basis of race and gender respectively. With so much textual constitutional protection to the right to vote, there is no doubt that it is a fundamental right, and that any law interfering with the exercise of that right is subject to strong justification under the compelling governmental interest standard of review.[731] The cases involving constitutional protection of the right to vote fall into three categories: (1) denial or qualification of the right to vote; (2) dilution of the right to vote; (3) restrictions on candidates and political parties. The equal protection clause has been the primary textual basis by which the Court has provided constitutional protection to the right to vote.[732]

1. Denial or Qualification of the Right to Vote

357. The qualifications for voting are established by state law for both state and federal offices. This is because the Constitution specifically provides that voters for Members of Congress shall have the same qualifications as voters for the lower house of the state legislature.[733] The states can constitutionally limit the franchise to persons who are at least 18 years of age, and all states do so. The states are not constitutionally required to limit voting to United States citizens and legal residents of the state, but

729. *Haig v. Agee*, 453 U.S. 280 (1981).

730. *Aptheker v. Secretary of State*, 378 U.S. 500 (1964). In an earlier case, the Court found that Congress had not authorized the State Department to deny passports to persons because of their "communist backgrounds." *Kent v. Dulles*, 357 U.S. 116 (1958).

731. *See Reynolds v. Sims*, 377 U.S. 533 (1964).

732. The right to vote means simply the right to vote in elections. The Constitution does not require that all important governmental positions must be elective, nor does it prevent the states from filling vacancies in elective positions by means other than election. *See* e.g., *Rodriguez v. Popular Democratic Party*, 457 U.S. 1 (1982), holding that it was constitutionally permissible for a state or territory to provide that a vacancy in a local legislative body caused by the death, resignation or removal of a legislator would be filled until the next regularly scheduled election by the political party with which the previous incumbent was affiliated.

733. Article I, s. 2 (House of Representatives), and Amend. XVII (Senators). It will be recalled that the President is elected indirectly by an Electoral College, and that each state prescribes the qualifications for voting for its Electors.

again all states do.[734] The states must allow all bona fide residents of the state to vote, and they cannot deny residency status to persons in military service on the ground that they may be required to leave the state under military orders.[735] The states cannot constitutionally require that a voter pay a "poll tax" in order to vote.[736]

Some states deny or qualify the right to vote to persons who have been convicted of serious criminal offenses,[737] and the Supreme Court has held that this is constitutionally permissible, as being specifically authorized by the text of the Fourteenth Amendment.[738]

358. The right to vote may also be violated when the state tries to limit the right to vote to "interested voters" in elections involving specialized units of local government. The Supreme Court has held that the state may do so only in regard to "special interest elections," and has defined "special interest election" narrowly to refer only to those elections involving specialized units that do not exercise "normal governmental authority." Thus, the Court has held unconstitutional a state law that limited the right to vote in school district elections to residents of the school district who either owned or leased taxable land in the district or who had children enrolled in the district's schools. The effect of the law was to deny the right to vote in school district elections to an unmarried man living with his parents. The Court held that this was unconstitutional because as a resident of the district, that person could have a real interest in the actions taken by the school board.[739] The Court has also held unconstitutional laws limiting the right to vote to property owners in elections involving the issuance of municipal

---

734. As discussed previously, the fundamental right of interstate travel precludes the states from imposing durational residency requirements on the right to vote, except for a brief period necessary to ensure the preparation of accurate voter lists. *See Dunn v. Blumstein*, *supra* , n. 723.

735. *Carrington v. Rush*, 380 U.S. 89 (1965). However, because residency may be made a requirement for voting, the right to vote in municipal elections may be limited to persons who reside within the municipality and not in an adjacent unincorporated area, notwithstanding that under state law, the municipality could exercise certain regulatory powers in the adjacent unincorporated area. *Holt Civic Club v. City of Tuscaloosa*, 439 U.S. 60 (1978).

736. The Twenty-Fourth Amendment specifically prohibits the imposition of a "poll tax" in Presidential and Congressional elections, and the Court has held that the imposition of a "poll tax" in an election for state or local officials is violative of equal protection. *Harper v. Virginia State Board of Elections*, 383 U.S. 663 (1966).

While the use of literacy tests as a voter qualification is not unconstitutional, Congress has prohibited the use of literacy tests because of the fact that they have frequently been used to discriminate against racial minority voters. Such a prohibition is within Congress' power to prevent racial discrimination in voting under the Fifteenth Amendment. *See Oregon v. Mitchell*, 400 U.S. 112 (1970).

737. Most provide for "restoration of civil rights" after a period of time has elapsed since the person has served the sentence for the crime, and restoration includes the right to vote.

738. *Richardson v. Ramirez*, 418 U.S. 24 (1974). Section 2 of the Fourteenth Amendment, enacted in the aftermath of the Civil War, prohibited the states from denying the vote to male citizens over 21 "except for participation in rebellion or other crime." The Court held that the phrase, "except [for] other crime," constituted specific authorization to the states to disqualify persons convicted of crimes from voting, and so upheld against equal protection challenge a state's disenfranchisement of persons convicted of felony offenses.

739. *Kramer v. Union Free School District*, 395 U.S. 621 (1969).

bonds by a municipally owned utility,[740] and in elections involving the issuance of general obligation bonds to finance certain municipal improvements.[741] However, it has upheld a state law permitting only landowners to vote in "water storage district" elections. These districts planned projects for water acquisition, conservation and distribution, and assessed charges for the use of water and for water projects on landowners in proportion to the benefit received. The Court emphasized that the "water storage district" did not exercise "normal governmental authority," and that its actions "disproportionately affected landowners."[742]

359. The Supreme Court has held that the right to vote does not include the right to vote by absentee ballot. However, when the state does provide for absentee ballot voting, restrictions on access to absentee ballot voting may be challenged as violative of equal protection under the rational basis standard of review. Applying that standard, the Court has upheld a law providing absentee ballots only to the physically handicapped and those who would be out of their home county on election day,[743] but has held unconstitutional as "wholly arbitrary" a law that allowed absentee ballots to persons absent from their home county, including persons held in jail in another county, but denied them to persons held in jail in their home county.[744] The Court has recently upheld the constitutionality of a state law requiring each voter to present a government-issued identification card as a condition of voting.[745]

360. A final aspect of voting disqualification relates to voting in political party primary elections. Some states provide for "open primaries," in which the voter can choose to vote in either party's primary election. Other states require voters to register as a party member in order to vote in that party's primary election. States taking the latter approach sometimes impose restrictions on primary voting that are designed to prevent voters who are affiliated with one party from voting for "weaker" candidates in the other party's primary election, so that their own party's candidate will have a better chance of winning the general election. The Court has held that this is a permissible objective generally, but that the particular restriction cannot unreasonably burden the right to vote in a party primary. On this basis, the Court has upheld a requirement that a voter register as a party member thirty days before the preceding general election, although this was some eleven months in advance of the next primary election,[746] but has held unconstitutional a law prohibiting a person from voting in a party primary

740. *Cipriano v. City of Houma*, 395 U.S. 701 (1969).
741. *Phoenix v. Kolodziejski*, 399 U.S. 204 (1970).
742. *Salyer Land Co. v. Tulare Lake Basin Water Storage District*, 410 U.S. 719 (1973). *See also Ball v. James*, 451 U.S. 355 (1981), where the Court upheld a law limiting voting in water district elections to landowners, notwithstanding that the water district in question had become a major supplier of hydroelectric power in the state.
743. *McDonald v. Board of Election Commissioners*, 394 U.S. 802 (1969). The law was challenged by inmates who were confined in jail while awaiting their trials.
744. *O'Brien v. Skinner*, 414 U.S. 524 (1974).
745. *Crawford v. Marion County Election Board*, 553 U.S. 181 (2008).
746. *Rosario v. Rockefeller*, 410 U.S. 752 (1973).

election if that person had voted in another party's primary election within the preceding twenty-three months.[747]

2. Dilution of the Right to Vote

361. Perhaps the most "politically significant" aspect of the Supreme Court's equal protection doctrine is the requirement of voting equality, or as it is popularly called, "one person, one vote." Under the requirement of voting equality, every person's vote in an election must have substantially the same weight as every other person's. This means that electoral districts for members of legislative bodies must be drawn in such a way that they contain substantially equal numbers of voters. While the equal protection clause does not require that they be drawn with "precise mathematical equality,"[748] it does require that they be drawn within a range of permissible deviation.

362. The Supreme Court first declared this principle in the early 1960s in constitutional challenges to the malapportionment of state legislatures. In many states, legislative districts had traditionally been drawn in such a way as to keep intact county and city boundaries and to reflect "communities of interest." The end result was that legislative districts in the less populated and rural areas of the state were comprised of substantially fewer persons than legislative districts in the more populated and urban areas of the state. This meant that the residents of the less populated legislative districts would have proportionately greater representation and weight of vote in the legislative body than the residents of the more populated legislative districts. After holding that constitutional challenges to legislative malapportionment were "justiciable,"[749] the Supreme Court went on to hold that legislative malapportionment violated the equal protection rights of voters in the more populated legislative districts. The Court emphasized that "legislators represent people, not trees," and that, "citizens, not history or economic interests cast votes," so that, "The equal protection clause requires that

747. *Kusper v. Pontikes*, 414 U.S. 51 (1973). The Court has also held unconstitutional under the First Amendment's guarantee of freedom of association, a state law that prohibited a political party from allowing persons who had not registered with either party (so-called independent voters) from voting in its party primary election. *Tashjian v. Republican Party of Connecticut*, 479 U.S. 208 (1986). Likewise, the Court has invalidated a state law requiring, contrary to the Democratic Party's rules, that delegates selected for the party's presidential nominating convention vote at the convention in accordance with the results of the state's "open presidential preference primary." *Democratic Party v. Wisconsin ex rel. LaFollette*, 450 U.S. 107 (1981).

748. Since Art. I, s. 2, cl. 3 requires that representation in the United States House of Representatives be entirely on the basis of population, the Supreme Court has held that Congressional districts within a state must be drawn "with precise mathematical equality." *Kirkpatrick v. Preisler*, 394 U.S. 526 (1969); *Karcher v. Daggett*, 462 U.S. 725 (1983). This requirement relates to the "Great Compromise" by which the House of Representatives would represent "people according to their respective numbers," while the Senate would represent the states as states in the national legislature. *See* Part II, Ch. 2.

749. *Baker v. Carr*, 369 U.S. 186 (1962). *See* the discussion para. 118, n. 134, *supra* .

a state make a good-faith effort to construct districts in both houses of its legislature as nearly of equal population as is practicable."[750]

363. In subsequent decisions, the Court defined "as nearly of equal population as is practicable" in terms of a range of permissible deviation between the most overrepresented district and the most underrepresented district. The Court has held that a maximum deviation of under 10% is "insignificant" and does not have to be justified.[751] It has also upheld a plan with a 16% maximum deviation that the state justified as an effort to keep political subdivision lines intact.[752] However, in another case, the Court invalidated a plan with a maximum deviation of 16.5% for state senate districts and 19.3% for state house districts. The Court found that the state's attempt to justify the plan in terms of maintaining county boundaries was insufficient, because counties did not have significant legislative powers and because the challengers presented an alternative plan that would have maintained county boundaries with less population deviation.[753]

As a result of the Court's decisions in this area, state legislative reapportionment following the decennial census,[754] is potentially subject to constitutional challenge under the equal protection clause, and such challenges occur almost as "of course."

364. The requirement that legislative districts be drawn "as nearly of equal population as is practicable" extends to a large number of local governmental bodies whose members are elected by district, such as a county governing board,[755] a junior

---

750. *Reynolds v. Sims*, 377 U.S. 533 (1964). The Court rejected the state's argument, drawing an analogy to the system of representation in the Congress, that it should be permitted to have representation in one house of the legislature based on factors other than population, such as political subdivisions. The Court noted that the system of representation in the Congress related to the fact that formerly sovereign states were binding themselves together in one national government. Political subdivisions of the states, by contrast, are not "sovereign," but are rather subordinate governmental units created by the state.

By the same token, a "county unit" system for the election of statewide officers, under which the candidate receiving the highest number of votes in each county obtained two votes for each representative to which the county was entitled in the lower house of the state legislature, was held unconstitutional, because counties were not represented in the state legislature in proportion to their population, and counties having the population of one-third of the state had a majority of "county units." *Gray v. Sanders*, 372 U.S. 368 (1963).

The Supreme Court has recently rejected a claim that legislative districts must be drawn on the basis of the population of those eligible or registered to vote rather than on the basis of total population. The Court noted that its precedents and the long-standing practice of all the states established that the state could draw its legislative districts based on total population without denying equal protection to those districts that had a larger population of voters eligible or registered to vote. *Evenwel v. Abbott*, 136 Sup.Ct. 1120 (2016).

In *Bush v. Gore*, 531 U.S. 98 (2000), the Court applied the principle of voting equality to hold unconstitutional Florida's method of recounting votes in disputed elections. *See* the discussion, *supra* , para. 60, n. 56.

751. *White v. Regester*, 412 U.S. 755 (1973); *Gaffney v. Cummings*, 412 U.S. 735 (1973).

752. *Mahan v. Howell*, 410 U.S. 315 (1973).

753. *Connor v. Finch*, 431 U.S. 407 (1977).

754. State constitutions typically require the reapportionment of the state legislature following the decennial census.

755. *Avery v. Midland County*, 390 U.S. 474 (1968).

college district,[756] and a municipal body that performed legislative functions.[757] However, it does not extend to election districts for state court judges, since the function of judges is not to represent people, but to administer and apply the law.[758]

365. The principle of voting equality only requires that each person's vote in an election for representative officials have substantially the same weight as the vote of any other person. It does not apply to limit the authority of the states to determine how officials shall be elected. Thus, it does not prevent the states from establishing multimember legislative districts or requiring that all representatives be elected at large,[759] or choosing to provide for appointment rather than election of members of a legislative body,[760] or providing that if no candidate for Governor receives a majority of the popular vote, that the Governor shall be selected by the legislature from the two candidates receiving the highest popular vote.[761] Nor does it prevent the states from imposing "supermajority" or "concurrent majority" requirements in elections, such as that a proposal to increase tax rates receive 60% voter approval in a referendum,[762] or that a new county charter could go into effect only if approved in a referendum by separate majorities of the voters in each city of the county, and by a majority of the voters living outside of the cities.[763]

366. It should also be noted that a legislative apportionment that satisfies the requirement of voting equality may be challenged on other constitutional grounds, such as that it intentionally discriminates against minority voters,[764] or that it was

756. *Hadely v. Junior College District*, 397 U.S. 50 (1970).
757. *Board of Estimate v. Morris*, 489 U.S. 688 (1989). This case involved a feature unique to the government of New York City. In addition to the elected City Council, the city charter provided for a Board of Estimate consisting of designated elected officials. Three officials, the city's mayor, controller and city council president, were elected to their offices on a city-wide basis. The other members were the presidents of each of the city's five boroughs, which varied widely in population, so that the residents of the city's least populous borough had a greater impact on the election of members of the Board than the residents of the city's most populous borough. The Board performed a variety of functions that more typically would have been performed by the city council, including zoning authority, fixing the salaries of city officers, and sharing some authority over the budget with the City Council. The Court held that the Board exercised sufficient legislative authority to bring the selection of its members within the equality of vote requirement.
758. *See Wells v. Edwards*, 409 U.S. 1095 (1973), *sum. Aff'g.*, 347 F.Supp. 453 (M.D.La. 1972). The federal Voting Rights Act, however, does apply to the election of state court judges, and judicial election districts are invalid under the Act if they unfairly dilute minority voting power. *Chisom v. Roemer*, 501 U.S. 380 (1991).
759. *Forston v. Dorsey*, 379 U.S. 433 (1965); *City of Mobile v. Bolden*, 446 U.S. 55 (1980). However, the use or retention of multimember districts or at-large elections is violative of the Fourteenth and Fifteenth Amendments if the court finds that this method of selection was intentionally established or retained to discriminate against minority voters. *White v. Regester*, 412 U.S. 755 (1973); *Rogers v. Lodge*, 458 U.S. 613 (1982). It is violative of the federal Voting Rights Act if it has the effect of diluting minority political power. *Thornburg v. Gingles*, 478 U.S. 30 (1986).
760. *Sailors v. Board of Education*, 387 U.S. 105 (1967).
761. *Fortson v. Morris*, 385 U.S. 231 (1966).
762. *Gordon v. Lance*, 403 U.S. 1 (1971).
763. *Town of Lockport v. Citizens for Community Action at the Local Level Inc.*, 430 U.S. 259 (1977).
764. *See* para. 313, n. 632, *supra* .

intentionally "politically gerrymandered," to dilute the voting strength of a minority political party.[765] A claim of "political gerrymandering" will be difficult to sustain in practice, and there is no reported case where such a claim has been sustained. The minority political party must show as a threshold matter that the legislative districts have consistently been drawn in such a way that it had been unfairly denied its chance to effectively influence the political process. If it surmounts this threshold burden, it must then show that the districts were consistently drawn in this way with the intention of depriving the party of its chance to effectively influence the political process. In *Vieth v. Jubelirer*,[766] four Justices took the position that claims of "political gerrymandering" were completely non-justiciable and should be dismissed under the political question doctrine. (*See* paragraphs 114–122, *supra*). A fifth Justice took the position that while such claims were difficult to sustain, a claim could be sustained in a case where it could be shown that the "political classifications" leading to the "gerrymander" "were applied in an invidious manner or in a way unrelated to any legitimate legislative objective." There were four dissents. Thus, five Justices ended up taking the position that such claims were not completely non-justiciable, but as stated above, such claims will be difficult to sustain in practice. In *League of United Latin Voters v. Perry*,[767] the Court again rejected a "partisan gerrymandering" challenge to a redistricting plan, with a Court majority indicating that such a challenge was either "non-justiciable" or could not be sustained in the absence of demonstrating a reliable standard for challenging "partisan gerrymandering."

3. Restrictions on Candidates and Political Parties

367. The states have the constitutional authority to prescribe the qualifications that candidates must have to run for public office, and that political parties must have to designate party candidates on the ballot. In the exercise of this authority, the states have a legitimate interest in limiting the number of candidates on the ballot in order to reduce the potential for voter confusion and to increase the likelihood that the candidate who is elected will have received a majority of the popular vote. However, restrictions on ballot access do impair the right of voters to cast a ballot for candidates of their choice, and thus are subject to equal protection challenge as interfering with the right to vote.[768]

368. The Court has held unconstitutional the imposition of ballot access fees, as applied to bar ballot access to an indigent candidate,[769] and any property ownership

765. *Davis v. Bandemer*, 478 U.S. 109 (1986).

766. 541 U.S. 267 (2004).

767. 548 U.S. 399 (2006).

768. Restrictions on ballot access, particularly those imposed on new political parties, also interfere with the First Amendment right of persons to associate for the expression of views and for concerted action in a particular campaign. Depending on the particular kind of restriction, the Court may employ either an equal protection analysis or a First Amendment analysis or both, but frequently either or both methods of analysis will lead to the same conclusion as to the constitutional permissibility or impermissibility of the challenged restriction.

769. *Lubin v. Panash*, 415 U.S. 709 (1974); *Bullock v. Carter*, 405 U.S. 134 (1972).

requirement as a condition to be a candidate for public office.[770] Here, any asserted governmental interest to support the requirement is clearly outweighed by the right of indigent persons to become candidates for public office and the right of voters to vote for them.

369. The Court has been more disposed to uphold "demonstrated support" requirements to obtain ballot access for independent candidates and candidates of minor or new political parties. The "demonstrated support" requirement advances the state's legitimate interest in limiting the number of candidates on the ballot for the reasons discussed above. Typically, the "demonstrated support" requirement requires that a political party must either have received a minimum percentage of the vote cast at the last general election, or failing that, must obtain a certain number of signatures from qualified voters related to the total vote cast at the last general election. Independent candidates and candidates of new parties must obtain the requisite number of signatures. If the particular "demonstrated support" requirement is reasonable and will not operate to impose serious barriers to ballot access for independent and minor or new party candidates, it will be held to be constitutional.

370. The Court has upheld "demonstrated support" requirements that simply require that the independent candidate or political party obtain a specified number of signatures by a reasonable time before the general election. Thus, the Court has upheld a signature requirement for minority parties (defined as parties with less than 2% of the total vote in the last general election for Governor) or new political parties, totaling 1% of the number of persons voting in the last gubernatorial election, approximately 22,000 votes in the particular case.[771] The Court has likewise upheld a requirement of obtaining signatures totaling 5% of the number of persons eligible to vote in the last election for the office in question, so that the required number of signatures would vary depending on the size of the electorate for the particular office.[772] And where the state holds a "blanket primary," in which voters may vote for any candidate regardless of the candidate's political affiliation, the state may limit participation in the general

770. *Turner v. Fouche*, 396 U.S. 346 (1970); *Quinn v. Millsap*, 491 U.S. 95 (1989).

771. *American Party of Texas v. White*, 415 U.S. 767 (1974). The candidates of the "major political parties," defined as a party whose candidate received more than 200,000 votes in the last gubernatorial election, could obtain ballot access by being nominated in a primary election. The signatories of the "minority political party" had to execute a notarized oath that they had not participated in any other party's primary or nomination process, and the required signatures had to be submitted 120 days before the general election.

772. *Jenness v. Fortson*, 403 U.S. 431 (1971).

elections to candidates who received their party's nomination in the primary, and who, in addition, have received at least 1% of the total vote in the "blanket primary."[773]

371. Where "demonstrated support" requirements cease to be reasonable and may operate to impose serious barriers to ballot access by independent and minor or new party candidates, is where they contain very large signature requirements, where they contain supplementary signature requirements, or where they couple signature requirements with early deadlines for collecting them. The Court has held unconstitutional a law that required new political parties seeking ballot access to maintain an elaborate party structure, to collect signatures totaling 15% of the votes cast in the last gubernatorial election, and to have the signatures filed by February for the November election.[774] In a series of cases coming from one state, Illinois, the Court has held unconstitutional the following restrictions on ballot access:

(1) a requirement that independent candidates in the Presidential election collect 25,000 signatures, with at least 200 signatures from each of fifty of the state's 102 counties;[775]
(2) a requirement that new political parties and independent candidates obtain 25,000 signatures to appear on the ballot for statewide elections, and that candidates for offices within a political subdivision such as a county, obtain signatures from at least 5% of the people who had voted in the previous election of that particular subdivision (as applied to the largest city in the state and the county in which it was located, Chicago and Cook County, candidates would need 35,000 signatures, more than was otherwise required for state office);[776]
(3) an amended version of that law, which changed the maximum for each political subdivision to 25,000, but required that for a multidistrict subdivision, such as Chicago and Cook County, the signatures would have to be obtained for both subdivisions, and here would require 50,000 signatures.[777]

---

773. *Munro v. Socialist Workers Party*, 479 U.S. 189 (1986). The federal Presidential campaign financing law allocates federal funding in a manner that favors the major parties over minor parties, and does not provide any funds for new parties or independent candidates. The Court has held that there was no constitutional objection to Congress allocating federal funding in this manner, since Congress could require "some preliminary showing of a significant modicum of support" as a condition for eligibility for public funds. *Buckley v. Valeo*, 424 U.S. 1, 96 (1976).

In a similar vein, the Court has upheld the constitutionality of a ban on "write-in" voting for candidates not on the ballot, where the electoral system provided for easy candidate access to the ballot until the cut-off date for the filing of nominating petitions, which was two months before the primary election. *Burdick v. Takushi*, 504 U.S. 428 (1992).

774. *Williams v. Rhodes*, 393 U.S. 23 (1968).

775. *Moore v. Ogilvie*, 394 U.S. 814 (1969).

776. *Illinois State Board of Elections v. Socialist Workers Party*, 440 U.S. 173 (1979).

777. *Norman v. Reed*, 502 U.S. 279 (1992). The Court upheld the 25,000 signature requirement as a condition for obtaining ballot access in each political subdivision in which the party wanted to run candidates.

The Court has also held unconstitutional a filing deadline for independent candidates that was set before the party primary election and seven months before the general election.[778]

372. The Court has held that restrictions on the right of an individual candidate to run for public office will not be evaluated with the same degree of scrutiny as restrictions on ballot access for independent candidates and minor and new political parties. It has upheld, for example, the constitutionality of a party affiliation law, under which a person who had registered as a member of a political party within a year of the preceding primary election or who had voted or run as a candidate in the party primary election, could not run as an independent candidate in the general election.[779]

E. A New Enumerated Right: The Right to Keep and Bear Arms

373. The Second Amendment to the Constitution provides that, "A well-regulated Militia, being necessary to the security of a free State, the right of the people to keep and bear arms shall not be infringed." The historical purpose of this provision was to prevent the federal government from abolishing the state militias that fought for Independence during the Revolutionary War and that were retained by the states following Independence. It was also contended, however, that the Second Amendment created a right on the part of individuals to keep and bear arms, so that gun control regulation was subject to constitutional challenge as violative of the Second Amendment. It should be noted that gun ownership is very important to a substantial number of American citizens who maintain that individual gun ownership is necessary for self-defense and as a means of deterring crime. This claim was much disputed by advocates of gun regulation, and the controversy was not resolved by the Supreme Court until 2008. In *District of Columbia v. Heller*,[780] the Court held 5-4, that the Second Amendment did create an individual right to keep and bear arms. The Court did not say that this right was a fundamental right for purposes of the two-tier standard of review, and did not go beyond saying that it was an "enumerated right," so that a gun control regulation could not be sustained under a "mere rational basis" analysis. In that case, the Court held unconstitutional a District of Columbia law that absolutely prohibited any possession of a loaded handgun in the home. The Court stated that, "Under any of the standards of scrutiny that we have applied to enumerated constitutional rights, banning from the home 'the most preferred firearm in the nation to keep and use for protection

---

778. *Anderson v. Celebrezze*, 460 U.S. 780 (1983).

779. *Storer v. Brown*, 415 U.S. 724 (1974). Conversely, a state cannot absolutely bar a person from access to the ballot as an independent candidate, but can only impose reasonable "demonstrated support" requirements. *See McCarthy v. Briscoe*, 429 U.S. 1317 (1976), where former Justice Powell issued an interim order requiring that a state place an independent candidate for President on the ballot, holding unconstitutional a state law requiring that presidential candidates belong to an organized political party.

A number of states and municipalities limit the number of terms that an individual can serve in executive and legislative offices. While no cases involving term limits have reached the Supreme Court, these laws have consistently been upheld as constitutional by the lower federal courts. *See* e.g., *Citizens for Legislative Choice v. Miller*, 144 F.3d 916 (6th Cir. 1998) (lifetime term limits for members of state legislatures); *Bates v. Jones*, 131 F.3d 843 (9th Cir. 1997) (same).

780. 554 U.S. 570 (2008).

of one's home and family' would fail constitutional muster under any standard."[781] But the Court went on to say that:

> Although we do not undertake an exhaustive historical analysis today of the full scope of the Second Amendment, nothing in our opinion should be taken to cast doubt on longstanding prohibitions on the possession of firearms by felons and the mentally ill, or laws forbidding the carrying of firearms in sensitive places such as schools and government buildings or laws imposing conditions and qualifications on the commercial sale of arms.[782]

The Court also pointed out that the right was limited to the use of "weapons of common usage by law-abiding persons" and did not extend to "dangerous and unusual weapons."[783] It may be assumed then that the right is limited to handguns and rifles.

For present purposes, it is sufficient to note that while the right to keep and bear arms has not been held to be a fundamental right for purposes of the two-tier standard of review, restrictions on gun ownership and usage, beyond those that the Court in *Heller* indicated were permissible, will be subject to at least an intermediate degree of scrutiny. The precise nature of this newly enumerated right remains to be determined, as challenges to gun regulation will come before the Court.

III. Social and Economic Legislation

A. Due Process and Equal Protection: The Rational Basis Standard of Review

374. Since most social and economic legislation does not affect fundamental rights, due process and equal protection challenges to such legislation are evaluated under the rational basis standard of review. Under this standard of review, the challenged law or classification will be held unconstitutional only if it can be shown that it is not reasonably related to the advancement of a legitimate governmental interest. As would be expected, under this standard of review, there is a considerable degree of judicial deference to legislative judgment and discretion. The Court will hypothesize purposes for the law or classification in issue, and there is no requirement that the government demonstrate that the hypothesized purpose was in fact the actual purpose. The legislature

781. *Ibid.*, at 628–629.
782. *Ibid.*, at 626–627.
783. *Ibid.*, at 627. The Court has recently held that the relevant question is whether a type of arms is in common use today, not whether the type of arms was in common use at the time of the Second Amendment's enactment. Without resolving the question, the Court held that "stun guns" could be protected arms under the Second Amendment. *Caetano v. Massachusetts*, 136 S.Ct. 1027 (2016).

also has broad discretion in concluding that a particular regulation or classification will advance the purpose for which it was adopted.[784]

375. In practice, the Court's application of the rational basis standard of review, while always deferential, will vary somewhat in the degree of deference depending on the importance of the particular interest involved. When the Court is dealing with governmental economic regulation of business enterprises, the application of the rational basis standard is extremely deferential, amounting to virtual non-reviewability. However, when the Court is dealing with laws or governmental action affecting individual liberty or property interests, such as restrictions on the right to work or classifications contained in social welfare legislation, the Court's application of the standard is somewhat less deferential. Most of the time, however, even with less deferential review, the challenged law or classification will still be upheld against due process or equal protection challenge. But sometimes the Court will invalidate a law or classification on the ground that, even with considerable deference to legislative judgment, the challenged law or classification is objectively unreasonable.

376. As stated above, when the Court is dealing with governmental economic regulation of business enterprises, the application of the rational basis standard amounts to virtual non-reviewability, and the challenged economic regulation will always be sustained against due process or equal protection challenge. Interestingly enough, in the early twentieth century, the Court applied the rational basis standard to challenges to governmental economic regulation with little deference at all, and used the due process and equal protection clauses to restrict significantly the power of the government to regulate the operation of the "market economy."[785] With the coming of the "Great Depression" in the 1930s, the Court did an "institutional turn-around," so to speak. Applying the same articulated rational basis standard, the Court upheld the constitutionality of governmental economic regulation against due process and equal protection challenges, overruling earlier cases to the contrary.[786] In the years thereafter, as the Court continued to uphold all economic regulation of business enterprises against due process and equal protection challenge, it is realistic to conclude that in this area, the

784. *See* generally the Court's discussion and application of the rational basis standard of review in *United States R.R. Retirement Board v. Fritz*, 449 U.S. 166, 174–179 (1980), and *Federal Communications Commission v. Beach*, 508 U.S. 307, 314–316 (1993).

785. This period was referred to as the "Lochner era," after *Lochner v. New York*, 198 U.S. 45 (1905), where the Court held unconstitutional as an improper interference with "freedom to contract" a state law prohibiting bakery workers from working more than 60 hours a week. At this time, the Court was applying the articulated rational basis standard of review to all due process and equal protection challenges, and had not yet developed a "two-tier" standard of review that distinguished between "fundamental" and "non-fundamental" rights. But the Court was applying the rational basis standard of review in a manner quite similar to the manner in which it now applies the compelling governmental interest standard of review in resolving constitutional challenges to laws or classifications that interfere with fundamental rights.

786. This "institutional turnaround" began with *Nebbia v. New York*, 291 U.S. 502 (1934), where the Court upheld against due process challenge a state milk price regulation that established minimum prices at which milk could be sold at retail. The stated purpose of the law was to increase the prices paid by distributors to farmers. While it is arguable that fixing prices at retail will not necessarily or even likely increase the prices paid to farmers, the Court held that the rational basis standard required that it defer to legislative judgment on this matter.

Court's application of the rational basis standard means complete non-reviewability.[787] The Court's current approach is illustrated by a recent case where the Court upheld against equal protection challenge a change in a property assessment under which property owners who were paying in installments were relieved of future payments, but property owners who had paid the entire assessment in a lump sum were not given any refunds for the amount paid.[788]

377. Outside of the area of economic regulation of business enterprises, that is, when the Court is dealing with governmental action affecting individual liberty and property interests, as we have said, the Court's application of the rational basis standard is somewhat "less deferential." In due process challenges, the Court will give somewhat more scrutiny to the legitimacy of the asserted governmental interest and to the effectiveness of the regulation in advancing the asserted interest. In equal protection challenges, the Court will give somewhat more scrutiny to the matter of whether the favored and disfavored groups are similarly situated with respect to the purpose of the underlying regulation, and if they are similarly situated, to the independent justification that the government has advanced for the differential treatment. However, despite the review being "less deferential," the Court usually will end up sustaining the challenged law or classification except for those relatively few circumstances in which the Court concludes that it is objectively unreasonable.

378. We will first illustrate the operation of "less deferential" rational basis review by a consideration of governmental restrictions on the right to work or to practice a profession, which is an important individual right, although not a "fundamental" one for purposes of the two-tier standard of review. The government must have a "rational basis" for refusing to license a person to practice a profession, and the Court has held violative of due process a state's refusal to license a person to practice law on grounds of "poor moral character," where the only purported basis of "poor moral character" was conduct in which the person had engaged fifteen years previously. The Court concluded that there was no "rational basis" between the person's prior conduct a number of years before and the person's present fitness to practice law.[789] On the other hand, the Court has held that there was no due process or equal protection

---

787. For cases illustrating complete judicial deference to legislative judgment in this area, *see* e.g., *Ferguson v. Skrupa*, 372 U.S. 726 (1963) (upholding against due process challenge a law prohibiting non-lawyers from engaging in debt-adjustment activities); *Railway Express Agency, Inc. v. New York*, 336 U.S. 106 (1947) (upholding against equal protection challenge a classification contained in a law prohibiting vehicles from carrying advertising that exempted business delivery vehicles carrying the name of the business); *Federal Communications Commission v. Beach*, 508 U.S. 307 (1993) (upholding against equal protection challenge, a provision contained in the federal cable regulation law, which exempted from the regulation satellite transmission systems serving subscribers in an apartment building or buildings under common ownership, but included in the regulation all other satellite transmission systems). *Fitzgerald v. Racing Association of Central Iowa*, 539 U.S. 558 (2003) (upholding against equal protection challenge a state's imposition of a higher tax rate on revenue from slot machines at racetracks than on revenue from slot machines on riverboat casinos).

788. *Armour v. City of Indianapolis*, 132 Sup.Ct. 2073 (2012).

789. *Schware v. Board of Bar Examiners of State of N.M.*, 353 U.S. 232 (1957). In practice, most states will permit licensing even of a person who has been convicted of a criminal offense in times past if that person is now rehabilitated and is presently "of good moral character."

violation resulting from a state law, enacted as a "consumer protection" measure, that prohibited the fitting of eyeglasses without a medical prescription. The effect of that law was to prevent opticians, as opposed to ophthalmologists and optometrists, from fitting eyeglasses, and the Court held that the legislature had a rational basis for doing so.[790] In another case, the Court upheld an employment rule of a municipal transit authority denying employment to persons who were on "methadone maintenance." Methadone is a transitional drug used to treat persons with addiction problems, and the Court held that it was not unreasonable for the transit authority to include persons on "methadone maintenance" within the category of "drug users," who were ineligible for employment with the transit authority.[791] The Court has also upheld a state law requiring public universities to develop standards for professors' instructional workloads and exempting matters relating to those standards from collective bargaining between public universities and faculty unions.[792]

379. The operation of "less deferential" rational basis review may also be illustrated by a consideration of two cases involving due process challenges to laws interfering with individual liberty and property rights, where the challenged law was carefully considered by the Court, but ultimately upheld. In one case, the challenged law required pharmacists who filled prescriptions for specified harmful drugs to send copies of the prescriptions to the state health department, where the information, including the patient's name, was retained on computers for five years, under strict nondisclosure requirements. The Court found that the requirement was rationally related to the asserted purposes of deterring the use of illegal drugs and aiding in the detection of illegal drug use. The Court also emphasized that the strict disclosure requirements reduced the likelihood that the information would be used improperly. For these reasons, the law did not violate the due process rights of the patients.[793] In the other case, a property owner living in the vicinity of a nuclear power plant challenged as violative of due process a federal law limiting the liability of nuclear power plants in the event of a "nuclear disaster" to USD 560,000,000. The purpose of the limitation on liability was to encourage private development of nuclear energy, and the Court

790. *Williamson v. Lee Optical of Oklahoma Inc.*, 348 U.S. 483 (1955). The law also contained an exemption for "ready-to-wear" eyeglasses, and the Court held that this exemption did not deprive the opticians of equal protection. The Court has emphasized that in making classifications in regulatory legislation, the legislature may decide to deal with the problem "one step at a time." Here, the legislature could reasonably conclude that the danger of "consumer fraud" or harm to health was not present with respect to "ready-to-wear" eyeglasses, or that the amount of "ready-to-wear" eyeglasses sold in the state was sufficiently small as not to be "worth the cost of regulation."

791. *New York City Transit Authority v. Beazer*, 440 U.S. 568 (1979).

792. *Central State University v. American Association of University Professors*, Central State University Chapter, 526 U.S. 124 (1999). The lower court had found that the state had failed to show any rational basis for singling out university faculty members as the only public employees precluded from bargaining over their workload. The Supreme Court held that under the rational basis standard of review, the state could properly conclude that collective bargaining over their workload by university faculty members would interfere with the legislature's efforts to ensure that a uniform workload policy for university faculty members would be in place by a certain date.

793. *Whalen v. Roe*, 429 U.S. 589 (1977).

held that the USD 560,000,000 limit was reasonable in light of the exceedingly small risk of occurrence of a nuclear accident involving claims in excess of USD 560,000,000, and the statutory commitment of Congress to provide additional relief in the event of an "extraordinary disaster."[794]

380. By far, the largest number of "less deferential" rational basis cases have involved equal protection challenges to classifications contained in governmental benefit programs that excluded certain groups of persons from the benefit. In most of these cases, the Court has upheld the classification against equal protection challenge, either on the ground that the legislature could reasonably conclude that the favored and disfavored groups were not similarly situated with respect to the purpose of the underlying benefit program, or more typically, on the ground that there was a sufficient independent justification for the differential treatment between the similarly situated groups.

381. The following are illustrative of such classifications that the Court has upheld against equal protection challenge:

(1) A maximum grant limitation on child welfare benefits, based on family size, coupled with a provision that benefits were not reduced by money earned by family members through gainful employment. The asserted purpose for the limitation was to encourage family members to seek gainful employment, and since the maximum amount of the grant was keyed to the minimum wage laws, an effort to maintain some semblance of equitable balance between families on welfare and those supported by an employed breadwinner.[795]
(2) The denial of "veterans benefits" to conscientious objectors who had performed alternative civilian service instead of military service during the Vietnam War, on the ground that they did not suffer the same disruption in their lives as did persons who had performed military service, and so were not similarly situated to the favored group with respect to the purpose of the underlying "veterans benefits" legislation.[796]
(3) The limitation of a federally provided "comfort allowance" for needy aged, blind and disabled persons confined in institutions to those persons who were confined in institutions that received other federal funds, on the ground that the federal government could reasonably decide to avoid expending federal resources on behalf of persons whose care and treatment were being fully provided for by state and local governments instead of by the federal government.[797]
(4) The grant of "spousal" benefits, in addition to the benefits provided to the child, to the wife of a retired or disabled worker with a child in her care, but not to the worker's former divorced wife with a child in her care, on the ground that Congress could have rationally assumed that divorced couples depend less on each other for financial support than couples who stay married, so that the favored group

---

794. *Duke Power Co. v. Carolina Environmental Study Group*, 438 U.S. 59 (1978).
795. *Dandridge v. Williams*, 397 U.S. 471 (1971).
796. *Johnson v. Robison*, 415 U.S. 361 (1974).
797. *Schweiker v. Wilson*, 450 U.S. 221 (1981).

and the disfavored group were not similarly situated with respect to the purpose of the underlying legislation.[798]

(5) Duration of relationship requirements which deny "surviving spouse and child" benefits to spouses and stepchildren whose relationships with the deceased worker were formed less than nine months before the worker's death, on the ground that the requirement was reasonably related to the purpose of discouraging people from entering into a marriage relationship in order to enable one spouse to claim benefits upon the anticipated early death of the other spouse.[799]

382. The operation of "less deferential" rational basis with respect to classifications contained in governmental benefit programs can further be illustrated by cases involving classifications contained in federal laws providing for "food stamps," which enable low-income persons to purchase food at little or no cost. Here, the Court has upheld some of the classifications, but has invalidated others as being objectively unreasonable. The Court has upheld the denial of "food stamps" to persons whose eligibility for "food stamps" was the result of being "on strike" against their employer, on the ground that Congress wanted to avoid undue favoritism to one side in a labor dispute.[800] The Court has also upheld a provision in the "food stamp" law which treated parents and children living together less favorably than distant relatives or strangers living together, on the ground that a policy of the law was to encourage common meal preparation, and Congress could reasonably conclude that it was easier for close relatives to accommodate their living habits to this policy than it would be for distant relatives or unrelated persons. In other words, Congress could reasonably conclude that the favored and disfavored groups were not similarly situated with respect to the underlying common meal preparation policy.[801]

383. On the other hand, the Court held unconstitutional an earlier rule that denied "food stamps" to unrelated persons living in the same household. The effect of the rule was to create two groups of persons who were identically situated with respect to the purpose of the underlying "food stamp" legislation.[802] The favored group consisted of "food stamp" eligible persons who were living alone or with relatives; the disfavored group consisted of "food stamp" eligible persons who were living together with unrelated persons. The government was unable to hypothesize any plausibly valid independent justification for the classification. The ban was directed at young people living together in what Congress had referred to as "hippie communes," and, as the Court emphasized, a desire to deny benefits to a politically unpopular group could not constitute a legitimate governmental interest under the rational basis standard of review. The government's assertion that the classification was necessary to prevent fraudulent applications for "food stamps" was summarily rejected by the Court, since whether the persons were related or not had no reasonable relationship to the propensity to commit fraud. Because there was no plausibly valid independent justification for the differential treatment between groups who were identically situated with respect

798. *Mathews v. De Castro*, 429 U.S. 181 (1976).
799. *Weinberger v. Salfi*, 422 U.S. 749 (1975).
800. *Lyng v. International Union*, 485 U.S. 360 (1988).
801. *Lyng v. Castillo*, 477 U.S. 635 (1986).
802. *United States Department of Agriculture v. Moreno*, 413 U.S. 528 (1973).

to the underlying purpose of the "food stamp" legislation, the classification was objectively unreasonable and so violative of equal protection. The Court also invalidated on due process grounds another provision of the law that denied food stamps to persons 18 years of age or older who had been claimed as a dependent child for federal income tax purposes by a taxpayer who was not a member of a household eligible for "food stamps." The denial extended for a one-year period after dependency had been claimed. The purpose of the ban was to deny "food stamps" to otherwise eligible college students, and the Court held that it was irrational to presume that they were not in need of "food stamps" solely because they had previously been claimed as dependents by their parents.[803]

384. Another example of a classification that the Court invalidated under the rational basis standard of review was one that resulted from the way in which a local tax assessor administered a state law requiring that all land be taxed at its "fair market value." The assessor valued the plaintiff's newly purchased land for tax purposes on the basis of its recent purchase price, but refused to reassess the lands of neighboring landowners to reflect their current market value. The result was that the plaintiff's land was assessed at eight to thirty-five times the value of neighboring land. In effect, the classifying factor was "recent sale of the property," and this classifying factor was not rationally related to and was actually inconsistent with the purpose of the underlying tax law that all property be assessed at its current market value. Thus, the classification was objectively unreasonable, and so was violative of equal protection.[804] However, a state taxing scheme that was designed to protect landowners from a tax increase due to an unrealized "paper increase" in the market value of the land was upheld against equal protection challenge. Under the taxing scheme, property tax assessments on the land were "frozen" as of a given date, and the land was reassessed only when something affirmatively happened, such as additional construction or improvement on the land or sale of the land. The scheme had the effect of creating two groups: the favored group consisted of landowners whose property had appreciated in value only because of market conditions, while the disfavored group consisted of landowners that had recently constructed upon the land or had recently acquired it. While the favored and disfavored groups may be considered to be similarly situated with respect to the purpose of the underlying tax law, there was an independent justification for the differential treatment, which was that owners should not have to pay taxes on unrealized "paper increases." The Court held that under the rational basis standard of review this was sufficient justification for the differential treatment.[805]

385. Some other cases involving the rational basis standard of review have arisen in the context of the Court's rejecting the contention that the particular interest involved should be treated as a "fundamental right" for purposes of the two-tier standard of due process and equal protection review. As discussed previously, the Court has held that important individual interests, such as education and housing, are not "fundamental rights" for this purpose.[806] But precisely because they are important interests, the Court has applied the rational basis standard with a somewhat greater

803. *United States Department of Agriculture v. Murry*, 413 U.S. 508 (1973).

804. *Allegheny Pittsburgh Coal Co. v. County Commission*, 488 U.S. 336 (1989).

805. *Nordlinger v. Hahn*, 505 U.S. 1 (1992).

806. *See* para. 333, n. 683, *supra* .

degree of scrutiny when dealing with laws that implicate these interests. Thus, while upholding a state law that allowed the landlord to bring an expedited action to recover possession of the property unless the tenant posted security for costs and that limited the defenses that the tenant could assert in that action, the Court invalidated a provision in the law requiring that the tenant post a bond for double the amount of rent due in order to take an appeal. The Court in effect held that the state could rationally treat actions to recover immediate possession of rental property differently from other actions, and could allow the landlord to obtain immediate possession, subject to the tenant's assertion of defenses to eviction at a later time. But the "double bond" requirement, according to the Court, was not rationally related to the asserted purpose of preventing frivolous appeals. Tenants who could post the bond could take the appeal, no matter how frivolous, and those who could not post the bond could not take the appeal, no matter how meritorious.[807]

386. Because education is not a "fundamental right" for purposes of the two-tier standard of review, equal protection challenges to state systems of school financing are evaluated under the rational basis standard of review, and have been upheld as being rationally related to the state's legitimate interest in preserving local control over school operations and expenditures. These systems of school financing relate to the fact that in every state primary and secondary education is administered by a number of autonomous local school districts, and financing for each school district is based on a combination of funds generated from taxes on property located within the school district, and funds received from the state government. Because the value of taxable property varies considerably from school district to school district, there will be a significant disparity between the amount of funds available for the education of each child depending on the property wealth of the school district in which the child lives. For equal protection purposes, this system of school financing creates a classification under which the favored group consists of children living in relatively "property rich" school districts and the disfavored group consists of children living in relatively "property poor" school districts.[808] In upholding the constitutionality of this system of school financing against equal protection challenge, the Court in effect has held that the state's interest in preserving local control over school, operations and expenditures was a sufficient independent justification for the differential treatment between the two classes of schoolchildren, so that the system of school financing satisfied the rational basis standard of review.[809]

387. However, the Court, again applying the articulated rational basis standard of review, has held unconstitutional a state law denying public school education to "undocumented" or "illegal" alien children. The Court was sharply divided in this 5-4 decision, with the dissenters insisting that under the rational basis standard of review,

---

807. *Lindsey v. Normet*, 405 U.S. 56 (1972).

808. Taxable property includes industrial property, commercial property, agricultural property, and residential property. Thus, school district wealth does not necessarily correlate with the socio-economic status of the people living in the school district. While school districts comprised of wealthy residential areas, as some suburban school districts are, will necessarily be relatively "property rich," so will school districts containing valuable industrial, commercial, or agricultural property, regardless of wealth of the persons residing there.

809. *San Antonio Independent School District v. Rodriguez*, 411 U.S. 1 (1973).

the state could reasonably conclude that it did not have the same responsibility to provide benefits for persons who were illegally in the United States as it did for persons lawfully present. The Justices in the majority used differing rationales to invalidate the restriction, but all of them emphasized the importance of education to these children, many of whom would be remaining in the United States, and the permanent harmful effects they would suffer if they were denied an education. It is fair to say that in this case, because of the importance of education, and the fact that the children were being denied an education completely, the Court majority applied the rational basis standard of review in a manner not at all dissimilar to the way that the Court applies the compelling governmental interest standard of review in "fundamental rights" cases.[810]

We see then that when evaluating due process and equal protection challenges to social and economic legislation under the rational basis standard of review, the Court will frequently reject the challenge. Nonetheless, we also see that in some cases the Court will invalidate the law or classification, especially when a law implicates important individual interests and when a classification contained in a law is found to be objectively unreasonable.

388. In a more recent case, *Lawrence v. Texas,*[811] the Court invalidated as violative of due process a state law prohibiting as "deviate sexual intercourse" anal or oral sex between persons of the same sex. The Court held that the due process clause prohibited a state from making criminal sexual conduct between consenting adults in private. The Court did not specifically discuss standards of review or specifically hold that the right of consenting adults to engage in sexual conduct in private was a fundamental right for constitutional purposes. Nonetheless, it emphasized that this right was a very important one and subjected the state's justifications for the law to very careful scrutiny.[812] The case stands as a precedent for challenging other laws that interfere with important personal interests, and indicates that the Court may invalidate such laws without finding that the personal interest constitutes a fundamental right.[813]

It is interesting to note that the Court's opinion in this case referred to decisions of the European Court of Human Rights recognizing the right of homosexual persons to engage in intimate sexual conduct under the European Convention on Human Rights.[814] It is very rare for the Court to look to decisions of foreign nations or

810. *Plyler v. Doe*, 457 U.S. 202 (1982).
811. *Lawrence v. Texas*, 539 U.S. 558 (2003).
812. The Court stated as follows: The case does involve two adults who, with full and mutual consent from each other, engaged in sexual practices common to a homosexual lifestyle. The petitioners are entitled to respect for their private lives. The State cannot demean their existence or control their destiny by making their private sexual conduct a crime. Their right to liberty under the Due Process Clause gives them the full right to engage in their conduct without intervention of the government. "It is a promise of the Constitution that there is a realm of personal liberty which the government may not enter (citation omitted). The Texas statute furthers no legitimate state interest which can justify its intrusion into the personal and private life of the individual."
813. The Court overruled its earlier decision in *Bowers v. Hardwick*, 478 U.S. 186 (1986), that rejected a constitutional challenge to a state's prohibition of "homosexual sodomy." The Court stated that the continuance of that case as a precedent "demeans the lives of homosexual persons," and that it was "not correct when it was decided and it is not correct today."
814. *Dudgeon v. United Kingdom*, 45 Eur.Ct.H.R. (1981), p. 52; *P.G. & I.H. v. United Kingdom*, App.No. 00044787/98, p. 56 (Eur.Ct.H.R., September 25, 2001).

international human rights tribunals, and its doing so may be recognition of the fact that the constitutional protection of individual rights now has taken on an international dimension.

We have earlier discussed *Lawrence* in the context of the "line of growth of constitutional doctrine relating to the unconstitutionality of discrimination against same-sex persons." And the Court's landmark decision in *Obergefell v. Hodges,* holding unconstitutional a ban on marriage for same-sex couples was based primarily on the due process clause. *See* paragraph 329, *supra*. While *Lawrence* and Obergefell are properly considered as cases invalidating discrimination n the basis of sexual orientation, the due process basis of those decisions indicates that due process may be relied on in other cases involving interference with personal liberties that do not rise to the status of fundamental rights.

B. The Takings Clause and the Contracts Clause

389. Specialized protection to certain forms of property interests is provided by the takings clause of the Fifth Amendment, which is incorporated into the Fourteenth Amendment, so as to be binding on the states, and the contracts clause of Article I, section 10, which applies only to the states. The Framers of the Constitution strongly believed in the institution of private property and were concerned about governmental expropriation of private property for public use. The Fifth Amendment's takings clause, however, recognizes the eminent domain power of the government to expropriate private property for public use, but specifically requires that when the government does so, it must pay the owner "just compensation." The Framers also feared that the states would enact laws canceling debts or otherwise providing debtor relief, and to prevent this from occurring, they promulgated the contracts clause of Article I, section 10, prohibiting the states from enacting any law "impairing the obligation of contracts."[815] These two clauses have limited application, but when applicable, they do operate to provide specialized protection to certain forms of property interests in particular circumstances. We will consider the takings clause and the contracts clause separately.

1. The Takings Clause

390. Takings clause doctrine requires that the taking be for a "public purpose." In theory, if the taking does not advance a "public purpose," the "forced sale" that is effected by the taking, even with the payment of compensation, is unconstitutional. However, the Supreme Court has held that the government has very broad discretion in defining the "public interest," and thus in deciding what constitutes a "public purpose" to justify the taking of private property for "public use." The taking may be considered to be for a "public purpose," even though the immediate effect of the taking is to benefit other private entities. In a capitalist economic system and market economy,

815. There is no comparable constitutional limitation applicable to the federal government, so that any constitutional challenge to the federal government's abrogation of either private or its own contractual obligations must be based on the due process clause or the takings clause. *See* e.g., *Lynch v. United States*, 292 U.S. 571 (1934); *United States v. Locke*, 471 U.S. 84 (1985); *Bowen v. Public Agencies Opposed to Social Security Entrapment*, 477 U.S. 41 (1986).

the "public interest" often cannot be separated from the "private interests" of particular private entities. Thus, the Court has held that the government may use the eminent domain power to eliminate "urban blight" and promote urban redevelopment, notwithstanding that the redevelopment is accomplished by the transfer of the expropriated property to private entities.[816] The Court has also held that where the Hawaii Legislature concluded that the concentration of land ownership in relatively few families, resulting from Hawaii's earlier land tenure system prior to the time it became a state, had an adverse effect on the operation of the residential land market, Hawaii could use its eminent domain power to buy up some of the land from the owners and then sell it to the persons who had been leasing the land.[817] Finally, the Court has held that the government may use the eminent domain power to promote economic development to the point of taking private property and turning it over to private entities that will be using the property for commercial purposes.[818] All that is required in practice then is that when the government uses the eminent domain power to take private property, it pays the owner "just compensation," and the courts have developed standards to determine what constitutes "just compensation" for takings clause purposes.[819]

391. Most of the takings clause cases today involve the situation where the government has not affirmatively exercised the eminent domain power, but has regulated the use of private property, and the owner of the property claims that the regulation amounts to a "taking" for constitutional purposes. If the regulation does amount to a "taking," the government must either abandon the regulation or pay the owner just compensation.

392. The claim that there has been a "regulatory taking," as it is called, has met with success only in the limited circumstances where the regulation amounts to a permanent physical occupation of the property, or where it completely deprives the property of all economic value in a manner that could not have been anticipated when the owner acquired the property. The Court has found a permanent physical occupation as a result of frequent and regular low-altitude flights of government airplanes over a person's land, concluding that the government had in effect taken an easement over

816. *Berman v. Parker*, 348 U.S. 26 (1954).
817. *Hawaii Housing Authority v. Midkiff*, 467 U.S. 229 (1984).
818. *Kelo v. New London*, 545 U.S. 469 (2005).
819. While most of the takings clause cases involve the taking of land, the takings clause also applies to governmental taking of other property. Thus, the government could not require that raisin growers set aside a portion of their raisins for the government, free of charge, as a condition for selling their raisins in interstate commerce. The government had to pay just compensation for the portion of the raisins that were to be set aside for governmental use. *Horne v. Department of Agriculture*, 135 Sup.Ct. 2419 (2015).

the land due to the frequency and regularity of the low-altitude flights.[820] The Court has also found a permanent physical occupation where a state regulatory body required that the owner of beachfront property give the public an easement of access to the beach from the property, as a condition for approval of the owner's request to construct a dwelling on the property,[821] where the federal government ruled that a privately owned lagoon had become a "navigable water" because of its connection to a bay, and required that the owners of the lagoon allow the public free access,[822] and where state law required privately owned apartment buildings to permit cable television equipment to be attached to the building for use by the tenants.[823]

393. The Court has held that a regulatory taking could also occur if the regulation completely deprives the property of all economic value. In the leading case on this issue, the owner had purchased two lots on beachfront land, 300 feet from the beach, intending to build a home on each lot. A subsequently enacted state law aimed at preventing erosion of the seashore, was applied to bar the building of homes that close to the beach. As a result of the law, the land was deprived of "any reasonable economic use." The Court held that this would amount to a regulatory taking unless the owner could reasonably have anticipated that the land could be made subject to this kind of regulation at the time it was acquired.[824] Cases where the regulation completely deprives the property of all economic value will be rare, but where this is so, the regulation may amount to a regulatory taking. However, in practice, the Court has not found a regulatory taking in other cases involving land development. In one case the Court

820. *United States v. Causby*, 328 U.S. 256 (1946). The Court held that the landowner was entitled to as much of the air space above the land as he had reasonably been using in connection with the operation of the land as a farm. In a later case, the Court held that the establishment of a governmental airport next to residential property could amount to a regulatory taking if the flights and operation of the airport made the property unusable for residential purposes. *Griggs v. Allegheny County*, 369 U.S. 84 (1962). The Court has very recently held that government-induced flooding of land, even of limited duration, can be compensable as a taking. *Arkansas Game and Fish Commission v. United States*, 133 S.Ct. 511 (2012).

821. *Nollan v. California Coastal Commission*, 483 U.S. 825 (1987). If the government had required that the owner of property give the public an easement over the property, there would be no question that this would be a regulatory taking. The Court held that requiring that the easement be given as a condition for governmental approval of the construction did not change the constitutional result. *See also Dolan v. City of Tigard*, 512 U.S. 374 (1994), where the Court found that the imposition of certain conditions on a landowner's permit to double the size of her plumbing and electrical supply store in the central business district, specifically that she dedicate to the city the flood plain portion of her lot to enable the city to improve the drainage system along the creek, and a 15-foot strip adjoining the floodplain for a public pedestrian/ bicycle path, constituted a "regulatory taking." The Supreme Court has recently held that the unconstitutional conditions doctrine required that the government's demand for "monetary exactions" as a condition of a land use permit must satisfy the requirement that the demand have an essential nexus and rough proportionality to the impacts of a proposed development. *Koontz v. St. Johns River Water Management District*, 133 S.Ct. 2586 (2013).

822. *Kaiser Aetna v. United States*, 444 U.S. 164 (1979).

823. *Loretto v. Teleprompter Manhattan CATV Corp.*, 458 U.S. 419 (1982).

824. *Lucas v. South Carolina Coastal Council*, 505 U.S. 1003 (1992). The particular case was remanded to the lower court with directions that it make findings concerning whether the regulation could have reasonably been anticipated by the owner at the time the land was acquired.

held that the land was not "deprived of any reasonable economic use," since the landowner could build a substantial residence on the property, although he was unable to develop it.[825] In a recent case, the Court dealt with the situation where state projects involved placing sand along beaches seaward from the mean high-water line, which was the boundary between the state's submerged land and the owners' properties. The property owners contended that the state's ownership of the new dry land to seaward deprived the owners of their right to accretion. The Court held that there was no regulatory taking, because the owners had no right to future accretions and to contact with the water that was superior to the state's right to fill in its submerged land, and any future seaward accretion became the property of the state.[826] The Court has also held that a moratorium on development of land for a period of time while the state is formulating a comprehensive land use plan for the areas does not necessarily amount to a regulatory taking. The question is whether, in light of all the circumstances the imposition of the moratorium for the period of time is reasonable.[827]

394. With these exceptions, the Court has rejected a wide variety of claims that regulations restricting certain uses of property and diminishing the economic value of the property amounted to a regulatory taking. In addition to conventional zoning and land use laws, which the Court has long held do not amount to a regulatory taking,[828] the Court has upheld against regulatory taking claims the following: the application of a landmark preservation law to prevent the construction of an office building atop a famous railroad station;[829] a subsidence prevention law that required coal companies to keep in place half of the coal located beneath dwellings and other protected structures;[830] an endangered species protection law that prohibited the sale of artifacts containing eagle parts;[831] rent control laws, limiting the amount of rent increases that the landlord could impose and the circumstances under which the landlord could evict

825. *Palazzolo v. Rhode Island*, 533 U.S. 606 (2001).
826. *Stop the Beach Renourishment, Inc. v. Florida Department of* Environmental *Protection*, 560 U.S. 702 (2010).
827. *Tahoe-Sierra Preservation Council, Inc. v. Tahoe Regional Planning Agency*, 535 U.S. 702 (2010).
828. *See Euclid v. Ambler Realty Co.*, 272 U.S. 365 (1926); *Goldblatt v. Town of Hempstead*, 369 U.S. 590 (1962); *Agins v. City of Tiburon*, 447 U.S. 255 (1980). When the particular use to which the property is being put causes harm to other property or is harmful to the public interest, regulation of the property in order to advance "a substantial public purpose" does not amount to a public taking. This proposition is cogently illustrated by *Miller v. Schoene*, 276 U.S. 272 (1928), where the Court held that the takings clause was not violated when the state required the destruction of ornamental cedar trees, without compensation, because they produced cedar rust that was fatal to apple trees, a very important industry in the state.
829. *Penn Central Transportation Co. v. New York City*, 438 U.S. 104 (1978).
830. *Keystone Bituminous Coal Association v. DeBenedictis*, 480 U.S. 470 (1987).
831. *Andrus v. Allard*, 444 U.S. 51 (1979).

the tenant;[832] and a state's use of interest on lawyers' trust accounts that could earn net interest for the clients to pay for legal services for poor persons.[833]

395. At the present time, then, the Court does not appear to be disposed to extend the scope of regulatory taking, and the takings clause has not operated to limit significantly the power of the government to regulate property use.[834]

2. The Contracts Clause

396. The contracts clause was earlier used by the Court to invalidate state laws that retroactively altered contractual arrangements between private persons and between private persons and the state, such as those contained in corporate charters. However, by the end of the nineteenth century, the Court was relying more on substantive due process to invalidate state laws interfering with contractual rights, and the contracts clause receded in importance. When the Court began upholding economic regulation against due process challenge during the "Great Depression" of the 1930s, it also held that the contracts clause did not impose an absolute bar to regulations that altered contractual arrangements between private persons, such as debtor relief laws. The Court held that the state could impose reasonable regulations that altered existing contractual arrangements during an "emergency situation," such as that brought about by the "Great Depression," as long as the regulation did not destroy the underlying contractual right itself. Thus, the Court upheld a "mortgage moratorium" law that extended the period in which the defaulting mortgagor could redeem the land after foreclosure, contrary to the provisions of the mortgage agreement, on condition that the mortgagor pay a reasonable part of the rental value of the land.[835] And some thirty years later, the Court upheld against contract clause objections a state law that altered the reinstatement rights of purchasers of land from the state. Under the previous law, there was no time limit during which the purchaser's reinstatement rights could be exercised, and this resulted in much land speculation and uncertainty over land

832. *Yee v. City of Escondido*, 503 U.S. 519 (1992); *Pennell v. City of San Jose*, 485 U.S. 1 (1988).

833. *Brown v. Legal Foundation of Washington*, 538 U.S. 216 (2003).

A regulated public utility is entitled to a reasonable rate of return on its investment. However, the states have broad discretion in determining utility rates, and it is highly unlikely that the state's use of a particular formula to determine rates will be held to amount to a regulatory taking. *See Duquesne Light Co. v. Barasch*, 488 U.S. 299 (1989).

834. In *Eastern Enterprises v. Apfel*, 524 U.S. 498 (1998), the Court was faced with a constitutional challenge to a federal law imposing retroactive liability on former coal mine operators in order to finance health benefits for miners who had worked for the operators before they went out of business. In a 5-4 decision, the Court held this retroactive imposition of liability to be unconstitutional. Four of the Justices took the position that the retroactive imposition of liability violated the Takings Clause, and one Justice took the position that it violated the Due Process Clause, while saying that it did not violate the Takings Clause. The effect of this division on the Court was that five Justices held that the retroactive imposition of liability did not violate the Takings Clause.

835. *Home Building and Loan Association v. Blaisdell*, 290 U.S. 398 (1934). However, the Court held unconstitutional a law that eliminated foreclosure remedies and did not require the mortgagor to pay anything during the time when the mortgagee could not foreclose on the property. *W.B. Worthen Co. v. Kavanagh*, 295 U.S. 56 (1935).

ownership. The Court held that the state could remedy this situation despite the resulting alteration of the state's contractual arrangements with the landowners.[836]

397. In more recent years, however, the Court has again invoked the contracts clause to invalidate particular laws that altered the state's own contractual arrangements with private entities and that altered contractual arrangements between private entities themselves. One case involved the New York-New Jersey Port Authority, which administers airports and other transportation facilities in the New York City-northern New Jersey metropolitan area. In 1962, the Port Authority decided to take over a privately owned bankrupt passenger railroad line, and in order to reassure the Authority's bondholders, the Authority agreed to limit the number of privately owned mass transit operations it would take over in the future. In 1974, the New Jersey legislature repealed the legislation that implemented the limitation agreement. The Court held that the repeal violated the contracts clause, because the state had contractually bound itself to limit its financial obligations with respect to taking over privately owned mass transit operations, and that it could not avoid its contractual commitment, simply because it wanted to spend the money to promote the "public welfare" rather than the "private welfare" of its creditors.[837]

398. Another case involved a state law that increased the financial obligations of private companies that had a preexisting pension plan for their employees and that had either terminated the plan or closed their business facility in the state. The law required that employees who had worked for such a company for more than ten years be granted benefits regardless of the provisions of the company's pension plan. The Court held that this law violated the contracts clause, because it substantially impaired the company's existing obligations and imposed unanticipated additional obligations despite the companies' justified reliance on actuarial calculations as to the amount of funding necessary to sustain the projected payouts from the pension fund. The Court also noted that the law was not enacted to deal with a general social problem, but focused on a limited number of employers who had voluntarily established pension plans for their employees.[838]

399. On the other hand, the Court held that the contract clause was not violated by a prohibition on oil and gas producers passing a severance tax increase on to consumers, even though preexisting contracts between some of the producers and their consumers required the consumers to reimburse the producers for all severance taxes. The Court emphasized that the law imposed a generally applicable rule of conduct

836. *City of El Paso v. Simmons*, 379 U.S. 497 (1965).

837. *United States Trust Co. v. New Jersey*, 431 U.S. 1 (1977).

838. *Allied Structural Steel Co. v. Spannaus*, 438 U.S. 234 (1978). *Compare Connolly v. Pension Benefit Guaranty Corp.*, 475 U.S. 211 (1986), where the Court upheld against due process and takings clause challenge a requirement in the federal law that comprehensively regulates employer pension plans to the effect that an employer who withdraws from a multiemployer pension plan pay into that plan's fund the withdrawing employer's proportionate share of the plan's "vested benefits" and the current value of its assets at the time of withdrawal. This was contrary to a provision contained in a particular multiemployer pension plan agreement that protected a withdrawing employer from incurring additional obligations. The Court emphasized that the employer was on notice that Congress was extensively regulating employer pension plans, and that subsequent legislation might be enacted imposing additional obligations on withdrawing employers.

applicable to all oil and gas producers, designed to protect consumers from excessive prices. This being so, the law's purpose was not to change the provisions of an existing contract, as in the two cases discussed above, and the fact that it had this incidental effect as to some producers did not undercut its broad regulatory purpose.[839] The Court has also held that a state law placing a limit on price increases that a natural gas supplier could charge a public utility under the "escalator clause" of a preexisting contract did not violate the contracts clause. This was because the contracting parties had recognized that their activities were subject to extensive governmental regulation, and the law advanced an important consumer protection interest.[840]

400. The results in these cases indicate that the contract clause is a specialized and limited restriction on state governmental regulation. It is violated only when the state acts unilaterally to avoid its own contractual obligations, or to retroactively modify the contractual arrangements between particular private entities, and there is not a sufficient public interest justification for the state's doing so. The contracts clause will not operate to restrict significantly the power of the states to enact generally applicable economic regulation.

IV. Procedural Due Process

401. The procedural component of the due process clause imposes certain requirements on the conduct of civil litigation in the courts and in adjudicative administrative proceedings. A principal requirement imposed by procedural due process is that the case be adjudicated before a fair and impartial tribunal. This requirement is violated when the decision-maker has a monetary interest in the outcome, such as where traffic offenses were adjudicated by a town's mayor, and a major portion of the town's revenue came from fines collected for traffic offenses,[841] or where a licensing body was given the authority to institute disciplinary proceedings against its professional competitors.[842] In a more recent case, the Court held that as a matter of due process, a state Supreme Court Justice was required to disqualify himself in a case involving a party who had contributed a very large amount of party to the justice's campaign for election to the court.[843]

The due process clause also applies in criminal cases, in addition to the specific constitutional guarantees afforded to persons accused of crime. In a very recent case, the Court held that when a judge earlier had a significant personal involvement as a prosecutor in a critical decision involving a criminal defendant's case, namely authorizing the prosecutor to seek the death penalty, the judge's failure to recuse himself from an appeal of a court's decision granting postconviction relief to the defendant violated

839. *EXXON Corporation v. Eagerton*, 462 U.S. 176 (1983).
840. *Energy Reserves Group, Inc. v. Kansas Power & Light Co* 459 U.S. 400 (1983).
841. *Ward v. Village of Monroeville*, 409 U.S. 57 (1972).
842. *Gibson v. Berryhill*, 411 U.S. 564 (1973).
843. *Caperton v. Massey Coal Co.*, 556 U.S. 868 (2009).

due process.[844] As a general proposition, procedural due process requires that a governmental body follow its own regulations, even though the governmental body would not have been required by due process to promulgate those regulations in the first place. [845] The Court has also held that procedural due process is violated by legal procedures that enable a creditor to seize the property of the alleged debtor without a prior hearing.[846] It has also held that an award of punitive damages in an amount that is grossly excessive in relation to the actual damages suffered, here 500 times the amount of actual damages, is violative of due process.[847] Finally, the Court has held that due process is violated by a state court holding that under its law of res judicata a person is bound by a prior adverse adjudication to which that person had not been a party.[848] However, the primary significance of procedural due process in practice has revolved around the question of entitlement to a "hearing." This question arises when the government takes action that interferes with a person's liberty or affects a person's property or a claimed property interest, and that person contends that the due process clause requires that there be some form of "hearing" to determine the facts on which the government's reasons for taking that action are predicated. When a person asserts a due process entitlement to a "hearing," there is a two-part inquiry. The first part of the inquiry relates to whether the particular interest that is affected by the governmental action constitutes a "liberty" or "property" interest for due process purposes. If it does not, then the due process clause is inapplicable, and no "hearing" of any sort is required. Conversely, if the particular interest does constitute a "liberty" or "property" interest

---

844. *Williams v. Pennsylvania*, 136 Sup.Ct. 1899 (2016).However, the fact that judges serving on an intermediate appellate court in the military justice system did not serve for a fixed term was held not to violate due process. The Court emphasized that some deference was due to Congress' balancing of the rights of servicepersons against the needs of the military, and that Congress had provided a number of safeguards to ensure the impartiality of military tribunals, as well as making all of their decisions subject to possible review by a court composed entirely of civilian judges who served fixed terms. *Weiss v. United States*, 510 U.S. 163 (1994).

845. *See Logan v. Zimmerman Brush Co.*, 455 U.S. 422 (1982), where a state administrative agency was held to have deprived a party filing an employment discrimination claim of due process when it dismissed the claim on the ground that it itself had failed to convene a fact-finding conference within the time required by law.

846. *See* e.g., *Snidach v. Family Finance Corp.*, 395 U.S. 337 (1969) (garnishment of wages); *North Georgia Finishing, Inc. v. Di-Chem, Inc.*, 419 U.S. 601 (1975) (attachment of assets). *See also United States v. Good Real Property*, 510 U.S. 43 (1993), holding that procedural due process is violated by the government's seizing property allegedly used for criminal purposes in a civil forfeiture proceeding, without prior notice and hearing.

847. *BMW of North America v. Gore*, 517 U.S. 559 (1996). *State Farm Mutual Automobile Insurance Co. v. Campbell*, 538 U.S. 408 (2003). In addition, as a matter of due process, the award of punitive damages cannot be based upon a jury's desire to punish the defendant for harming persons who are not before the court in the particular case. *Philip Morris v. Williams*, 549 U.S. 346 (2007).

848. *Richards v. Jefferson County*, 517 U.S. 793 (1996).

for due process purposes, then procedural due process requires that there must be some form of "hearing" as a condition to the government's taking that action.[849]

402. The second part of the inquiry relates to what form this "hearing" must take, or as it is sometimes put, "what process is due"? Depending on various factors, due process may require the full panoply of procedures of an adjudicative proceeding, referred to as a full evidentiary hearing,[850] or may require no more than "minimum procedural fairness," which is informal notice of the reasons why the government is taking the action in issue, and an informal opportunity to defend. The factors to be considered and balanced in determining the nature of the "hearing" required by procedural due process are: (1) the importance of the interest that will be affected by the governmental action; (2) the risk of an erroneous deprivation of that interest through the procedures that the government wishes to use, and the probable value, if any, of additional or substitute procedural safeguards; (3) the government's interest, including the function involved and the fiscal and administrative burdens that the additional or substitute procedural requirement would entail.[851]

403. Governmental interference with a person's "liberty" interests (other than by a criminal prosecution) may occur in essentially two ways. First, the government may be depriving the person of freedom of action by physically restraining the person, such as by a nonvoluntarily commitment to a mental institution.[852] Second, the

849. Analytically, the same inquiry must be made whenever a substantive due process claim is asserted, and sometimes the question of what constitutes a "liberty" or "property" interest arises in both a substantive and procedural context. *See* e.g., *Paul v. Davis*, 424 U.S. 693 (1976) (circulation by police of flyers listing persons as "active" shoplifters did not implicate "liberty" interest protected by due process clause, so that resulting harm to individual's reputation did not violate individual's substantive due process rights, and procedural due process did not require that police conduct a "hearing" to determine whether person was an "active shoplifter"). In practice, however, the issue of whether a particular individual interest is a protected "liberty" or "property" interest for due process purposes most frequently arises in the context of the assertion of a procedural due process claim.

850. This would include adequate notice of the charge, a neutral decision-maker, the opportunity to present evidence and to confront and cross-examine opposing witnesses, the right to be represented by counsel, and the right to a decision based on the record and a statement of reasons for the decision.

851. *See Mathews v. Eldridge*, 424 U.S. 319 (1976). A temporary suspension of a police officer who was charged with a felony without a pre-suspension hearing was held not to violate due process. In this circumstance, due process requires only that an adequate post-suspension hearing be provided. *Gilbert v. Homar*, 520 U.S. 924 (1997). So too, a thirty day delay in a hearing to recover on a claim challenging the on-the-spot imposition of a fine for a parking violation does not violate due process. *City of Los Angeles v. David*, 538 U.S. 715 (2003).

852. In this circumstance, as might be expected, the due process clause requires a full evidentiary hearing and may impose burden of proof requirements. For example, an adult cannot be involuntarily committed to a mental institution without a finding, based on at least a standard of "clear and convincing evidence," that the person is dangerous to himself or others. *Addington v. Texas*, 441 U.S. 418 (1979). However, when children are committed to state mental institutions at the request of their parents, the due process clause only requires that there be a "fair review" of their condition at the time of admission, which consists of an inquiry by a neutral fact finder to determine if the legal criteria for commitment were met in the case of the particular child. *Parham v. I.R.*, 442 U.S. 584 (1979).

government may be depriving the person of freedom of action by prohibiting the person from engaging in certain activities, such as the practice of a profession, or the purchase of alcoholic beverages. "Property" interests for due process purposes include not only the traditional forms of "property," such as land and movable property, but also certain governmental entitlements and benefits and other "property" interests recognized by state law.[853] Whenever a party asserts that a particular interest constitutes a "property" interest for due process purposes, it is necessary to determine whether this interest has in fact been established as a "property" interest by the government or is recognized as a "property" interest under state law.

404. We will now discuss the Court's determination of what individual interests constitute protected "liberty" and "property" interests for due process purposes, and as applicable, the matter of "what process is due" with respect to governmental interference with particular "liberty" or "property" interests.

405. We will begin with a consideration of employment interests that are dependent upon governmental action, such as the practice of a licensed profession or governmental employment. Once an individual has been licensed to practice a profession, that license represents a valuable property right, and if the government seeks to revoke the license, it must provide the licensee with a full evidentiary hearing.[854] A "hearing," probably one that amounts to a full evidentiary hearing, is also required when the government initially refuses to issue the license, since the effect of the government's refusal to license is to prevent the person from practicing that person's chosen profession.[855]

406. Governmental employment, like private employment, is considered contractual in nature, so a governmental employee does not have a "property" right in that employment for due process purposes. Thus, the governmental employer, in the same manner as a private employer, can terminate the employment in accordance with the employment contract, and is not required to provide the employee with a "hearing" on the matter of termination.[856] However, if the governmental employer has established an "expectation of continued employment," such as by the adoption of a formal or informal tenure system at a public university, the employee does have a "property" interest for due process purposes, and the employment cannot be terminated without a "hearing."[857] The question in this circumstance is whether the government has established an "expectation of continued employment." If, for example, the

---

853. Certain "liberty" interests, such as the right to practice a profession, also constitute "property" interests, because they produce economic advantage for the person.

854. In re Ruffalo, 390 U.S. 544 (1968).

855. *See Willner v. Committee on Character & Fitness*, 373 U.S. 96 (1963), where the Court held that the procedural due process rights of an applicant seeking admission to the practice of law were violated when he was denied a hearing to confront charges of unfitness that were made against him by the investigating agency.

856. *Board of Regents v. Roth*, 408 U.S. 564 (1972) (refusal to review university instructor on one-year contract).

857. *Perry v. Sindermann*, 408 U.S. 593 (1972). The Court did not decide on what kind of "hearing" due process required, because the claim that the university had established an informal tenure system had yet to be determined. It may be assumed that the "hearing" required by due process would be a full evidentiary hearing, since universities that have formal tenure systems employ the academic equivalent of a full evidentiary hearing in tenure revocation proceedings.

governmental employer has defined the terms of so-called permanent employment in such a way as to preclude any claim of "expectation of continued employment," the employee does not have a "property" interest in continued employment, and is not entitled to a hearing upon termination.[858] But once the government in fact has established an "expectation of continued employment," such as by a state civil service law providing that "classified civil servants" can only be discharged "for cause," there is a "property" interest for due process purposes, and the due process clause, not the provisions of state law, determine "what process is due." In other words, while the government is not required to create a "property" interest in continued employment, once it has created such an interest, any action it takes to interfere with that interest is subject to the "hearing" and other requirements of procedural due process.[859]

407. The Court has held that the employee's interest in the "expectation of continued employment," once such an expectation has been created, is of sufficient importance that as regards the question of "what process is due," some kind of "hearing" must be provided prior to termination, and a full evidentiary hearing must be provided post-termination. At the pre-termination "hearing," there must be oral or written notice of the charges against the employee, an explanation of evidence supporting the charges, and an opportunity for the employee to reply to the charges. The matter need not be definitively resolved prior to termination, and the employee's rights are considered to be adequately protected by the post-termination full evidentiary hearing.[860]

408. Where the government has established a benefits program, persons who have been awarded benefits under the program may have a protected "property" interest in the continued receipt of those benefits. This will occur where the government has by law set forth eligibility criteria for the benefit, so that persons meeting the eligibility criteria may be said to have a legal "entitlement" to the benefit. Where this is so, the government must provide some form of "hearing" when it seeks to terminate a person's "entitlement" to that benefit.[861] The Court has held that because welfare benefits provide "the very means by which a person needs to live," the government may not terminate welfare benefits unless it provides a full evidentiary hearing prior to termination.[862]

858. *Bishop v. Wood*, 426 U.S. 341 (1976). Even though the city police officer was classified as a "permanent" employee, the lower court found that the city law regulating governmental employment gave the city manager the authority to discharge employees, subject to certain "procedural" rights that had been followed in the particular case.

859. *Cleveland Board of Education v. Loudermill*, 470 U.S. 532 (1985). As the Court emphasized, "property" for due process purposes cannot be defined by the procedures provided by state law for its "deprivation."

860. *Cleveland Board of Education v. Loudermill*, 470 U.S. 532 (1985). *See also Arnett v. Kennedy*, 416 U.S. 134 (1974), where the Court held that discharge procedures for a nonprobationary federal civil service employee satisfied due process. Under those procedures, the employee received notice of the charges, was entitled to reply to them orally or in writing, and to submit affidavits to the official authorized to remove him. The employee was also entitled to a post-termination hearing.

861. There has been no case in which the Court has held that a person has a protected "property" interest in the initial receipt of governmental benefits. However, the federal government and the states frequently provide procedures for administrative and judicial review of denial of claims to initial entitlement to certain governmental benefits.

862. *Goldberg v. Kelley*, 397 U.S. 254 (1970).

However, with respect to the termination of other kinds of "entitlements," the Court has held that due process is satisfied by a post-termination hearing, which in practice generally has many of the features of a full evidentiary hearing.[863] The Court has also held that when a municipally owned public utility provided that electrical service could only be terminated "for cause," it was required to provide a "hearing" to customers before service was terminated for nonpayment of disputed utility bills.[864]

409. Turning now to "liberty" interests, the Court has held that an individual's interest in driving an automobile is a protected "liberty" interest for due process purposes. Thus, the Court has held unconstitutional a state law that automatically revoked the driver's license of an uninsured motorist who was involved in an accident unless the motorist posted security to cover the damages claimed by the other parties to the accident. As a matter of due process, the state was required to provide some form of "hearing" to determine whether there was a reasonable basis for concluding that the uninsured motorist was "at fault" in the accident and so could be liable for damages.[865]

Governmental action that interferes with a person's ability to do something that the person had previously been able to do, such as purchasing alcoholic beverages, constitutes an interference with a "liberty" interest for due process purposes. Thus, a governmental body could not constitutionally prohibit the selling of alcoholic beverages to persons it had designated as "excessive drinkers," in the absence of some form of

---

863. *See Mathews v. Eldridge*, 424 U.S. 319 (1976) (termination of disability benefits). *Compare O'Bannon v. Town Court Nursing Center*, 447 U.S. 773 (1980), where the Court held that residents of a nursing home did not have an "entitlement" in the nursing home's continued eligibility to receive the federal funds that paid for their care in the nursing home, although the residents would have to move to another nursing home if the nursing home's eligibility for those funds was terminated. *See also American Manufacturers Mutual Insurance Co. v. Sullivan*, 426 U.S. 40 (1999), holding that where, under state workers' compensation law, an employee was entitled to "reasonable and necessary" medical treatment, and where there was a requirement that disputes over the reasonableness and necessity of particular treatment had to be resolved before an employer's obligation to pay arose, injured employees did not have a "property interest" in the payment of the benefits.

864. *Memphis Light, Gas & Water Division v. Craft*, 436 U.S. 1 (1978).

865. *Bell v. Burson*, 402 U.S. 535 (1971). However, the Court has held that when a driver refuses to take a chemical test or breath analysis for alcohol use while driving the vehicle, the state may summarily suspend the driver's license so long as it provides for a prompt post-suspension administrative hearing. At that hearing, it must be determined whether the police officer who requested the driver to take the test had reasonable grounds to believe that the driver was intoxicated, whether the driver in fact was the person arrested by the officer, and whether the driver refused to take the test. *Mackey v. Montrym*, 443 U.S. 1 (1979).

The Court has also upheld temporary suspension of licenses to engage in certain activities pending a prompt post-suspension administrative hearing. *See Hodel v. Virginia Surface Mining and Reclamation Ass'n.*, 452 U.S. 264 (1981) (suspension of surface mining permit pending review of allegations that operator was violating environmental regulations); *Berry v. Barchi*, 443 U.S. 55 (1979) (suspension of race-horse trainer's license when one of his horses was found to have been drugged prior to a race).

"hearing" at which the person's status as an "excessive drinker" could be determined.[866] The Court has also held that schoolchildren have a protected "liberty" interest in continued attendance at the school and in being free from corporal punishment. Thus, a public school cannot suspend or expel children or administer corporal punishment without following "minimum due process" by giving the child notice of the charge and the opportunity to be heard in defense.[867] A recent interesting case raised the question of whether a naturalized American citizen had a protected liberty interest in her marriage that entitled her to seek judicial review of a consular officer's decision denying her husband's application for a visa on the ground that he was a former civil servant in the Taliban regime in Afghanistan. Four Justices held that she had a protected liberty interest, three held that she did not, and two found that there was no need to decide the question, since the notice that she did receive satisfied due process. T he result was that the question of a protected liberty interest was not resolved, but the American citizen lost her due process claim.[868]

410. Persons who are incarcerated in prison or subject to incarceration because of conviction for crime still have certain "liberty" interests for due process purposes. These "liberty" interests are the strongest when they relate to release from incarceration. Many states provide that persons convicted of crime may be placed on probation in lieu of being imprisoned or may be released from prison on parole prior to the completion of their sentence. When the state has provided for probation or parole, it has established a "liberty" interest for due process purposes, and when it seeks to revoke a person's probation or parole, it must provide a "hearing" for determining the facts that are necessary to support the asserted basis for revocation. The "hearing" need not be a full evidentiary hearing, but must provide a "fair procedure" by which the person can demonstrate that the probation or parole should not have been revoked.[869] By the same token, when the state provides for "good-time" credits that could result in the inmate's earlier release from prison, but also provides that these credits can be forfeited for

866. *Wisconsin v. Constantineau*, 400 U.S. 433 (1971). *Compare Paul v. Davis*, 424 U.S. 693 (1976), where an injury to a person's reputation caused by the government's distribution of a flyer listing him as an "active shoplifter" was held not to amount to a "liberty" interest for due process purposes. And since the state can constitutionally require that all convicted sex offenders be listed on a sex offender registry based on the fact of their conviction, an offender claiming not to be "currently dangerous" is not entitled to a hearing to establish that fact. Any constitutional challenge must be to the substantive requirement that the offender be listed on the registry without regard to whether the offender is "currently dangerous." *Connecticut Department of Public Safety v. Doe*, 538 U.S. 1 (2003).

867. *Goss v. Lopez*, 419 U.S. 565 (1975); *Ingraham v. Wright*, 430 U.S. 651 (1977).

Public universities typically have formalized procedures applicable to the suspension and expulsion of students, which are likely to satisfy due process requirements. In *Board of Curators v. Horowitz*, 435 U.S. 78 (1978), the Court held that the procedures followed by a medical school in dismissing a student on academic grounds satisfied due process, emphasizing that the decision rested upon the academic judgment of the medical school officials.

868. *Kerry v. Dinn*, 135 S.Ct. 2128 (2015).

869. *Gagnon v. Scarpelli*, 411 U.S. 778 (1973) (revocation of probation); *Morrissey v. Brewer*, 408 U.S. 471 (1972) (revocation of parole).

"serious misbehavior," there must be a "fair procedure" hearing on the issue of forfeiture.[870]

411. The Court has held that the transfer of an inmate from one prison facility to another does not implicate a protected "liberty" interest, because such transfers are discretionary with the prison authorities, and do not change the nature of the inmate's confinement.[871] However, the involuntary transfer of an inmate from a prison facility to a mental hospital does change the nature of the inmate's confinement, and so implicates a protected "liberty" interest. In order for the government to effectuate such a transfer, there must be a "hearing" to determine whether the statutory conditions for such a transfer have been satisfied. This "hearing" must include notice to the inmate of the intended transfer and the inmate's right to contest it, the opportunity for the inmate to be heard in person and to present evidence and witnesses, the opportunity to confront and cross-examine opposing witnesses except where good cause exists for limiting confrontation, the right to have the decision made by an independent decision-maker, a written statement by the decision-maker detailing the evidence and reasons supporting the transfer, and the assistance of an independent advisor, who need not be a lawyer.[872] The Court has also held that while substantive due process does not prohibit the prison authorities from administering an antipsychotic drug to an inmate without the inmate's consent, procedural due process does require that there be a "hearing" on the matter in accordance with procedures similar to those required for the involuntary transfer of an inmate to a mental institution.[873]

412. For a review of problems of aliens, we refer to Chapter 5 of this Part, and for the constitutional protection of minorities with U.S. citizenship, to Chapter 2, §4.

---

870. *Wolff v. McDonnell*, 418 U.S. 539 (1974). *Compare Sandin v. Conner*, 515 U.S. 472 (1995), holding that an inmate did not have a "liberty" interest in being free from disciplinary segregation within the prison for a limited period of time.

871. *Meachum v. Fano*, 427 U.S. 215 (1976).

872. *Vitek v. Jones*, 445 U.S. 480 (1980).

873. *Washington v. Harper*, 494 U.S. 210 (1990). In that case, the Court upheld the procedures provided by the state, which included a hearing before a panel of medical professionals and prison officials who were not involved in the inmate's current treatment, and the inmate's right to seek judicial review of the decision by filing a petition in the state court. As a substantive constitutional matter, the Constitution permits the government involuntarily to administer antipsychotic drugs to a mentally ill defendant facing serious criminal charges in order to render that defendant competent to stand trial, but only if the treatment is medically appropriate, is substantially unlikely to have side effects that may undermine the fairness of the trial, and, taking account of less intrusive means, is significantly necessary to further important governmental trial-related interests. *See Sell v. United States*, 539 U.S. 166 (2003).

Procedural due process also requires that the state provide a judicial or administrative procedure by which a prison inmate can obtain redress for the intentional violation of his "liberty" or "property" interests by prison officials and employees. *See Hudson v. Palmer*, 468 U.S. 517 (1984).

Chapter 3. Judicial Control of Administrative Action

413. In the American constitutional system, judicial review of administrative action is best understood as a specific application of the broader principle of judicial review of governmental action. Since it has long been established that the federal courts have the power under Article III to review and declare unconstitutional laws and executive action, it would have been inconsistent with this fundamental principle of American constitutionalism to exempt the actions of administrative agencies from judicial review or to treat judicial review of administrative action in a substantially different way from judicial review of governmental action generally. The nature of judicial review of administrative action, which includes judicial review both of rule-making and of adjudication,[874] has been adapted to the regulatory function performed by administrative agencies and to the way that this regulatory function is performed. But at the core of judicial review of administrative action is the concept that it is the responsibility of courts to ensure that administrative agencies comply with the Constitution and with the provisions of the laws that they have been directed to administer by Congress. Minimally then, judicial review of administrative action means that the courts must determine whether the action taken by the administrative agency is consistent with the Constitution and consistent with the jurisdiction and authority that have been conferred upon the agency by Congress. The court must also determine whether the agency has complied with legally required procedures and whether its decision is reasonable and supported by the administrative record on which the decision was based.

414. As a general proposition, all administrative action is presumptively subject to some form of judicial review. A number of the laws establishing administrative agencies expressly provide for judicial review of their actions,[875] and the Administrative Procedure Act authorizes judicial review in all cases except where "statutes preclude judicial review," or "agency action is committed to agency discretion by law."[876] The Supreme Court has stated that these exceptions under the Act are to be construed narrowly, and that, "only upon a showing of clear and convincing evidence of a contrary

874. These claims may be between private entities or between a private entity and agency officials. An agency's internal regulations will ensure that when the claim involves a private entity and an agency official, there will be a separation of "enforcement" and "adjudication." The claims are adjudicated in the first instance by an Administrative Law Judge, an agency employee whose sole responsibility is to adjudicate claims.

875. Some of these laws provide for judicial review of agency action in the federal courts of appeal rather than in the federal district courts. These include actions of the National Labor Relations Board, the Federal Trade Commission, and the Federal Energy Regulatory Commission. Most actions of the Federal Communications Commission can only be reviewed in the United States Court of Appeals for the District of Columbia Circuit. Unless a specific law provides otherwise, judicial review of agency action must be sought in a federal district court, with an appeal to the federal Court of Appeals exercising jurisdiction over appeals from that district court.

876. 5 U.S.C. sec. 701(a).

legislative intent should the courts restrict access to judicial review."[877] However, because of the large number of administrative agencies and their myriad activities of rule-making, adjudication, and informal agency action, there will be a significant number of actual cases in which judicial review is in fact precluded, although these cases represent only a very small fraction of the total cases in which parties seek judicial review of actions taken by administrative agencies. Our discussion will be divided into three parts: (1) preclusion of judicial review; (2) standing to obtain judicial review; (3) the scope of judicial review.

§1. Preclusion of Judicial Review

415. Preclusion of judicial review refers to preclusion of any review of the action that the agency has taken except for the claim that such action is violative of the Constitution. The Supreme Court has been unwilling to interpret any law as containing the "clear intent" of Congress to preclude judicial review of constitutional claims involving administrative action, and has stated that a "serious constitutional question" would arise if Congress should attempt to do so.[878]

416. Under section 701 of the Administrative Procedure Act, judicial review of agency action may be precluded if: (1) the relevant statute precludes judicial review of a particular agency action; or (2) the particular agency action sought to be reviewed "is committed to agency discretion by law." The difference between these two bases of preclusion of judicial review has been stated by the Supreme Court as follows: "The former applies when Congress has expressed an intent to preclude judicial review. The latter applies in different circumstances; even where Congress has not affirmatively precluded review, review is not to be had if the statute is drawn so that a court would have no meaningful standard against which to judge the agency's exercise of discretion."[879]

417. With respect to the first basis of preclusion, since there must be a showing of "clear and convincing evidence of legislative intent to restrict access to judicial review," it is only in very limited circumstances that the courts will find that the relevant statute precludes judicial review of the agency action, although such circumstances sometimes do occur. The following are examples of the relevant statute precluding judicial review. The National Labor Relations Act precludes judicial review of dismissal of unfair labor practices complaint pursuant to informal settlement between Board's

877. *Abbott Laboratories v. Gardner*, 387 U.S. 136, 141 (1967). The President is not an "administrative agency" for purposes of the Administrative Procedure Act, and action committed to the President's discretion by Congress is not subject to review under the Act. *Dalton v. Specter*, 511 U.S. 462 (1994). Claims that the President acted without statutory authority or in violation of the Constitution are, of course, subject to judicial review in an ordinary lawsuit.

878. *See Webster v. Doe*, 486 U.S. 592 (1988), where the Court held that the National Security Act of 1947 precluded judicial review of employee termination decisions of the Director of the CIA, except for the claim that the termination of the employee was unconstitutional. *Compare Weinberger v. Salfi*, 422 U.S. 749 (1975), where the Court found that judicial review of a constitutional claim was precluded by one part of the applicable federal law, but not by another, and so proceeded to determine the merits of the claim.

879. *Heckler v. Chaney*, 470 U.S. 821, 830 (1985).

general counsel and employer.[880] The Interstate Commerce Act precluded judicial review of the Interstate Commerce Commission's decision not to initiate an investigation into the legality of a railroad's seasonal rate increase.[881] The Postal Reorganization Act precludes judicial review of decision of Board of Governors of the United States Postal Service to remove the Postmaster General.[882] The Parole Reorganization Act precludes judicial review of Bureau of Prison's decision to refuse to move for reduction of a prisoner's sentence in federal court.[883] The Court has also found partial statutory preclusion of judicial review in certain circumstances.[884]

418. This situation is clearly illustrated by *Webster v. Doe*,[885] where an employee of the CIA who was terminated because of his homosexual orientation sought judicial review of the termination decision under the Administrative Procedure Act. The employee contended that the action of the Director in terminating him was "arbitrary, capricious, an abuse of discretion, or otherwise not in accordance with law," within the meaning of section 706(2)(A) of the Administrative Procedure Act. The relevant provision of the National Security Act of 1947, section 102(c), provided that: "The Director of Central Intelligence may, in his discretion, terminate the employment of any officer or employee of the Agency whenever he shall deem such termination necessary or advisable in the interests of the United States." The Supreme Court held that the above language, which says "deem[s] necessary" rather than "is necessary," "fairly exudes deference to the Director, and appears to us to foreclose the application of any meaningful judicial standard of review."[886]

In the same vein, the Supreme Court has held that when a party seeks judicial review of an administrative agency's decision not to take certain action, the presumption should be that the decision not to take action is "committed to agency discretion by law" and so not subject to judicial review. The presumption can be overcome only where the applicable law has provided "guidelines for the agency to follow in exercising its enforcement powers." This case arose out of rather grotesque circumstances. Convicted murderers, who had been sentenced to death by lethal injection, brought

880. *National Labor Relations Board v. United Food and Commercial Workers Union*, 484 U.S. 112 (1987).

881. *Southern Railway Co. v. Seaboard Allied Milling Corp.*, 442 U.S. 444 (1979).

882. *Carlin v. McKean*, 823 F.2d 620 (D.C. Cir. 1987).

883. *Turner v. United States Parole Commission*, 810 F.2d 612 (7th Cir. 1987).

884. *See Block v. Community Nutrition Institute*, 467 U.S. 340 (1984), where the Court found that a federal law that comprehensively regulated milk marketing was intended to preclude ultimate consumers of dairy products from obtaining judicial review of milk marketing orders issued by the Secretary of Agriculture. The law would not preclude judicial review by milk handlers and other entities involved in the milk marketing system. *Compare Thunder Basin Coal Co. v. Reich*, 510 U.S. 200 (1994), where the Court held that a federal law's statutory review scheme precluded the federal courts from hearing pre-enforcement challenges to the law and that judicial review would be available only after the administrative agency issued a final order. In *United States v. Bean*, 537 U.S. 1 (2002), the Court held that judicial review was not available to review the Secretary of the Treasury's refusal to consider a gun dealer's application for relief from a statutory prohibition against his possession or receipt of firearms, because the applicable statute only permitted judicial review of an affirmative denial of the dealer's application for relief.

885. *Webster v. Doe*, *supra* , n. 878.

886. *Ibid.*, at 600.

an action under the Administrative Procedure Act against the Food and Drug Administration, claiming that the drugs that would be used by the states to carry out the lethal injections had not been tested and approved by the agency for use in human executions.[887] They sought an order requiring the agency to take certain actions with respect to those drugs, which the agency had previously refused to take. The Supreme Court held that the agency's decision not to take any action with respect to those drugs was "committed to agency discretion by law," relying on the presumption stated above, and finding no enforcement guidelines in the applicable law to overcome that presumption.[888] In another case, the Court held that where an administrative agency did not have statutory authorization to review the decision of an intermediary body's refusal to reopen a reimbursement determination, the party denied reimbursement could not bring a federal court action seeking judicial review of the intermediary body's refusal to reopen.[889] Attempts by states to argue that federal law requires various agencies of the federal government to reimburse them for the costs of incarcerating and educating illegal aliens have been rejected by the federal Courts of Appeal as involving a matter that is "committed to agency discretion by law."[890]

Under section 706(1) of the Administrative Procedure Act, federal courts are authorized to "compel federal agency action unlawfully withheld or unreasonably delayed." This provision is narrowly construed and applies only where the plaintiff asserts that an agency failed to take a discrete action that it is required to take.[891]

419. In deciding whether an action is "committed to agency discretion by law," then, the question is "whether there is law to apply." Analytically, the question is the same whether judicial review is sought of action that an agency has taken or of the failure of the agency to take action, but in the latter situation, as stated above, there is a presumption that the decision not to take action is "committed to agency discretion by law," so the courts are more likely to find that judicial review is precluded. Again, because of the voluminous actions taken by the large number of federal administrative agencies, there will be a significant number of cases in practice where the courts will

887. *Heckler v. Chaney*, 470 U.S. 821, 830 (1985).

888. *See also Lincoln v. Vigil*, 508 U.S. 182 (1993), where the Court held that an agency's decision to shift funds contained in a lump-sum appropriation from one program to another was "committed to agency discretion by law." *Compare Dunlop v. Bachowski*, 421 U.S. 560 (1975), where the Court found that there were sufficient guidelines in the applicable law to permit judicial review of the decision of the Secretary of Labor to refuse to institute a suit to set aside a union election claimed to be in violation of that law.

889. *Your Home Visiting Nurse Services v. Shalala*, 525 U.S. 449 (1999).

890. *See* e.g., *State of New Jersey v. United States*, 91 F.2d 463 (3d Cir. 1996).

891. *See* e.g., *Norton v. Southern Utah Wilderness Alliance*, 542 U.S. 55 (2004), holding that this provision did not apply to allow a challenge to the Secretary of the Interior's identification of certain public lands as "wilderness study areas."

find that the challenged action is "committed to agency discretion by law."[892] However, this should not obscure the fact that most of the time the courts will find that judicial review of agency action is not precluded on this basis.

§2. Standing to Obtain Judicial Review

420. Section 702 of the Administrative Procedure Act authorizes judicial review by any "person suffering legal wrong because of agency action, or adversely affected or aggrieved by agency action within the meaning of a relevant statute." A person seeking judicial review of administrative action must, of course, satisfy the "case or controversy" requirements of standing in the same manner as any person seeking judicial review of governmental action generally. In the judicial review of administrative action context, the plaintiff must show injury in fact having a fairly traceable causal connection to the challenged [administrative] action that is likely to be redressed by a favorable decision. Thus, where the party seeking judicial review of administrative action fails to demonstrate a direct, identified and differentiated injury that is fairly traceable to the challenged administrative action, the party lacks standing to challenge that action.[893]

421. However, there is an additional requirement for standing to seek judicial review of administrative action. Since the party seeking such review must be "adversely affected or aggrieved" by agency action within the meaning of a relevant statute, the party must show that he or she is within the zone of interests sought to be protected

---

892. For a few illustrative lower court cases, *see* : State of North Dakota ex Rel. *Board of University and School Lands v. Yeutter*, 914 F.2d 1031 (8th Cir. 1990) (decision by Secretary of Agriculture to waive conditions for participation in land conservation program); Local 2855, *AFGE (AFL-C/O) v. United States*, 602 F.2d 574 (3d Cir. 1979) (decision of Department of Army to contract out to private concern services previously performed by government employees); *Woodsmall v. Lyng*, 816 F.2d 1241 (8th Cir. 1987) (federal agency's evaluation of creditworthiness of applicants for loan under government program and denial of loan for lack of creditworthiness); *Board of Trade of City of Chicago v. Securities Exchange Commission*, 883 F.2d 525 (7th Cir. 1989) (order of Securities Exchange Commission allowing proprietary trading system to deal in options on government securities without requiring it to register as "exchange"); *Scalise v. Thornburgh*, 891 F.2d 640 (7th Cir. 1989) (Attorney-General's denial of requests from American citizens incarcerated abroad for transfers to American prisons).

893. *See* e.g., *Lujan v. National Wildlife Federation*, 497 U.S. 871 (1990), where members of a wildlife federation group were found to lack standing to challenge a "land withdrawal review" "program of the Bureau of Land Management," because they only alleged that they made recreational use of land "in the vicinity" of the land covered by the agency's actions, and did not allege that they made recreational use of the land actually covered by the agency's actions.

by the substantive law on which the party is relying to challenge the agency action.[894] The zone of interests requirement is clearly illustrated by *Air Courier Conference of America v. American Postal Workers Union, AFL-CIO*.[895] There, a union representing postal employees challenged an action of the United States Postal Service that permitted private couriers to engage in some mailing operations that competed with the operations of the Service. Federal law gave the Postal Service a postal monopoly by excluding private carriers, and a provision of that law permitted the Postal Service to suspend the restrictions on private carriers "upon any mail route when the public interest requires the suspension." The union sought judicial review of that action, contending that the Service was not justified in concluding that the particular suspension of the monopoly was "required by the public interest." While the postal employees admittedly satisfied the "injury in fact" requirement, because the increased competition resulting from the participation of private couriers in mailing operations could affect their employment opportunities, the Court held that they did not satisfy the "zone of interests" test. The Court found that Congress's purpose in enacting the laws providing for a postal monopoly was not to protect jobs with the Postal Service, but rather to provide the receipt of necessary revenues for the Postal Service itself. Thus, the postal employees were not within the zone of interests protected by the postal monopoly laws, and did not have standing to seek judicial review of the actions of the Postal Service under those laws.

422. On the other hand, the Court held that the zone of interests test was satisfied when securities brokers, underwriters, and investment bankers challenged the action of the Comptroller of the Currency in allowing a national bank to conduct discount brokerage activities inside and outside the bank's home state. They challenged the Comptroller's action as violative of a law regulating the operation of branch banks by a national bank, and the Court found that the underlying purpose of that law was to prevent national banks from gaining a monopoly control over credit and money through branch banking. Since the plaintiffs would be competing with the national banks in providing discount brokerage services, they were "competitors who allege an injury that implicates the policies of the [Act]." Thus, they were within the zone of interests protected by the law and could seek judicial review of administrative action that could result in harm to their competitive position.[896] Similarly, in an earlier case, data processors were held to come within the zone of interests protected by a federal law that prohibited banks from engaging in any activity other than banking services, and so had standing to challenge an action of the Comptroller of the Currency that permitted

894. This requirement does not apply where there is a specific statutory provision authorizing judicial review by a given class of persons or by "any person affected by the agency action." Congress can confer standing on an administrative official to seek judicial review of agency action as a "person affected by the agency action," but in the absence of such authorization, an administrative official generally cannot seek judicial review of agency action. *See* Director, Office of Worker's Compensation Programs, *Department of Labor v. Newport News Shipbuilding and Dry Dock Co.*, 514 U.S. 122 (1995) (Director of the Department of Labor's Office of Worker's Compensation Programs could not seek judicial review of agency action substantially lessening an employer's obligation to pay benefits to an injured employee, who did not seek judicial review of that action).

895. 498 U.S. 517 (1991).

896. *Clarke v. Securities Industries Association*, 479 U.S. 388 (1987).

banks to provide data processing services to their customers and to other banks.[897] And in another case, the Court found standing for tenant farmers who were eligible for federal agricultural subsidies to challenge an action of the Secretary of Agriculture permitting assignment of those benefits to secure rent for farmland. They contended that landlords would rely on the new regulation to demand advance assignment of the federal benefits as a condition to obtaining a lease, thereby making the plaintiffs dependent on the landlord for their supplies. The zone of interests test was satisfied, because one of the purposes of the federal act allegedly violated by the Secretary was to protect the interests of tenant farmers against landlords.[898] In its most recent decision on "zone of interests," the Court held that the owner of land near the site of a proposed Indian casino who brought a suit challenging the decision of the Secretary of the Interior to acquire the site on behalf of the tribe arguably fell within the "zone of interests" regulated by the federal law that authorized acquisition of the land to foster an Indian tribe's economic development.[899]

423. As these cases indicate, ordinarily the party seeking judicial review of administrative action will be able to satisfy the zone of interests' requirement, but in some cases, such as *Air Courier*, the party will not, and this must be recognized as an additional requirement for standing to seek judicial review of administrative action.[900]

897. *Association of Data Processing Service Organizations v. Camp*, 397 U.S. 150 (1970). Other cases finding "zone of interest" standing for competitors to challenge actions of the Comptroller of the Currency permitting banks to engage in activities arguably prohibited by bank regulation laws are *Investment Company Institute v. Camp*, 401 U.S. 617 (1971), and *Arnold Tours, Inc. v. Camp*, 400 U.S. 45 (1970).

898. *Barlow v. Collins*, 397 U.S. 159 (1970). For more recent cases where the Court found that the zone of interests test was satisfied, *see* : *Bennett v. Spear*, 520 U.S. 154 (1997) (water districts whose use of water was adversely affected by lake level restrictions imposed by administrative agency in order to protect endangered species could challenge action as violative of Endangered Species Act, even though the districts were seeking to prevent application of environmental restrictions rather than to implement such restrictions); *Federal Election Commission v. Akins*, 524 U.S. 11 (1998) (group of voters who opposed the policies of a particular organization could challenge Federal Election Commission's refusal to require the organization to make disclosures concerning its membership, contributions and expenditures as violative of Federal Election Campaign Act); *National Credit Union Administration v. First National Bank and Trust Co.*, 522 U.S. 479 (1998) (competing financial institutions could challenge membership policies of federal credit unions as violative of Federal Credit Union Act).

899. *MATCH-E-BE-NASH-SHE-WISH Band of Pottawatomi v. Patchak*, 132 Sup.Ct. 2199 (2012).

900. In regard to judicial review of administrative action, the ripeness limitation, discussed earlier in connection with limitations on judicial review generally, relates primarily to concerns about the abstract posture in which the issue may be presented. So, where the challenged rule was clear, and the party challenging it could be charged with a violation if it acted in a certain way, the question was "ripe" for judicial review in advance of a violation. *Abbott Laboratories v. Gardner*, 387 U.S. 136, 141 (1967). However, in *National Park Hospitality Association v. Department of the Interior*, 538 U.S. 803 (2003), the Court found that a challenge to a policy statement of the National Park Service that a federal law establishing rules governing certain government contracts did not apply to concession contracts was not ripe in the absence of a concrete dispute about a particular concession contract.

§3. The Scope of Judicial Review

424. There are essentially two parts to judicial review of the actions of administrative agencies: (1) determination of legal questions, such as the constitutional validity of the action taken by the agency or the agency's statutory authority to take such action; (2) the supportability of the agency's action on the basis of the record compiled in the proceedings before the agency.

425. Section 706 of the Administrative Procedure Act provides that the reviewing court shall "decide all relevant questions of law, interpret constitutional and statutory provisions, and determine the meaning or applicability of the terms of an agency action." While the courts' review of constitutional questions arising in connection with agency action obviously is the same as its review of constitutional questions arising with respect to legislation or executive action generally, its review of other legal questions arising in connection with agency action may be affected by the agency's interpretation of the law that it is administering. Suppose that there is a question of whether a provision of the law that the agency is administering applies to a particular activity that the agency seeks to regulate. In such a circumstance, the Supreme Court has said that the court should first consider whether "Congress has directly spoken to the precise question at issue." If the court concludes that Congress has done so, then that is the end of the matter, since both the courts and the agency "must give effect to the unambiguously expressed intent of Congress." If, however, the court concludes that the law is silent or ambiguous with respect to the particular issue, then the question for the court is "whether the agency's answer is based on a permissible construction of the statute."[901]

There have been a large number of recent cases involving judicial deference to administrative interpretation. The following rulings have been upheld on the basis of judicial deference. Agency ruling establishing reasonable time frames for state or locality to act on wireless facility siting applications.[902] Interpretation by Environmental Protection Agency that Clean Water Act,[903] authorized Agency to employ a cost-benefit analysis in setting national performance standards under the Act.[904] Determination by Federal Communications Commission that cable companies' broadband internet service was not a "telecommunications service" under 47 U.S.C. sec. 153(46).[905] Interpretation by Equal Employment Opportunity Commission that law prohibiting employment discrimination against persons with disabilities was not violated by denial of employment to person whose disability on the job would pose a direct threat to his health.[906] Interpretation by Social Security Administration of statutory term "disabled" to mean

901. The above-quoted language is taken from the Court's decision in Chevron, *U.S.A. v. Natural Resources Defense Council*, 467 U.S. 837, 842–843 (1984), which is a "landmark" case on the question of judicial deference to administrative interpretation.

902. City of Arlington, *Texas v. Federal Communications Commission*, 133 S.Ct. 1863 (2013).

903. 33 U.S.C. sec. 1326(b).

904. *Entergy Corporation v. Riverkeeper, Inc.*, 556 U.S. 208 (2009).

905. *National Cable & Telecommunications Association v. Brand X Internet Services*, 545 U.S. 967 (2005).

906. *Chevron U.S.A. v. Echazabal*, 536 U.S. 73 (2002).

an inability to work for at least twelve months.[907] Interpretation by Social Security Administration of statutory term "disabled" to mean that a claimant was not "disabled" where claimant remained physically and mentally able to do her previous work without investigating whether that work existed in significant numbers in the national economy.[908] Interpretation by Federal Communications Commission that its statutory authority to regulate rates charged for "attachments" to utility poles' by telecommunications carriers and by cable television system included attachments that provided co-mingled cable television and high-speed Internet service and attachments that provided wireless telecommunications.[909] Interpretation of statute by United States Customs Service that garment manufactured abroad that was "baked" to maintain crease and avoid wrinkles was "improved by operation [not] incidental to the assembly process" and so was not eligible for partial duty exemption.[910] Interpretation of statute by Comptroller of Currency that statutory term "interest" included late payment fees imposed by credit card companies.[911] Interpretation by Secretary of Health and Human Services of regulation relating to reimbursement of hospital's medical costs as not including costs that were borne by hospital's medical schools.[912] In two recent cases, the Supreme Court applied "*Chevron*" deference to uphold a determination by the Board of Immigration Appeals that a statute addressing eligibility for cancellation of removal required each alien to satisfy the requirement of residence in the United States individually, without imputation of a parent's years of residence,[913] and a determination by the Social Security Administration with reference to state intestacy law that children conceived posthumously by in vitro fertilization after the wage-earner's death were not entitled to child's insurance benefits.[914] The same test applies to determine whether an agency's issuance of a regulation is within its statutory authority. Where the law is silent or ambiguous, the courts will give deference to the agency's interpretation of the statute as authorizing it to issue the regulation in question.[915]

In other words, if the legal question is not resolved by the "unambiguously expressed intent of Congress," there is considerable judicial deference to the agency's interpretation of the law that it is administering. So long as that interpretation is a reasonable one, the court must accept it, and may not require a different interpretation in light of its view of the overall purpose of the regulatory law. As a practical matter,

---

907. *Barnhart v. Walton*, 535 U.S. 212 (2002).
908. *Barnhart v. Thomas*, 540 U.S. 20 (2003).
909. *National Cable & Telecommunications Association v. Gulf Power Co.*, 534 U.S. 327 (2002).
910. *United States v. Haggar Apparel Co.*, 526 U.S. 380 (1999).
911. *Smiley v. Citibank*, 517 U.S. 735 (1996).
912. *Thomas Jefferson University v. Shalala*, 512 U.S. 504 (1997).
913. *Holder v. Martinez Gutierrez*, 132 Sup.Ct. 2011 (2012).
914. *Astrue v. Capato*, 132 Sup.Ct. 2021 (2012). *See also Conkright v. Frommert*, 559 U.S. 506 (2010), holding that the requirement of judicial deference applied to agency's subsequent interpretation of law notwithstanding that original interpretation had been set aside by a court.
915. *See* e.g., *Edelman v. Lynchburg College*, 535 U.S. 106 (2002) (Equal Employment Opportunity Commission regulation providing that where a charge has been timely filed within the limitations period, the charge can be verified after the period for filing a charge has expired); *New York v. Federal Energy Regulatory Commission*, 535 U.S. 1 (2002) (Federal Energy Regulatory Commission regulation including "unbundled" retail transmissions of energy within scope of "open access" requirements).

in such a case, the question is whether the intention of Congress on the matter in issue is unambiguous, and some cases will be found where the courts have found that the agency's interpretation of the law was contrary to unambiguous Congressional intent. The following cases are based on a finding of contrary to unambiguous Congressional intent. Express language of Voting Rights Act was contrary to determination of Attorney-General that Act applied to matters that affected the authority of elected public officials.[916] Expressed intent of Congress in Paperwork Reduction Act was that Office of Management and Budget did not have authority to review regulations of other agencies mandating public disclosure of information by regulated agencies.[917] Secretary of Labor's eligibility regulations for "black lung" claims violated statutory provision that eligibility standards not be "more restrictive" than standards existing as of a certain date.[918] Express language of Federal Credit Union Act that credit union membership shall be limited to groups having a "common bond" of occupation or association was contrary to determination of National Credit Union Administration that federal credit union could be made up of multiple unrelated employer groups.[919] The text, structure, purpose and history of Age Discrimination in Employment Act, along with its relationship to other federal laws, required rejection of Equal Employment Opportunity Commission's interpretation that law prohibited employer from favoring an older employee over a younger one.[920] The Supreme Court has also held that the federal Food, Drug and Cosmetic Act, taken as a whole, evidenced Congressional intent to deny the Food and Drug Administration the authority to regulate tobacco products.[921]

In three very recent cases the Court found that the administrative agency's interpretation of the applicable statute was not entitled to *Chevron* deference. In *King v. Burwell*,[922] the Court found that the Internal Revenue Service's interpretation that the term "an exchange established by the state" for purposes of entitlement to tax credits for purchase of health insurance did not include an exchange established by the federal government was not entitled to *Chevron* deference, where statutory language was ambiguous and gave the federal government the direction to establish exchanges where a state opted not to do so. In *Michigan v. Environmental Protection Agency*,[923] the Court found that the Environmental Protection Agency had interpreted the Clean Air Act,[924] unreasonably when it deemed the cost of complying with the regulation irrelevant in determining whether the regulation was "appropriate and necessary." And in *Encino Motocars, LLC v. Navarro*,[925] the Court found that the Department of Labor's regulation was not entitled to *Chevron* deference on the question of whether service

916. *Presley v. Etowah County Commission*, 502 U.S. 491 (1992).
917. *Dole v. United Steelworkers of America*, 494 U.S. 26 (1990).
918. *Pittson Coal Group v. Sebben*, 488 U.S. 105 (1988).
919. *National Credit Union Administration v. First National Bank & Trust Co.*, 522 U.S. 479 (1998).
920. *General Dynamics Land Systems, Inc. v. Cline*, 340 U.S. 541 (2004).
921. *Food and Drug Administration v. Brown & Williamson Tobacco Corp.*, 529 U.S. 120 (2000). Congress subsequently amended the law to give the Food and Drug Administration the authority to regulate tobacco products.
922. 135 S.Ct. 2480 (2015).
923. 135 S.Ct. 2699 (2015).
924. 42 U.S.C. sec. 7412(n)(1)(A).
925. 136 S.Ct. 2117 (2016).

advisors employed by an automobile dealership were exempt from overtime provisions of federal law, where the regulation was issued without the reasoned explanation that was required in light of the Department's change from its longstanding position that service advisors were exempt from these provisions.

426. The second component of the scope of review relates to the supportability of the agency's action on the basis of the record compiled in the proceedings before the agency. There are two standards of review articulated in section 706(2) of the Administrative Procedure Act and the laws establishing administrative agencies. For formal rule-making and adjudication, the "substantial evidence" standard applies: the action of the agency may be set aside if it is "unsupported by substantial evidence." For informal agency action, the "arbitrary and capricious" standard applies: the action of the agency may be set aside if it is "arbitrary, capricious, an abuse of discretion, or otherwise not in accordance with law."[926]

However, the law establishing the agency may specify the standard of review, both for rule-making and adjudication and for informal agency action. Sometimes, the law will use the "substantial evidence" standard, and sometimes it will use the "arbitrary and capricious" standard. If the law establishing the agency sets forth a standard of review, that standard controls; the provisions of the Administrative Procedure Act distinguishing between formal and informal agency action only apply in the absence of an otherwise applicable standard.[927]

427. It is questionable how much actual difference there is between the application of the two standards in practice. Under section 706 of the Act, the reviewing court must review the whole record in every case, but at the same time it would be expected that there would be a good deal of deference to the findings and conclusions of the administrative agency under either standard. The Supreme Court has defined "substantial evidence" review with reference to the sufficiency of the evidence to take a case to a jury. (In the United States, civil cases, as well as criminal cases, are usually tried by a jury.) If the evidence before the jury is so one-sided, that the jury could reasonably decide the case only in favor of one of the parties, the case does not go to the jury, and the judge directs a verdict in favor of that party. According to the Supreme Court, there is "substantial evidence" to support a decision of an administrative agency if the evidence is "enough to justify, if the trial were to a jury, a refusal to direct a verdict when the conclusion sought to be drawn from it is one of fact for the jury."[928] The Court has defined the "arbitrary and capricious" standard as follows:

> To make this finding the court must consider whether the decision was based on a consideration of the relevant factors and whether there has been a clear error in judgment ... Although this inquiry into the facts is to be searching and careful,

926. For these purposes, any action other than formal rule-making or adjudication constitutes informal agency action, and is subject to review under the "arbitrary and capricious" standard. *See Citizens to Preserve Overton Park v. Volpe*, 401 U.S. 402, 410 (1971).
927. In a very few laws, Congress has provided for de novo review of the agency's actions by the courts.
928. *Illinois Central Railroad Co. v. Norfolk & Western Ry. Co.*, 385 U.S. 57, 66 (1966).

the ultimate standard of review is a narrow one. The court is not empowered to substitute its judgment for that of the agency.[929]

While the formulations of the two standards differ, both standards embody the concept of reasonableness, with the "substantial evidence" standard perhaps requiring a bit more scrutiny by the courts. Nonetheless, both standards require deference to the findings and conclusions of the administrative agencies, and in practice most of the time the action of the administrative agency will be sustained under either standard.[930]

428. Where the reviewing court sets aside the action of the administrative agency on the ground that it is not supportable in the record, the case is returned to the administrative agency for further proceedings. These may include additional fact-findings, and it is possible that, following the additional fact-finding and reconsideration, the administrative agency will make the same decision.

929. *Citizens to Preserve Overton Park v. Volpe*, 401 U.S. 402,416 (1971).

930. For a recent case involving the application of the "arbitrary and capricious" standard, *see Federal Communications Commission v. Fox Stations, Inc.,* 556 U.S. 502(2009), where the Court upheld a finding of the Commission that "indecent language" in a broadcast included "fleeting expletives." However, in another recent case, *Judulang v. Holder*, 556 U.S. 42(2011), the Court held that a "comparable grounds" rule (whether a charged deportation ground had a close analogue to the list of exclusion grounds) of the Board of Immigration Appeals for determining whether an alien was eligible for discretionary relief from deportation was "arbitrary and capricious" and so was invalid.

Chapter 4. Legal Position of Aliens

429. The best way to analyze the rights of aliens under the Constitution and laws of the United States is to draw a sharp distinction between aliens who have been admitted to the United States for permanent residence and aliens who are seeking entry into the United States or who may be temporarily in the United States. On the one hand, there are virtually no constitutional restrictions on the power of Congress to regulate the entry and stay in the United States of aliens seeking entry and aliens who have not been admitted to the United States for permanent residence. On the other hand, aliens who have been admitted to the United States for permanent residence are entitled to a high degree of constitutional and legal protection. They can only be deported for specified grounds in accordance with legal proceedings that satisfy all the requirements of procedural due process. They cannot be subject to discrimination by the states where they reside except with respect to "political matters," such as voting, jury service, and "policy-making and policy-executing" governmental employment. However, respect for Congress' plenary power over immigration and naturalization has resulted in judicial deference to Congressional action even with respect to aliens who have been admitted to permanent residence, and the Supreme Court has upheld the constitutionality of federal laws that effect a degree of discrimination against resident aliens in comparison to citizens.

§1. Control of Entry of Aliens

430. Since every nation has the inherent power to control its borders, the Supreme Court has been reluctant to impose any constitutional limits on the power of Congress to control the entry of aliens into the United States. It is well settled that aliens cannot assert a constitutionally protected "liberty" interest in obtaining admission into the United States, and that they have no constitutional right to a "due process" type of hearing before being denied admission.[931] The Court has also upheld against First Amendment challenge a federal law authorizing the denial of a visa to an alien who was invited to speak in the United States because of the alien's political views.[932]

431. Congress, however, has long provided that an alien who is denied admission to the United States at a port of entry is entitled to a hearing, at which it is to be

931. *Shaughnessy v. United States ex rel. Mezei*, 345 U.S. 206 (1953). However, under current law Congress has provided for a hearing for some aliens denied admission to the United States, and this hearing is conducted under the same rules that govern deportation hearings. *See* para. 433, *infra* .

932. *Kleindienst v. Mandel*, 408 U.S. 753 (1972). In *Jean v. Nelson*, 472 U.S. 846 (1985), Haitian refugees seeking admission to the United States contended that the immigration officials ordered them held in custody rather than releasing them on parole pending the determination of their status because of their race. The Court did not reach the question of whether constitutional prohibitions against racial discrimination applied to governmental action with respect to aliens seeking admission to the United States, finding that the applicable federal statute prohibited the alleged racial discrimination in the circumstances presented.

determined whether or not the alien is entitled to admission to the United States.[933] The alien applying for admission is interviewed by an immigration officer. If the immigration officer finds that the alien is inadmissible on illegal entry or lack of proper documentation grounds, the officer shall order the alien removed without further review unless the alien indicates either an intention to apply for asylum[934] or a fear of persecution.[935] If the alien applying for admission so indicates, the officer refers the alien for interview by an asylum officer. In other cases, the immigration officer must

---

933. 8 U.S.C. sec. 1225. The grounds for exclusion of aliens are set forth in 8 U.S.C. sec. 1182. They are numerous and are classified as follows: (1) health-related grounds; (2) criminal and related grounds; (3) security and related grounds; (4) likely to become a public charge; (5) seeking employment without certification; (6) illegal entry and immigration violation; (7) lack of proper documentation; (8) immigrants permanently ineligible for citizenship; (9) aliens previously removed; and (10) miscellaneous grounds, such as intention to practice polygamy, engaging in international child abduction, and being a former American citizen who has renounced American citizenship for the purpose of avoiding taxation by the United States.

In *Sale v. Haitian Centers Council*, 509 U.S. 155 (1993), the Supreme Court held that there was no entitlement to an exclusion hearing until the alien actually reached the border. The Court thus upheld a Presidential interdiction order under which the United States Coast Guard intercepted vessels illegally transporting passengers from Haiti to the United States and returned the passengers to Haiti without first determining whether any passenger was entitled to enter the United States as a "refugee."

934. An alien is considered a "refugee" eligible for asylum under 8 U.S.C. sec. 1101(a)(42)(A) if the alien "has suffered persecution in the past or has a well founded fear of persecution on account of race, religion, nationality, membership in particular social group, or political opinion, or can show objectively reasonable fear of such prosecution in the future." *See* e.g., *Angoucheva v. I.N.S.*, 106 F.3d 781 (7th Cir. 1997); *Grupee v. Gonzales*, 400 F.3d 1026 (7th Cir. 2005). "Persecution on the basis of political opinion" includes having been forced to undergo an abortion or involuntary sterilization or resistance to coercive population control. A "refugee" does not include a person who has himself engaged in such persecution of another person. For a recent Supreme Court case, interpreting the "persecutor bar," *see Negusie v. Holder*, 555 U.S. 511 (2009), where the Court held that an alien's intent and motivation were relevant to the issue of whether the alien assisted in the persecution and that the bar did not apply if the alien was coerced into assisting in the persecution. The procedure for applying for asylum is set forth in 8 U.S.C. sec. 1158.

935. However, since an alien denied admission on this basis is held in custody pending actual deportation, the alien may in effect seek judicial review of that decision by applying for a writ of habeas corpus. Judicial review in the habeas corpus proceeding is limited to the questions of whether the petitioner is an alien, whether the petitioner was denied admission on this basis, and whether the petitioner can prove by a preponderance of the evidence that the petitioner is an alien lawfully admitted for permanent residence, or has been admitted as a refugee or has been granted asylum. 8 U.S.C. sec. 1252(d)(e)(2). In addition, in some limited circumstances, the courts have found that the denial of admission to the particular alien was not authorized by law. *See* e.g., *Hill v. Immigration and Naturalization Service*, 714 F.2d 1470 (9th Cir. 1983) (exclusion of a person as a homosexual was improper without a medical certification of psychopathic personality, sexual deviation or mental defect; today, of course, as a constitutional matter, no person can be denied admission on the basis of sexual orientation); *Allende v. Shultz*, 845 F.2d 1111 (1st Cir. 1988) (denial of a visa to widow of former Chilean President invited to speak in the United States on the basis that her presence would cause harm to American foreign policy is improper).

make a determination whether the alien is clearly and beyond a doubt entitled to be admitted. If the immigration officer does not make a favorable determination for admission, the alien is detained for a proceeding under 8 U.S.C. 1229a. This proceeding is called a removal proceeding and governs both the admission of aliens to the United States and the deportation of aliens who have been admitted. (*See* paragraph 433). As a result, aliens who have been denied admission have substantially the same procedural rights as aliens facing deportation proceedings. However, if the alien is an applicant for admission, the alien has the burden of establishing clearly and beyond doubt that the alien is entitled to be admitted or establishing by clear and convincing evidence that the alien is lawfully present in the United States pursuant to a prior admission.

§2. Deportation of Aliens

432. The deportation of an alien is considered a civil proceeding designed to rid the United States of statutorily defined "undesirable aliens." However, although deportation does not amount to criminal punishment for constitutional purposes, it is, in the case of an alien admitted for permanent residence, a severe penalty, and so is subject to the constitutional requirements of due process of law.[936] Congress has specified the grounds for deportation and has provided for the full panoply of procedural protections in deportation proceedings. While these procedural protections were provided in the context of the threatened deportation of aliens who have been admitted for permanent residence, they apply to all deportation proceedings, and thus benefit aliens who are temporarily in the United States, such as those who are in the United States on student or visitor visas, and claim entitlement to remain in the United States.

433. The applicable federal law, 8 U.S.C. sec. 1227, lists five broad categories of deportable aliens, and these categories can be divided into two general classes: aliens deportable for acts committed prior to entry, and aliens deportable for acts committed since their entry. Acts committed prior to entry include acts that would have justified exclusion at the time of entry,[937] illegal entry into the United States, participation in Nazi persecutions or genocide, and involvement in fraudulent marriage in order to secure entry of a person into the United States. Acts committed since the entry of the alien include subversive activity and activity endangering the security of the United States, conviction of a crime or crimes involving moral turpitude within five years after entry, conviction of violation of a law relating to a controlled substance or illegal weapon, crimes of domestic violence and violations of certain protection orders, convictions of violation of security laws and terrorist activities, becoming a public charge within five years from the date of entry from causes not shown to have

936. As the Supreme Court has stated: "This Court has not closed its eyes to the drastic deprivations that may follow when a resident of this country is compelled by our Government to forsake all the bonds formed here and to go to a foreign land where he often has no contemporary identification." *Woodby v. Immigration and Naturalization Service*, 385 U.S. 276, 285 (1966).

937. *See* para. 430, n. 933, *supra* .

arisen since entry, assisting in illegal entry of other aliens, and failing to meet reporting requirements as to the alien's immigration status.[938]

434. Deportation proceedings, now called removal proceedings, are conducted before an immigration judge and begin with service on the alien of an order to show the cause why the alien shall not be deported.[939] This order will contain a statement of the charges of deportability. In these proceedings, the alien is entitled to be represented by counsel engaged at the alien's own expense. An interpreter will be provided if the alien does not understand English. The proceeding is conducted in substantially the same manner as a judicial proceeding, with cross-examination and compulsory process for obtaining testimony. The government has the burden of proving by clear and convincing evidence that the alien is removable, and the decision must be based on reasonable, substantial and probative evidence.[940] If the immigration judge orders deportation, the decision may be appealed to the Board of Immigration Appeals. The decision of that body is subject to judicial review in a United States Court of Appeals.[941] However, in 1996 Congress enacted a law that denied the Court of Appeals jurisdiction to review a final order of removal against an alien who is removable for the commission

---

938. Aliens admitted in nonimmigrant status, such as students, are subject to deportation if they have failed to maintain nonimmigrant status or otherwise failed to comply with the conditions of their admission.

939. Deportation proceedings, now called removal proceedings, are governed by 8 U.S.C. sec. 1229, and implementing regulations issued by the Attorney-General. Judicial review of removal orders is governed by 8 U.S.C. sec. 1252. These procedures are very detailed, and only the main provisions have been discussed in this section.

Congress has specifically mandated that aliens convicted of an "aggravated felony" or of two crimes involving "moral turpitude" be detained pending the deportation hearing, and the Supreme Court has held that this provision is constitutional. *Demore v. Kim*, 538 U.S. 510 (2003). Otherwise, Congress has given the Attorney-General broad discretion to determine whether and on what terms an alien arrested on suspicion of being removable should be released pending the removal hearing.

In recent years, thousands of minor aliens have been arrested on suspicion of being removable. In the absence of a parent or guardian in the United States, they have for the most part been placed in juvenile detention facilities, and the Supreme Court has held that this practice does not violate their constitutional rights. *Reno v. Flores*, 507 U.S. 292 (1993).

940. This is now the statutory standard. 8 U.S.C. sec. 1229(c)(3)(A). The statutory standard is similar to, but slightly less stringent, than the former "clear, unequivocal and convincing evidence" standard, which is the standard required for denaturalization proceedings. *See Woodby v. Immigration and Naturalization Service*, 385 U.S. 276 (1966).

941. *See* e.g., *Drakes v. Zimski*, 240 F.3d 246 (3rd Cir. 2001); *Vasquez-Velezmoro v. United States Immigration and Naturalization Service*, 281 F.3d 693 (8th Cir. 2002). The Courts of Appeal have held that they can consider constitutional questions on direct appeal from the removal order, *see* Vasquez-Velezmoro, *supra* ; *Lara-Ruiz v. Immigration and Naturalization Service*, 241 F.3d 934 (7th Cir. 2001), and the Supreme Court has held that Congress did not intend to prohibit aliens subject to a removal order from filing a petition for a writ of habeas corpus in the federal court in order to assert constitutional and statutory challenges to the removal order. *See Deboris Calcano-Martinez v. Immigration and Naturalization Service*, 533 U.S. 348 (2001). As a practical matter then, aliens removable on this ground can obtain a judicial determination of constitutional and statutory questions presented in the proceedings, but the only question that really matters is whether they have been convicted of an "aggravated felony."

of certain "aggravated felonies." In such a case, once the Court of Appeals determines that the alien was convicted of a crime that constitutes an "aggravated felony" under the statute, it must dismiss the appeal.

Where the Court of Appeals has jurisdiction to hear the appeal, it may not set the Board's decision aside if the Board has made no error of law and if reasonable, substantial, and probative evidence on the record, considered as a whole, supports its factual findings.[942] Once the alien has been found to be removable, a final order of removal is entered, and the Attorney-General must arrange for the alien's removal to a country willing to receive the alien. The alien is detained in custody pending removal. However, the Supreme Court has held that after a six-month period, where there is no significant likelihood of removal in the foreseeable future because there is no country willing to take the alien, the alien must be released from detention.[943]

§3. Discrimination Against Aliens Admitted for Permanent Residence

435. The Supreme Court has said that aliens as a class are a prime example of a "discrete and insular minority," since they are not entitled to vote. It has thus held that state laws discriminating against aliens are "suspect" and so must be analyzed under the highly restrictive "compelling governmental interest" standard of review. Applying that standard, the Court has held unconstitutional state laws denying welfare benefits to aliens,[944] barring aliens from all state governmental employment,[945] prohibiting aliens from engaging in the practice of law or other professions,[946] and denying alien

942. *See Howard v. Immigration and Naturalization Service*, 930 F.2d 432, 434 (5th Cir. 1991); *Gao v. Ashcroft*, 299 F.3d 266 (3rd Cir. 2002).

943. *Zadvydas v. Davis*, 533 U.S. 678 (2001). This holding also applies to aliens who had been found inadmissible for entry into the United States and ordered detained pending their removal. *Clark v. Martinez*, 543 U.S. 371 (2005). The Attorney-General is given the discretion to cancel an order of removal for a narrow class of aliens: (1) permanent resident aliens who have lived in the United States for five years and other aliens who have resided in the United States for seven years, who have not been convicted of an aggravated felony; (2) aliens who have resided in the United States for 10 years, have been of good moral character, who have not been convicted of serious crimes, and whose removal would result in exceptional hardship to a citizen or permanent resident spouse, parent or child of the alien; and (3) in very limited cases to a battered spouse or parent of a battered child. 8 U.S.C. sec. 1229b. The Supreme Court has held that conviction for misdemeanor drug offenses does not constitute an "aggravated felony" for purposes of the Attorney-General's discretion. *Carachuri-Rosendo v. Holder*, 130 Sup.Ct. 2577 (2010).

944. *Graham v. Richardson*, 403 U.S. 365 (1971).

945. *Sugarman v. Dougall*, 413 U.S. 634 (1973).

946. Application of Griffiths, 413 U.S. 717 (1973).

college students financial aid unless they had affirmed their intention to apply for citizenship as soon as they were eligible.[947]

436. The Court has recognized a "governmental function" exception to the general rule prohibiting discrimination against resident aliens by the states. It has held that just as the states may constitutionally deny aliens the right to vote and to hold public office or to serve on juries, the states may exclude aliens from governmental employment involving the "formulation, execution or review of broad public policy."[948] Such positions have been held to include police officers,[949] public school teachers,[950] and probation officers.[951] Apart from this exception, however, all state laws discriminating against aliens have been held to be unconstitutional.

437. When it comes to actions of the federal government, however, the plenary power of Congress over immigration and naturalization has shaped the Court's view of the constitutional permissibility of discrimination against resident aliens by the federal government. The Court has held that because of Congress' plenary power over immigration and naturalization, there should be extreme judicial deference to Congress' actions with respect to resident aliens. Thus, the Court, applying the less restrictive "rational basis" standard of review, has upheld the constitutionality of federal laws effecting the identical discrimination against resident aliens that was held unconstitutional when engaged in by the states.[952]

---

947. *Nyquist v. Mauclet*, 432 U.S. 1 (1977). In that case, as in others, the Court also emphasized that state discrimination against aliens interferes with Congress' plenary power to control the admission of aliens into the United States. In this connection, *see also Toll v. Moreno*, 458 U.S. 1 (1982), holding unconstitutional a state university rule that refused to treat as "residents" of the state students who had been admitted to the United States on a special nonimmigrant visa issued to employees of certain international organizations and their immediate families. In *Plyler v. Doe*, 457 U.S. 202 (1982), the Court, applying the less restrictive "rational basis" standard, held violative of equal protection a state law denying public school education to "undocumented" or "illegal" alien children. *See* para. 386, *supra* .
948. The Court has held that with respect to such positions, the less restrictive rational basis standard of review applies, which means in practice that the exclusion of aliens from such positions will be held to be constitutional.
949. *Foley v. Connelie*, 435 U.S. 291 (1978).
950. *Ambach v. Norwick*, 441 U.S. 68 (1979).
951. *Cabell v. Chavez-Salido*, 454 U.S. 432 (1982).
952. *See Matthews v. Diaz*, 426 U.S. 67 (1976) (welfare benefits); *Hampton v. Mow Sun Wong*, 426 U.S. 88 (1976) (federal governmental employment). In *Hampton*, the Court held that the President or Congress rather than the federal Civil Service Commission had to make the determination that the national interest required a ban on the employment of aliens in the federal civil service. President Ford subsequently issued an executive order barring aliens from federal government employment. The executive order was upheld against constitutional challenge by the lower federal courts, and the Supreme Court refused to review the question.

Part V. Specific Problems

Chapter 1. War, Treaty and Foreign Affairs Powers

§1. Federal Foreign Affairs Powers

438. It is well settled that under the President's power to "receive Ambassadors and other public Ministers," only the President can recognize a foreign government. Thus, the courts cannot review the President's refusal to recognize a foreign government, although that foreign government would be entitled to recognition under principles of international law. For example, American Presidents refused to recognize the "communist government" of the Soviet Union until 1933, although it came to power in 1917, and they likewise refused to recognize the "communist government" of China, which came to power in 1949, until 1978. The President also can suspend diplomatic relations with any foreign government.[953]

The Court has also held that Congress did not act unconstitutionally in granting preferential immigration status to legitimate children and their parents and out-of-wedlock children and their mothers while denying this status to out-of-wedlock children and their mothers.[954] While, as we have seen, discrimination on the basis of out-of-wedlock status is generally subject to an "important and substantial" relationship standard of review, since the discrimination here involved Congress' plenary power over immigration, it was tested only under the rational basis standard of review and was upheld.

It will be recalled that in discussing "Fifth Amendment equal protection," we said that whatever is a violation of the Fourteenth Amendment's equal protection clause on the part of the states is also a violation of the Fifth Amendment's due process clause on the part of the federal government unless there is a federal interest justifying differential treatment on the part of the federal government. This proposition is illustrated most clearly by the Court's differing conclusions as to the constitutionality of

953. Because only the President can recognize a foreign government, the Court held that Congress could not require that when a child was born to American parents in Jerusalem, that child's passport list the place of birth as "Jerusalem, Israel." It has long been the practice of American Presidents to refuse to recognize Israel's annexation of Jerusalem, and for that reason the State Department has refused to list the place of birth of the child as "Jerusalem, Israel." *Zivotofsky v. Kerry*, 125 Sup.Ct. 2076 (2015).

954. *Fiallo v. Bell*, 430 U.S. 787 (1977).

discrimination against aliens when practiced by the states and when practiced by the federal government.

439. The President, with the concurrence of two-thirds of the Senate, has the power to enter into a treaty with a foreign government on behalf of the United States.[955]

It should be noted in this connection, however, that as a matter of American constitutional law, a treaty stands only on the same footing as federal legislation. So, if a treaty is irreconcilable with subsequent federal legislation, the subsequent legislation controls, even though this effective repeal of the treaty may put the United States in violation of its obligations under international law.[956] The President's power over foreign affairs has given rise to another form of international commitment by the United States, the executive agreement. The use of an executive agreement rather than a treaty enables the President to by-pass the Senate, and the question of the constitutionality of executive agreements as regards the President and the Senate has not yet been resolved by the Supreme Court.[957]

---

955. Typically, the President initials a treaty with a foreign government on behalf of the United States, and then submits the treaty to the Senate for ratification. Depending on the subject matter of the treaty, it may be self-executing or it may require implementing Congressional legislation.

The treaty power is an independent power, so that the subject matter of the treaty need not otherwise be within the scope of federal power. *Missouri v. Holland*, 252 U.S. 416 (1920). This principle is not very important today, since the scope of federal power, especially the power to regulate interstate commerce, is now very extensive, and any matter that is covered by a treaty is likely to otherwise be within federal power.

956. *Chae Chin Ping v. United States* (The Chinese Exclusion Case), 130 U.S. 581 (1889). This result is deemed to follow from the language of the Supremacy Clause, Art. VI, s. 2, which refers to "[t]he Constitution and the Laws of the United States which shall be made in Pursuance thereof, and all Treaties made, or which shall be made, under the Authority of the United States."

957. For example, while, as stated above, a subsequent treaty would prevail over a prior irreconcilable statute, it is doubtful whether this would be true for an executive agreement. The prior statute would prevail.

A number of international commitments of the United States, including the General Agreement on Tariffs and Trade (GATT), have been concluded by executive agreement rather than by treaty. An international agreement was also used by President Reagan to enter into a claims settlement agreement with Iran as a part of the conditions for the release of American hostages. That agreement required the United States to terminate all suits brought against Iran in American state and federal courts, to nullify existing attachments obtained in connection with such suits, and to prohibit future litigation against Iran.

However, as regards their effect on inconsistent state law, executive agreements have the same effect as a treaty and supersede inconsistent state law.[958]

§2. Federal War Powers

440. Under Article II, section 2, the President is the "Commander in Chief of the Army and Navy of the United States, and of the militia of the several States when called into the actual Service of the United States."

The most controversial question concerning Presidential and Congressional power—and one that is not likely ever to be resolved by the Supreme Court—involves the power over war and military intervention. This question arises because the Constitution gives both Congress and the President specific powers relating to war and military intervention. As stated above, the President is Commander-in- Chief of the Armed Forces. Under Article I, section 8, Congress has the power to "declare War, grant letters of Marque and Reprisal, and make Rules concerning Captures on Land and Water," to "raise and support Armies," to "provide and maintain a Navy," to "make Rules for the Government and Regulation of the land and naval Forces," and to "regulate the state militias and to call them into federal service." Thus, both the President and Congress have powers with respect to war and military intervention, and these powers can conflict with respect to particular military action.

441. It should be noted that there is no provision in the Constitution which restricts in any way military intervention on the part of the United States, and as far as the Constitution is concerned, of course, it is completely irrelevant that a particular military intervention by the United States may violate international law. For example, in the 2003 invasion of Iraq by the United States, President Bush initiated the action despite the failure of the United Nations Security Council to adopt a resolution specifically authorizing the use of military force against Iraq in order to secure its compliance with prior Security Council Resolutions. Thus, in the United States the only constitutional question regarding war and military intervention relates to separation

958. As the Supreme Court stated in *United States v. Belmont*, 301 U.S. 324, 331 (1937): "[i]n the case of all international compacts and agreements ... complete power over international affairs is in the national government and is not and cannot be subject to any curtailment or interference on the part of the several states." In that case and in the later case of *United States v. Pink*, 315 U.S. 203 (1942), the Court upheld the Litinov Agreement between the United States and the then Soviet Union. The Litinov Agreement took the form of an executive agreement, under which the United States agreed to recognize the Soviet government and in return the Soviet Union assigned to the United States the Soviet Union's interests in certain Russian properties located abroad that had been expropriated by the Soviet Union. The United States would use these assets to payoff claims by the United States and American citizens against the Soviet Union. The claims of American citizens against the Soviet Union were to be superior to the claims of foreign creditors. One of the expropriated properties included the New York branch of a Russian insurance company. The United States filed its claim against the property in a New York state court, which refused to enforce the Litinov Agreement. The Supreme Court held that under the Supremacy Clause, an executive agreement had "similar dignity" with a treaty as the "supreme law of the land," and thus prevailed over inconsistent state law.

of powers and a possible conflict between the exercise of Congressional power and the exercise of Presidential power.

442. The separation of powers issue is avoided, of course, whenever the particular military intervention is authorized by Congress. Congress may authorize military intervention by a formal declaration of war, as it did against the Axis powers in World War II, following the bombing of Pearl Harbor, or by a concurrent resolution granting authority to the President to take military action, as Congress did prior to the commencement of the Gulf War in 1991.[959] Congress also adopted concurrent resolutions in 2001, authorizing President Bush to initiate military action against the Taliban regime in Afghanistan and in 2003, authorizing the President to initiate military action against the Saddam Hussein regime in Iraq.

It has been assumed that no question of separation of powers is involved when the President as Commander-in-Chief commits the United States to military intervention that is specifically called for under the nation's treaty obligations: the ratification of the treaty by the Senate satisfies the requirement of Congressional authorization for the military action taken by the President pursuant to the treaty.[960]

443. In addition, Congress can preempt any military action by the President through the use of its appropriations power under Article I, section 8, to specifically prohibit the use of appropriated funds for a particular military action or for any other particular purpose. No President has ever asserted the authority to expend appropriated funds contrary to a restriction specifically imposed on the use of such funds by Congress.[961] For example, for a period of time Congress specifically prohibited any use of appropriated funds to provide assistance to the "contras" in Nicaragua. However, where Congress appropriates funds without specific restrictions, as, for example, in the annual general appropriation for the Department of Defense, the President can use these funds for any "defense" purpose, including military intervention.

444. Coming back to the question of whether the President can constitutionally order military intervention without Congressional authorization, the argument in favor of Presidential power to do so rests on his power as Commander-in-Chief of the Armed

---

959. President Eisenhower also obtained Congressional authorization by joint resolution prior to sending troops into the Formosan Straits in 1955 and into Lebanon in 1958. In 1994, when President Clinton prepared to send an American-led force to Haiti in order to restore the Aristide government, he did not seek Congressional authorization. American military involvement in Korea in 1950 was pursuant to a resolution of the United Nations Security Council, and the American troops served as part of a United Nations force that was led by an American commander. In more recent times, American military involvement in Bosnia and Kosovo was as part of a North Atlantic Treaty Organization (NATO) force, and President Clinton did not seek Congressional authorization for either involvement.

960. If, for example, the former Soviet Union had launched an attack against a NATO ally during the "cold war" period, the President would be required by American obligations under the NATO Treaty to commit troops to the defense of the NATO ally.

961. Note again that the legislation containing such a restriction must be signed by the President or passed over his veto. However, as discussed in Part II, the President does not have a "line item veto," and could be faced with the difficult choice of approving the appropriations bill with the restriction in its entirety or vetoing the bill and engaging in a "test of wills" with the Congress over military appropriations. As a practical matter, the President will usually approve the appropriations bill despite the inclusion of a restriction with which he may disagree.

Forces. It is further argued that if Congress disagrees with an anticipated or ongoing military intervention, such as that involved in the Vietnam War, it could prohibit the use of appropriated funds to support such intervention. All the while that the nation was engaged in the Vietnam War, Congress continued to vote the appropriations requested by the President for the Department of Defense budget, a substantial amount of which was being used to carry on the war. In fact, it could be contended that Congressional approval of the President's appropriation request, with the knowledge that such funds were going to be used to carry on the war, constituted Congressional approval of the war for constitutional purposes.

445. The contrary view typically draws a distinction between different kinds of military intervention. It would say that military intervention under the President's Commander-in-Chief power is limited to "emergency-type" or "short-term" situations, such as an armed attack on the United States or a threat to American citizens or property in a foreign country. This basis for military intervention was relied on by President Reagan when he sent American troops into Grenada in 1983, claiming that the safety of Americans attending a medical school in Grenada was in danger, with the result that a government favorable to Cuba was overthrown. This basis for military intervention could also support the bombing of Libya by President Reagan in 1986 in reprisal for alleged Libyan responsibility for a terrorist attack in Germany in which American servicepersons were killed, and the sending of troops into Panama by President Bush in 1990 to capture General Noriega and bring him to trial in the United States for alleged violations of American drug laws.[962] However, under this view, the President could not rely on his Commander-in-Chief power to commit the United States to an ongoing military conflict, such the Vietnam War. This view maintains that only Congress, by a formal declaration of war, or other specific authorization, could make such a commitment to an ongoing military conflict on behalf of the United States.

446. The question of the constitutional power of the President as Commander-in-Chief of the Armed Forces to commit the United States to an ongoing military intervention without specific Congressional authorization is not likely to be resolved by the only tribunal that could authoritatively do so: the Supreme Court. As we saw in Part II, Chapter 5, §2, there are a number of limitations on judicial review in the United States, one of which is the political question doctrine. Certain kinds of constitutional questions are not considered appropriate for judicial resolution by the courts, and these are referred to as "non-justiciable political questions." Where a question involves a conflict between Congress and the President over a matter of foreign affairs or military intervention, the federal courts, including the Supreme Court if the issue should come before it, are likely to treat it as a "non-justiciable political question," saying that the President and Congress should "resolve it as coequals," or at least that the courts will not resolve it until an irreconcilable conflict between Congress and the President is presented.[963] Again, if Congress disagrees with the President's action in committing the United States to an ongoing military intervention, it can require the termination of such intervention by prohibiting the use of appropriated funds to support it. For example, if Congress had the "political will" to challenge

962. Again, there is no concern as a constitutional matter whether such military intervention is in violation of international law.

963. *See* paras. 119, 120, *supra* .

President Johnson and later President Nixon over American military involvement in Vietnam, it could have simply prohibited the use of appropriated funds to support any action in connection with such intervention except to terminate it. Since Congress was unwilling to do so, the courts were also unwilling to resolve the constitutional question of Presidential authority.[964]

447. As this discussion indicates, in the American constitutional system, it is the Congress that has the final authority to determine whether there will be ongoing American military intervention in any circumstance. But Congress must exercise this authority by invoking its appropriations power to specifically prohibit the use of appropriated funds for the military intervention in issue. As stated above, no American President has ever asserted the authority to expend appropriated funds contrary to a specific restriction imposed on the use of such funds by Congress, and any President who violated such a restriction would be subject to impeachment. In this situation then, the answer to the constitutional question thus becomes a political one rather than a judicial one.

At the present time, such a situation is highly unlikely to occur, since as indicated by recent American military involvement in Iraq and Afghanistan, Congress has authorized such involvement by concurrent resolution and has supported it by providing the funds requested by the President.

In the War Powers Resolution of 1973, enacted over President Nixon's veto, Congress attempted to exercise a degree of control over the President's commitment of American troops to a foreign military intervention by requiring the President to submit a report to Congress within 48 hours. The submission of the report triggers a sixty-day period, during which the troops must be removed unless Congress has declared war or has specifically authorized the use of military force, or has extended the period. Congress also can direct the removal of the troops within the sixty-day period by means of a concurrent resolution. In the Grenada intervention, President Reagan made the required report within forty-eight hours and withdrew the troops within sixty days. President Bush did the same in connection with the Panama intervention.

There are a number of constitutional problems with the War Powers Resolution, including the fact that it directly interferes with the President's power as Commander-in-Chief to respond to "emergency-type" situations, and that it amounts to an impermissible "legislative veto" insofar as it allows Congress to overturn Presidential action by means of a concurrent resolution instead of by means of legislation. *See* Part II, Chapter 3, paragraph 78, *supra*. The Resolution stands on stronger constitutional grounds insofar as it declares that the intervention must come to an end after sixty days unless Congress has declared war or authorized the military action: the power to declare war includes the power to define what is a "war," and it is not unreasonable for Congress to conclude that after military involvement has continued for more than

964. In a number of cases arising in the lower federal courts during the Vietnam period, the courts usually invoked the political question doctrine to avoid deciding the constitutional question. The few courts that reached the constitutional question on the merits found Congressional authorization for the war in Congress' appropriating funds to support it and/or in the Gulf of Tonkin Resolution of 1964. The Supreme Court refused to review any of the lower court decisions, so the constitutional question was never authoritatively resolved.

sixty days, there is a "war" for constitutional purposes. However, the "constitutional remedy," so to speak, is for Congress to prohibit the use of appropriated funds to support this "war," and, in the absence of such action by Congress, the courts will invoke the political question doctrine to refuse to decide the question of whether the President is constitutionally required to remove the troops after sixty days.

448. During the military action by the United States against the Taliban regime in Afghanistan, initiated after the attacks of September 11, 2001, a number of combatants fighting with the Taliban were captured by American troops. Those who were suspected of having ties to al Qaeda (the terrorist group believed to have been responsible for the attacks of September 11, 2001) were transferred to detention facilities at Guantanamo, an American military base off the coast of Cuba. The United States has occupied this base since 1903 pursuant to a lease agreement executed with the newly independent Republic of Cuba in the aftermath of the Spanish-American War. The lease agreement recognizes the continuance of the "ultimate sovereignty" of Cuba over the leased area, but provides that during the period of operation of the base by the United States, the United States shall exercise "complete jurisdiction and control over the leased area." President Bush, in the exercise of his powers as Commander-in-Chief of the Armed Forces, took the position that al Qaeda was "engaged in armed conflict with the United States" and that those combatants having ties to al Qaeda are "unlawful enemy combatants." President Bush also took the position that the Guantanamo detainees were not entitled to prisoner of war status and so could be subject to interrogation and could be held in detention indefinitely. Some of the detainees sought to challenge the legality of their detention by filing a writ of habeas corpus in a federal court in the United States. They alleged that they had not been a combatant against the United States and had never engaged in any terrorist acts. In a landmark decision, the Supreme Court has held that the federal habeas corpus statute[965] conferred a right to judicial review of the President's detention of aliens at Guantanamo. The Court based its decision on the fact that the United States exercises plenary and exclusive jurisdiction over Guantanamo, that the government conceded that an American citizen held at the base could bring a habeas corpus action, and that the habeas corpus statute does not draw any distinction between Americans and aliens held in federal custody.[966]

One of the persons detained at Guantanamo was found to be an American citizen, and the military authorities transferred him from Guantanamo to a military facility in the United States. He filed a petition for a writ of habeas corpus in a federal court, challenging the legality of his detention. A federal appeals court held that since he had been captured on the battlefield, the court would not question the facts contained in the government's affidavit stating that he was an "unlawful enemy combatant." As a result, the court ruled that he was not entitled to the appointment of a lawyer and could be held in detention indefinitely.[967] In another landmark decision, the Supreme Court reversed. The Court held that while Congress had authorized the President to detain

965. 28 U.S.C. secs. 2241 et seq. The statute has granted federal district courts "within their respective jurisdictions" the authority to hear applications for a writ of habeas corpus by any person who claims to be held "in custody in violation of the Constitution or laws or treaties of the United States."

966. *Rasul v. Bush*, 542 U.S. 466 (2004).

967. *Hamdi v. Rumsfeld*, 296 F.3d 278 (3rd Cir. 2003).

as an "enemy combatant" an American citizen captured on the battlefield,[968] due process required that he be given a meaningful opportunity to contest the factual basis for that detention before a neutral decision maker. Specifically due process required that: (1) he be given notice of the factual basis for his classification as an "unlawful enemy combatant;" (2) he be given a fair opportunity to rebut the government's factual assertions; (3) the determination of his status be made by a neutral decision-maker.

In this case, Justice O'Connor, writing for the Court, stated: "Striking the proper constitutional balance here is of great importance to the Nation during this period of ongoing conflict. But it is equally vital that our calculus not give short shrift to the values this country holds dear or to the privilege that is American citizenship. It is during our most challenging and uncertain moments that our nation's commitment to due process is most severely tested; and it is in these times that we must preserve our commitment at home to the principles for which we fight abroad."[969] If it is determined that the detainee was not an "unlawful enemy combatant," then the government must either charge him with a criminal offense (in which case he would have all the procedural rights of any person charged with a crime) or release him from custody.[970]

449. A federal statute, 10 U.S.C. secs. 821, 836, authorizes the President to establish military commissions to try persons for violations of the laws of war. The term, "laws of war" finds its source in international law and prohibits certain conduct by "belligerents" that violates accepted standards of military conduct. Following the terrorist attacks on the United States of September 11, 2001, President Bush, exercising his powers as Commander-in-Chief of the Armed Forces, and pursuant to Congressional authorization under 10 U.S.C. secs. 821, 836, issued a military order authorizing the trial before military commissions of non-citizens who are or were members of al Qaeda, or who have engaged in, aided or abetted, or conspired to commit acts of international terrorism, or acts in preparation for, that have caused, threaten to cause, or have as their aim to cause, injury to or adverse effects on the United States, its citizens, national security, foreign policy or economy, or who have knowingly harbored a member of al Qaeda or a terrorist. He subsequently issued military orders establishing military commissions and rules for the conduct of trials before military commissions. In still another landmark decision involving Presidential power in the "war on terrorism," the Supreme Court held that President Bush's order establishing military commissions and the rules governing their operation was not authorized by 10 U.S.C. secs. 821, 836, and that the procedures for trial before the military commission violated federal

968. Because the Court found that Congress had provided the President with such authorization, the Court found it unnecessary to pass on the President's claim that he had the power under Art. II to order such detention without Congressional authorization.

969. 542 U.S. at 532.

970. The detainee here was released from custody on condition that he renounces his American citizenship and return to Saudi Arabia, where he had lived most of his life. The government had also arrested an American citizen in the United States and transferred him to a military facility in the United States, claiming that he had been involved with Al Qaeda in Pakistan and Afghanistan and was sent to the United States to engage in terrorist activity. He also brought an action for a writ of habeas corpus, but the Supreme Court dismissed the action on the ground that he had filed it in the wrong federal court. *Rumsfeld v. Padilla*, 542 U.S. 426 (2004). The government chose to transfer him to the United States for trial before a United States District Court, where he was convicted of terrorism-related offenses.

laws and treaties. The Court further held that the President's assertion of his powers as Commander-in-Chief was invalid, since it was in direct conflict with Congressional law and federal treaties.[971]

There has been little constitutional experience with military commissions in the United States. At the time of the Civil War, the Supreme Court held that it was unconstitutional to try an American citizen civilian before a military commission for an alleged crime committed in an American state. The Court emphasized that he was not a belligerent (it was charged that he was aiding the Confederacy against the Union) and that he could be tried in the civilian courts.[972] There were two cases involving trial before military commissions in World War II, both involving belligerents, and the Supreme Court held that such trials were permissible. In one case, German soldiers were landed from a submarine off the coasts of New York and Florida. They shed their military uniforms and proceeded in civilian dress to various points in the United States, where they planned to engage in spying and acts of espionage. They were captured and tried before a military commission for violations of the laws of war. The Supreme Court held that their trial before a military commission was constitutionally permissible. The Court emphasized that they were belligerents, since they were members of the German armed forces, and that since they had shed their uniforms, they were unlawful belligerents, subject to trial and punishment by military tribunals for violations of the laws of war, such as spying and sabotage.[973] The other case involved a trial before a military commission in the Philippine Islands (at that time an American possession) of the Japanese commander in the Philippines, who was charged with and convicted of violations of the laws of war, relating to crimes committed by his troops against prisoners of war and against the civilian population. The Supreme Court held that Congress had the power to provide for the establishment of a military commission to try crimes committed abroad by belligerents engaged in war with the United States and that the offenses for which he was convicted constituted a violation of the laws of war.[974]

Finally, the Court has held that Congress could not constitutionally bar Guantanamo detainees from filing a petition for a writ of habeas corpus to contest the legality of their detention. Such an action was held to violate the provisions of Article I, section

---

971. *Hamdan v. Rumsfeld*, 548 U.S. 557 (2006). As discussed previously, the Court earlier held that where there was a direct conflict between the exercise of Congressional power and the exercise of Presidential power, at least in matters not directly involving military action or foreign affairs, the exercise of Congressional power must prevail. Part II, Ch. 4, *supra* . The decision in this case extends that principle to a direct conflict involving military action, at least with respect to the President's action in establishing military commissions.

Congress has since enacted a new law relating to the establishment of military commissions, which provided more procedural rights to the defendant in proceedings before a military commission, and the government has instituted proceedings before military commissions against a few of the Guantanamo detainees.

972. *Ex parte Milligan,* 71 U.S. 2 (1866).

973. *Ex parte Quirin*, 317 U.S. 1 (1942).

974. *Application of Yamashita*, 327 U.S. 1 (1946).

2, clause 9, which prohibits suspension of the privilege of habeas corpus, and the Court held that the "suspension" clause applied to the Guantanamo detainees.[975]

450. We see then that in the "war on terrorism," the Supreme Court has interpreted the Constitution and federal law as circumscribing Presidential power and providing at least some degree of constitutional protection to alleged "terrorists" held at Guantanamo.[976]

§3. The Question of State Powers in Foreign Affairs

451. In the area of foreign affairs, as might be expected, federal power is paramount. Upon Independence, that aspect of the sovereignty of the British Crown pertaining to foreign affairs did not devolve upon each of the states, but upon the "Union of States" that was waging the Revolutionary War and that eventually concluded the peace with Great Britain. Since sovereignty over foreign affairs never belonged to the states, it is deemed in American constitutional theory to be inherent in the federal government that was subsequently established by the Constitution. Thus, the federal government has the inherent power to conduct the foreign affairs of the Nation, and

975. *Boumediene v. Bush*, 553 U.S. 41 (2008). The law that the Court invalidated provided that the detainees could contest their status as an "unlawful enemy combatant" before a Defense Department Tribunal, with very limited review by the United States Court of Appeals for the District of Columbia. The Court held that this process was not a constitutionally sufficient substitute for habeas corpus.

976. While President Obama tried to close Guantanamo, Congress blocked him from doing so, and inmates continue to be housed at the facility.

In the latest effort to deal with the "war on terrorism," President Trump has issued an executive order suspending for ninety days entry into the United States nationals from seven countries, Iran, Syria, Sudan, Libya, Iraq. Somalia, and Yemen, that have been "associated with a heightened risk of terrorism." The order also suspends for 120 days the United States refugee program suspends entry of nationals from Syria indefinitely.

Numerous lawsuit have been filed in a number of federal courts, challenging the legality of the executive order on statutory and constitutional grounds. The order has been put on hold by two Federal Courts of Appeals. The matter has not been resolved at the time preparation of the monograph has been completed.

as regards the constitutional allocation of federal and state power, the foreign affairs power is an exclusive federal power.[977]

452. But even here, the principle of state sovereignty comes into play. Since the states have the general regulatory and taxation power, an exercise of state power is not necessarily unconstitutional merely because it could have an effect on foreign affairs. Rather it is that whenever an exercise of state power does affect foreign affairs, that exercise of state power may be more likely to conflict with an exercise of federal power, and so be invalidated as a matter of federal supremacy. In addition, even in the absence of such a conflict, certain exercises of state power affecting foreign affairs may be found to be constitutionally invalid as an improper interference with federal power over foreign affairs. Finally, the Constitution restricts to a limited degree the states' power to impose taxes on foreign commerce.

453. The most typical way by which the federal government preempts state regulation affecting foreign affairs is by a treaty or executive agreement. The treaty power is an exclusive federal power: the President is authorized to enter into treaties on behalf of the United States with the concurrence of two-thirds of the Senate, and the states are expressly prohibited from entering into treaties.[978] The treaty power is an independent power, so that the subject matter of the treaty need not otherwise be within the scope of federal power.[979] Finally, while some treaties by their nature are executory and require implementing legislation before they can take effect, self-executing treaties take effect immediately upon ratification by the Senate, and require no further legislative action.[980]

---

977. The war power is also an exclusive federal power, in that under Art. I, s. 10, a state cannot, without the consent of Congress, "engage in war, unless actually invaded, or in such imminent danger as will not admit of delay." At the time of the adoption of the Constitution, each state had its own militia, and the states' entitlement to have a militia to protect against attack and domestic violence was recognized in the Constitution. Under Art. I, s. 8, cl. 16, however, Congress was given the power to regulate state militias, and under Art. II, s. 2, the President has the power to call them up for federal service. As a practical matter, the state militia, or National Guard, as it is called today, is sometimes used to deal with domestic problems, such as riot control, and is sometimes called into federal service (a number of National Guard units were mobilized during the Gulf War and the Iraq war, and have been mobilized in the current war in Afghanistan). Under Art. IV, s. 2, the federal government has the responsibility to "protect each state against invasion, and [upon request of the Legislature or Governor] domestic violence." State governors have sometimes requested the President to send federal troops into the state to deal with riot-type situations.

978. The states may, however, with Congressional approval, enter into compacts with foreign nations, as they may with sister states. A "compact" for these purposes is a less formal arrangement than a treaty. Pursuant to this authorization, some American states have entered into compacts with neighboring Canadian provinces and with Mexico.

979. *Missouri v. Holland*, 252 U.S. 416 (1920). In that case, the Court upheld a treaty between the United States and Great Britain, protecting birds migrating between Canada and the United States, although legislation dealing with the identical subject matter had previously been held to be beyond federal legislative authority. Now that the power of the federal government over interstate and foreign commerce has been construed so broadly, such legislation would be upheld as a proper exercise of the federal commerce power. As this example indicates, the fact that the treaty power is an independent power is no longer very significant in practice.

980. *See Foster v. Neilson*, 27 U.S. 253 (1829).

454. Once a treaty takes effect, it is enforceable by private persons, and under the Supremacy Clause, a treaty prevails over inconsistent state law. This principle was involved in one of the earliest cases decided by the Supreme Court, where the Court held that the treaty between the United States and Great Britain ending the Revolutionary War, which contained a provision for the restitution of property confiscated during the War, operated to revive a debt of an American citizen to a British subject that had been confiscated under a Virginia law.[981] Ever since that case, private persons, aliens and citizens alike, have been able to rely on federal treaties to challenge inconsistent provisions of state law.[982]

455. State regulation affecting foreign affairs may also be invalidated as an improper interference with federal power over foreign affairs. For example, federal control over foreign affairs dictates that what is considered an "act of state" under federal law must be recognized as such by state courts in litigation coming before them.[983] Likewise, state laws providing for the forfeiture of a decedent's estate where an alien heir's home state would not allow American citizens reciprocal rights of inheritance have been invalidated as "an intrusion by the State into the field of foreign affairs which the Constitution entrusts to the President and the Congress."[984] Still another example of a state regulation invalidated as an improper interference with federal power over foreign affairs was California's attempt to impose a property tax on cargo containers of Japanese companies, which were used exclusively in international trade and which were based, registered, and subject to full value property taxes in Japan.[985]

---

981. *Ware v. Hylton*, 3 U.S. 199 (1796).

982. The cases often involve treaties giving foreign nationals inheritance rights, which supersede state law interfering with those rights. *See* e.g., *Hauenstein v. Lynham*, 100 U.S. 483 (1879); *Kolovrat v. Oregon*, 366 U.S. 187 (1961). As stated previously, an executive agreement also prevails over an inconsistent provision of state law. *See* para. 438, *supra.*

983. *Banco Nacional de Cuba v. Sabbatino*, 376 U.S. 398 (1964). In that case, the Court held that under the federal definition of the "act of state" doctrine, the Cuban government's expropriation of American property in Cuba would be recognized, so that a state court was compelled to recognize the validity of that expropriation in a suit in which the effect of the expropriation was in issue. In *Crosby v. National Foreign Trade Council*, 530 U.S. 363 (2000), the Court held that a Massachusetts law restricting the authority of state agencies to purchase goods or services with companies doing business with Myanmar was an unconstitutional interference with the power of the federal government over foreign affairs and conflicted with a federal law imposing certain sanctions on Myanmar. Similarly, in *American Insurance Association v. Garamendi*, 539 U.S. 396 (2003), the Court held that a California law requiring insurance companies doing business in the state to disclose information about all insurance policies sold in Europe between 1920 and 1945 interfered with the President's efforts to resolve Holocaust-era insurance claims by encouraging European governments and insurance companies to make voluntary settlements.

984. *Zschernig v. Miller*, 389 U.S. 429, 432 (1968).

985. *Japan Lines, Ltd. v. Los Angeles County*, 441 U.S. 434 (1979). This is my explanation of the actual basis of the holding, although the stated basis of the holding was that the imposition of the tax violated the negative aspect of the commerce clause. Nonetheless, the Court discussed the "international complications" that could result from state taxes on instrumentalities of foreign commerce, and observed that such taxes could "impair federal uniformity in an area in which federal uniformity is essential."

456. Finally, Article I, section 10, prohibits the states, without the consent of Congress, from taxing imports or exports and from imposing tonnage duties. The purpose of this restriction was to provide the federal government with a reliable tax base that would not be eroded by overlapping state taxation. The import-export restriction has now been interpreted as prohibiting only discriminatory state taxation. The states can impose general taxes on goods produced in the state, notwithstanding that the goods may be destined for foreign export, and likewise can impose general taxes on goods that have been imported into the state from a foreign country.[986]

457. As the above discussion indicates, it is in the area of foreign affairs that federal power is most likely to displace state power. But even in this area, there is still considerable scope for state regulation affecting foreign affairs, so long as that regulation is not inconsistent with a federal treaty or executive agreement and does not improperly intrude upon federal power over foreign affairs.

986. *See Michelin Tire Corp. v. Wages*, 423 U.S. 276 (1976). Earlier cases holding that imports could not be taxed so long as they remained in the "original package" were overruled in *Michelin Tire*. Thus, a state may impose its general property tax on imported goods to be used in the importer's factory in the state. *Limbach v. Hooven & Allison Co.*, 466 U.S. 353 (1984).

Chapter 2. Taxing and Spending Power

458. As discussed previously (*See* Part II, Chapter 2, paragraph 50), Article I, section 8, includes the taxing and spending power among the powers of Congress relating to the operation of the federal government. The taxing and spending power is very comprehensive, and the Constitution imposes only a few specific limits on Congress' exercise of this power. As regards the taxing power, customs duties and excise taxes must be uniform throughout the United States,[987] and no tax or duty may be imposed on exports from any state.[988] As regards the spending power, appropriations for military purposes cannot be longer than for two years,[989] and there must be a "regular statement and account of the receipts and expenditures of all public monies.[990] There are no substantive limits on Congress" exercise of the spending power,[991] and when Congress allocates federal funds to the states, it has broad authority to condition the receipt of those funds on compliance with federal policies, so long as the states have a realistic choice of whether or not to accept the federal funds.[992]

The states, it will be recalled, succeeded upon Independence to the sovereignty formerly exercised by the British Crown over domestic matters, and so possess the general taxation power (*See* Part III, Chapter 1, paragraph 138). The only limits that the Constitution specifically imposes on the states' taxation power, in order to protect the federal government's revenue base, are that the states cannot tax imports or exports and cannot, without the consent of Congress, impose tonnage duties.[993] However, as has been discussed previously, the commerce clause and the due process clause impose some significant limitations on the power of the states to tax interstate and foreign commerce.[994]

987. Article I, s. 8.
988. Article I, s. 9. Under the Sixteenth Amendment, Congress is specifically authorized to impose an income tax from "whatever source derived without apportionment among the several states and without regard to any census or enumeration." This amendment was necessary because of a provision in the original Constitution that required a "head tax" to be apportioned among the states on the basis of their population according to the census.
989. Article I, s. 8. Since Congress enacts appropriations bills annually, this provision has become irrelevant.
990. Article I, s. 9.
991. *Charles G. Steward Machine Co. v. Davis*, 301 U.S. 548 (1937).
992. *See* para. 154, *supra* .
993. *See* para. 455, *supra* .
994. *See* paras. 183–187, *supra* .

Chapter 3. Emergency Laws

459. The Constitution does not recognize any concept of "emergency laws." All laws must be enacted by Congress in accordance with the procedures specified in Article I, section 7, and in American constitutional theory, Congress and the President must deal with an "emergency" under the powers granted to them by the Constitution. Following the terrorist attack on the United States of September 11, 2001, President Bush declared that the United States was now engaged in a "war on terrorism." The "war on terrorism," however, must be carried out within the constraints of the Constitution, which as pointed out above, does not recognize any concept of "emergency laws." Nor does the Constitution grant to the President any independent power to deal with an "emergency" and any laws that Congress enacts or any action that the President takes to deal with an "emergency" are subject to challenge in the courts as being prohibited by the Constitution. It is within this constitutional framework that the government of the United States must wage the "war on terrorism."

460. However, in waging the "war on terrorism," the federal government used its plenary control over immigration (*See* Part IV, Chapter 5 paragraph 428, *supra*) to take certain actions against temporary visitor aliens from predominantly Muslim Middle Eastern and South Asian countries where there is a "suspected terrorist presence." It will be recalled that there are virtually no constitutional restrictions on the power of Congress to regulate the entry and stay of temporary visitor aliens, such as students and tourists, who have not been admitted for permanent residence. Temporary visitor aliens who are out-of-status, such as those who have violated the terms of their admission or whose visa has expired, are "illegal aliens" and subject to detention and removal.[995] In practice, however, prior to the September 11 attacks, the federal Immigration and Naturalization Service (Now the Immigration and Customs Enforcement Agency, which is a part of the Department of Homeland Security), the federal agency charged with enforcing immigration laws, had not undertaken a major effort to do so and to deport "illegal aliens." There has been a large influx into the United States of "illegal aliens," many from Mexico, and they and other "illegal aliens" are vital to the American economy, because they do many of the lowest-level jobs that Americans and resident aliens are unwilling to take. The Immigration and Naturalization Service had also been lax in enforcing actual deportation orders.

All of the nineteen terrorists involved in the September 11 attacks were from Middle Eastern countries (fifteen were from Saudi Arabia, all were admitted as temporary visitors. and sixteen of the nineteen were out-of-status). As a part of the "war on terrorism," the federal government undertook certain actions against temporary visitor aliens from the predominantly Moslem Middle Eastern and south Asia countries where there was a "suspected terrorist presence." In the immediate aftermath of the September 11 attacks, the government arrested a number of temporary visitor aliens, primarily for immigration violations, and refused to release them on bail or to deport them until it "cleared them of links to terrorism."[996] The government also refused to disclose their

995. They are entitled to a hearing, *see* para. 433, *supra* , but the only question to be determined at the hearing is whether they are out-of-status.

996. It also held some persons on criminal charges and others as "material witnesses."

identities.[997] The chief hearing officer for the Immigration and Naturalization Service issued an order closing the immigration hearings of more than 600 "special interest" cases.[998] The Immigration and Naturalization Service began to enforce actual deportation orders, but at the direction of the Attorney-General, only against nationals of countries where there was a "suspected terrorist presence." Finally, the Attorney-General issued an order requiring temporary visitor aliens from eighteen mostly Arab and Moslem countries to be interviewed, photographed and fingerprinted by the Immigration and Naturalization Service.

Again, it must be emphasized that the government was able to undertake these actions because the federal government has plenary power over immigration, and because these actions involved temporary visitor aliens, who have little in the way of legal rights and only a limited entitlement to remain in the United States.

997. A federal appeals court held that the identities of the detained persons and the circumstances of their detention were exempt from disclosure under the federal Freedom of Information Act as "information compiled for law enforcement purposes" *See Center for National Security Studies v. Department of Justice*, 331 F.3d 918 (D.C. Cir. 2003).

998. One federal appeals court held that the closure order violated the First Amendment right of the public to attend legal proceedings, *Detroit Free Press v. Ashcroft*, 303 F.3d 681 (6th Cir. 2002), but another federal appeals court upheld the government's claim of the need for secrecy. *North Jersey Media Group, Inc. v. Ashcroft*, 308 F.3d 198 (3rd Cir. 2002). Shortly after these cases were decided, the government announced that there were no more "special interest" cases in which the hearing would be closed.

Chapter 4. The Relationship Between Church and State

461. Although the Supreme Court has sometimes referred to the Establishment Clause as creating a "wall of separation" between church and state, it is obviously not possible for the government to avoid any degree of involvement whatsoever with religion, nor should the government do so. The Court has noted on many occasions that the Establishment Clause does not require that the government be hostile toward religion, nor does it require that the government discriminate against religious institutions in the provision of governmental services that are available to the public as a whole. Rather the current view of the nature of the Establishment Clause is that it requires that the government pursue a policy of complete official neutrality toward religion.[999] There is complete official neutrality toward religion, for example, when the police direct traffic at Sunday church services, in the same manner as they would at any large gathering likely to create traffic problems. Likewise, complete official neutrality is not breached when the government opens up public facilities for expression and permits religious groups to have equal access to those facilities. And in certain circumstances, the government can include the religious with the secular in the receipt of a governmental benefit.[1000]

Because permitting religious groups equal access to public facilities does not amount to an "establishment of religion," the government's denial of equal access to public facilities to religious groups is a content-based exclusion that violates the First Amendment's guarantee of freedom of expression. So, a public university may not exclude student group wishing to use a designated public forum for religious worship and discussion.[1001] And where a school district permitted after-hours use of school facilities for "social, civic and recreational purposes" by private organizations, it could not prohibit such use of school facilities by private organization for the showing of film "considering family life and childrearing from Christian perspective."[1002] The

999. "The established principle [is] that the government must pursue a course of complete official neutrality toward religion." *Wallace v. Jaffree*, 472 U.S. 38, 60 (1985).

1000. Typically, the benefit such as a tax exemption is provided to organizations that carry on "religious, charitable, and educational activities." *See* e.g., *Walz v. Tax Commission of City of New York*, *infra* , para. 467, n. 1026. And as we will *see* subsequently, *infra* , paras 469–471. In many circumstances, the government can include children attending sectarian schools and their parents in benefits provided to children attending public schools.

1001. *Widmar v. Vincent,* 454 U.S. 263 (1981).

1002. *Lamb's Chapel v. Center Moriches Union Free School District*, 508 U.S. 384 (1993).

facilities also must be open for a private Christian organization that wanted to use the facilities for religious activities for children.[1003]

462. The government breaches the requirement of complete official neutrality toward religion when the purpose or effect of governmental action is to favor one religion over another religion[1004] or to favor religion in the sense of belief in a Supreme Being over nonreligion.[1005] The "classic meaning" of the Establishment Clause has been stated by the Supreme Court as follows: Neither a state nor the Federal Government can set up a church. Neither can pass laws which aid one religion, aid all religions, or prefer one religion to another. Neither can force nor influence a person to go to or to remain from church against his will or force him to profess a belief or disbelief in any religion. No person can be punished for entertaining or professing religious beliefs or disbeliefs, for church attendance or nonattendance. No tax in any amount, large or small, can be levied to support any religious activities or institutions, whatever they may be called, or whatever form they may adopt to teach or practice religion. Neither a state nor the Federal Government can, openly or secretly, participate in the affairs of any religious organizations or groups and vice versa.[1006]

463. The Court, however, has gone beyond the "classic meaning" of the Establishment Clause to invalidate a number of laws and governmental actions that violate the principle of complete official neutrality toward religion. The Court has promulgated a three-part test to determine whether a challenged law or governmental action violates the Establishment Clause. Under this test, referred to as the *Lemon* test,[1007] a law or governmental action violates the Establishment Clause if either: (1) it was undertaken for a religious rather than a secular purpose; or (2) its primary effect, regardless of its purpose, is to advance or inhibit religion; or (3) it fosters an excessive entanglement between government and religion.

1003. *Good News Club v. Milford Central School*, 533 U.S. 98 (2001).*See also* Board of *Education of Westside Community Schools v. Mergens*, 496 U.S. 226 (1990), upholding a federal law prohibiting school districts receiving federal funds from discriminating against religiously oriented groups in regard to access to school facilities. Other cases involving the equal access of religious groups to public facilities include *Capitol Square Review Advisory Board v. Pinette*, 515 U.S. 753 (1995) (Christmas season display of cross in plaza in front of state capitol that had been dedicated as a public forum); *Rosenberger v. University of Virginia*. 515 U.S. 819 (1995) (where public university paid printing costs of student publications, it could not refuse to pay printing costs of religiously oriented student publication).

1004. For an example of such a case, *see Larson v. Valente*, 456 U.S. 228 (1982), where a state law requiring charitable organizations to register, but exempting organizations that received at least half of their funds from members, was held unconstitutional as applied to require registration of a religious organization that received more than half of its funds from nonmembers. The "half the funds from non-members" rule was characterized as creating a preference between religions, and so violated the Establishment Clause.

1005. *See* e.g., *Texas Monthly, Inc. v. Bullock*, 489 U.S. 1 (1989), where the Court held violative of the Establishment Clause an exemption from the state sales tax for "periodicals that are published or distributed by a religious faith and that consist wholly of writings promulgating the teaching of the faith and books that consist wholly of writings sacred to a religious faith."

1006. *Everson v. Board of Education*, 330 U.S. 1, 15–16 (1947).

1007. The test takes its name from *Lemon v. Kurtzman*, 403 U.S. 602 (1971), the case in which it was first promulgated in its precise form. The test, however, reflected the "cumulative criteria developed by the Court over many years" in Establishment Clause cases.

464. Under the first or "religious purpose" element of the *Lemon* test, a law or governmental action that was undertaken for a religious purpose violates the Establishment Clause regardless of whether its effect is to advance religion within the meaning of the second element of the Lemon test. So, a state law requiring a "period of silence or voluntary prayer" for public school students at the start of the school day, which the trial court found was enacted for the religious purpose of "returning voluntary prayer to the public schools," was unconstitutional regardless of whether or not it had the effect of "advancing religion."[1008] Likewise, a state law that prohibited the teaching of the biological theory of evolution in the public schools was found, "on the basis of the historical evidence surrounding its enactment" to have been enacted for the purpose of forbidding the teaching of a biological theory that conflicted with "fundamentalist" religious doctrine.[1009] In the same vein, a state law that prohibited the teaching of the theory of evolution in the public schools unless accompanied by instruction in "creation science," was found to have been enacted for the purpose of changing the school curriculum in order to advance a particular religious doctrine that rejected the factual basis of evolution and embodied the religious belief that a supernatural creator was responsible for the creation of humankind. Thus, it too failed the "religious purpose" element of the *Lemon* test. Crucial to the finding that the law was enacted for a religious purpose was a determination that so-called creation science was not a science at all, but a religious doctrine masked as "science."[1010]

465. Under the second or "religious effect" element of the Lemon test, the Court has invalidated a number of traditional practices in the public schools on the ground that they have the effect of advancing religion, such as school-sponsored prayers,[1011] Bible reading,[1012] and the posting of a copy of the Ten Commandments in public school classrooms.[1013] The Court has also held that the Establishment Clause prohibits a public

---

1008. *Wallace v. Jaffree*, 472 U.S. 38 (1985). A "moment of silence" requirement is not "inherently religious," even if some students observe the requirement by engaging in silent prayer. Thus, such a requirement, if it was not enacted for a religious purpose, would likely be sustained against Establishment Clause challenge as having both a secular purpose and a secular effect. *See also McCreary County v. American Civil Liberties Union*, 545 U.S. 844 (2005), where the Court found that a county's purpose in creating a "Foundations of American Law" display that included the Ten Commandments along with the Bill of Rights and other historical documents was to promote the Ten Commandments with its religious message, and so violated the Establishment Clause. In the absence of this religious purpose, the display likely would have been found to have a secular purpose and effect, and so would not be held to violate the Establishment Clause. *See Van Orden v. Perry*, *infra* , para. 465, n. 1020.

1009. *Epperson v. Arkansas*, 393 U.S. 97 (1968).

1010. *Edwards v. Aguillard*, 482 U.S. 578 (1987).

1011. *Engle v. Vitale*, 370 U.S. 421 (1962). This includes officially sponsored prayer at a public school commencement. *Lee v. Weisman*, 505 U.S. 577 (1992). In this 5-4 decision, the Court rejected the contention that a "ceremonial prayer" at a public school commencement did not have the effect of advancing religion. In *Santa Fe Independent School District v. Doe*, 530 U.S. 290 (2000), the Court held unconstitutional a public high school's policy of permitting the student body to vote to have prayers at athletic contests and to select a student to deliver the prayers.

1012. *School District of Abington Township v. Schempp*, 374 U.S. 203 (1963).

1013. *Stone v. Graham*, 449 U.S. 39 (1980).

school's "released time" program in which religious groups provide teachers to conduct religious classes on the school premises for students who wish to attend them.[1014] Outside of the school context, under this element of the *Lemon* test, the Court has invalidated regulatory laws that were found to have the effect of favoring religion over nonreligion, such as a law that entitled an employee to take time off work on the day that the employee observed as the sabbath,[1015] and a law that gave churches the power to prevent the issuance of a liquor license to a business that would be located within 500 feet of the church.[1016]

466. The more difficult "religious effect" cases are those involving laws or governmental action that presently advance a secular purpose and have a secular effect, but that, because of the historical interaction between the "religious" and the "secular" with respect to the matter in issue, have some "religious effect" as well. One example of such a law is a law requiring businesses to close on Sundays.[1017] There is no doubt that historically the adoption of these laws was motivated by religious considerations, but their retention in more modem times advances the secular purpose of providing a uniform day of rest for all employees. The fact that the uniform day of rest coincides with the Christian sabbath in a society that is predominantly Christian is deemed to confer only an "incidental benefit" on religion that is not sufficient to outweigh the primarily secular purpose and effect of the law. Thus, the Court has held that "Sunday closing laws" do not violate the Establishment Clause.[1018] Similarly, Christmas, despite its historically religious origin, is observed primarily as a secular holiday in the United States. It is the "national holiday of gift-giving," so to speak. For this reason, the Court has held that the inclusion of a nativity scene, a Christian religious symbol, in a

1014. *McCollum v. Board of Education*, 333 U.S. 203 (1948). The public schools, however, may establish a "released time" program under which students leave the school for a specified period of time during the school day to attend religious instruction in non-school facilities. The Court held that such a "released time" program constitutes an "accommodation of religion" that is not prohibited by the Establishment Clause. *Zorach v. Clauson*, 343 U.S. 306 (1952). In *Board of Education v. Kiryas Joel Village School District*, 512 U.S. 687 (1994), the Court held unconstitutional as creating an impermissible "religious effect" a state's effort to establish a school district embracing only the boundaries of a specific religious community, so that the district could provide remedial education for the children of the religious community who otherwise attended sectarian schools.

1015. *Estate of Thornton v. Caldor, Inc.*, 472 U.S. 703 (1985). The effect of the law was to advance religion, since the only employees who could choose their day off were employees who wanted to observe that day as their sabbath. A law giving all employees the right to choose their day off would not violate the Establishment Clause, notwithstanding that it would enable many employees to take off the day that they observed as their sabbath.

The federal law prohibiting employment discrimination on the basis of race, sex, religion and the like, requires employers to make a limited accommodation for an employee's religious beliefs, so long as this can be done "without undue hardship on the conduct of the employer's business." This limited accommodation requirement has been construed very narrowly by the Supreme Court, in apparent recognition that a broader construction of that requirement would raise serious Establishment Clause problems. *See Trans World Airlines, Inc. v. Hardison*, 432 U.S. 63 (1977).

1016. *Larkin v. Grendel's Den*, 459 U.S. 116 (1982).

1017. While these laws have were widespread in times past, today they have been repealed in most states and localities.

1018. *McGowan v. Maryland*, 366 U.S. 420 (1961).

governmentally sponsored Christmas holiday display, containing a Santa Claus, Christmas trees, toy animals, and the other secular symbols of Christmas, does not have the "religious effect" of "endorsing Christianity," and so does not violate the Establishment Clause.[1019] But the display on public property of a nativity scene, standing alone, during the Christmas holiday season, does have the "religious effect" of "endorsing Christianity," and so violates the Establishment Clause.[1020]

467. The relevance of historical practice to the matter of "religious effect" under the second element of the *Lemon* test is also reflected in regard to what has been called "secular deism." Precisely because of the historical significance of religion in American life, there have long been references to "God" in governmental ceremonies and activities, such as the reference to "One Nation Under God" in the official Pledge of Allegiance, the national motto of "In God We Trust" placed on American currency, official documents and public buildings, and the traditional opening of court sessions with, "God Save this Honorable Court." These official references to "God" do not have the effect of advancing religion for purposes of the second element of the *Lemon* test, because they may be considered to reflect the traditional role of religion in American life, and because through long usage in a secular context, they have lost their religious significance.[1021] So too, the Supreme Court has held that the opening of sessions of Congress and other legislative bodies with prayer does not violate the Establishment Clause, because this practice was followed by Congress at the time the First Amendment was adopted.[1022]

468. The third or "excessive" "entanglement" element of the *Lemon* test precludes governmental involvement in religious matters and in the internal affairs of religious bodies. Under this element of the *Lemon* test, the civil courts may not become involved with matters of religious doctrine or policy, but must defer to the resolution of these

---

1019. *Lynch v. Donnelly*, 465 U.S. 668 (1984).

1020. *Allegheny County v. American Civil Liberties Union*, 492 U.S. 573 (1989). In that case, the Court also held that the display of a Chanukah menorah, a Jewish religious symbol, as part of a "Salute to Liberty" display next to a large Christmas tree and a "Salute to Liberty" sign, did not have the "religious effect" of "endorsing Judaism," and so did not violate the Establishment Clause. *See also Van Orden v. Perry*, 545 U.S. 677 (2005), where the Court held that the display of a monument donated by a private organization that was inscribed with the Ten Commandments on the grounds of the Texas state capitol, along with seventeen other monuments and twenty-one historical markers commemorating the "people, ideals and events that compose Texan identity," had a primary secular effect and did not violate the Establishment Clause. Since the Ten Commandments is a "quintessential religious symbol," its display alone, like the display of a nativity scene alone, would have a primarily religious effect and so would violate the Establishment Clause.

1021. *See* the discussion of this point by the late Justice Brennan in his concurring opinion in *Abington Township School District v. Schempp*, 374 U.S. 203, 303–304 (1963), where he refers to these practices as having been "interwoven so deeply into the fabric of our civil policy that [their] present use may well not present the type of involvement which the First Amendment prohibits."

1022. *Marsh v. Chambers*, 463 U.S. 783 (1983). In *Greece v. Galloway*, 134 S.Ct. 1811 (2014), the Court held that there was no constitutional requirement that the prayers of a legislative body be nonsectarian or ecumenical, and that so long as the opportunity to deliver the prayers was open to clergy or laypersons of any persuasion, there was no constitutional violation resulting from the fact that in a town that was predominantly Christian most of the prayers were Christian prayers.

issues by the highest tribunal of a hierarchical church authority. Thus, the courts cannot interfere with the decisions of the appropriate ecclesiastical authority within the church as to what persons are entitled to serve as ecclesiastical officials.[1023] Nor may they become involved in disputes between church factions over control of church property, with each faction claiming to have the "true faith." Again, the courts must defer to the determination of which group has the "true faith" that has been made by the highest tribunal of a hierarchical church organization.[1024] However, where the form of church organization is congregational rather than hierarchical, the courts may, consistent with the Establishment Clause, apply general principles of contract and property law to determine which of the contending factions is entitled to the church property.[1025] The Court has also applied this element of the *Lemon* test "in reverse," so to speak, to uphold against Establishment Clause challenge a state law that included property used for religious purposes in a general tax exemption for property used for educational or charitable purposes. According to the Court, the inclusion of property used for religious purposes in the general tax exemption promoted "benevolent neutrality" toward religion and avoided the "entanglement" that could result from governmental valuation of church property for tax purposes and enforcement of the tax against church property.[1026]

469. We will now consider the extent to which the Establishment Clause precludes the government from providing financial assistance to institutions operated by religious organizations. The Court has had no difficulty in upholding the constitutionality of governmental financial assistance to those institutions that perform secular functions of the same type as those performed by purely secular institutions, such as church-affiliated hospitals.[1027] Likewise, the Court has held that most church-affiliated colleges and universities are sufficiently similar to secular universities in their operation and academic program, so that governmental assistance directly tied to their secular educational functions is not violative of the Establishment Clause.[1028] Finally, the Court has held that the Establishment Clause was not violated by the government's inclusion of religiously affiliated organizations in a program of grants to private organizations

1023. *See Serbian Eastern Orthodox Diocese v. Milivojevich*, 426 U.S. 696 (1976); *Gonzalez v. Roman Catholic Archbishop of Manila*, 280 U.S. 1 (1929).
1024. *See Watson v. Jones*, 80 U.S. 679 (1871); *Kedroff v. St. Nicholas Cathedral*, 344 U.S. 94 (1952); *Presbyterian Church v. Hull Church*, 393 U.S. 440 (1969).
1025. *Jones v. Wolf*, 443 U.S. 595 (1979).
1026. *Walz v. Tax Commission of City of New York*, 397 U.S. 664 (1970).
1027. *Bradfeld v. Roberts*, 175 U.S. 291 (1899).
1028. *See Tilton v. Richardson*, 403 U.S. 672 (1971) (federal construction grants to church-affiliated colleges and universities for buildings and facilities used exclusively for secular educational purposes); *Hunt v. McNair*, 413 U.S. 734 (1973) (state-issued revenue bonds that could be used by church-affiliated colleges and universities to borrow funds to finance construction of facilities used for secular purposes); *Roemer v. Board of Public Works of Maryland*, 426 U.S. 736 (1976) (grants to defray part of expense of educating students in private colleges and universities, including grants to religiously affiliated institutions that had given "adequate assurance that funds would be used for a secular purpose").

to provide counseling for the prevention of adolescent sexual relations and care for pregnant adolescents and adolescent parents.[1029]

470. However, the Establishment Clause severely restricts the power of the government to provide financial aid to sectarian elementary and secondary schools. Since these schools are necessarily permeated by religious teaching, any form of direct governmental aid to these schools, such as a per pupil grant, will necessarily have the effect of advancing religion, and so will violate the "religious effect" element of the *Lemon* test. In order to avoid the "religious effect" problem, any program of governmental educational assistance that includes sectarian schools must take the form of providing a benefit to sectarian school students along with public school students, and insofar as it involves instructional assistance, must be limited to secular instruction.

471. The Court has held that the government does not violate the Establishment Clause when it transports students to sectarian schools as well as to public schools, because the important public purpose of ensuring the safety of schoolchildren is served by having all children transported to school at public expense.[1030] By the same token, school lunch programs and the like can include sectarian school students, because in this circumstance the school is merely a conduit for the distribution of a governmental benefit to children.[1031] The Court has also held that the government may provide sectarian school students with textbooks in secular subjects, as it does for students in the public schools.[1032] And there is no violation of the Establishment Clause when the state allows all parents to take a tax deduction for educational expenses, notwithstanding that most of the deductions will be taken for tuition payments made by parents who are sending their children to sectarian schools.[1033] However, if the state only allows a tax deduction for school tuition paid by parents whose children are attending private or sectarian schools, this is considered direct governmental subsidization of sectarian school tuition, and is unconstitutional.[1034]

472. Governmental efforts to assist sectarian schools in providing education in secular subjects present Establishment Clause problems, but these efforts may be

1029. *Bowen v. Kendrick*, 487 U.S. 589 (1988). The grant was challenged on the ground that the organizations would use the grants to advance their religious views on adolescent sexual relations. The Court held that there was no reason to assume that the organizations would not carry out the secular function in a "lawful secular manner," and that if a particular organization used the grant in an improper manner, the grant could be revoked.

1030. *Everson v. Board of Education*, 330 U.S. 1 (1947).

1031. *See Wolman v. Walter*, 433 U.S. 229 (1977), where the Court held that the state could provide diagnostic services in which state employees tested individual children for particular health and educational problems in the sectarian schools.

1032. *Board of Education v. Allen*, 392 U.S. 236 (1968). In *Zobrest v. Catalina Foothills School District*, 509 U.S. 1 (1993), a sharply divided Court held 5-4, that where a school district provided sign-language interpreters for deaf students in the public schools, it was not prohibited by the Establishment Clause from providing a sign-language interpreter for a deaf student who transferred to a sectarian school.

1033. *Mueller v. Allen*, 463 U.S. 388 (1983). *See also Witters v. Washington Department of Services for the Blind*, 474 U.S. 481 (1986), where the Court held that the Establishment Clause was not violated where a blind student used state payments provided to blind students for educational purposes to attend a religiously affiliated college for the purpose of pursuing a religious vocation.

1034. *Committee for Public Education and Religious Liberty v. Nyquist*, 413 U.S. 756 (1973).

constitutionally permissible depending on the manner in which the assistance is provided. The government may not pay or supplement the salaries of teachers employed by the sectarian schools to teach secular subjects.[1035] This is because the "religious effect" element of the *Lemon* test requires that the government act to ensure that the assistance will in fact be limited to secular subjects, and governmental efforts to satisfy this requirement are likely to violate the "excessive entanglement" element of the *Lemon* test.[1036] However, the Court has held that the state may send public school teachers into the sectarian schools to provide remedial services and "supplemental secular instruction" to sectarian school students.[1037] This kind of assistance was held to fall on the side of "aid to the child" rather than on the side of "aid to the school," and so was constitutionally permissible. Moreover, since the instruction would be provided entirely by public school teachers without any involvement on the part of the sectarian school itself, there would be no problem with "excessive entanglement."[1038]

Finally, since this kind of assistance was limited to the provision of remedial services and "supplemental secular instruction," the Court found that it did not impermissibly subsidize the religious mission of the schools by relieving them of costs

1035. *Lemon v. Kurtzman*, 403 U.S. 602 (1971).The government may reimburse parochial schools for expenses incurred in complying with state law requirements designed to ensure that parochial school students are receiving an adequate secular education, such as expenses incurred in connection with state-administered educational tests. *Committee for Public Education and Religious Liberty v. Regan*, 444 U.S. 646 (1980). However, the government may not provide the parochial schools with an unrestricted lump-sum grant, purportedly designed to reimburse the parochial schools for the expenses mandated by state law. *Levitt v. Committee for Public Education*, 413 U.S. 472 (1973).

1036. In *Lemon*, the state supplemented the salaries of teachers of secular subjects in the sectarian schools. It required submission of financial data by the schools and examination of school records, and imposed restrictions on the teachers receiving the supplements to ensure that they were teaching only secular subjects. The Supreme Court held that the teacher salary supplement scheme violated the "excessive entanglement" element of the *Lemon* test, noting that: "A comprehensive, discriminating, and continuing state surveillance will inevitably be required to ensure that [the statutory] restrictions are obeyed and the First Amendment otherwise respected.... These prophylactic contacts will involve excessive and enduring entanglement between state and church." 403 U.S. at 619.

1037. *Agostini v. Felton*, 521 U.S. 203 (1997).

1038. In so holding, the Court specifically overruled its earlier decisions in *Aquilar v. Felton*, 473 U.S. 402 (1985), and *School District of Grand Rapids v. Ball*, 473 U.S. 373 (1985). In *Aquilar*, the Court held that while the provision of remedial services for sectarian school students was constitutionally permissible as constituting "aid to the child," the provision of those services within the sectarian school itself created an impermissible "symbolic union" between church and state, and so was constitutionally impermissible. As a result, the remedial services had to be provided in separate facilities outside of the sectarian school, either in public school buildings or in governmentally operated "portables" on the sectarian school grounds. This rationale was repudiated in *Agostini*, and now the remedial services can be provided in the sectarian schools themselves. In *Ball*, the Court held unconstitutional, again under "symbolic union" rationale, a "shared time" program under which public school teachers went into the sectarian schools and taught certain "enrichment" subjects that were designed to supplement the "core curriculum" of the sectarian schools. With the abandonment of the "symbolic union" rationale, the holding in *Ball* was effectively overruled as well.

they otherwise would have borne in educating their students or by providing a financial incentive to undertake sectarian education.

Similarly in *Mitchell v. Helms*,[1039] the Court held that it was constitutional for the state to include sectarian schools in a program in which public funds were used to purchase instructional equipment and materials, such as media material and computer software, that were loaned to the students. The materials and equipment had to be "secular, neutral and non-ideological." Private schools were required to include in their application how they would use the materials. The Court was highly fragmented on the question of whether it was constitutionally permissible to use public funds in this way. Four Justices maintained that the program was constitutionally permissible, since the aid was allocated on the basis of neutral, secular criteria and was available to both sectarian and secular beneficiaries on a non-discriminatory basis. Five Justices were of the view that the program also had to contain safeguards to prevent diversion of the materials for religious use. But two of these Justices concluded that the program did contain sufficient Justices, while three concluded that they did not. Since six Justices agreed on different grounds that the program was constitutional, it was upheld. But the holding that emerges from the case, expressing the views of five Justices, and thus a majority of the Court, was that such a program must contain sufficient safeguards to prevent diversion of the materials for religious use.[1040] There has been great controversy over whether it is permissible for the government to provide "school vouchers" for parents that they may use either for a free education at a public school or to defray tuition at private and sectarian schools. When this question came before the Court, the Court was highly fragmented, but held 5–4, that in certain circumstances, the state could provide tuition vouchers that schoolchildren could use at sectarian schools. In that case, the state had adopted a program that provided financial assistance to parents of low-income children attending poorly performing urban public schools. The program contained a number of different forms of financial assistance, including attendance at "community" and "magnet" schools. It also included tuition vouchers for private sectarian and non-sectarian schools. The Court majority said that while the state could not provide aid directly to sectarian schools, it could establish "programs of true private choice, in which government aid reaches [religious] schools only as a result of the genuine and independent choices of private individuals." The majority found that the particular program of financial assistance was a "program of true private choice" and so did not violate the Establishment Clause. The position of the dissenting Justices was that the Establishment Clause prevented the state from using public funds to pay tuition at sectarian schools and that it was irrelevant that the funds got to the schools on the basis of the parents' private choices.

1039. 530 U.S. 393 (2000).

1040. In this case, the six Justices who joined in the holding that the program was constitutionally permissible agreed that the holding on this point overruled the earlier holdings in *Meek v. Pittenger*, 421 U.S. 349 (1975), and *Wolman v. Walter*, 433 U.S. 229 (1977), to the effect that the government could not constitutionally loan any instructional materials to children attending sectarian schools. In *Wolman v. Walter*, the Court also held that it was unconstitutional to use public funds to provide for transportation for field trips by sectarian students. In light of *Mitchell v. Helms*, it would seem to be constitutionally permissible to use public funds to provide for transportation for field trips that were of a purely secular nature.

Because the decision was based on the matter of "true private choice," the result was not a sharp departure from earlier cases holding that it was constitutionally permissible for the state to provide certain benefits to children attending sectarian schools, as opposed to providing aid to school itself. However, the decision furnishes a model of a constitutionally permissible voucher program and gives guidance as to how the state can filter money to sectarian institutions through the "genuine and independent choices of private individuals." At the same time, the decision imposes detailed requirements on the adoption of such a program, and the decision has not led to the adoption of such programs in many states or school districts.

473. We see then that the Establishment Clause stands as a significant obstacle to governmental efforts to promote religion in the United States. The Establishment Clause prohibits a large number of governmental practices that have the purpose or effect of favoring religion, including most officially sponsored prayer and religious displays, and most forms of governmental financial aid to parochial schools. Because of the Establishment Clause, the government must pursue a policy of complete official neutrality toward religion, and the Establishment Clause has been the primary method of protecting religious freedom in the American constitutional system.

Selected Bibliography

I. General Treatises and Casebooks

Erwin Chemerinsky. *Constitutional Law: Principles and Policies*. 5th ed. New York: Aspen Law and Business, 2015

Kathleen M. Sullivan & Noah Feldman. *Constitutional Law*. 19th ed. New York: Foundation Press, 2016.

Jesse H. Choper, Richard H. Fallon, Yale Kamisar Jr., Steven H. Shiffrin, Michael C. Dorf & Frederick Schauer, *Constitutional Law.* 12th ed. St. Paul, Minnesota: West Publishing Co., 2011.

John E. Nowak & Ronald D. Rotunda. *Constitutional Law.* 8th ed. St. Paul, Minnesota: West Publishing Co., 2015.

Laurence H. Tribe. *American Constitutional Law.* 3rd ed., vol. 1. New York: Foundation Press, New York, 2000.

II. American Constitutional History

Akhil R. Amar. *The Bill of Rights: Creation and Reconstruction*. New Haven, Connecticut: Yale University Press, 1998.

Jack M. Balkin. "'Wrong the Day It Was Decided': Lochner and Constitutional Historicism." *Boston University Law Review* 85 (2005): 677.

Edward Corwin. *Corwin on the Constitution*. 2 vols., R. Loss (ed.), Ithaca, New York: Cornell University Press, 1981, 1987.

David P. Currie. *The Constitution in the Supreme Court.' The First Hundred Years, 1789–1888*. Chicago, Illinois: University of Chicago Press, 1985.

Richard H. Fallon, Jr. *The Dynamic Constitution: An Introduction to American Constitutional Law*. New York: Cambridge University Press, 2004.

M. Farrand. *Records of the Federal Convention of 1787*. ed. New Haven, Connecticut: Yale University Press, 1966.

Bernard Schwartz. *The Bill of Rights: A Documentary History*. New York: Chelsea House Publishers, 1971.

Charles Warren, *The Supreme Court in United States History*. 3 vols. Boston, Massachusetts: Little, Brown and Company, 1922–1924.

Cordon S. Wood. *The Creation of the American Republic, 1776–1787*. Chapel Hill, North Carolina: University of North Carolina Press, 1969.

III. The Federal Government: The Powers of Congress and the President

David Barron & Martin S. Lederman. "The Commander in Chief at the Lowest Ebb- Framing the Problem, Doctrine, and Original Understanding." *Harvard Law Review* 121 (2008): 689.

David Barron & Martin S. Lederman. "The Commander In Chief at the Lowest Eb – A Constitutional History." *Harvard Law Review* 121 (2008): 941.

Alexander M. Bickel. "Congress, The President and the Power to Wage War." *Chicago-Kent Law Review* 48 (1971): 131.

Charles L. Black, Jr. *Impeachment: A Handbook*. New Haven, Connecticut: Yale University Press, 1974.

Curtis A. Bradley & Trevor W. Morrison. Historical Glass and the Separation of Powers, *Harvard Law Review* 126 (2012) 411.

Jessica Bulman-Pozen. Federalism as a Safeguard of Separation of Powers, *Columbia* Law Review 112 (2012) 459

Erwin Chemerinsky. "How Should We Think About Bush *v.* Gore?." *Loyola University Chicago Law Journal* 34 (2002): 1.

George J. Clark. "Military Tribunals and the Separation of Powers." *University of Pittsburgh Law Review* 63 (2002): 837.

Richard H. Fallon, Jr. Interpreting Presidential Powers. *Duke Law Journal 63* (2013) 347.

A. Michael Froomkin. "The Imperial Presidency's New Vestments." *Northwestern University Law Review* 88 (1994): 1346.

Michael J. Gerhardt. *The Federal Impeachment Process*. Princeton, New Jersey: Princeton University Press, 1996.

Lawrence Lessig & Cass R. Sunstein. "The President and the Administration." *Columbia Law Review* 94 (1994): 1.

Thomas W. Merrill. "The Constitutional Principle of Separation of Powers." *Supreme Court Review* (1991): 225.

Deborah J. Merritt, "Commerce." *Michigan Law Review* 94 (1995): 674.

Saikrishna B. Prakash & Steven G. Calabresi. "The President's Power to Execute the Laws." *Yale L.J.* 104 (1994): 541.

Saikrishna B. Prakash. "The Separation and Overlap of War and Military Powers." *Texas Law Review* 87 (2008): 299.

Zachary S. Price. *Vanderbilt Law Review* 67 (2014): 1045.

Donald H. Regan. "How to Think About the Federal Commerce Power and Incidentally Rewrite United States *v.* Lopez." *Michigan Law Review* 94 (1995): 554.

Peter M. Shane & Harold H. Bruff. *The Law of Presidential Power*. Durham, North Carolina: Carolina Academic Press, 1988.

Robert Stem. "The Commerce Clause and the National Economy, 1933–1946." *Harvard Law Review* 59 (1946): 645.

Robert Stem. "The Commerce Clause Revisited -The Federalization of Intrastate Crime." *Arizona Law Review* 15 (1973): 271.

Peter L. Strauss. "The Place of Agencies in Government: Separation of Powers and the Fourth Branch." *Columbia Law Review* 84 (1984): 573.

Kathleen M. Sullivan. "Dueling Sovereignties: U.S. Term Limits *v.* Thornton." *Harvard Law Review* 109 (1995): 78.

Cass R. Sunstein. "Impeaching the President." *University of Pennsylvania Law Review* 147 (1998): 279.

IV. Judicial Review

Lea Brilmayer. "The Jurisprudence of Article III. Perspectives on the Case or Controversy Requirement." *Harvard Law Review* 93 (1979): 297.

Charles D. Kelso & R. Randall Kelso. "Standing to Sue: Transformations in Supreme Court Methodology, Doctrine and Results." *University of Toledo Law Review* 28 (1996): 93.

Erwin Chemerinsky. "The Rhetoric of Constitutional Law." *Michigan Law Review* 100 (2002): 2008.

David P. Currie & Frank I. Goodman. "Judicial Review of Federal Administrative Action: Quest for the Optimum Forum." *Columbia Law Review* 75 (1975): 1.

Christopher F. Edley, Jr. "Ch. 4, Scope of Judicial Review." In *Administrative Law*. New Haven, Connecticut: Yale University Press, 1990.

Richard H. Fallon, Jr. "As-Applied and Facial Challenges and Third Party Standing." *Harvard Law Review* 113 (2000): 1321.

Matthew D. Adler. "Rights, Rules, and the Structure of Constitutional Adjudication: A Response to Professor Fallon." *Harvard Law Review* 113 (2000): 1371.

Martha A. Field. "Abstention in Constitutional Cases: The Scope of the Abstention Doctrine." *University of Pennsylvania Law Review* 122 (1974): 1071.

Martha A. Field. "The Eleventh Amendment and Other Immunity Doctrines." *University of Pennsylvania Law Review* 126 (1978): 515.

William A. Fletcher. "The Structure of Standing." *Yale Law Journal* 98 (1988): 221.

Michael J. Gerhardt. "Rediscovering Nonjusticiability: Judicial Review of Impeachments After Nixon." *Duke Law Journal* 44 (1994): 231.

Louis Henkin. "Is There a 'Political Question' Doctrine?." *Yale Law Journal* 85 (1976): 597.

John C. Jeffries, Jr. "In Praise of the Eleventh Amendment and Section 1983." *Virginia Law Review* 84 (1998): 47.

Henry P. Monaghan. "Constitutional Adjudication: The Who and When." *Yale Law Journal* 82 (1973): 1363.

Jonathan Remy Nash. "Standing's Expected Value." *Michigan Law Review* 111 (2013): 1283.

Martin H. Redish. "Judicial Review and the Political Question." *Northwestern University Law Review* 79 (1985): 1031.

John G. Roberts. "Article III Limits on Statutory Standing." *Duke Law Journal* 42 (1993): 1219.

Fritz W. Scharpf. "Judicial Review and the Political Question Doctrine: A Functional Analysis." *Yale Law Journal* 75 (1966): 517.

Robert A. Sedler. "The Assertion of Constitutional Jus Tertii: A Substantive Approach." *California Law Review* 70 (1982): 1308.

Robert A. Sedler. "Standing and the Burger Court: An Analysis and Some Proposals for Legislative Reform." *Rutgers Law Review* 30 (1977): 863.

Robert A. Sedler. "Younger and Its Progeny: A Variation on the Theme of Equity, Comity and Federalism." *University of Toledo Law Review* 9 (1978): 681.

Symposium. "Judicial Review: Blessing or Curse? Or Both? A Symposium in Commemoration of the Bicentennial of Marbury *v.* Madison" (Contributions by Michael Kent Curtis, Davison M. Douglas, Daniel A. Farber, Jeffrey Goldworthy, Thomas C. Grey, Kenneth L. Karst, Sanford Levinson, Frank I. Michelman, Robert F. Nagel, Michael J. Perry, L.A. Powe, Jr., William G. Ross, Suzanna Sherry and Mark Tushnet). *Wake Forest Law Review* 38 (2003): 313.

Harry H. Wellington. "The Nature of Judicial Review." *Yale Law Journal* 91 (1982): 486.

V. The American Federal System: Federal and State Power

Federalism

Bradford R. Clark. "Putting the Safeguards Back into the Political Safeguards of Federalism." 80 *Texas Law Review* 327 (2001).

Michael W. McConnell, "Federalism: Evaluating the Framers' Design." *University of Chicago Law Review* 54 (1987): 1484.

Robert A. Sedler. "The Constitution and the American Federal System." *Wayne Law Review* 55 (2009): 1487.

Laurence H. Tribe. "Intergovernmental Immunities in Litigation, Taxation and Regulation." *Harvard Law Review* 89 (1976): 682.

Laurence H. Tribe. "Clear Statement Rules, Federalism and Congressional Regulation of States." *Harvard Law Review* 107 (1994): 1941.

Mark *v.* Tushnet. "Federalism and the Traditions of American Political Theory." *Georgia Law Review* 19 (1985): 981.

Herbert Wechsler. "The Political Safeguards of Federalism: The Role of the States in the Composition and Selection of the National Government." *Columbia Law Review* 54 (1954): 543.

Foreign Affairs

Curtis A. Bradley & Martin S. Flaherty. "Executive Power, Essentialism and Foreign Affairs." *Michigan Law Review* 102 (2004): 545.

Stephen Breyer. *Making Our Democracy Work.* New York: Alfred A. Knopf Co., 2010.

Louis Henkin. *Foreign Affairs and the United States Constitution.* 2nd ed. Mineola, New York: Foundation Press, 1996.

Charles A. Lofgren. "United States *v.* Curtiss-Wright Export Corporation: An Historical Reassessment." *Yale Law Journal* 83 (1973): 1.

John E. Nowak & Ronald D. Rotunda. "A Comment on the Creation and Resolution of a 'Non-Problem': Dames and Moore *v.* Regan, the Foreign Affairs Power, and the Role of the Court." *U.C.L.A. Law Review* 29 (1982): 1101.

Nicholas Q. Rosenkranz. "Executing the Treaty Power." *Harvard Law Review* 118 (2005): 1867.

Abraham Sofaer, War. *Foreign Affairs and Constitutional Power.* Cambridge, Massachusetts: Ballinger Publishing Co., 1976.

John C. Yoo. "War. Responsibility and the Age of Terrorism." *Stanford Law Review* 57 (2004): 793.

Federal Power

Jesse H. Choper. "The Scope of National Power Vis-a-Vis the States: The Dispensability of Judicial Review." *Yale Law Journal* 86 (1977): 1552.

Jesse H. Choper & John C. Yoo. "The Scope of the Commerce Clause After Morrison." *Oklahoma City Law Review* 25 (2000): 843.

Martha A. Field. "Garcia v, San Antonio Metropolitan Transit Authority: The Demise of a Misguided Doctrine." *Harvard Law Review* 99 (1985): 84.

Steven G. Gey. "The Myth of State Sovereignty." *Ohio State Law Journal* 63 (2002): 1601.

Lawrence Lessig. "Translating Federalism: United States *v.* Lopez." *Supreme Court Review* (1995): 125.

Deborah J. Merritt. "The Third Translation of the Commerce Clause: Congressional Power to Regulate Social Problems." *George Washington Law Review* 66 (1998): 1206.

H. Jefferson Powell. "The Oldest Question in Constitutional Law." *Virginia Law Review* 79 (1993): 633.

Ronald H. Rotunda. "The Doctrine of Conditional Preemption and Other Limitations on Tenth Amendment Restrictions." *University of Pennsylvania Law Review* 132 (1984): 289.

William W. Van Alstyne. "The Second Death of Federalism." *Michigan Law Review* 83 (1985): 1709.

State Power

Jesse H. Choper & Tung Yin. "State Taxation and the Dormant Commerce Clause: The Object-Measure Approach." *Supreme Court Review* (1998): 193.

Brannon P. Denning. "Extraterritoriality and the Dormant Commerce Clause. a Doctrinal Post-Mortem." *Louisiana Law Review* (2013): 979.

Julian N. Eule. "Laying the Dormant Commerce Clause to Rest." *Yale Law Journal* 91 (1982): 425.

Walter Hellerstein. "Is 'Internal Consistency' Foolish? Reflections on an Emerging Commerce Clause Restraint on State Taxation." *Michigan Law Review* 87 (1988): 138.

William B. Lockhart. "A Revolution in State Taxation of Commerce?." *Minnesota Law Review* 65 (1981): 1025.

Bradford Mank. "The Supreme Court's New Public-Private Distinction Under the Dormant Commerce Clause." *Hastings Constitutional Law Quarterly* 37 (2009).

Donald H. Regan. "The Supreme Court and State Protectionism: Making Sense of the Dormant Commerce Clause." *Michigan Law Review* 84 (1986): 1091.

Ferdinand P. Schoettle. "Commerce Clause Challenges to State Taxes." *Minnesota Law Review* 75 (1991): 907.

Robert A. Sedler. "The Negative Commerce Clause as a Restriction on State Regulation and Taxation: An Analysis in Terms of Constitutional Structure." *Wayne Law Review* 31 (1985).

Gary J. Simson. "Discrimination Against Non-Residents and the Privileges and Immunities Clause of Article IV." *University of Pennsylvania Law Review* 128 (1979): 379.

Jonathan D. Varat. "State 'Citizenship' and Interstate Equality." *University of Chicago Law Review* 48 (1981): 457.

VI. Constitutional Protection of Individual Rights: General Considerations

Bruce Ackerman. *Before the Next Attack: Preserving Civil Liberties in an Age of Terrorism*. New Haven, Connecticut: *Yale University Press*, New Haven, Connecticut 2006.

Lawrence A. Alexander & Frederick Schauer. "On Extrajudicial Constitutional Interpretation." *Harvard Law Review* 110 (1997): 1359.

Jack M. Balkin, "Living Originalism."*Harvard University Press*, Cambridge, Massachusetts, 2011

Jack M. Balkin & Sanford Levinson. "The Canons of Constitutional Law." *Harvard Law Review* 111 (1998): 963.

Randy E. Barnett. "Scrutiny Land." *Michigan Law Review* 106 (2008): 1479.

Robert W. Bennett. "'Mere' Rationality in Constitutional Law: Judicial Review and Democratic Theory." *California Law Review* 67 (1979): 1049.

Scott D. Bice. "Rationality Analysis in Constitutional Law." *Minnesota Law Review* 65 (1980): 1.

Robert H. Bork. *The Tempting of America*. New York, New York: Free Press, 1990.

Paul Brest. "The Fundamental Rights Controversy: The Essential Contradictions of Normative Constitutional Scholarship." *Yale Law Journal* 90 (1981): 1063.

Alan E. Brownstein. "How Rights Are Infringed: The Role of Undue Burden Analysis in Constitutional Doctrine." *Hastings Law Journal* 54 (1994): 867.

Erwin Chemerinsky. "Rethinking State Action." *Northwestern University Law Review* 80 (1985): 503.

John Hart Ely. "The Supreme Court 1977 Term -Foreword: On Discovering Fundamental Values." *Harvard Law Review* 92 (1978): 5.

John Fee. "The Formal State Action Doctrine and Free Speech Analysis." *North Carolina Law Review* 83 (2005): 569.

Charles Fried. "Constitutional Doctrine." *Harvard Law Review* 107 (1994): 1140.

Robert J. Glennon & John E. Nowak. "A Functional Analysis of the Fourteenth Amendment's 'State Action' Requirement." *Supreme Court Review* (1976): 221.

Joseph D. Grano. "Judicial Review and a Written Constitution in a Democratic Society." *Wayne Law Review* 28 (1981): 1.

Gerald Gunther. "The Supreme Court, 1971 Term -Foreword: In Search of Evolving Doctrine on a Changing Court: A Model for a Newer Equal Protection." Harvard Law Review 86 (1972): 1.

Kenneth L. Karst. "The Fifth Amendment's Guarantee of Equal Protection." *North Carolina Law Review* 55 (1977): 541.

Jules Lobel. "The War on Terrorism and Civil Liberties." *University of Pittsburgh Law Review* 63 (2002): 767.

Ira C. Lupu. "Untangling the Strands of the Fourteenth Amendment." *Michigan Law Review* 77 (1979): 981.

Michael J. Perry. "Modem Equal Protection: A Conceptualization and Appraisal." *Columbia Law Review* 79 (1979): 1023.

Ronald D. Rotunda. "Runyon *v.* McCrary and the Mosaic of State Action." *Washington University Law Quarterly* 67 (1989): 47.

Robert A. Sedler. "The Legitimacy Debate in Constitutional Adjudication: An Assessment and a Different Perspective." *Ohio State Law Journal* 44 (1983): 93.

Laurence H. Tribe. "Taking Text and Structure Seriously: Reflections on Free Form Method in Constitutional Interpretation." *Harvard Law Review* 108 (1995): 1221.

VII. Constitutional Protection of Individual Rights: Equality and the Protection of Minorities

Racial Equality

Alexander T. Alienkoff. "A Case for Race-Consciousness." Columbia Law Review 91 (1991): 101.

Derrick Bell. *Race, Racism and American Law*. 6th ed., New York: Aspen Publishers, 2004.

Selected Bibliography

Robert W. Bennett. "Reflections on the Role of Motivation Under the Equal Protection Clause." *Northwestern University Law Review* 79 (1984–1985): 1009.

Charles L. Black, Jr. "The Lawfulness of the Segregation Decisions." *Yale Law Journal* 69 (1960): 421.

Paul Brest. "Affirmative Action and the Constitution: Three Theories." *Iowa Law Review* 72 (1987): 281.

Barbara J. Flagg. "Enduring Principles: On Race, Process and Constitutional Law." *California Law Review* 82 (1994): 935.

Charles Fried. "Metro Broadcasting, Inc. *v.* FCC: Two Concepts of Equality." *Harvard Law Review* 104 (1990): 107.

Joel Goldstein. "Beyond Bakke: Grutter-Gratz and the Promise of Brown." *St. Louis University Law Journal* 48 (2004): 899.

Lino A. Graglia. "'Affirmative Action', Past, Present and Future." *Ohio Northern Law Journal* 23 (1996): 1207.

Samuel Issacharoff. "The Constitutional Contours of Race and Politics." *Supreme Court Review* (1995): 45.

Randall Kennedy. "For Discrimination: Race, Affirmative Action, and the Law." *paperback* (2013).

Michael J. Klarman. "Brown, Racial Change, and the Civil Rights Movement." *Virginia Law Review* 80 (1994): 7.

Michael J. Klarman. "Brown, Originalism and Constitutional Theory." *Virginia Law Review* 81 (1995): 1881.

Michael J. Klarman. *From Jim Crow to Civil Rights: The Supreme Court and the Struggle for Racial Equality*. New York, New York: Oxford University Press, 2004.

Michael J. Perry. "The Disproportionate Theory of Racial Discrimination." *University of Pennsylvania Law Review* 125 (1977): 540.

Richard H. Pildes. "Institutional Formalism and Realism in Constitutional and Public Law." *Supreme Court Review (2013: 1*

Michael Rosenfeld. "Decoding Richmond: Affirmative Action and the Elusive Meaning of Constitutional Equality." *Michigan Law Review* 87 (1989): 1729.

Eric Schnapper. "Perpetuation of Past Discrimination." *Harvard Law Review* 96 (1983): 828.

Robert A. Sedler. "The Constitution and the Consequences of the Social History of Racism." *Arkansas Law Review* 40 (1987): 677.

Robert A. Sedler. "The Constitution and School Desegregation: An Inquiry into the Nature of the Substantive Right." *Kentucky Law Journal* 68 (1979–1980): 879.

Robert A. Sedler. "Affirmative Action, Race and the Constitution: From Bakke to Grutter." Kentucky Law Journal 92 (2003–2004): 219.

David A. Strauss. "Discriminatory Intent and the Taming of Brown." *University of Chicago Law Review* 56 (1989): 935.

William W. Van Alstyne. "Rites of Passage: Race, the Constitution, and the Supreme Court." *University of Chicago Law Review* 46 (1979): 775.

Gender Equality

Katherine M. Franke. "The Central Mistake of Sex Discrimination Law: The Disaggregation of Sex From Gender." *University of Pennsylvania Law Review* 144 (1995): 1.

Ann E. Freedman. "Sex Equality, Sex Differences and the Supreme Court." *Yale L.J.* 92 (1983): 913.

Ruth Bader Ginsburg. *Constitutional Aspects of Sex-Based Discrimination*. St. Paul, Minnesota: West Publishing Company, 1974.

Leo Kanowitz. "'Benign' Sex Discrimination: Its Troubles and Their Cure." *Hastings Law Journal* 31 (1980): 1379.

Herma Hill Kay. "Equality and Difference: The Case of Pregnancy." *Berkeley Women's Law Journal* 1 (1985): 1.

Hernia Hill Kay. "Models of Equality." *University of Illinois Law Review* 39 (1985).

Sylvia A. Law. "Rethinking Sex and the Constitution." *University of Pennsylvania Law Review* 132 (1984): 955.

Christine A. Littleton. "Reconstructing Sexual Equality." *California Law Review* 75 (1987): 1279.

Katherine MacKinnon. "Reflections on Sex Equality Under Law." *Yale Law Journal* 100 (1991): 1281.

Reva B. Siegel. "She and the People: The Nineteenth Amendment, Sex Equality, Federalism and the Family." *Harvard Law Review* 115 (2002): 947.

Kathleen M. Sullivan. "Constitutionalizing Women's Equality." The Record 56 (2001): 22.

Wendy W. Williams. "The Equality Crisis: Some Reflections on Culture, Courts and Feminism." *Women's Law Reporter* 7 (1982): 175.

Other Forms of Group Discrimination

Akhil R. Amar. "Attainder and Amendment: Romer's Rightness." Michigan Law Review 95 (1996): 203.

Harry D. Krause. *Illegitimacy: Law and Social Policy*. Indianapolis, Indiana: Bobbs-Merrill Co., 1971.

Martha L. Minow. "When Difference Has Its Home: Group Homes for the Mentally Retarded, Equal Protection, and Legal Treatment of Difference." *Harvard Civil Rights-Civil Liberties Law Review* 22 (1987): 111.

Cass R. Sunstein. "Homosexuality and the Constitution."

Craig M. Bradley. "The Right Not to Endorse Gay Rights: A Reply to Sunstein." Indiana Law Journal 70 (1994): 1, 29.

Other Forms of Group Discrimination

Akhil R. Amar. "Attainder and Amendment: Romer's Rightness." *Michigan Law Review* 95 (1996): 203.

Pamela S. Karlan. "Loving Lawrence." *Michigan Law Review* 102 (2004): 1447.

Harry D. Krause. *Illegitimacy: Law and Social Policy*. Indianapolis, Indiana: Bobbs-Merrill Co., 1971.

Martha L. Minow. "When Difference Has Its Home: Group Homes for the Mentally Retarded, Equal Protection, and Legal Treatment of Difference." *Harvard Civil Rights-Civil Liberties Law Review* 22 (1987): 111.

Cass R. Sunstein. "Homosexuality and the Constitution."

Craig M. Bradley. "The Right Not to Endorse Gay Rights: A Reply to Sunstein." *Indiana Law Journal* 70 (1994): 1, 29.

Cass R. Sunstein. "Liberty After Lawrence." *Ohio State Law Journal* 65 (2004): 1059.

Laurence H. Tribe. "Lawrence *v.* Texas: The 'Fundamental Right' That Dare Not Speak Its Name." *Harvard Law Review* 117 (2004): 1893.

Citizenship and the Rights of Aliens

Alexander M. Bickel. "Citizenship in the American Constitution." *Arizona Law Review* 15 (1973): 369.

Jesse H. Choper. "Discrimination Against Aliens." *Supreme Court Trends and Developments* 4 (1983).

Gittel Gordon, Charles Gordon & Stanley Mailman. *Immigration Law and Procedure*. rev. ed., with annual supplements, New York: Matthew Bender Co., 1998.

Stephen H. Legomsky. "Immigration, Federalism, and the Welfare State." *U.C.L.A. Law Review* 42 (1995): 1453.

Earl M. Maltz. "Citizenship and the Constitution: A History and Critique of the Supreme Court's Alienage Jurisprudence." *Arizona State Law Journal* 28 (1996): 1135.

Gerald M. Rosberg. "The Protection of Aliens from Discrimination by the National Government." *Supreme Court Review* (1977): 275.

VIII. Constitutional Protection of Individual Rights - Freedom of Expression

Lawrence A. Alexander. "Low Value Speech." *Northwestern University Law Review* 83 (1989): 547.

C. Edwin Baker. "Harm, Liberty and Free Speech." *Southern California Law Review* 70 (1997): 979.

Randall P. Beznanson. "Institutional Reckless Disregard for Truth in Public Defamation Actions Against the Press." *Iowa Law Review* 90 (2005): 887.

Vincent A. Blasi. "Towards a Theory of Prior Restraint: The Central Linkage." *Minnesota Law Review* 66 (1981): 11.

Vincent A. Blasi. "Justice Holmes and the Marketplace of Ideas." *Supreme Court Review* 2004 (2004): 1.

Lee Bollinger. *Images of a Free Press*. Chicago, Illinois: University of Chicago Press, 1994.

Robert F. Bouchard. *Guidebook to the Freedom of Information and Privacy Acts*. New York, New York: Boardman Co., 1980.

Paul H. Brest. "Protecting Academic Freedom Through the First Amendment." *Texas Law Review* 66 (1988): 1359.

Elena Kagan. "Regulation of Hate Speech and Pornography After *R.A. V.*" *University of Chicago Law Review* 60 (1993): 873.

Alex Kozinski & Henry Banner. "Who's Afraid of Commercial Speech?." *Virginia Law Review* 76 (1990): 627.

Douglas O. Linder. "Freedom of Association After Roberts *v.* United States Jaycees." *Michigan Law Review* 82 (1984): 1878.

Katherine MacKinnon. "Pornography, Civil Rights and Speech." *Harvard Civil Rights-Civil Liberties Law Review* 20 (1985): 1.

William Marshall. "Free Speech and the 'Problem of Democracy.'" *Northwestern University Law Review* 89 (1994): 191.

Barry P. McDonald. "Speech and Distrust: Rethinking the Content Approach to Protecting Freedom of Expression." *Notre Dame Law Review* 81 (2006): 1347.

Selected Bibliography

Henry P. Monaghan. "First Amendment Due Process." *Harvard Law Review* 83 (1970): 518.

Henry P. Monaghan. "Overbreadth." *Supreme Court Review* (1981): 1.

Melvin B. Nimmer. "The Meaning of Symbolic Speech Under the First Amendment." *University of California at Los Angeles Law Review* 21 (1973): 29.

John E. Nowak & David A. Farber. "The Misleading Nature of Public Forum Analysis: Content and Context in First Amendment Adjudication." *Virginia Law Review* 70 (1984): 1219.

Robert C. Post. "Between Governance and Management: The History and Theory of the Public Forum." *University of California at Los Angeles Law Review* 34 (1987): 1713.

Robert C. Post. "Recuperating First Amendment Doctrine." *Stanford Law Review* 47 (1995): 1249.

Robert C. Post. "Reconciling Theory and Doctrine in First Amendment Jurisprudence." *California Law Review* 88 (2000): 2353.

L.A. Scan Powe, Jr. *American Broadcasting and the First Amendment.* Berkeley: University of California Press, 1987.

David H. Rabban. "The Emergence of Modern First Amendment Doctrine." *University of Chicago Law Review* 50 (1983): 1205.

Martin H. Redish. *Freedom of Expression: A Critical Analysis.* Charlottesville, Virginia: Michie Company, 1984.

Frederick Schauer. "Commercial Speech and the Architecture of the First Amendment." *University of Cincinnati Law Review* 56 (1988): 1181.

Frederick Schauer. *Free Speech: A Philosophical Enquiry.* Cambridge, England, and New York, New York: Cambridge University Press, 1982.

Frederick Schauer. "The Phenomenology of Speech and Harm." *Ethics* 103 (1993): 635.

Frederick Schauer. "The Boundaries of the First Amendment: A Preliminary Exploration of Constitutional Salience." *Harvard Law Review* 117 (2004): 1765.

Robert A. Sedler. "The First Amendment in Litigation: The 'Law of the First Amendment.'" *Washington & Lee Law Review* 48 (1991): 457.

Robert A. Sedler. "The 'Law of the First Amendment' Revisited." *Wayne Law Review* 58 (2013): 1003.

Steven Shiffrin. "The First Amendment and Economic Regulation: Away from a General Theory of the First Amendment." *Northwestern University Law Review* 78 (1984): 1212.

David Skover & Ronald Collins. "The Pornographic State." *Harvard Law Review* 107 (1994): 1374.

Rodney Smolla. "Rethinking First Amendment Assumptions About Racist and Sexist Speech." *Washington & Lee Law Review* 47 (1990): 171.

Geoffrey R. Stone. "Content Regulation and the First Amendment." *William & Mary Law Review* 25 (1983): 189.

Nadine Strossen. "The Convergence of Feminist and Civil Liberties Principles in the Pornography Debate." *New York University Law Review* 62 (1987): 201.

Cass R. Sunstein. "Pornography and the First Amendment." *Duke Law Journal* (1986): 589.

Cass R. Sunstein. *Democracy and the Problem of Free Speech.* New York: Free Press, 1993.

Cass R. Sunstein. "The First Amendment in Cyberspace." *Yale L.J.* 104 (1995): 1757.

Symposium. "Thoughts on Commercial Speech: A Roundtable Discussion." *Loyola Law Review* 41 (2007): 333.

Symposium. "Emerging Media: Technology and the First Amendment." *Yale Law Journal* 104 (1994): 1611.

William W. Van Alstyne. *Interpretation of the First Amendment.* Durham, North Carolina: Duke University Press, 1984.

Eugene Volokh. "Speech as Conduct: Generally Applicable Laws, Illegal Courses of Conduct, Situation-Altering Utterances, and the Uncharted Zones." *Cornell Law Review* 90 (2005): 1277.

Samuel Walker. *Hate Speech: The History of an American Controversy.* Lincoln, Nebraska: University of Nebraska Press, 1994.

Jonathan Weinberg. "Broadcasting and Speech." *California Law Review* 81 (1993): 1101.

IX. Constitutional Protection of Individual Rights - Freedom of Religion

Alan Brownstein. "Protecting the Liberty of Religious Institutions," *Journal of Contemporary Legal Issues* 21 (2013) 201.

Jesse H. Choper. "The Rise and Decline of Constitutional Protection of Religious Liberty." *Nebraska Law Review* 70 (1991): 651.

Jesse H. Choper. "The Establishment Clause and Aid to Parochial Schools – An Update." *California Law Review* 75 (1987): 6.

Jesse H. Choper. *Securing Religious Liberty.* Chicago, Illinois: University of Chicago Press, 1995.

John H. Garvey. "Churches and the Free Exercise of Religion." *Notre Dame Journal of Law, Ethics & Public Policy* 4 (1990): 567.

Selected Bibliography

John H. Garvey. "Free Exercise and the Values of Religious Liberty." *Connecticut Law Review* 18 (1986): 779.

Kent Greenawalt. "Religion as a Concept in Constitutional Law." *California Law Review* 72 (1984): 753.

Philip Kurland. "The Origins of the Religion Clauses of the Constitution." *William & Mary Law Review* 27 (1986): 839.

Douglas Laycock. "Formal, Substantive, and Disaggregated Neutrality Toward Religion." *DePaul Law Review* 39 (1990): 993.

Ira C. Lupu. "Where Rights Begin: The Problem of Burdens on the Free Exercise of Religion." *Harvard Law Review* 102 (1989): 933.

William P. Marshall. "In Defense of Smith and Free Exercise Revisionism." *University of Chicago Law Review* 58 (1990): 308.

William P. Marshall. "'We Know It When We See It': The Supreme Court and Establishment." *Southern California Law Review* 59 (1986): 495.

Michael W. McConnell. "Accommodation of Religion." *Supreme Court Review* 1 (1985).

Michael W. McConnell. "Religious Freedom at a Crossroads." *University of Chicago Law Review* 59 (1992): 115.

Michael J. Perry. "Freedom of Religion in the United States: Fin de Siècle Sketches." *Indiana Law Journal* 75 (2000): 295.

Leo Pfeffer. "Freedom and/or Separation, The Constitutional Dilemma of the First Amendment." *Minnesota Law Review* 64 (1980): 561.

Robert A. Sedler. "Essay: The Protection of Religious Freedom Under the American Constitution." *Wayne Law Review* 53 (2007): 817.

Robert A. Sedler. "Understanding the Establishment Clause: The Perspective of Constitutional Litigation." *Wayne Law Review* 43 (1997): 1317.

Robert A. Sedler, "Understanding the Establishment Clause: A Revisit." *Wayne Law Review* 59 (2013) 589.

Steven H. Shiffrin. "The Pluralistic Foundations of the Religion Clauses." *Cornell Law Review* 90 (2004): 9.

Gary J. Simson. "The Establishment Clause in the Supreme Court: Rethinking the Court's Approach." *Cornell Law Review* 72 (1987): 905.

William W. Van Alstyne. "What Is an 'Establishment of Religion'?." *North Carolina Law Review* 65 (1987): 909.

X. Constitutional Protection of Individual Rights - Liberty and Property Rights

Fundamental Rights

Robert A. Burt. "The Constitution of the Family." *Supreme Court Review* (1979): 329.

Jesse H. Choper. "Consequences of Supreme Court Decisions Upholding Individual Constitutional Rights." *Michigan Law Review* 83 (1984): 1.

William Cohen. "Equal Treatment for Newcomers: The Core Meaning of National and State Citizenship." *Constitutional Commentary* 1 (1984): 9.

Robert Dixon. "Reapportionment Perspectives: What Is Fair Representation?." *American Bar Association Journal* 51 (1965): 319.

Melvyn R. Durchslag. "Salyer, Ball and Holt: Reappraising the Right to Vote in Terms of Political Interest and Vote Dilution." *Case Western Law Review* 33 (1982): 1.

Martha Field. "Abortion Law Today." *Journal of Legal Medicine* 14 (1993): 3.

John H. Garvey. "Children and the Idea of Liberty." *Kentucky Law Journal* 68 (1979–1980): 809.

Ruth Bader Ginsburg. "Some Thoughts on Autonomy and Equality in Relation to Roe *v.* Wade." *North Carolina Law Review* 63 (1985): 375.

Brace C. Hafen. "The Constitutional Status of Marriage, Kinship and Sexual Privacy." *Michigan Law Review* 81 (1983): 463.

Yale Kamisar. "Physician-Assisted Suicide: The Problems Presented by the Compelling, Heartwrenching Case." *Journal of Criminal Law and Criminology* 88 (1998): 1121.

Kenneth L. Karst. "Foreword, Equal Citizenship Under the Fourteenth Amendment." *Harvard Law Review* 91 (1977): 1.

Kenneth L. Karst. "Freedom of Intimate Association." *Yale Law Journal* 89 (1980): 624.

Thomas R. McCoy. "Recent Equal Protection Decisions of the Supreme Court - Fundamental Right to Travel or 'Newcomers' as a Suspect Class?." *Vanderbilt Law Review* 28 (1975): 987.

Robert McKay. "Reapportionment: Success Story of the Warren Court." *Michigan Law Review* 67 (1968): 223.

Philip L. Martin. "The Supreme Court and State Legislative Apportionment: The Retreat from Absolutism." *Valpariso University Law Review* 9 (1974): 31.

Michael W. McConnell. "The Right to Die and the Jurisprudence of Tradition." *Utah Law Review* 1997 (1997): 665.

David D. Meyer. "Lochner Redeemed: Family Privacy After Troxel and Carhart." *University of California at Los Angeles Law Review* 48 (2001): 1125.

Martha Minow. "Which Question? Which Lie? Reflections on the Physician Assisted Suicide Case." *Supreme Court Review* (1997): 1.

Michael J. Perry. "Substantive Due Process Revisited." *Northwestern University Law Review* 71 (1976): 417.

Richard Posner. "The Uncertain Protection of Privacy by the Supreme Court." *Supreme Court Review* 1979 (1979): 173.

Donald H. Regan. "Rewriting Roe *v.* Wade." *Michigan Law Review* 77 (1979): 1569.

Carl E. Schneider. "State Interest Analysis in Fourteenth Amendment 'Privacy' Law: An Essay on the Constitutionalization of Social Issues." *Sl Law & Contemporary Problems* 79 (1988).

Peter H. Schuck. "The Thickest Thicket: Partisan Gerrymandering and Judicial Regulation of Politics." *Columbia Law Review* 87 (1987): 1325.

Robert A. Sedler. "Abortion, Physician-Assisted Suicide and the Constitution: The View from Without and Within." *Notre Dame Journal of Law. Ethics & Public Policy* 12 (1998): 529.

Mark *v.* Tushnet. "Permissible Gun Regulation After *Heller*: Some Speculation About Method and Outcomes." *U.C.L.A. Law Review* 56 (2009): 1425.

Eugene Volokh. "Implementing the Right to Keep and Bear Arms for Self-Defense: An Analytical Framework and a Research Agenda." *U.C.L.A. Law Rev.* 56 (2009): 1443.

J. Harvie Wilkinson III & G. Edward White. "Constitutional Protection for Personal Lifestyles." *Cornell Law Review* 62 (1977): 562.

Economic and Social Legislation

C. Edwin Baker. "Property and Its Relation to Constitutionally Protected Liberty." *University of Pennsylvania Law Review* 134 (1986): 741.

Edward L. Barrett, Jr. "The Rational Basis Standard of Equal Protection Review for Ordinary Legislation." *Kentucky Law Journal* 68 (1980): 845.

William H. Chine, III. "The Supreme Court's Treatment of Wealth Classifications Under the Fourteenth Amendment." *Supreme Court Review* 289 (1975).

Richard Epstein. *Takings: Private Property and the Power of Eminent Domain.* Cambridge, Mass: Harvard University Press, 1985.

Gilbert L. Finnell, Jr. "Public Access to Coastal Public Property: Judicial Theories and the Taking Issue." *North Carolina Law Review* 67 (1989): 627.

Robert J. Glennon. "Taxation and Equal Protection." *George Washington Law Review* 58 (1990): 261.

Ronald J. Krotoszynski, Jr. "Expropriatory Intent: Defining the Proper Boundaries of Substantive Due Process and the Takings Clause." *North Carolina Law Review* 80 (2002): 713.

Robert G. McCloskey. "Economic Due Process and the Supreme Court: An Exhumation and Reburial." *Supreme Court Review* 34 (1962).

Frank L. Michelman. "Takings 1987." *Columbia Law Review* 88 (1988): 1600.

Lawrence G. Sager. "Tight Little Islands: Exclusionary Zoning, Equal Protection and the Indigent." *Stanford Law Review* 21 (1969): 767.

Gary J. Simson. "Abortion, Poverty and the Equal Protection of the Laws." *Georgia Law Review* 13 (1979): 606.

Kathleen M. Sullivan. "Unconstitutional Conditions." *Harvard Law Review* 102 (1989): 1413.

Mark *v.* Tushnet. "The Newer Property: Suggestions for a Revival of Substantive Due Process." *Supreme Court Review* (1975): 261.

James H. Wilkinson, III. "The Supreme Court, the Equal Protection Clause and the Three Faces of Constitutional Equality." *Virginia Law Review* 61 (1975): 945.

Procedural Due Process

Richard H. Fallon. "Some Confusions About Due Process, Judicial Review, and Constitutional Remedies." *Columbia Law Review* 93 (1993): 309.

Jerry L. Mashaw. *Due Process in the Administrative State.* New Haven, CT: Yale University Press, 1985.

Jerry L. Mashaw. "The Supreme Court's Due Process Calculus for Administrative Adjudication in Mathews *v.* Eldridge." *University of Chicago Law Review* 44 (1976): 28.

Henry P. Monaghan. "Of 'Liberty' and 'Property.'" *Cornell Law Review* 62 (1977): 401.

Robert L. Rabin. "Job Security and Due Process: Monitoring Administrative Discretion Through a Reasons Requirement." *University of Chicago Law Review* 44 (1976): 60.

Rodney A. Smolla. "The Reemergence of the Right-Privilege Distinction in Constitutional Law." *Stanford Law Review* 35 (1982): 69.

Timothy P. Terrell. "'Property', 'Due Process' and the Distinction Between Definition and Theory in Legal Analysis." *Georgetown Law Journal* 70 (1982): 861.

William W. Van Alstyne. "Cracks in 'The New Property': Adjudicative Due Process in the Administrative State." *Cornell Law Review* 62 (1977): 445.

Stephen F. Williams. "Liberty and Property: The Problem of Government Benefit." *Journal of Legal Studies* 12 (1983): 3.

Table of Cases

The numbers given are paragraph numbers.

Table of Cases

Table of Cases

Table of Cases

Table of Cases

Table of Constitutional Provisions

The numbers given are paragraph numbers.

Table of Statutes

The numbers given are paragraph numbers.

Index

The numbers given are paragraph numbers.

Index

Index

Index